Pathmarks

This is the first time that this seminal collection of fourteen essays by Martin Heidegger (originally published in German under the title *Wegmarken*) has appeared in English in its complete form. The volume includes new or first-time translations of seven essays and thoroughly revised, updated versions of the other seven. Among the new translations are such key essays as "On the Essence of Ground," "On the Question of Being," and "Hegel and the Greeks."

Spanning a period from 1919 to 1961, these essays have become established points of reference for all those with a serious interest in Heidegger. Now edited for the first time by an experienced Heidegger translator and scholar, they will prove an essential resource for all students of Heidegger, whether they work in philosophy, literary theory, religious studies, or intellectual history.

William McNeill is Assistant Professor of Philosophy at DePaul University in Chicago. His translations include *The Concept of Time*, *The Fundamental Concepts of Metaphysics* (with Nicholas Walker), and *Hölderlin's Hymn "The Ister"* (with Julia Davis). An experienced Heidegger translator and scholar, he has also published numerous essays on Heidegger.

MARTIN HEIDEGGER

Pathmarks

EDITED BY
WILLIAM McNEILL

CAMBRIDGE
UNIVERSITY PRESS

CAMBRIDGE UNIVERSITY PRESS
Cambridge, New York, Melbourne, Madrid, Cape Town, Singapore,
São Paulo, Delhi, Dubai, Tokyo

Cambridge University Press
32 Avenue of the Americas, New York, NY 10013-2473, USA

www.cambridge.org
Information on this title: www.cambridge.org/9780521439688

First published 1998
10th printing 2009

A catalog record for this publication is available from the British Library

Library of Congress Cataloging in Publication data
Heidegger, Martin, 1889–1976.
[Weigmarken, English]
Pathmarks / Martin Heidegger ; edited by William McNeill.
p. cm.
Includes bibliographical references (p.).
ISBN 0-521-43362-2 (hb.) – ISBN 0-521-43968-X (pb.)
1. Philosophy. 2. Ontology. I. McNeil, William (William A.)
II. Title.
B3279.H48W413   1998
193 – dc21   97-22565
CIP

ISBN 978-0-521-43362-4 Hardback
ISBN 978-0-521-43968-8 Paperback

Transferred to digital printing 2010

In Memoriam
KURT BAUCH

Our fruitful friendship, based in our mutual participation in lectures and seminars on art history and philosophy, stood the test of time.

The encouragement received from our close companionship of thoughtful inquiry moves me to dedicate this collection of texts – a series of stops under way in the single question of being – to my deceased friend. – M. H.[1]

Contents

Editor's Preface

The present collection brings together for the first time in English a series of key texts by Martin Heidegger published in German under the title *Wegmarken*. Together the texts span more than forty years of Heidegger's thought, and include some of his most important and best-known writings. Not all of the texts were originally conceived as essays; rather, they encompass a range of genres that also includes critical review, public address, letter, contribution to a commemorative *Festschrift*, and edited excerpts from a lecture course. The reference section at the end of the volume provides further details of the original format, date of publication, and subsequent editions of each piece.

In addition to bringing together in a single volume revised and updated versions of existing translations, the present volume includes translations of several texts previously unavailable in English: Heidegger's review of Karl Jaspers's *Psychology of Worldviews* (1919/21), his edited excerpts "From the Last Marburg Lecture Course" (1928), and the essay "Hegel and the Greeks" (1958). A number of new translations also appear here for the first time: "On the Essence of Ground" (1929), "Plato's Doctrine of Truth" (1931/32, 1940), "Postscript to 'What Is Metaphysics?'" (1943), and "On the Question of Being" (1955).

The present volume is a translation of volume 9 of the *Gesamtausgabe*, or Complete Edition of Heidegger's works, published by Vittorio Klostermann (Frankfurt am Main, 1976). This German edition includes for the first time a select number of marginal notes and remarks that Heidegger recorded in his own first edition of *Wegmarken*, or in separate publications of the individual texts. As in the German edition, these notes appear as footnotes indicated by a, b, c, and so on, together with an indication of the edition in which they originally appear. Further information on the principles of selection used and on the dating of the marginalia is provided in the German editor's Postscript, which appears in translation at the end of this volume.

In addition to these marginalia, the *Gesamtausgabe* edition also provides the original, numbered notes to the essays "On the Essence of Ground" and "Hegel and the Greeks," and to "Phenomenology and Theology," which, together with the review of Karl Jaspers's *Psychology of Worldviews*, is new to the *Gesamtausgabe* edition of *Wegmarken*. The *Gesamtausgabe* edition also provides a series of numbered notes to the "Postscript to 'What Is Metaphysics?'," intended to indicate the original version of that text, which was altered in a number of places in the fifth edition (cf. the German editor's Postscript).

Remaining numbered notes are those of the editor or translator(s) of the English edition, and are indicated by (Ed.) or (Trans.), respectively. The editor has also indicated a number of places where the text of the *Gesamtausgabe* edition differs from that of the first, 1967 edition of *Wegmarken*. It is not certain that all such changes have been noted. Furthermore, because of the number of different editions that have appeared of some of the individual texts, it was not possible to check and compare all variations. All numbered notes appear as endnotes.

The numbers in the text in brackets refer, where relevant, to the original pagination of the first edition of *Wegmarken*.

An effort has been made to standardize translations as far as possible throughout the text. Thus, in twelve of the fourteen essays, the German *Sein* is rendered as "being," and *das Seiende* as "a being" or "beings," depending on context (occasionally as "an entity" or "entities" to avoid confusion). In the remaining two essays, "On the Essence of Truth" and "Introduction to 'What Is Metaphysics?'," *Sein* has been rendered as "Being" (capitalized) at the translators' request.

I owe a sincere debt of gratitude to David Farrell Krell and John Sallis, who persuaded me to take on this project and who have remained as consultant editors throughout. Their advice, assistance, and encouragement have been invaluable. I am especially grateful to all the translators who have contributed to this volume and have worked with me in updating and revising their existing translations. Thanks also to my assistants Chris Leazier and Dan Price, and to DePaul University for the provision of two summer research grants and a period of leave that have enabled me to see this long and arduous project through to completion. Last but not least, thanks to Terence Moore, Executive Editor of Humanities at Cambridge University

Press, for his infinite patience, and to Mary Byers, my production and copy editor, for her thorough work on the project.

William McNeill
DePaul University, 1997

Preface to the German Edition

This volume of already published texts (cf. References at the end of the book) seeks to bring to attention something of the path that shows itself to thinking only on the way: shows itself and withdraws.

Presumably this is a path leading to *The Vocation of the Matter of Thinking*. The vocation brings nothing new. For it leads us before the oldest of the old. It demands our abode within the ever-sought-after Sameness of the Same.

The path leading into this abode prevents our describing it like something that lies facing us. Whoever attempts to start out on this path is helped only by the unceasing endeavor to locate by discussion (to find at its locale) what the word "being" once revealed as something to be thought, what it may once perhaps conceal as something thought.

Whoever sets out on the path of thinking knows least of all concerning the matter that – behind and over beyond him, as it were – determines his vocation and moves him toward it.

Whoever lets himself enter upon the way toward an abode in the oldest of the old will bow to the necessity of later being understood differently than he thought he understood himself.

Yet this necessity is grounded in the possibility that a free realm continues to be granted in which the claim of what is handed down by history may play its role. It could also be that history and what it hands down to us may be leveled out into the uniform storage of information and as such made useful for the inevitable planning needed by a humanity under control.

Whether thinking will then come to an end in a bustle of information, or whether a descensional passage [*Unter-Gang*] into the protection offered by its provenance, concealed from thought itself, is reserved for its vocation remains the question. It now directs thinking into a region this side of pessimism and optimism.

Freiburg im Breisgau, early summer 1967

Comments on *Karl Jaspers's* Psychology of Worldviews

Translated by John van Buren[1]

A "fitting" orientation for a positive and illuminating critical review of this work published by Jaspers is *not* available in the current inventory of our scientific and philosophical knowledge. Making such an admission right at the outset may serve as an appropriate indication of the originality and significance of Jaspers's achievement. This critical review will attempt to orient itself in a fitting manner to the immanent intentions of Jaspers's work and follow up on them. Some preliminary reflections on the scope of this course of inquiry and on the range of its claims will also help us to characterize the actual object to be dealt with in the following comments, and will thus be far from an otiose discussion of possible methods.

Jaspers's work developed out of a concern with psychology as a whole (5), and psychology is supposed to allow us to see "what the human being is" (ibid.). The psychology of worldviews, which is a "part" of the whole of psychology with its own specific nature and function, attempts to mark out the "limits of our psychical life," and thereby provide a clear and comprehensive horizon for our psychical life. Marking out such limits is, more precisely, a type of observation in which we comprehensively examine the being of the human mind in its substantial totality and classify its ultimate positions. And this means "marking out that domain of which we already possess a conceptual understanding at present" (6). Psychology of worldviews is only *one* way of acquiring a "basis" for understanding the whole of our psychical life, the other way being given in "general psychology" (a doctrine of principles and categories, a methodology for gaining knowledge in psychology). According to the way in which it is undertaken by Jaspers, this type of observation, which gives us an understanding and overview of the basic capacities and tendencies of psychical, mental life as a whole, already in itself has – apart from being evaluated in terms of its primary purpose – also a positive significance for knowledge in psychiatry as well in the human sciences. For it expands our "natural" psychological understanding, rendering it more receptive and versatile, i.e., more perceptive regarding the nuances, dimensions, and different levels of our psychical being.

But the concrete tendency of Jaspers's work – its concern with the whole of psychology, i.e., with acquiring the fundamental domain of psychology and its horizon of *principles* – should in fact already be seen as "philosophical." Psychology of worldviews is not supposed to develop a positive worldview and impose it on others. Rather, by understanding and classifying the positions, processes, and stages of our psychical life, this type of observation is meant to provide us with "clarifications and possibilities that can serve as means to our self-reflection (in our worldviews)" (Foreword). It is in this way that the aforementioned direction of Jaspers's inquiry, namely, gaining access to psychology as a whole, is assigned its ultimate goal. The way in which the first set of tasks gets carried out is simultaneously the way to fulfill the second set of real, philosophical tasks. And, in turn, this orientation to the goal of philosophizing, which is described by Jaspers in a particular manner, provides fundamental guidance for his preoccupation with the problem of psychology.

This critical review intends to deal with the principles at work in Jaspers's book. Thus we will not be focusing on particularities in the content of this text, or on the individual components of Jaspers's classificatory schemata, so that we can, for instance, modify these and replace them with others. Our goal is not to add supplementary content or insert missing "types." What is important is rather to define the "how" of this philosophical review in regard to its basic approach and in relation to the problems that it intends to broach. In providing this definition, we will simultaneously be limiting the range of claims that we can make.

The basic approach of this critical review lies in its attempt to free up the real tendencies of Jaspers's work. In doing so, it seeks to bring into sharper focus both the primary direction in which Jaspers's problems tend and the basic motivations for this direction. Here we will determine to what extent Jaspers's approach to his tasks, his choice of methods, and his way of employing these methodological means to carry out his tasks are really in keeping with the underlying tendencies of his inquiry and the directions in which these tendencies discernibly point us. We will also examine whether the motivations and tendencies of Jaspers's inquiry have themselves been shaped radically enough in line with the tentative orientation to philosophizing that lies at the basis of his inquiry. Accordingly, every type of critical review oriented to fixed standards will remain out of play for us. Jaspers's observations will not be confronted with the aid of a finished philosophy that has been established on some secure foundation, or evaluated in terms of their distance from a consummate objective systematics in the field of philosophical problems. Nor are they to be assessed in relation to a fixed ideal of scientific and philosophical rigor in methodology. Where such standards have become available in one's philosophizing, a type of critical review oriented to fixed standards is not only justifiable but may also even be urgently needed, and all the more so when the work under discussion is experienced as unsettling, provocative, and challenging. But this kind of critical review has been ruled out at present insofar as Jaspers's investigation will not be judged with the help of such ideas as "the absolute validity of truth," "relativism," and "skepticism." This type of assessment will be avoided precisely because the following comments endeavor to sharpen our consciences regarding the need to inquire into the genuine sense of the "history of ideas," and return radically to the original genetic motivations in this history that led to the establishment of such epistemological ideals in philosophy. We need to determine anew whether these ideals satisfy the fundamental sense of philosophizing, or whether they do not rather lead a shadowy life that has hardened into a long, degenerate, and spurious tradition, and that has never been appropriated in an original manner. It is certain that such sharpening of the conscience cannot be taken care of, or approached in any genuine manner whatsoever, by "creating" a "new" philosophical program; rather, it must be enacted in a very concrete manner in the form of a destruction that is directed precisely to what has been handed down to us in the history of ideas. This task is tantamount to explicating the original motivational situations in which the fundamental experiences of philosophy have arisen. And these experiences are to be understood as having undergone theoretical development and refinement in the establishment of the aforementioned epistemological ideals. In this regard, the meaning of the term "theory" is itself geared precisely to its origin (cf. Plato, Aristotle). The "idea" that we have of the meaning and scope of this task is such that it can scarcely be overestimated. To the contrary, we will come to see *what* is concretely "necessary" in philosophy precisely *by restricting ourselves to this task* and consciously abandoning aspirations to "creative" philosophizing that are in fact traditional, even if somewhat historically open-ended.

If this critical review emphatically rules out any intention of assessing Jaspers's work with fixed, highly refined points of reference that have demonstrably not, however, been appropriated in any radical sense, it is likewise very suspicious of all indulgent "philosophies of life" that make claims to free thinking and an apparent primordiality. "Philosophy of life" will be called into question by analyzing it to show that the basic philosophical motive that comes to expression in it does so in a hidden manner, is hardly able to be grasped with the meager inventory of concepts available to philosophy of life, and in fact manifests itself in a degenerate form.

Refraining from the type of critical review that brings into play fixed standards to orient itself means anything but an uncritical approach that advocates an ambivalent syncretism that is blind to differences and subjects everything to mediation. A definite orientation is also to be found in the basic approach that will be adopted and enacted in this review. The essential characteristic of this approach is expressed precisely in the "how" of our persisting in it. And this "how" of our critical attitude always remains subject to a type of appropriation that must constantly renew itself in the form of a destruction. Our critical review is phenomenological in the genuine sense, but it is not "without presuppositions" in the bad sense. Here one turns what is immediately "on hand" in one's objective historical, intellectual situation into the in-itself of the "things themselves." One fails to see what is characteristic of all intuition, namely, that it is enacted in the context of a definite orientation and an anticipatory preconception of the respective region of experience. Thus, when one shuns constructivistic points of view that are foreign to the subject matter, and is concerned with immediacy only in this respect, one's intuition can all too easily fall prey to a certain blindness regarding the fact that its own motivational basis is itself in the end not primordial. The meaning of primordiality does not lie in the idea of something outside of history or beyond it; rather, it shows itself in the fact that thinking without presuppositions can itself be achieved only in a self-critique that is historically oriented in a factical manner. An incessant enactment of our concern for achieving primordiality is what constitutes primordiality. (The term "historical"[2] is used here in a sense that will become somewhat more explicit in the course of the following reflections.) Thinking without presuppositions is here intended to be taken in a philosophical sense and not in a specifically scientific sense. The path that leads to the "things themselves" treated in philosophy is a long one. Thus the excessive liberties taken recently by many phenomenologists in their use of essential intuition appear in a very dubious light, and are hardly in line with the "openness" and "devotion" to the things themselves preached by these phenomenologists. It might just be the case that even the directions of inquiry in which we could find access to the things themselves of philosophy lie covered over for us, and that what is thus necessary is a radical kind of deconstruction and reconstruction, i.e., a genuine confrontation with the history that we ourselves "are." And this confrontation would be something that is enacted within the very meaning of philosophizing. In the end, it is just this precisely oriented detour and the type of roundabout understanding enacted in it that make up *the* path to the things themselves. In connection with the fundamental question of the "I am," we need to ask ourselves if it is not high time to determine whether we have really so thoroughly come to terms with that which we ourselves purportedly "have" and "are." Are we, rather than taking firm hold of the most important questions in a philosophically rigorous manner, generating an unspeakable hustle and bustle in our concerns for the preservation of culture, though we never actually get around to applying ourselves to this task? Are we today troubling ourselves with peripheral matters that were transformed into fundamental problems by an earlier form of intellectual industriousness that searched too *broadly* for all objects of philosophical investigation? Thinking phenomenologically without presuppositions denotes a certain approach and orientation, and this is neither mere sport nor prophetic pageantry that promises the salvation of the world. In a critical review guided by this type of thinking, it involves exploring the nature of the intuitive experiences lying at the basis of the author's initial approach to the respective problems and the conceptual explication of such an approach (experience is to be understood here in a phenomenological sense). This "intuition" that grounds the author's approach is interrogated in a critical fashion regarding its primordiality, its motivation, its tendencies, and the extent to which it is genuinely enacted and seen through to the end.

In adopting this kind of basic critical approach to free up the respective work under investigation, to explore its internal features, and finally to examine these features with regard to the way in which their intrinsic meaning actually shows itself, one constantly runs the risk of missing the mark, i.e., being led down unintended paths, or singling out and highlighting tendencies of thought that were treated at random. The more we go wrong in this respect, the less value there is in communicating a positive critical review to others, and the more the value of such communication is limited to the function of clarifying for oneself what one has ventured to do. But whatever the plight of this communication may be, its claims must be restricted to *calling something to the attention of others*. This is ultimately the predicament of all philosophizing regarding its intention of having an effect in the world of others.

The "positive" side of this critical review consists simply in raising problems and understanding what is intended in Jaspers's work in a "more precise" manner. And it might just be the case that "more precise" means something other than simply achieving a progressively clearer conceptual presentation of what is intended in this work. Though always guided by a fundamental orientation, the "preliminary work" that we need to do is radically destructive, and in our opinion it involves such great difficulties and perhaps even prolonged tediousness that we will not be able to venture putting forward any finished results in this review. It will suffice if we can call attention to, and discuss, one or another decisive experiential motivation for Jaspers's explication of the phenomena he deals with.

An explication of both aforementioned directions in which Jaspers's book moves, namely, the preliminary one (establishing the science of psychology as a whole) and the real one (providing clarifications and possibilities that can serve as means to self-reflection), will allow us to proceed in the direction of those problems that are to be highlighted in this critical review. Psychology of worldviews marks out the limits of the human soul. The movement of our lives in worldviews is supposed to be understood from the standpoint of "limit-situations" (246). "Some kind of influence on all aspects of our psychical life must occur in the experience of these limits, and here everything will in one way or another presumably be a determining factor for the worldview of a human being" (6). Marking out such limits allows us to gain a "clear horizon" for the whole of our psychical life. Here we find a preoccupation with providing a regional definition of the whole of our psychical life that has never before been accomplished or even attempted along such paths and with such breadth. In its initial approach, it works with a certain basic aspect of psychical life, namely, that it has limits. In psychical life, there are "limit-situations" to which certain "reactions" are possible, and these reactions to the structural antinomies of limit-situations take place in the "vital process" of psychical life, which functions as their medium (247). The *Dasein* of our mental life, i.e., its existence or "being there," arises through antinomies (304).[3] In this way of posing the problem of psychical life in psychology of worldviews, we find a certain understanding of psychical life. Prior to Jaspers's initial approach to the problem of psychical life, this psychical life is for its part implicitly seen from the point of view of a certain traditionally expressed preconception about it: namely, the soul has limits, i.e., limit-situations, in the experience of which an "influence" *must* occur on the play of mental forces that make up our Dasein. From the point of view of the underlying tendency that actually guides Jaspers's problem of psychical life, is it at all feasible for him to adopt this preconception about the basic aspect of psychical life? In other words, is this preconception really in keeping with the underlying tendency of Jaspers's problem of psychical life? Are not unexamined presup*positions* introduced here in an illegitimate manner? Is the task of gaining access to

6

psychology as a whole promoted in a radical fashion? Can this task be posed at all in such an isolated manner? Such questions must be confronted and dealt with by means of fundamental reflection. To begin with, we need to see but one thing: namely, *a preconception about psychical life, which is expressed in a particular manner, is already given and at work in Jaspers's initial approach to the problem of psychical life.*

Psychology of worldviews is not supposed to work out a doctrine of life and impose it on others; rather, its goal is "to give clarifications and possibilities that can serve as means to self-reflection." This work of clarification means clarification *of* "life," and here "life" is seen in some manner. In Jaspers's initial approach to this clarification, in the techniques he uses for it, and in the nature and scope of his goals here, life itself is *forced to appear under a certain aspect* for those who are appropriating such clarifications. If possibilities are disclosed, they are possibilities *under* a certain articulated aspect of our life and psychical existence, and *for the sake of* it. A notion of the essential meaning of the "how" of life itself is expressed in this aspect. However much Jaspers made the attempt to undertake everything in the nonprejudicial attitude of mere observation, it is nonetheless the case that, when we go to understand what he has presented in his observations and use it in our own self-reflection, we are required to adopt, and acquiesce in, certain basic approaches to the way in which life and the self are to be intended. If genuine psychology is supposed to allow us to see "what the human being is" (5), then the initial manner in which it actually poses the problem must from the start harbor within it certain preconceptions about the sense of being that belongs to this whole of our psychical, mental Dasein, and then again preconceptions about the possible "how" in accordance with which this life, having now been clarified, is supposed to be lived, i.e., preconceptions about the basic sense of that in which such things as "possibilities" can in any sense be brought to light.

However, in seeing these particular preconceptions that accompany Jaspers's investigations, we should not be tempted to undertake a philosophically feeble and sterile type of sham critique in which we would now reproach Jaspers for having *contradicted* his own intentions, maintaining on the basis of this charge that his intentions could never be realized in the concrete, and arguing that his whole project is thus "refuted in principle" and "dealt with." This type of criticism always claims a formal type of superiority in argumentation, but it thereby fails to take up the productive possibility of returning in a positive fashion to the thoughts in question and understanding them in a deeper sense. What our critical review of Jaspers's work really needs to do is to highlight his preconceptions in a *still more* precise manner, to delve into the motivation, the sense, and the scope of the direction of inquiry that led to such preconceptions, and to become aware of what is *demanded* by the very sense of these preconceptions, even though the author himself may not have actually understood these demands in an explicit manner. In other words, we must ultimately evaluate Jaspers's preconceptions with regard to the philosophical relevance and primordiality of their immanent intentions.

What these problems indicate and lead us to acknowledge is that preconceptions "are" at work "everywhere" in the factical experience of life (and therefore also in the sciences and in philosophizing), and that what we need to do is simply, as it were, join in the experience of these preconceptions wherever they operate, as they do, for example, in providing direction for any fundamental type of knowledge about something. Moreover, we need simply to proceed in light of how such preconceptions themselves call for their own clarification. It is by proceeding in this manner that the concrete context in which we enact some form of understanding (e.g., a particular science) can be made genuinely transparent. In other words, our method can be made more appropriate. All problems of preconception are problems of "method," and such problems differ in each case according to the primordiality, the tendencies, the regional orientation, and the theoretical level of the preconceptions in question. We cannot but give ourselves an initial understanding of method along with our preconceptions of the subject matter. Method arises together with these preconceptions and out of the same source. A definition of the concept of "method" must work with a formally indicative meaning (e.g., "way") and thereby remain open to being shaped concretely in actual research. In obtaining these concrete definitions of method, we must at the same time also get rid of any prejudices that may have found their way into them by means of the formally indicative meaning of method with which we have been working. If method is from the start cut to the measure of specific, isolated problems in the subject matter of a particular science, and is nonetheless taken to be a technique that can be applied anywhere, one loses the possibility of understanding method in a primordial manner in each particular case of research. One becomes blind to the fact that one's own way of proceeding is loaded down with this particular approach. When objects are approached by way of a specifically oriented mode of apprehension, and when this mode of apprehension is, whether explicitly or not, understood and used as a technique, i.e., basically as a means of defining these objects that is not, however, restricted to them, it might turn out that these objects become lost for good by being forced to conform to a particular type of apprehension that is alien to them. And, consequently, the copious use of "methods" and possible variants of these methods would only continue to miss the very objects of which one actually intends to gain knowledge.

Our investigation of the aforementioned problem of preconception in Jaspers's work endeavors to demonstrate that his approach to the problems in question *requires* a more radical type of reflection on method. This is the case not only because it should be possible for the underlying tendency of these problems to be realized in a more consistent and genuine manner, but also and primarily because the object that has been apprehended in these preconceptions is in fact what it is only by virtue of a primordially immanent "method." This method is part of the object's very makeup, and is not something merely foisted on the object from the outside. If one is not aware of this problem of explication in a "rigorous" enough manner, one can, to be sure, nonetheless still wind up actually intending the object in some manner, but a kind of surrogate will, without further explanation, have been inserted into one's intuition and concepts. This surrogate will then henceforth constantly make demands on us to treat it from different sides in order to master it in knowledge (we are motivated to do this on the basis of real acts of intending the object, but these intentions do not get involved with the object and grasp it). The surrogate finally becomes so intrusive that it passes itself off as the genuine phenomenon, whereas the possibility of actually experiencing the authentic phenomenon vanishes and continues to exist merely in words. "We have no dominant method, but rather now this one, now that one" (11), and, according to Jaspers, this is supposed to be the case within the basic approach of "mere observation."

The object actually investigated in Jaspers's work can be defined in formal indication as our *existence* [Existenz]. Having such a formally indicated meaning, this concept is intended to point to the phenomenon of the "I am," i.e., to the sense of being in this "I am" that forms the starting point of an approach to a context of fundamental phenomena and the problems involved there. In formal indication (which should be seen to make up the fundamental methodological sense of all philosophical concepts and their relationships, though this will not be explained in more detail here), any uncritical lapse into a particular interpretation of existence – for example, Kierkegaard's or Nietzsche's – ought to be avoided from the start, so that we can free up the possibility of pursuing a genuine sense of the phenomenon of existence and explicate what comes to the fore in this pursuit. In an exegesis of Kierkegaard's thought, Jaspers writes: "The consciousness of our existence arises precisely through our consciousness of situations of antinomy" (217). Limit-situations shed light on our vital Dasein. "It is in limit-situations that the most intense consciousness of existence flares up, and this consciousness is a consciousness of something absolute" (245). "Limit-situations are experienced as something ultimate for human life" (274). With this critical analysis of limit-situations (202–47) we come to the solid core that sustains the whole of Jaspers's work. It should be possible to develop the previously outlined problems of preconception and method to some extent in connection with this concrete and indeed most powerful section of Jaspers's investigation. (Though a student of Kierkegaard and Nietzsche, Jaspers displays in this section a very rare talent and energy, giving these free play in his breakdown and treatment of "psychical states," and compiling the respective phenomena in a valuable, even if only classificatory, manner.)

There are certain crucial situations "that are bound up with our very humanity, and that are unavoidably given for our finite Dasein" (202). As soon as human beings attempt to attain certainty about the totality of the world and life, they find themselves faced with ultimate forms of incompatibility. "We and our world are split apart in the form of an antinomy" (203). "The structural antinomy of our Dasein [the world and we ourselves, i.e., the objective and subjective sides of this split] poses a limit for any objective worldview" (?), and the "subjective" (?) counterpart of this limit is a type of "suffering that is bound up with all human life" (204). "Struggle, death, chance, and guilt" are "particular instances" of this "universal" nature of limit-situations (ibid.). Certain reactions to these situations of antinomy are possible, i.e., particular ways in which human beings attempt to cope with these situations and find some kind of security in the face of them. "When human beings advance beyond their finite situations in order to see them within the whole," they see "oppositions" and "processes of destruction" everywhere. "Insofar as everything objective is able to be conceptually expressed, [these oppositions] can be thought of as contradictions" (203f.). Here destruction means a type of destruction that lies in the rationality of contradiction. "As antinomies, contradictions remain at the limit of our knowledge about the infinite. Thus the concepts of infinity, limit, and antinomy belong together" (205). The concepts of antinomy and limit derive their meaning from a definite or, we should rather say, indefinite aspect of the infinite. It is from our experience of antinomy that there arises in us a vital will to unity (213). "We see experiences of 'unity' again and again, and it is precisely the most intense thinkers of antinomy who in their paradoxical expressions readily teach us about this kind of mystical and vital unity" (215). The life of the mind is itself a kind of life that is oriented to unity (213). Human beings "always find themselves on paths leading to the infinite or the whole" (204).

It should by now be sufficiently clear that it is from this initial preconception about "the whole" ("unity," "totality") that all talk of "destruction," "division," and "opposition" derives its sense. Human beings stand within antinomies insofar as they see themselves in the "whole" and thus have a preconception of *this* aspect of life, seeing themselves essentially to be inserted into this whole as something ultimate, and experiencing their Dasein as something "surrounded" by this unbroken "medium." Antinomies destroy and bifurcate, and our experience of them amounts to standing within limit-situations, only because all this is initially viewed from the vantage point of our approach to the flowing stream of life as a whole. Regarding the genesis of their meaning, even concepts have their origin in the whole of life. "And if antinomy, infinity, limit, and the Absolute are concepts that revolve around the same thing" (245), this is likewise the case with the concept of totality. These concepts not only revolve around the same thing, but also derive their meaning from it, i.e., their conceptual structure or perhaps lack thereof, as well as their appropriateness or perhaps inappropriateness for promoting a conceptual understanding of what they are supposed to grasp and express. We are told nothing definite about what this "seeing within the whole" and this experience of antinomies within an infinite reflection are supposed to mean. At any rate, this is a type of "thinking" or "seeing" that gets its motivation from the above-mentioned preconception about the whole, and its approach, tendencies, and scope are oriented to this preconception. It is only on the basis of *this* particular preconception that the notion of "attaining certainty about the totality" has any meaning.

It might seem as though the point of our exposition of Jaspers's central, guiding preconception is to demonstrate that his position belongs under the rubric of "philosophy of life." This kind of approach is indeed possible. And it could possibly draw upon the *particular focus* that Heinrich Rickert has used in his recently published critical review of various philosophies of life. This critical review and others like it cannot but meet with approval whenever they in principle affirm the need for the rigorous "formation" of concepts, i.e., whenever they see it from the vantage point of an ideal of philosophical knowledge that is incontestable in the formal sense that it stresses the importance of rigorous conceptuality, while the concrete approach that one should take to this ideal is left open for discussion. But Rickert tells us nothing about the "how" of this formation of concepts, about the way in which philosophical concepts get their structure, and about the basic intention of conceptual explication in philosophy. Assuming that all one's talk about concept-formation and all the structural characteristics of concepts one has extracted from the workings of concept-formation in particular sciences have a validity that is nonprejudicial in more than a simply formal sense, and this is something that needs to be investigated, it might turn out to be the case that in rightly stressing the importance of concept-formation one nonetheless has failed to give due attention precisely to *the real* problem, namely, the one arising from the fact that the work of "differentiating the meaning of forms" begins with the "material" with which one is dealing. How is the material in question actually there for us, how do we actually "have" it there before us, and what does gaining access to it really mean? When our conceptualization of the material takes its motivation from this access to, and having of, the material, and when it persists in them, how is it constituted? Here the *positive* tendencies of philosophy of life need to be examined to see if a certain radical tendency toward philosophizing is not indeed ventured in it, even if this happens in a covert manner and with the help of a means of expression that was borrowed from tradition rather than being fashioned in an original manner. Here we would have to examine above all the high point of philosophy of life in Dilthey, to whom all those who came later are indebted for their important insights, though these inferior offspring actually misunderstood his real intuitions, and he himself was not even able to achieve real insight into them. In this regard, it is with an eye to the radical tendency toward philosophizing in philosophy of life that our critical review is pursuing its course of analysis. It is important to see that philosophy of life, which developed out of a genuine orientation to the history of ideas, tends – whether explicitly or not – in the direction of the phenomenon of existence, though the same cannot be said for the type of philosophy of life found in specialized literati. (Because this point is of importance for a positive evaluation of philosophy of life, it can be formulated and indicated in rough fashion by defining the "vague" concept of life with reference to two principal tendencies in its meaning, though these are themselves ambiguous. However, regarding the need for a radical treatment of the problem of life, we run the risk here of expecting too much from individual philosophies of life when considered separately. We find in contemporary philosophy of life a widespread and vociferous but nebulous emphasis on orienting our Dasein to the immediate reality of life, and to the need for enriching, fostering, and intensifying life. That is, we encounter the now common and extensively cultivated way of speaking about life, a feeling for life, lived experience, and experiencing. All this is a symptom of a certain intellectual situation, which involves a tangled interplay of motives deriving from the history of ideas and arising from the most varied types of experience. It is this interplay of motives that has led to the predominance of the current interest in the reality of mental life and to the interpretation of life primarily from the point of view of the human sciences, even though biological concepts of life have not been completely eradicated here. The characteristic feature of this intellectual situation is perhaps precisely a muddled interplay of biological, psychological, social-scientific, aesthetic-ethical, and religious concepts of life. It is in this muddled fashion that problems in contemporary philosophy are predominantly centered on "life" as the "primordial phenomenon" in one of two ways. Either life is approached as the fundamental reality, and all phenomena are seen to lead back to it, so that everything and anything is understood as an objectification and manifestation "of life." Or else life is seen as the formation of culture, and this formation is thought to be carried out with reference to normative principles and values. The meaning of this watchword "life" should be allowed to remain ambiguous, so that it is able to indicate for us all the different phenomena that are intended in it. Here we need to single out two directions in the sense of this term that have led the way in shaping its meaning, and in which we find expressed a tendency toward the phenomenon of existence.

(1) Life is understood as objectifying in the widest sense, as an act of creative formation and achievement, as an act of going out of itself, and thus – though this is not clearly spelled out – as something like our "*being there*" ["Da sein"] *in* this life and *as* this life.

(2) Life is understood as experiencing, as having an experience, understanding, appropriating, and thus – though again the connection is left unexplained – as something like our "*being there*" *in* such experiencing.)

The progress that Jaspers's work makes lies in the fact that his classification of the phenomena, which have not previously been made available in this manner, has called our attention to the problem of existence in a much more concentrated fashion, and has in connection with this moved the problems of psychology into more fundamental domains. Its philosophical shortcoming with respect to the need for actually getting down to work and delving into the problems it broaches is clearly visible in the fact that Jaspers persists in a certain untested opinion. He thinks that the preconception about "the whole" that was highlighted above can help him get a handle on the phenomenon of existence, and that he can understand this phenomenon precisely by means of those concepts already available to him in his intellectual milieu.

Keeping in mind the positive tendency of Jaspers's work that is directed toward the phenomenon of existence, we now need to discuss the above-mentioned preconception of this work with regard to the methodological consequences of its structure for making the phenomenon of existence visible and conceptually understanding it. How does the meaning of this phenomenon get articulated when such a preconception forms the starting point of one's inquiry?

It is only with reference to the infinite whole of life that the particular framework of such concepts as the "limits of life," "limit-situations," "structural antinomies," "reactions," and "vital process" can be understood to have the function that they do in Jaspers's scheme of classification. The very meaning of this conceptual framework somehow depends on an initial approach to the whole of life, and the contexts of meaning that Jaspers describes are always ultimately related back to this whole.

The way in which this preconception about the whole of life functions in conceptually articulating the basic meaning of the phenomenon of "existence" can be brought into relief in the following manner. In its teleological contexts, the biological life of the body is an intensive infinity; i.e., "things never come . . . to an end" here (289). This infinity stands in contrast to the kind of limitlessness found in the possible data that can be gathered about an individual being (e.g., a stone). "The *life of the mind* possesses the same kind of infinity that the life of the body does" (ibid.). Here, too, we never come to an end when we attempt to understand the contexts in which the human mind lives. "The medium here is the psychical. But in this psychical realm we find not only the *life* of the mind but also a mere *limitlessness* of phenomena that is similar to the limitlessness of facts available in the individual forms of lifeless matter. The infinity of this life of the mind is there [*ist da*] for us, whether we deal with this life in general terms, or deal with it in the concrete and unique form of an individual person. This intensive infinity of the mind, i.e., this infinity in which it lives, stands in contrast to the limitlessness of the mind in which it has a chaotic character. . . ." (289). When we attempt to understand life, we find only the finite and the particular. But we can see that behind all this something is astir as its driving force, namely, a movement that is oriented in the direction of the infinite. Since life is "motion," the essence of mental life lies in the fact that it is always "on the way to the actualization of its qualities" (290).

Our examination of these claims is not meant to be focused on the question as to whether the different aspects of the meaning of infinity that have been gleaned from the reality of *bodily* life can be so freely applied to the "life of the mind." For (understood on the level of the distinctions with which Jaspers himself works) the limitlessness of data about an individual being (or limitless progression in knowing and defining it) and the limitlessness of teleological contexts in the organic world (or never coming to an end in defining the organic world) do not in any sense differ with respect to the meaning of infinity. They tell us absolutely nothing about the meaning of the infinity that belongs to life as such. The objective "concept" of infinity, which has apparently been obtained specifically from the unity of *biological* objects, is claimed for the life of the mind as well, but in such a way that, when Jaspers goes on to define the life of the mind further, a different notion of life intervenes. In looking at the life of the mind, one notices a movement toward the infinite "behind it." Does "infinite" mean here limitless progression in our attempt to understand actual human lives, i.e., understand their purposeful contexts, or is a completely different sense of infinity introduced here? What is meant by "infinite" here is certainly not the limitlessness of the individual "products and appearances" of the human mind. In connection with the notion of infinity, the essence of the mind is defined as a "way." Here the direction toward the infinite, which is experienced "behind" the life of the mind, clearly means a type of infinity that lies in the sense of enactment and relational tendency belonging to certain acts. This type of infinity is then somehow equated with the sense of "infinity" obtained from the objective, external observation of biological unities of life. However, this objective concept of infinity (i.e., the infinity related to a type of objectifying, *theoretical understanding* that is concerned with material or organic objects) is not sufficiently explained. And regarding the new sense of infinity (i.e., an infinity relative to the immanent sense of tendencies found in the context of the enactment of acts that have a certain direction), no attempt is made to obtain it from the "movement of life" itself and to define it conceptually on the basis of this movement. Nor has it been shown that these two fundamentally different concepts of infinity can be equated with each other in such a cursory manner. For, in establishing this connection between them, one presumably decides an issue of crucial importance. If the "mere observation" of Jaspers's investigations can proceed along these lines, this is only because of the preconception involved here, which initially takes an objectifying approach to "life" itself as a whole. Both concepts of infinity, each of which is already vague on its own, are made to reflect each other in a muddled fashion when the talk comes around to the notions of "infinite whole" and "infinite process." Jaspers in fact approaches life as a whole by means of a preconception in which life is, with respect to the intentional sense of its relational tendency, thought of as a thing-like object: i.e., "it is there," a process in motion (motion means: intentionally directed; and process, "taking place" in the manner of an occurrence). Life is *something given* in the objective medium of psychical being, it occurs there, and it is a process that takes place there before itself.

Life as a whole is the "encompassing" region in which processes of composition and decomposition run their course. That a certain "direction"
is ascribed to the driving forces, processes, and phenomena of movement
generally does not change the slightest thing in the basic aspect of life that
is described here as an encompassing realm and as a flowing "stream" that
bears all movements within itself. Even if one professes to reject metaphysics, one still owes it to oneself – if it is indeed true that "dodging the
issues" should have no place in philosophy – to give some kind of explanation of the objective sense and the mode of being on the basis of which
this whole, or psychical stream, is intended. When one talks about how
every attempt to understand life or a "part" of it is able to grasp only finite
aspects, this is only an expression of the fact that life is initially approached
as an undivided realm that, in conformity with the idea we have of it, can
eventually be grasped in its totality.

Every attempt to understand life is forced to turn the surge and flux
of the aforementioned process into a static concept and thereby *destroy*
the essence of life, i.e., the restlessness and movement (again understood
more as an occurrence than as a directedness to something) that characterize
life's actualization of its ownmost qualities. Such argumentation works with
the objective concept of infinity that is related to *theoretical understanding*.
In putting forth its poorly grounded demonstration that a stilling of the
psychical stream "takes place" objectively in this manner, it believes itself
to have thereby ascertained something of importance about the possibility
of understanding "life" with respect to the precise sense of enactment that
belongs to its acts. But, in fact, one has here forgotten to begin one's
investigation by first of all taking a close look at the sense of these contexts
of enactment. Instead, one at the same time takes a "concept" to be, as it
were, an objective and thing-like apparatus that inevitably breaks apart the
unbroken psychical medium to which it is applied. This characteristically
Bergsonian line of argumentation suffers from its own kind of paralysis, and
it does so in a twofold sense. Apart from the fact that problems concerning
meaning, concepts, and language are approached only from a very narrow
perspective that focuses on objective, reifying concepts, these problems
are allowed to remain on the level of a very crude and vague treatment,
which contributes nothing toward that type of treatment in which one
would attempt to define the fundamental sense of life and lived experience
as a whole. And instead of using this "glut on the market" to provide
oneself with an air of profound philosophy (such talk about ineffability easily
gives the impression that one has actually gazed upon ineffable realms), it
is high time that we found genuine problems to deal with. When one

has actually succeeded in discovering new contexts of phenomena, as is the case in Jaspers's investigation, such a backward theory of expression is unnecessary. However little Jaspers has defined the concept of life as a whole with precision, we can nonetheless glean from it what is decisive for the context of problems under discussion, namely, the function that "life" has. It is *the* realm, *the* fundamental reality, and the one all-encompassing domain into which Jaspers inserts all the phenomena that he examines.

Since the point of this critical review is to discuss the central, guiding preconception in Jaspers's work with respect to *what* is intended in it and *how* it is intended, as well as to examine this preconception more specifically with regard to whether it is appropriate for conceptually defining the phenomenon of existence and for providing us with the fundamental kind of objectivity in which this conceptual definition ought to be carried out, we now need to understand the functional sense of this preconception more concretely than we have up to this point.

"Understood from the standpoint of its worldviews, life is played out within the subject-object split" (248). "The primal phenomenon of experience lies in the fact that objects stand opposite the subject." "Where no objects stand opposite us, so that every content of our experience disappears and cannot be spoken about, and yet something is still experienced, here we speak of the mystical in the broadest possible sense" (19). Insofar as the life of the mind lies in the restlessness and movement of taking up different positions and then abandoning them, "it is also, as something infinite, beyond the subject-object split." "The mystical is both alpha and omega" for the human mind (305). Due to all the movement involved with it, the mystical is the only thing in which the Absolute can be grasped without being an object. "From those limits that *encompass* all spheres of the subject-object split as the mystical (and here the mind does not flee into the mystical as a refuge, but rather constantly undergoes it and thereby finds that its proper sphere lies in movement), there falls an ineffable light on all *particulars* within the subject-object split, an indefinable meaning that is constantly pressing forward into form" (305; emphases added). The various types of mental life include certain kinds of movements that do not merely take place "between subject and object," but rather "stand at the same time beyond both of them and form the basis of the split between them" (307 n.; 388ff.). "Whereas most of the psychical phenomena we are able to describe are described within a subject-object split as properties of the subjective side or the objective side of this split, there are other kinds of psychical experiences in which the subject-object split either has not yet appeared or has been superseded" (392). What comes to be experienced in this supersession of the subject-object split is not something objectively marked off and removed from us; rather, it is characterized by a certain infinity from which arise driving forces that give direction to life (action, thinking, and artistic creation) (393). The subject-object split is itself "the very essence of human understanding" (426). "It is essentially within the form of this subject-object split that human beings live, and they never come to rest here, but are always striving after some kind of goal, purpose, value, or good" (202).

The whole of life is that from which all forms break forth into the light of day, and it is *what* "splits" itself asunder in this way. If we are to understand how the preconception that guides Jaspers's work basically gets worked out in concrete terms, the main thing we need to consider is that he always describes this "splitting asunder" precisely as the *primal phenomenon of psychical life*. It constitutes the fundamental meaning of the relation between subject and object (and here the concepts of subject and object each contain a whole multiplicity of phenomena, so that in the former, for example, we find the soul, the ego, lived experience, personality, the psychophysical individual [cf. 21]). This splitting asunder makes sense only insofar as we begin with the notion of that which is not split asunder, and approach it as the underlying reality. So as to avoid misunderstandings about the methodological intentions of our examination of the preconception that guides Jaspers's work, it should be clearly noted that the question as to whether one understands this whole in a metaphysical sense or avoids this kind of interpretation, as Jaspers himself wants to do, is irrelevant in the present context.

Our examination is not focused on the question of whether and in what way one could prove that this whole really exists in this or that sense of reality, or on what grounds its reality might possibly be posited as an idea. The really important thing here is much rather the functional sense of that which is initially put forth in Jaspers's preconception. He intends it to be the realm in which everything takes place or occurs, and it is accordingly an object that ultimately requires a theoretical, observational "attitude" as the correlative way of understanding it and as the basic sense in which it comes to be experienced by us. This means that the fundamental characteristic of the objective correlate of this theoretical attitude lies in the fact that it is an objective *thing*. Everything that has been split asunder, all movements, and all actions and reactions break forth into the light of day from out of this whole, pass through it, and return to it. It is from this context that the subject, one of the two basic components of the primal split, essentially derives its meaning. The subject is that in which life itself and its "driving forces" are "anchored" (24); i.e., it is basically characterized as a limited individuation of life itself, which always comes to expression only imperfectly in such individuations. "Life nowhere produces a concrete individual without remainder" (290).

The central, guiding preconception that supports everything in Jaspers's work will now be discussed on a fundamental level as a preconception. If such an adjudication of this preconception is to be what we intend it to be, then it can only mean that we must carry out a type of examination that is demanded by the very sense of this preconception. And our examination must accordingly focus on the question of whether the motivation that leads to the formation of the full sense of this preconception actually enjoys the level of primordiality that is claimed for it. The full sense of any phenomenon includes the following intentional characteristics: the intentional relation, the intentional content, and the intentional enactment (here "intentional" must be understood in a completely formal sense, so as to avoid any special emphasis on a *theoretical* sense of the intentional relation, and it is this specific meaning of "intentional" that is so easily suggested when one understands intentionality as "thinking about" [*Meinen von*"] or, correlatively, as "being-thought"). Our treatment of these intentional characteristics that make up the sense of any phenomenon should not consist of arranging them as an aggregate or succession of moments that have been tallied up. Rather, their sense derives from a structural context of relationships that varies in each case according to the levels and directions of experience involved. This context of relationships and the shifts of emphasis that occur here should not be understood as a "result" or as a momentary "addendum," but as the authentic factor that comes to light in the phenomenological articulation of the above-mentioned intentional characteristics. In turn, this authentic factor is itself to be understood precisely as a kind of prestruction in one's own existence. Such prestruction is in each case enacted and actualized in the current facticity of one's life in the form of a self-appropriation. It discloses and holds open a concrete horizon of expectations about which one is anxiously concerned [*bekümmerungshaften Erwartungshorizonts*], and which one develops in each particular context of enacting it.

Whence and in what way does the preconception under discussion make its appearance? Which motives would lead one to make it the starting point of one's inquiry, and to see it through to the end? What is the nature of these motives? Jaspers does not raise these questions. Were he to call to mind his own guiding preconception, he would find such questions about it empty and inconsequential. However, an attempt will not be made here to persuade him of their importance. It is up to him to decide whether he can "go on" without raising these questions, and to what extent these questions might not arise precisely from the kind of "infinite reflection" that constitutes the "genuine" sense of mental life and thus also scientific life. As is, Jaspers works more with what he has taken over from the intellectual history of his own present, doing this in part unconsciously, and in part by way of reflective appropriation. He has his eye specifically on what is of importance in this intellectual history for his special project of endeavoring to establish the science of psychology as a whole. Regarding the approach that he initially takes in his preconception, Jaspers would be able to say the following: Life as a whole is a central, guiding idea for me, and I need only look around to see that this life is somehow or other simply there for me wherever I go. This uniform and unbroken whole, this ultimate harmony, which transcends all oppositions, encompasses all life, and is free of all fragmentation and destruction – this is what guides my experience. I see all particulars in its light, all genuine illumination comes from it, and it marks out in advance the fundamental domain of sense on the basis of which everything I encounter comes to be determined and understood as something that develops and breaks forth out of this life, eventually sinking back into it again. This whole provides me with the essential articulation of those objects that I have attempted to observe and classify in my work.

The actual motivational basis from which this preconception thus arises is a fundamental experience of the whole of life in which we keep this whole before our gaze in the form of an idea. In a very formal sense, this experience can be defined as a "fundamental aesthetic experience." This means that the relational sense belonging to the primary type of experience that initially gives us the object called "life" actually consists of gazing upon something, observing it, and striving after it. We are not saying here that Jaspers "subscribes" to an "aesthetic" worldview. I know nothing about this. His worldview could just as well be an essentially moral one, supposing that such hackneyed philosophical coinage still means anything. Yet it is possible here that, without allowing himself to be placed before an antinomy, Jaspers does indeed gain access to the essential thing for him, i.e., the Absolute, within a fundamental aesthetic attitude, and sets about classifying it in the same manner. It is likewise possible that his view of life that focuses on the full "vehemence" and "force" of the "vital process" is an aesthetic one, even if the content of this "process" is understood to be of an ethical nature. Life "is there" as something that we have by means of looking at it, and it is by means of this kind of having that we gain possession of it in the sense of a whole that encompasses everything. Here Jaspers would perhaps on principle make the following reply: For me, it is indeed precisely a matter of simple observation, and what is observed must then be an object in the basic sense of being an observed object. There is no other way of proceeding here. In response, the following needs to be said: This formal type of argumentation remains from the start empty so long as we have not answered an important question, namely, does not the formal sense of theoretical understanding allow itself to be deformalized into very individual and concrete ways of understanding? And this question cannot be answered in a formally deductive manner, but rather only by starting from particular contexts of phenomena and allowing ourselves to be guided by them. It *could* be that, in accord with its sense, observation always has a theorizing character, but this does not necessarily entail that the sense of being belonging to what is observed must as such become accessible primarily within observation. And it is this simple point that we have been stressing in our examination of Jaspers's preconception. The relational sense of the *initial giving* of the object is not also the relational sense of the explication that has come across this pregiven object. Accordingly, the mere observation that has been used throughout Jaspers's work, and that extends all the way to the preconception in which the actual object of investigation is given, has in no way been justified by Jaspers as the appropriate method of explication. The basic experience in which the actual object is initially given needs to be examined regarding its full sense, and it must prescribe for us the genuine structure of explication. "Observation" in Jaspers's sense might be a fitting approach, but it also might not be. An answer to this question will be obtained in the following discussion, but for the time being it will take the form of making visible the problems involved here. To this end, that which Jaspers has taken up in the preconception of his work must be discussed in more concrete terms.

The whole of life, i.e., life *itself*, is something about which we can say nothing directly (288). But it must indeed be intended by us somehow, since our consciousness of our existence arises precisely from the fact that we look *to* the whole of life. When human beings "see [their finite situations] within the whole," when they "want to attain certainty about the totality of things," they have the experience that the objective world and their subjective action are split apart in the form of an antinomy. "Insofar as the driving forces in worldviews move human beings," and insofar as human beings are somehow "concerned about something essential," "they always find themselves on the way to the infinite or the whole." It is "*in view of* the infinite" that human beings find themselves in antinomies. Antinomies are oppositions, but they are oppositions "*from* the *point of view* of the Absolute and value." Antinomy is "destruction." When this destruction is experienced, it is experienced along with the "unity" or whole that is breaking apart in one way or another. The essence of the human mind is "the will to unity." Insofar as all processes of destruction are able to be formulated in a rational manner, they can be thought of as contradictions: for example, death contradicts life, whereas chance contradicts necessity as well as meaning (203ff.). But struggle, death, and chance are at the same time described also as limit-situations; i.e., we can experience struggle and death as limits in our consciousness of that whole which somehow exceeds life. "Struggle is a fundamental form of all existence" (227). "No existence is whole" (229), and that is why human beings must struggle if they want to live. This struggle "never lets a particular individual come to rest in any state of wholeness." "The process of life would cease without struggle" (227). Moreover, transitoriness holds for all *reality*. Every experience and all of our current conditions fade away into the past. Human beings are constantly changing (229). Experiences, individual human beings, a people, a culture – all of these fall prey to death. "The relation that human beings have to their own deaths is different from their relations to all other forms of transitoriness. Only the absolute nonbeing of the world is a comparable notion." "Only the perishing of their own being or of the world in general has a *total* character for human beings" (230). A "lived relation to death" is not to be confused with "universal knowledge about death." This lived relation is there in one's life only "when death has appeared as a limit-situation in one's experience," i.e., only when one's possible "consciousness of limit and infinity" (231) has not been left undeveloped.

We shall not at this point enter into a critical commentary on the various limit-situations that Jaspers has listed as concrete instances of the universal concept. We can also put aside for now the question of whether the concepts of "finite situation," "limit-situation," and "situation" have been explained in such a way that they accomplish something of significance for a real philosophical understanding of them. The following related questions may be left out of consideration as well: Do all of the concrete limit-situations mentioned above satisfy the "universal concept" of limit-situation in the same sense? Do universal concepts that can be applied to such concrete situations exist in any sense? To what extent is concrete knowledge of antinomies different from a "lived relation" to oppositions? How does the one arise from the other? Can these *experienced* antinomies – antinomies that are experienced *as* limit-situations, or antinomies that are experienced *in* limit-situations (this distinction has not been clearly worked out) – really be "rationally formulated" and thought of as "contradictions" without further ado? Do they not thereby lose their genuine sense? And, on the other hand, is it not precisely this theorizing reinterpretation that initially makes it possible for Jaspers to treat the concrete instances as contradictions that can be, as it were, lined up in a row for observation? We will also leave undiscussed the question of whether the concrete limit-situations stand in particular relations to each other when they are experienced, and to what extent it is precisely these concrete limit-situations that should properly be spoken of as limit-situations. Even if it is supposed to be "mere observation," I consider that which Jaspers puts forward about concrete limit-situations (in line with their fundamental significance within the total sphere of phenomena he intends to deal with, and to have emphasized this is precisely his main contribution) to be not in the least worked out in a fitting conceptual manner. That is the reason why a critical commentary focused on the particulars of Jaspers's work would all too easily run the risk of imputing to him views and meanings that he would not be willing to see as his own. In pursuing this type of critical commentary, we always move around in uncertainties so long as the basic context from which the phenomena and concepts in question have arisen is not more clearly visible. That is why critical observations always find themselves referred back to the problem of preconception.

Where are the intellectual motives to be found in a factical sense for the initial approach that Jaspers takes in his preconception? It is not difficult to recognize the historically "contingent" origin of the concept of the Absolute that he uses in his "observations." This concept represents a syncretism in which the Kantian doctrine of antinomies and its guiding concept of infinity are combined with Kierkegaard's concept of the Absolute, which has been "cleansed" of its specifically Lutheran religious sense and its particular theological meaning in this regard. Furthermore, these two components, which derive from very different basic preconceptions, are transplanted into that vagueness that arises from the concept of life we described above. More precisely, they are in fact viewed primarily on the basis of this vagueness. In the course of his general discussion of limit-situations, Jaspers at one point suddenly makes the comment about his "observations" that they amount to "only a presupposition for understanding a psychology of types of mental life, and are not yet themselves psychology" (204). But what then are they? Logic or sociology (2f.)? What is it that we strive after in these "observations" that are supposed to provide us with the fundamental presuppositions, and how do we strive after it?

It is possible that Jaspers wants these observations to be understood in a very formal sense. But then what is really needed is a discussion of the meaning of this "formal" factor, and here we need to raise the following questions. To what extent does this formal factor prejudice the observations that deal with concrete material? To what extent does it not do this? In what way can prejudice be avoided? In turn, to what extent can we obtain this formal sense only by means of beginning in a distinctive manner with that which is factically, concretely, and historically available to us, and then explicating this experiential point of departure in a particular way? To what extent does the conceptual expression found in actual understanding revoke the formal, and do this in such a manner that here concept-formation does not mean that we bring to light a theoretical theme for some merely theoretical purpose, but rather that our experience itself is illuminated through interpretation, and that we call attention to this experience in communication with others?

Jaspers's preconception has now been described in terms of its functional sense (its initial objective, factual approach to an intended realm), as well as in terms of the sense of its basic attitude (its aesthetic point of view) and its origin (its undiscussed adoption from the intellectual history of Jaspers's present situation). At this point, we need to examine Jaspers's preconception with regard to the question of whether it does in fact intend or even *can* intend that which it really wants to bring into view and understand, namely, phenomena of our existence. We need to ask whether it can in any sense simply put us into the situation of *being able* to enact a questioning about our existence and about the sense of the phenomena that are found there. Or does the fullest and most proper sense of Jaspers's preconception actually move us away from this situation? Might it be the case that, if this preconception dominates our thinking, *it will never be possible for us even to "circle round" the phenomenon of existence*?

What kind of explanation is required for our "existence"? From what was noted in our introductory comments on this problem, it should be obvious that we are not of the opinion that one can approach the problem of existence directly. This problem is characterized precisely by the fact that it is lost sight of when approached in this way (i.e., when one attempts to avoid all detours in a purportedly superior fashion). Even laying out the very specific *problem of our initial approach* that belongs precisely to the problem of existence, and doing this in a way that satisfies the most rigorous conceptual requirements, is out of the question here, given especially the restricted context of our approach in this critical review. But we should make the preliminary remark that the meaning of this problem of our initial approach is such that it cannot be settled through empty formalistic reflections. And it is just as pressing to underscore that this problem should not be considered something "out of the ordinary" and "novel" that allows us to raise a new commotion in philosophy and to curry favor with the hustle and bustle of an avant-garde culture that is at bottom really hungry for other things, even if it does display wonderful religious antics.

In line with the specific aim of this commentary, we wish only to call the reader's attention to a few themes, and thereby point to *the persistence of a problem*.

Using formal indication (a particular methodological level of pheno-menological explication that will not be dealt with further here, though some understanding of it will be gained in what follows), we can make the following remarks in order to provide an initial approach to this problem (an approach that, according to its very meaning, must in turn be decon-structed).

"Existence" is a determination of something. If one wants to character-ize it in a regional fashion, though in the end this characterization actually proves to be a misinterpretation that leads us away from the real sense of existence, it can be understood as a certain manner of being and thus as a particular sense of "is" that "is," i.e., has, the essential sense of the (I) "am." And we have this (I) "am" in a genuine sense, not through thinking about it in a theoretical manner, but rather by enacting the "am," which is a way of being that belongs to the being of the "I." Understood in this way, the being of the self has the formally indicative meaning of existence. Here we are given a clue as to where we must find the sense of existence as the particular "how" of the self (of the I). What turns out to be important here is accordingly the fact that I *have myself*, i.e., the basic experience in which I encounter myself as a self. Living in this kind of experience, and gearing myself to *its* very sense, I am able to question after the sense of my "I am." This having-myself is ambiguous in many different respects, and this di-versity found in its meaning must be understood specifically with reference to *historical* contexts rather than with reference to contexts of classification that have been elevated to the stature of regions within an autonomous system. In the archontic sense belonging to the enactment of our basic experience of the "I am," an experience that concerns precisely me myself in a radical manner, we find that this experience does not experience the "I" as something located in a region, as an individuation of a "universal," or as an *instance* of something. Rather, this experience is the experience of the "I" as a self. When we keep purely to this enactment of our experience, it be-comes clear that the notion of a region or an objective realm is quite foreign to the "I." We see that each time we attempt to give a regional definition of the "I" (a definition that arises from a preconception about such things as a stream of consciousness or a nexus of experience), we thereby "efface" the sense of the "am" and turn the "I" into an object that can be ascertained and *classified* by inserting it into a region. *Consequently, there is a need for radical suspicion* (and the appropriate investigations as well) *about all preconceptions that objectify by means of regions, about the contexts of concepts that arise from such preconceptions, and about the various avenues through which these concepts arise.*

When it has the sense of "is," the sense of being [*Seinssinn*] has developed from objectively oriented experiences that have been explicated in "theoretical" knowledge, and in which we always somehow or other say of *something* that it "is something." The object here need not be classified expressly within a particular scientific realm that has been worked out through the special logic of the science in question. Rather, it usually takes the form of the nontheoretical "objectivity" that belongs to *what is of significance to us* in our experience of the environing world, the social world we share with each other, and also the world of the self. In factical life, I have dealings of one sort or another with what is of significance to me, and to these "dealings with" there corresponds a unique sense of objectivity that can be understood phenomenologically. When the sense of existence is investigated in terms of its origin and our genuine basic experience of it, we see that it is precisely *that* sense of being that cannot be obtained from the "is" we use to explicate and objectify our experience in one way or another when we acquire knowledge about it. The sense of human existence is to be obtained rather from its own basic experience of having itself in an *anxiously concerned* manner. This having is enacted *prior to* whatever knowledge about it we might later acquire by objectifying it with the "is," and such knowledge is in fact inconsequential for this enactment. If I seek this objectifying knowledge, the attitude of observation will become central for me. All my explications will then have an objectifying nature, but they will put me at a remove from existence and from a genuine having of it (anxious concern).

The "I" should be understood here as the full, concrete, and historically factical self that is accessible to itself in its historically concrete experience of itself. It is not synonymous with the notion of the empirical subject as the possible subject matter of theoretical observation in psychology. In this kind of objectivity, which is understood more or less as a realm of "physical" processes that occur, the "soul" has been eclipsed in a fundamental sense. That is, whenever *this* kind of psychology has begun with *this* kind of object, it has never once brought the "soul" experientially into view, so that it could be given in a preliminary way as an object for further investigation.

Insofar as the "I am" is *something* that can be articulated into "he, she, it is" (or further, "is something"), existence can be spoken of in a formal manner as a particular sense of being and as a particular "how" of being. Here we should also take note of the fact that the "is" in "he, she, it is" (each of which must be understood in the concrete at any particular time) can in turn have different meanings, and these differences mark out a multiplicity of contexts of life and realms of objects. For example, "he is" can be taken in the sense of being present and occurring in nature as it is represented objectively (a multiplicity of objects and relations). Or "he is" can have the sense that he plays a role in the social world he shares with others around him. This sense is expressed, for example, in the trivial question, "What does X do in Y?" The "was" and the "will" that belong to this "is" in connection with the "he" have their own meanings that are crucial for the "is."

But the basic experience of having-myself is not available to one without further ado, nor is it a kind of experience that is aimed at the "I" in such general terms. Rather, if one is to be at all capable of experiencing the specific sense of the "am" and appropriating it in a genuine manner, the enactment of one's experience must have its origin in the full concreteness of the "I," and it must be directed back to this "I" by way of a particular kind of "how." Such experience is not a type of immanent perception that is pursued with a theoretical purpose in mind and is intent on observing the qualities of "psychical" processes and acts that it finds present. To the contrary, the experience of having-myself in fact extends historically into the past of the "I." This past is not like an appendage that the "I" drags along with itself; rather, it is experienced as the past of an "I" that experiences it historically within a horizon of expectations placed in advance of itself and for itself. And here the "I" also has itself in the form of a self. To explicate phenomenologically the "how" of this enactment of experience according to its basic *historical* sense is the task that is most important for us in the whole complex set of problems we face concerning phenomena of existence. Little is to be gained by an external view of the psychical in which one emphasizes that past and future act in conjunction with each other within "*consciousness*," if past and future are understood here as effective states of affairs. In dealing appropriately with this task, we need to understand that the nature of explication lies in the enactment of interpretation. The essential characteristic of the *explicata* involved here is found in the fact that they are *hermeneutical* concepts, to which we have access only in a constant renewal of interpretation that constantly begins anew. It is in this way that we must bring these *explicata* to their genuine level of "precision" and maintain them in it, though such precision cannot be compared to other kinds of conceptual refinement with a different orientation.

In the above-mentioned basic experience that is related to the I, the facticity of this I is decisive. Lived *hic et nunc*, and enacted accordingly in a situation within intellectual history, one's own factical experience of life also brings to enactment one's basic experience of the I that arises from it, remains within it, and returns to the factical. But this factical experience of life, in which I can have myself in different ways, is itself not anything like a region in which I am located, or a universal that gets individuated in my self. According to the "how" of its own enactment, this experience is rather an essentially "historical" phenomenon. However, it is not primarily an objective historical phenomenon (my life happening as something that takes place in the present), but rather a phenomenon of *historical enactment* that experiences itself in such enactment. When, in accord with the relational sense of one's experience, one is directed historically to one's self, the context of this experience also has a historical nature in accord with its sense of enactment. The "historical" is here not the correlate of theoretical and objective historical observation; rather, it is both the content *and* the "how" of the anxious concern of the self about itself, from which the former certainly cannot as such be detached. This having-oneself arises from *anxious concern*, is maintained in it, and tends toward it. And in this anxious concern, the specific past, present, and future of the self are not experienced as temporal schemata for objectively classifying facts; rather, they are experienced within a nonschematic sense of anxious concern that has to do with the enactment of experience in its "how." Accordingly, the phenomenon of existence discloses itself only in a radically historical and essentially anxiously concerned manner of enacting our experience and striving after such enactment. This enactment is not oriented to the attitude of observation, and it does not aim at that classification that objectifies the phenomenon of existence within a region. It is itself not something extraordinary and removed; rather, it has to be enacted in our factical experience of life as such and appropriated from out of such factical experience. And this is supposed to happen not merely once in a momentary and isolated fashion, but rather again and again in a constant renewal of anxious concern that is of necessity motivated by concern for the self as such, and is moreover oriented in a historical manner. In accord with its fundamental sense, "conscience" is understood here as the enactment of conscience, and not merely in the sense of occasionally having a conscience about something (*conscientia*). Conscience is a historically defined "how" of experiencing the self (the history of this "concept" needs to be examined in connection with the problem of existence, and this is not just an academic problem, even if it is already a pressing problem when approached in such a way). In indicating this connection between the sense of historical experience and the sense of the phenomenon of conscience, we are not giving the concept of the historical a broader meaning; rather, we are understanding it in such a way that it is being returned to the authentic source of its sense. And this is also the factical though concealed source from which historical experience in the sense of the development of objective historical knowledge (the historical human sciences) arises. The historical is today almost exclusively something objective, i.e., an object of knowledge and curiosity, a locus providing the opportunity to glean instructions for future action, an object for objective critique and rejection as something antiquated, a fund of materials and examples to be collected, a conglomeration of "instances" for systematic observations dealing with the universal. Since we are unable to see phenomena of existence today in an authentic manner, we no longer experience the meaning of conscience and responsibility that lies in the historical itself (the historical is not merely something of which we have knowledge and about which we write books; rather, we ourselves are it, and have it as a task). Thus even the motives for returning to the historical by way of our own history are inactive and hidden from us.

In its relation to what it experiences, our concrete and factical life-experience has of itself a characteristic tendency to fall away into the "objective" kinds of significance in the experienceable world around it. This falling away is the reason why the sense of being belonging to these objective kinds of significance becomes predominant for us. Thus it is understandable that, regarding its sense of being, the self quickly becomes experienced as having an objectified kind of significance (personality, ideal type of humanity), and within this experiential orientation comes to be understood theoretically and takes on meaning in philosophy. The more the experienced and known past works its way into our own present situation in the form of an objective tradition, the more the self is understood in this objectified manner. As soon as we see that factical life is characteristically loaded down with tradition in this way (tradition can be understood here in many different senses), and that the most pernicious effects of this loading down are mainly to be found precisely in the resulting experiences of having-oneself in the world of the self, we are led to the insight that the concrete possibility of bringing phenomena of existence into view and explicating them in a genuine kind of conceptuality can be opened up for us *only when* the concrete tradition experienced as still at work in one form or another has been deconstructed with an eye to the question of the ways and means of explicating our actual experience of the self, and when as a result of this destruction the basic experiences that have become the effective motives of our thought have been brought into relief and discussed regarding their primordiality. According to its very sense, this kind of destruction always remains inseparable from concrete, fully historical, anxious concern for one's own self.

The self is what it is in its relations to the world of the self, the world it shares with others, and the environing world. The sense of these directions of experience is ultimately historical and inseparable from the world of the self. When phenomenology first erupted onto the scene with its specific aim of appropriating the phenomena of *theoretical* experience and knowledge in a new and primordial manner (the *Logical Investigations*, i.e., a phenomenology of theoretical *logos*), the goal of its research was to win back an unspoiled seeing of both the sense of those objects that are experienced in such theoretical experiences and, correlatively, the sense of "how" these objects become experienced. But if we are to understand the philosophical sense of the tendencies of phenomenology in a radical manner, and appropriate them genuinely, we must not merely carry out research in an "analogical" fashion on the "other" "domains of experience" (the aesthetic, ethical, and religious domains) that we, following one philosophical tradition or another, have partitioned off from one another. Rather, we need to see that experiencing in its fullest sense is to be found in its authentically factical context of enactment in the historically existing self. And this self is in one way or another the ultimate question of philosophy. It will not do to bring in the notion of the person on occasion and *apply* to it philosophical results that were arrived at under the guidance of one philosophical tradition or another. To the contrary, the concrete self should be taken up into the starting point of our approach to philosophical problems, and brought to "givenness" at the genuinely fundamental level of phenomenological interpretation, namely, that level of interpretation that is related to the factical experience of life as such. From these unavoidably terse remarks one thing should have become clear: namely, the authentic phenomenon of existence refers us to the enactment of that way of access to it that is appropriate for it. We come to have the phenomenon of existence only within a certain "how" of experiencing it, and this "how" is something that has to be achieved in a specific manner. It is precisely this "*how*" of appropriation and, moreover, the "how" of our *initial approach* to the enactment of such appropriation that are decisive.

That our factical, historically enacted life is at work right within "how" we factically approach the problem of "how" the self, in being anxiously concerned about itself, appropriates itself – this is something that belongs originally to the very sense of the factical "I am."

Insofar as the phenomenon of existence and the problem that it poses are intended in this form, the question of how we should enact our initial approach and access will *constantly* stand before us in the starting point of our approach to this problem of existence whenever we have understood it in a genuine way. Our question about this "how" is the problem of method, though not the method for a knowledge of objects that defines them with reference to regions, or for a classification of diverse kinds of objects that are given in advance for us and can likewise be given in advance throughout the course of our classifying. Rather, method means here the method belonging to our interpretive, historically enacted explication of concrete and fundamental experiential modes of having-oneself in a factically and anxiously concerned manner.

We are here able to give only a rough indication of the questions that phenomenology urgently needs to address in order to clarify its philosophical sense and work out its position today. These questions, as listed below, must be answered not through abstract formal reflections, but rather in the course of concrete research.

(1) In regard to the problem of existence we have touched on, to what extent does the basic phenomenological attitude which first burst onto the scene with Husserl, and which is a philosophical attitude that cannot be learned by rote as a technique – to what extent does it preserve the most radical origin that can be assigned to the meaning of philosophy? To what extent does it explicitly preserve the decisive orientation that essentially pervades and directs philosophy's concern about all problems?

(2) To what extent does "history" get appropriated here in such a way that it is seen to be more than just a discipline in philosophy? To what extent do we gain an understanding of the fact that the historical is, according to its very sense, originally already there for us right within our philosophical problems, and that accordingly the problem of the relationship between the history of philosophy and systematic philosophy is at bottom a pseudo-problem, even if one believes oneself to have "solved" it with formalistic ruses?

(3) If we have appropriated the basic sense of the phenomenological attitude in a genuine way, to what extent would we sooner have it misused in any other type of intellectual and literary nonsense than have it misused to supply a forced orthodox dogmatics with its apologetic principles, a "perversion" for which a desire has recently begun to stir in phenomenology

(and be this dogmatics, in its tenets, ever so praiseworthy and today still ever so misunderstood as the dogmatics of the Middle Ages, which was, according to *its own* sense, a genuine type of dogmatics)?

Returning to our central problem of preconception, it now becomes clear that, insofar as it aims at the phenomenon of existence, Jaspers's preconception is unsuitable for realizing its own underlying intention. Such is the case both in regard to the functional sense of this preconception (it initially posits that on the basis of which and within which we are to *observe* our existence as concrete life, and it posits it as a whole with essentially regional characteristics) and in regard to the sense of the basic experience that motivates the preconception (the attitude of looking ultimately upon this whole, harmony, and unity of life, inserting phenomena into it in a businesslike fashion, and remaining all the while unconcerned about the world of one's self).

However, the full sense of Jaspers's preconception is not only unsuitable for realizing its own underlying intention that is at work in it; rather, it actually *runs counter to* this intention. For, regarding the intentional relational sense of its understanding, this orientation toward a region puts us at a remove from the phenomenon of existence, which, according to its sense, cannot be formulated and classified in regional terms. And, regarding the sense of the enactment of its fundamental (formally) aesthetic attitude, this orientation does not let the self's anxious concern about itself emerge in a crucial sense as that which first gives direction to and characterizes all problems, their objectivity, and their explication.

If we can now show concretely that in Jaspers's work "method" remains essentially at the level of a technical managing and classifying that, according to its relational sense, is characterized by the businesslike insertion of phenomena into a region, and if we can also show here that "method" is thus from the start not raised as a problem, it will become clear to us from this that Jaspers's method is indeed in keeping with the structure of his preconception, only that it thereby places itself *in opposition to* its very own intention of penetrating to phenomena of existence.

Jaspers characterizes the attitude of his method as mere observation. What is it supposed to accomplish? "The object of all observation is simply that which exists and is there for us so far in human experience. All observation has the tendency to take this as the whole" (329). Do "that which exists and is there [*da ist*] for us so far," "Dasein," and "so far" have the same meaning for any and every type of observing? Jaspers wants to observe "what life is" (250). This is what observation is supposed to teach us about. Observation stands "in the service of burgeoning life" (ibid.). The object that observation pursues is that whole that is initially approached in Jaspers's preconception, as well as the variety of concrete forms that belong to this whole. As observation, which is in itself not creative, it looks only to what is there before it. But how exactly is "life" there for us? And how do we obtain that which exists and is there for us so far? Phenomena of life are after all not like the pieces on a checkerboard that we now need to rearrange. That which is there for us so far, i.e., that which exists in life as something available and knowable, always exists and is "there" in various types of understanding and conceptual expression that have brought about this "being there" [*Dasein*]. After taking up what is given in this kind of interpretive understanding of life, and adopting it as that which actually exists and is really there for us, Jaspers in turn proceeds to organize and classify it in the specific context of understanding with which he works. This should already be clear to us from our previous attempts to make Jaspers's underlying preconception explicit. If our pursuit of phenomena of life merely looks at "what is there," is it at all capable of taking a single step without treating what is there for us so far in a specific context of understanding? Even if we expressly relinquish the claim that our observation is observation *per se* or the only possible kind of observation, our observing of phenomena of life is *historical*, insofar as it must inevitably be interpretive. It is "historical" not merely in the superficial sense of being valid only for a particular age; rather, according to the characteristic sense of its ownmost enactment, it has something essentially historical for its object. One needs to get clear on the nature of this interpretation, if one wants to understand "observation" as a method and recommend it as such.

The fact that today we live in a quite peculiar manner from, in, and with history is surely at the very least something that also exists and "is *there*" for us, if it is not indeed an essential factor of our times. This is the case even if "psychology" has not at all noticed it yet, and if philosophy has taken note of it only within an objective and external orientation. However, any use of observation that intends to get at phenomena of existence must regard precisely this fact of our times as something that needs to be "understood."

It might just be the case that phenomena of life, which are "historical" in accord with their own basic sense, can themselves become accessible to us only in a "historical" manner. And here we need to answer the following question. Does the objectifying kind of understanding in the discipline of history represent the most authentic and radical way of formulating our historical experience in theory? Or is it not the case that, when this question is seen in its inseparable connection with the problem of existence, we are confronted by the problem of finding a method of interpreting our existence in a primordially historical manner? Thus another question arises here. In enacting and explicating this type of interpretation that aims at phenomena of our existence, would we in any sense be calling for anything like the setting up of types? Would this not rather be quite unsuitable for interpreting our existence? Whenever this approach is brought into play, does it not result in essentially skewing the real direction in which understanding should move, since all work with types and any esteem for them always remains within a surreptitious aesthetic attitude? In the present context, it is only important for us to see here how two things *go together:* on the one hand, Jaspers's supposed intention of pursuing *observation*, one that treats phenomena of life as a variety of types and forms, or concretions and instances, which have been stripped of their proper historical provenance; and, on the other hand, his *previously described preconception.* What this shows us is that Jaspers does not see that the historical is a fundamental characteristic of the sense of our existence. Consequently, neither has the problem of method, with respect to its basic meaning and the nature of its point of departure, been geared to the historical in his work.

The other features exhibited by Jaspers's method, namely, the treatment of the question of conceptual expression and the question of "systematics," are also based on his underlying preconception, i.e., on the initial approach to life as a region and the observational attitude toward this region. Life is an infinite flowing whole, but since concepts are forms that bring life to a standstill, it is impossible to grasp life and truly understand it.

The inexpressibility of the soul has often and enthusiastically been asserted in connection with the impossibility of completely grasping the individual. However, it is of crucial importance here to ask which concept of the individual lies at the basis of this problem of conceptual expression. Instead of constantly reformulating the well-worn saying, "*individuum est ineffabile*" [the individual is inexpressible], in new ways, it might be about time to ask the following kinds of questions. What exactly is "*fari*" [expressing] supposed to mean here? What kind of understanding is supposed to come to expression? Is it not the case that what lies at the basis of this dictum is a particular way of understanding the individual which is ultimately based on aesthetic, external observation of the "whole person"? Does not this kind of observation still remain in effect even when personality is "understood" immanently in psychology, since the objective, pictorial point of view remains operative here (cf. Dilthey, for example)?

The manner in which Jaspers selects his "method" and interprets it finds its motivation in the first place in his preconception, but it goes back in particular to that influence of Max Weber and Kierkegaard that Jaspers himself expressly mentions. However, in both cases this happens by way of a fundamental misunderstanding of the real intentions of these thinkers, a misunderstanding that gets its motivation from Jaspers's own preconception. What turned out to be important for Jaspers in Weber's work was firstly his distinction between scientific observation and the promotion of values in worldviews, and secondly the connection he made between the most concrete kind of historical research and systematic thinking (13). I can only understand what Jaspers means here by "systematic" thinking to be Weber's attempt to develop a genuine type of rigorous conceptual expression that would be appropriate to the meaning of his own science. But this means that for Weber the problem of method was *an urgent problem* specifically *in the domain of his very own science*, and in fact only here. That he himself benefited in an essential way from subscribing to the particular theory of science and conceptuality that he did reveals only how clearly he saw the importance of the following two things: on the one hand, the fact that his science is a historical human science of culture ("sociology" is "an empirical science of human action"); and, on the other hand, the fact that Rickert's investigations provide the theoretical and scientific foundations particularly for the historical sciences of culture. This is why Weber had a certain right simply to adopt Rickert's investigations. He essentially never went any further here. He needed to be guided by this kind of approach in his own science, even though it contained a specific problem of method within it. However, one misunderstands the true scientific vehemence of Weber's thought when one simply carries *this* approach over into psychology and, moreover, into one's attempts to get at the *whole* of psychology, i.e., into one's "observations" about basic *principles* that at bottom have a completely different structure than the type of observations Weber pursued. To emulate Weber truly would rather be to strive just as radically and incessantly as he did to achieve a genuine "systematic" mastery in one's own field of psychology and, more particularly, with reference to the problem of working out the whole of psychology as a science. Objective economic processes and human actions as seen in the context of the development of intellectual history are surely from the start something other than worldviews and "ultimate positions of psychical life," i.e., phenomena of existence. At the very least, one really needs to ask whether the attitude, method, and conceptual structures of sociology can be transferred from this science (taken, moreover, in the sense of Weber's very specific conception of it) to Jaspers's problem of the nature of psychology, which he broaches, moreover, for the sake of pursuing specifically *philosophical* intentions.

Furthermore, we need to examine that distinction between scientific observation and value which likewise has a very specific sense in Weber's thought, and which again derives from his own concrete science. Can one make it a requirement also in the sphere of philosophical knowing without any further discussion? If the meaning of objectivity in philosophical knowledge has not been clarified beforehand, we can decide nothing about the role of this distinction in philosophy.

Concerning Kierkegaard, we should point out that such a heightened consciousness of methodological rigor as his has rarely been achieved in philosophy or theology (the question of where he achieved this rigor is not important here). One loses sight of nothing less than the most important aspect of Kierkegaard's thought when one overlooks this consciousness of method, or when one's treatment of it takes it to be of secondary importance.

Jaspers falls under the spell of a deception when he thinks that it is precisely in mere observation that he would achieve the highest degree of noninterference in the personal decisions of his readers, and would thus free these individuals for their own self-reflection. On the contrary, by presenting his investigations as mere observations he indeed appears to avoid imposing on his readers *particular* worldviews, i.e., the ones that he has described, but he pushes his readers into believing that his unexamined preconception (life as a whole) and the essential kinds of articulation corresponding to it are something obvious and noncommittal, whereas it is rather precisely in the meaning of these concepts and the "how" of interpreting that everything is really decided. Mere observation does not give us what it wants to, namely, the possibility of radical reexamination, decision, and, what is synonymous with these, an intense consciousness of the methodological necessity of questioning. We can set genuine self-reflection free in a meaningful way only when it is there to be set free, and it is there for us only when it has been rigorously awoken. Moreover, it can be genuinely awoken only if the Other is in a certain way relentlessly compelled to engage in reflection, and thereby sees that one's appropriation of the objects treated in philosophy is inseparably bound up with a certain rigor in the enactment of method. All sciences fall short of this kind of rigor, since in the sciences it is only the demand for objectivity that is important, whereas in philosophy what belongs together with the matters treated is the philosophizing individual and (his) notorious poverty. One can call something to the attention of others, and compel them to engage in reflection, only by traveling a stretch of the way oneself.

Jaspers might be able to justify his having allowed the problem of method to recede into the background by pointing out that he did not endeavor to provide a "general psychology" in his investigations. Certainly, all problems cannot be dealt with in one fell swoop. But in fundamental investigations dealing with principles the successive treatment of problems is no mere juxtaposition of them. Any individual problem in philosophy bears within itself directives for us to follow forward and backward into contexts of principles. It is a sign precisely of Jaspers's misunderstanding and undervaluation of the real problem of method that he approaches problems in psychology of worldviews under the assumption that this psychology is a separate science. He fails to see that "general psychology" and "psychology of worldviews" cannot be separated from each other in this way, and that both of these together cannot be separated from fundamental problems in philosophy.

Though Jaspers has only gathered up and depicted what "is there," he has nonetheless gone beyond mere classification by bringing together in a new way what has already been available to us, and this must be evaluated positively as a real advance. However, if it is to be capable of effectively stimulating and challenging contemporary philosophy, his method of mere observation must evolve into an "infinite process" of radical questioning that always includes itself in its questions and preserves itself in them.

APPENDIX

Familiarity with Jaspers's book is assumed. A detailed report has been avoided because this book does not, in a good sense, allow itself to be reported on without simply paraphrasing its different parts. Otherwise the clarity that Jaspers has striven for, and fully attained in many parts, would be missing from the reader's representation and understanding of his book. This is also why certain changes in the various parts of the book that have turned out to be rather sprawling would be welcome in a new edition. These parts could remain as they are, if only Jaspers would show us in his subsequent investigations that a clear preliminary presentation of the phenomena in question is really already a head start, as it were, for the philosophical explication that follows.

But one change or another may very well be apropos in the following areas.

(1) The Introduction (pp. 1–31) can be left out altogether without this impairing the reader's understanding of the body of the book, or else it must be rewritten and limited to §1, §2, and the section from p. 31 to p. 37. The latter belongs among the best parts of the book, and it makes possible a more fundamental understanding and analysis of principles. It is only in a fundamental investigation of principles that §3 (pp. 14–31) could be

developed in a way that is appropriate to the sense of the phenomena in question.

(2) It would be more germane to the subject matter of the book if Chapter III (Types of Mental Life) were placed at the beginning, and if Chapter I (Attitudes) and Chapter II (Worldviews) were also allowed to emerge, as it were, from out of the "vital forces" that are presented in Chapter III. Jaspers characterizes these attitudes and worldviews as "emanations" (189) of vital forces. It would be even more effective to organize Chapter III and "divide it up" into parts in such a way that Chapter I and Chapter II were taken up and contained right in the middle of it.

(3) It would be more in accordance with the way in which Jaspers actually proceeds in his book if the methodological expression "psychology of understanding" were specified as a "*constructive* psychology of understanding" ("constructive" is meant here in a positive sense as a formation of types that draws these types out of intuitive understanding, and which is enacted and developed in a manner that is always appropriate to such understanding). The problem of understanding has been left undiscussed in our critical observations because such questions remain unripe for discussion so long as the problem of the historical that was roughly indicated in our "comments" has not been laid hold of at its roots and lifted up into the center of philosophical problems. The same goes for the notion of "ideas as driving forces."

Phenomenology and Theology

Translated by James G. Hart and John C. Maraldo[1]

PREFACE

This little book contains a lecture and a letter.

The lecture "Phenomenology and Theology" was given on March 9, 1927, in Tübingen and was again delivered on February 14, 1928, in Marburg. The text presented here forms the content of the immediately reworked and improved second part of the Marburg lecture: "The Positivity of Theology and Its Relation to Phenomenology." In the Introduction to *Being and Time* (1927) §7, pp. 27ff., one finds a discussion of the notion of phenomenology (as well as its relation to the positive sciences) that guides the presentation here.

The letter of March 11, 1964, gives some pointers to major aspects for a theological discussion concerning "The Problem of a Nonobjectifying Thinking and Speaking in Today's Theology." The discussion took place at Drew University in Madison, New Jersey, on April 9–11, 1964.

These texts were published for the first time in *Archives de Philosophie*, vol. 32 (1969), pp. 356ff., with an accompanying French translation.

This little book might perhaps be able to occasion repeated reflection on the extent to which the Christianness of Christianity and its theology merit questioning; but also on the extent to which philosophy, in particular that presented here, merits questioning.

Almost one hundred years ago there appeared simultaneously (1873) two writings of two friends: the "first piece" of the *Thoughts Out of Season* of Friedrich Nietzsche, wherein "the glorious Hölderlin" is mentioned; and the "little book" *On the Christianness of Today's Theology* of Franz Overbeck, who established the world-denying expectation of the end as the basic characteristic of what is primordially Christian.

39

To say both writings are unseasonable also in today's changed world means: For the few who think among the countless who reckon, these writings intend and point toward that which itself perseveres before the inaccessible through speaking, questioning, and creating.

For a discussion of the wider realm of investigation of both writings, see Martin Heidegger, "Nietzsche's Word: 'God Is Dead,' " in *Holzwege* (1950), pp. 193ff.; and "European Nihilism" and "The Determination of Nihilism in the History of Being" in *Nietzsche*, vol. II, pp. 7–232 and 233–96. Both texts were published separately in 1967.

Freiburg im Breisgau, August 27, 1970

❧

The popular understanding of the relationship between theology and philosophy is fond of opposing faith and knowledge, revelation and reason. Philosophy is that interpretation of the world and of life that is removed from revelation and free from faith. Theology, on the other hand, is the expression of the credal understanding of the world and of life – in our case a Christian understanding. Taken as such, philosophy and theology give expression to a tension and a struggle between two worldviews. This relationship is decided not by scientific argument but by the manner, the extent, and the strength of the conviction and the proclamation of the worldview.

We, however, see the problem of the relationship *differently* from the very start. It is for us rather a question about the *relationship of two sciences*.

But this question needs a more precise formulation. It is not a case of comparing the factical circumstances of two historically given sciences. And even if it were, it would be difficult to describe a unified state of affairs regarding the two sciences today in the midst of their divergent directions. To proceed on a course of comparison with respect to their factical relationship would yield no *fundamental* insight as to how Christian theology and philosophy are related to one another.

Thus what is needed as a basis for a fundamental discussion of the problem is an ideal construction of the ideas behind the two sciences. One can decide their possible relationship to one another from the possibilities they both have as sciences.

Posing the question like this, however, presupposes that we have established the idea of science in general, as well as how to characterize the modifications of this idea that are possible in principle. (We cannot enter into this problem here; it would have to be taken up in the prolegomena to our discussion.) We offer only as a guide the following formal definition of science: science is the founding disclosure, for the sheer sake of disclosure, of a self-contained region of beings, or of being. Every region of objects, according to its subject matter and the mode of being of its objects, has its own mode of possible disclosure, evidence, founding, and its own conceptual formation of the knowledge thus arising. It is evident from the idea of science as such – insofar as it is understood as a possibility of Dasein – that there are two basic possibilities of science: sciences of beings, of whatever is, or ontic sciences; and *the* science of being, the ontological science, philosophy.

Ontic sciences in each case thematize a given being that in a certain manner is always already disclosed *prior* to scientific disclosure. We call the sciences of beings as given – of a *positum* – positive sciences. Their characteristic feature lies in the fact that the objectification of whatever it is that they thematize is oriented directly toward beings, as a continuation of an already existing prescientific attitude toward such beings. Ontology, or the science of being, on the other hand, demands a fundamental shift of view: from beings to being. And this shift nevertheless keeps beings in view, but for a modified attitude. We shall not go into the question of the method of this shift here.

Within the circle of actual or possible sciences of beings – the positive sciences – there is between any two only a relative difference, based on the different relations that in each case orient a science to a specific region of beings. On the other hand, every positive science is *absolutely*, not relatively, different from philosophy. Our thesis, then, is that *theology is a positive science, and as such, therefore, is absolutely different from philosophy.*

Hence one must ask how theology is related to philosophy in the light of this absolute difference. It is immediately clear from the thesis that theology, as a positive science, is in principle closer to chemistry and mathematics than to philosophy. Put in this way, we have the most extreme formulation of the relationship between theology and philosophy – one that runs counter to the popular view. According to this popular view, each of the sciences [philosophy and theology], to a certain extent, has as its theme the same area: human life and the world. But they are guided by different points of view. The one proceeds from the principle of *faith*, the other from the principle of *reason*. However, our thesis is: Theology is a positive science and as such is absolutely different from philosophy.

The task of our discussion will be to characterize theology as a positive science and, on the basis of this characterization, to clarify its possible relationship to philosophy, which is absolutely different from it.

Note that we are considering theology here in the sense of Christian theology. This is not to say that Christian theology is the only theology. The most central question is whether, indeed, theology in general is a science. This question is deferred here, not because we wish to evade the problem, but only because that question cannot be asked meaningfully until the idea of theology has been clarified to a certain extent.

Before turning to the discussion proper, we wish to submit the following considerations. In accordance with our thesis, we are considering a positive science, and evidently one of a particular kind. Therefore a few remarks are in order about what constitutes the positive character of a science as such.

Proper to the positive character of a science is: first, that a being that in some way is already disclosed is to a certain extent come upon as a possible theme of theoretical objectification and inquiry; second, that this given *positum* is come upon in a definite prescientific manner of approaching and proceeding with that being. In this manner of procedure, the specific content of this region and the mode of being of the particular entity show themselves. That is, this disclosure is prior to any theoretical apprehending, although it is perhaps implicit and not thematically known. Third, it is proper to the positive character of a science that this prescientific comportment toward whatever is given (nature, history, economy, space, number) is also already illuminated and guided by an understanding of being – even if it be nonconceptual. The positive character can vary according to the substantive content of the entity, its mode of being, the manner in which it is prescientifically disclosed, and the manner in which this disclosedness belongs to it.

The question thus arises: Of what sort is the positive character of theology? Evidently this question must be answered before we can be in a position to determine its relation to philosophy. But setting down the positive character of theology will not yet sufficiently clarify its status as a science. We have not yet arrived at the full concept of theology as a science, but only at what is proper to it as a positive science. If thematizing is supposed to adjust the direction of inquiry, the manner of investigation, and the conceptuality to the particular *positum* in each case, it is more to the point here to identify the specific scientific character belonging to the specific positive character of theology. Therefore, only by identifying the positive *and* the scientific character of theology do we approach this discipline as a positive science and acquire the basis for characterizing its possible relationship to philosophy.

Thus our consideration obtains a threefold division:

a) the positive character of theology;
b) the scientific character of theology;
c) the possible relation of theology, as a positive science, to philosophy.

a) THE POSITIVE CHARACTER OF THEOLOGY

A positive science is the founding disclosure of a being that is given and in some way already disclosed. The question arises: What is already given for theology? One might say: What is given for Christian theology is Christianity as something that has come about historically, witnessed by the history of religion and spirit and presently visible through its institutions, cults, communities, and groups as a widespread phenomenon in world history. Christianity: the given *positum*; and hence theology: the science of Christianity. That would evidently be an erroneous characterization of theology, for theology itself belongs to Christianity. Theology itself is something that everywhere in world history gives testimony to its intimate connection with Christianity itself as a whole. Evidently, then, theology cannot be the science of Christianity as something that has come about in world history, because it is a science that itself belongs to the history of Christianity, is carried along by that history, and in turn influences that history.

Is theology therefore a science that itself belongs to the history of Christianity in the way that every historical [*historische*] discipline is itself a historical [*geschichtliche*] appearance, namely, by representing the historical development of its consciousness of history? If this were the case, then we could characterize theology as the self-consciousness of Christianity as it appears in world history. However, theology does not belong to Christianity merely because, as something historical, the latter has a place in the general manifestations of culture. Rather, theology is a knowledge of that which initially makes possible something like Christianity as an event in world history. Theology is a conceptual knowing of that which first of all allows Christianity to become an originarily historical event, a knowing of that which we call Christianness pure and simple. Thus we maintain that *what is given for theology (its positum) is Christianness*. The latter decides the form theology will take as the positive science that thematizes it. The question arises: what does "Christianness" mean?

We call faith Christian. The essence of faith can formally be sketched as a way of existence of human Dasein that, according to its own testimony – itself belonging to this way of existence – arises *not from* Dasein or

43

spontaneously *through* Dasein, but rather from that which is revealed in and with this way of existence, from what is believed. For the "Christian" faith, that being which is primarily revealed to faith, and only to it, and which, as revelation, first gives rise to faith, is Christ, the crucified God. The relationship of faith to the cross, determined in this way by Christ, is a Christian one. The crucifixion, however, and all that belongs to it is a historical event, and indeed this event gives testimony to itself as such in its specifically historical character only for faith in the scriptures. One "knows" about this fact only *in believing*.

That which is thus revealed in faith is, in accordance with its specific "sacrificial" character, imparted specifically to individual human beings factically existing historically (whether contemporaneous or not), or to the community of these individuals existing as a community. The imparting of this revelation is not a conveyance of information about present, past, or imminent happenings; rather, this imparting lets one "part-take" of the event that is revelation (= what is revealed therein) itself. But the part-*taking* of faith, which is realized only in existing, is *given* as such always only through faith. Furthermore, this "part-taking" and "having part in" the event of the crucifixion places one's entire existence [*Dasein*] – as a Christian existence, i.e., one bound to the cross – before God. And thereby the existence struck by this revelation is revealed to itself in its forgetfulness of God. Thus – and again I speak only of an ideal construction of the idea – being placed before God means that existence is reoriented in and through the mercy of God grasped in faith. Thus faith understands itself only in believing. In any case, the believer does not come to know anything about his specific existence, for instance, by way of a theoretical confirmation of his inner experiences. Rather, he can only "believe" this possibility of existence as one which the Dasein concerned does not independently master, in which it becomes a slave, is brought before God, and is thus born *again*. Accordingly, the proper existentiell meaning of faith is: *faith = rebirth*. And rebirth does not mean a momentary outfitting with some quality or other, but a way in which a factical, believing Dasein historically exists in *that* history which begins with the occurrence of revelation; in *that* history which, in accord with the very meaning of the revelation, has a definite uttermost end. The occurrence of revelation, which is passed down to faith and which accordingly occurs in faithfulness itself, discloses itself only to faith.

Luther said, "Faith is permitting ourselves to be seized by the things we do not see" (*Werke* [Erlangen Ausgabe], vol. 46, p. 287). Yet faith is not something that merely reveals that the occurring of salvation is something happening; it is not some more or less modified type of knowing.

Rather, faith is an appropriation of revelation that co-constitutes the Christian occurrence, that is, the mode of existence that specifies a factical Dasein's Christianness as a particular form of destiny. *Faith is the believing-understanding mode of existing in the history revealed, i.e., occurring, with the Crucified.*

The totality of this being that is disclosed by faith – in such a way, indeed, that faith itself belongs to the context of its disclosure – constitutes the character of the *positum* that theology finds before it. *Presupposing* that theology is enjoined on faith, out of faith, and for faith, and *presupposing* that science is a *freely* performed, conceptual disclosure and objectification, theology is constituted in thematizing faith and that which is disclosed through faith, that which is "revealed." It is worthy of note that faith is not just the manner in which the *positum* objectified by theology is already disclosed and presented; faith itself is a theme for theology. And not only that. Insofar as theology is enjoined upon faith, it can find sufficient motivation for itself only in faith. If faith would totally oppose a conceptual interpretation, then theology would be a thoroughly *inappropriate* means of grasping its object, faith. It would lack something so essential that without this it could never become a science in the first place. The necessity of theology, therefore, can never be deduced from a purely rationally constructed system of sciences. Furthermore, faith not only motivates the intervention of an interpretive science of Christianness; at the same time, faith, as rebirth, is *that* history to whose occurrence theology itself, for its part, is supposed to contribute. Theology has a meaning and a legitimacy only if it functions as an ingredient of faith, of this particular kind of historical occurrence.

By attempting to elucidate this connection [between theology and faith], we are likewise showing how, through the specific positive character of theology, i.e., through the Christian occurrence disclosed in faith as faith, the scientific character of the science of faith is prefigured.

b) THE SCIENTIFIC CHARACTER OF THEOLOGY

Theology is the science of faith.

This says several things:

(1) Theology is the science of that which is disclosed in faith, of that which is believed. That which is believed in this case is not some coherent order of propositions about facts or occurrences which we simply agree to – which, although theoretically not self-evident, can be appropriated because we agree to them.

(2) Theology is accordingly the science of the very comportment of believing, of faithfulness – in each case a revealed faithfulness, which cannot possibly be any other way. This means that faith, as the comportment of believing, is itself believed, itself belongs to that which is believed.

(3) Theology, furthermore, is the science of faith, not only insofar as it makes faith and that which is believed its object, but because it itself arises out of faith. It is the science that faith of itself motivates and justifies.

(4) Theology, finally, is the science of faith insofar as it not only makes faith its object and is motivated by faith, but because this objectification of faith itself, in accordance with what is objectified here, has no other purpose than to help cultivate faithfulness itself for its part.

Formally considered, then, faith as the existing relation to the Crucified is a mode of historical Dasein, of human existence, of historically being in a history that discloses itself only in and for faith. Therefore theology, as the science of faith, that is, of an intrinsically *historical* [geschichtlichen] mode of being, is to the very core a *historical* [historische] science. And indeed it is a unique sort of historical science in accord with the unique historicity involved in faith, i.e., with "the occurrence of revelation."

As conceptual interpretation of itself on the part of faithful existence, that is, as historical knowledge, theology aims solely at that transparency of the Christian occurrence that is revealed in, and delimited by, faithfulness itself. Thus the goal of this historical science is concrete Christian existence itself. Its goal is never a valid system of theological propositions about general states of affairs within one region of being that is present at hand among others. The transparency of faithful existence is an understanding of existence and as such can relate only to existing itself. Every theological statement and concept addresses itself in its very content to the faithful existence of the individual in the community; it does *not* do so subsequently, on the basis of some practical *"application."* The specific content of the object of theology demands that the appropriate theological knowledge never take the form of some free-floating knowledge of arbitrary states of affairs. Likewise, the theological transparency and conceptual interpretation of faith cannot found and secure faith in its legitimacy, nor can it in any way make it easier to accept faith and remain constant in faith. Theology can only render faith more difficult, that is, render it more certain that faithfulness cannot be gained through the science of theology, but solely through faith. Hence theology can permit the serious character of faithfulness as a "graciously bestowed" mode of existence to become a matter of conscience. Theology "can" perform this; i.e., it is capable of this, but it is *only possibly* that it may have this effect.

In summary, then, theology is a *historical science*, in accordance with the character of the *positum* objectified by it. It would seem that with this thesis we are denying the possibility and the necessity of a *systematic* as well as a *practical* theology. However, one should note that we did not say that there is only "historical theology," to the exclusion of "systematic" and "practical" theology. Rather our thesis is: Theology as such is historical as a science, regardless of how it may be divided into various disciplines. And it is precisely this characterization that enables one to understand why and how theology originally divided into a systematic, a historical (in the narrower sense), and a practical discipline – not in addition, but in keeping with the specific unity of its theme. The philosophical understanding of a science is, after all, not achieved by merely latching on to its factical and contingent, pregiven structure and simply accepting the technical division of labor in order then to join the various disciplines together externally and subsume them under a "general" concept. Rather, a philosophical understanding requires that we question beyond the factically existing structure and ascertain *whether* and *why* this structure is demanded by the essence of the science in question and to what extent the factical organization corresponds to the idea of the science as determined by the character of its *positum*.

In reference to theology it thus becomes evident that, because it is a conceptual interpretation of Christian existence, the content of all its concepts is essentially related to the Christian occurrence as such. *To grasp the substantive content and the specific mode of being of the Christian occurrence, and to grasp it solely as it is testified to in faith and for faith, is the task of systematic theology.* If indeed faithfulness is testified to in the *scriptures*, systematic theology is in its essence *New Testament theology*. In other words, theology is not systematic in that it first breaks up the totality of the content of faith into a series of *loci*, in order then to reintegrate them within the framework of a system and subsequently to prove the validity of the system. It is systematic not by constructing a system, but on the contrary by *avoiding* a system, in the sense that it seeks solely to bring clearly to light the intrinsic σύστημα of the Christian occurrence as such, that is, to place the believer who understands conceptually into the history of revelation. The more historical theology is and the more immediately it brings to word and concept the historicity of faith, the more is it "systematic" and the less likely is it to become the slave of a system. The radicality with which one knows of this task and its methodological exigencies is the criterion for the scientific level of a systematic theology. Such a task will be more certainly and purely accomplished the more directly theology permits its concepts and conceptual schemes to be determined by the mode of being and the specific substantive content of *that* entity which it objectifies. The more unequivocally theology disburdens itself of the application of some philosophy and its system, the more *philosophical* is its own radical scientific character.

On the other hand, the more systematic theology is in the way we have designated, the more immediately does it found the *necessity of historical theology in the narrower sense* of exegesis, church history, and history of dogma. If these disciplines are to be genuine *theology* and not special areas of the general, profane historical sciences, then they *must* permit themselves to be guided in the choice of their object by systematic theology correctly understood.

The Christian occurrence's interpretation of itself as a historical occurrence also implies, however, that its own specific historicity is appropriated ever anew, along with an understanding, arising from that historicity, of the possibilities of a faithful existence [*Dasein*]. Now because theology, as a systematic as well as a historical discipline, has for its primary object the Christian occurrence in its Christianness and its historicity, and because this occurrence specifies itself as a mode of existence of the believer, and existing is action, πρᾶξις, *theology in its essence has the character of a practical science.* As the science of the action of God on human beings who act in faith it is already "innately" homiletical. And for this reason alone is it possible for theology itself to constitute itself in its factical organization as practical theology, as homiletics and catechetics, and not on account of contingent requirements that demand, say, that it apply its theoretical propositions to a practical sphere. *Theology is systematic only when it is historical and practical. It is historical only when it is systematic and practical. And it is practical only when it is systematic and historical.*

All of these characteristics essentially hang together. The contemporary controversies in theology can turn into a genuine exchange and fruitful communication only if the problem of theology as a science is followed back to the central question that derives from considering *theology as a positive science:* What is the ground of the specific unity and necessary plurality of the systematic, historical, and practical disciplines of theology?

We can add a few clarifications to this sketchy outline of the character of theology by showing what theology is *not.*

Etymologically regarded, theo-logy means: science of God. But God is in no way the object of investigation in theology, as, for example, animals are the theme of zoology. Theology is not speculative knowledge of God. And we hit upon the concept of theology no better when we expand the theme and say: The object of theology is the all-inclusive relationship of God to man and of man to God. In that case theology would be the philosophy or the history of religion, in short, *Religionswissenschaft*. Even less is it the psychology of religion, i.e., the science of man and his religious states and experiences, the analysis of which is supposed to lead ultimately to the discovery of God in man. One could, however, admit that theology does not coincide in general with speculative knowledge of God, the scientific study of religion, or the psychology of religion – and still want to stress that theology represents a special case of the philosophy and history of religion, etc., namely, the philosophical, historical, and psychological science of the Christian religion.

Yet it is clear from what we have said that systematic theology is not a form of the philosophy of religion applied to the Christian religion. Nor is church history a history of religion limited to the Christian religion. In all such interpretations of theology the idea of this science is abandoned from the very beginning. That is, it is *not* conceived with regard to the specific positive character of theology, but rather is arrived at by way of a deduction and specialization of nontheological sciences – philosophy, history, and psychology – sciences that, indeed, are quite heterogeneous to one another. Of course, to determine where the limits of the scientific character of theology lie, i.e., to determine how far the specific exigencies of faithfulness itself can and do press for conceptual transparency and still remain faithful, is both a difficult and a central problem. It is tied most closely to the question about the original ground of the unity of the three disciplines of theology.

In no case may we delimit the scientific character of theology by using an *other* science as the guiding standard of evidence for its mode of proof or as the measure of rigor of its conceptuality. In accord with the *positum* of theology (which is essentially disclosed only in faith), not only is the access to its object unique, but the evidence for the demonstration of its propositions is quite special. The conceptuality proper to theology can grow only out of theology itself. There is certainly no need for it to borrow from other sciences in order to augment and secure its proofs. Nor indeed can it attempt to substantiate or justify the evidence of faith by drawing on knowledge gained from other sciences. *Rather, theology itself is founded primarily by faith*, even though its statements and procedures of proof formally derive from free operations of reason.

Likewise, the shortcomings of the nontheological sciences with respect to what faith reveals is no proof of the legitimacy of faith. One can allow "faithless" science to run up against and be shattered by faith only if one already faithfully holds fast to the truth of faith. But faith misconceives itself if it then thinks that it is first proven right or even thereby fortified when the other sciences shatter against it. The substantive legitimacy of all theological knowledge is grounded in faith itself, originates out of faith, and leaps back into faith.

On the grounds of its specific positive character and the form of knowing which this determines, we can now say that theology is a fully autonomous ontic science. The question now arises: How is this positive science, with its specific positive and scientific character, related to philosophy?

c) THE RELATION OF THEOLOGY, AS A POSITIVE SCIENCE, TO PHILOSOPHY

If faith does not need philosophy, the *science* of faith as a *positive* science does. And here again we must distinguish: The positive science of faith does not need philosophy for the founding and primary disclosure of its *positum*, Christianness, which founds itself in its own manner. The positive science of faith needs philosophy only in regard to its scientific character, and even then only in a uniquely restricted, though basic, way.

As a science theology places itself under the claim that its concepts show and are appropriate to the being that it has undertaken to interpret. But is it not the case that that which is to be interpreted in theological concepts is precisely that which is disclosed only through, for, and in faith? Is not that which is supposed to be grasped conceptually here something essentially inconceivable, and consequently something whose content is not to be fathomed, and whose legitimacy is not to be founded, by purely rational means?

Nevertheless, something can very well be inconceivable and never primarily disclosable through reason without thereby excluding a conceptual grasp of itself. On the contrary: if its inconceivability as such is indeed to be disclosed properly, it can only be by way of the appropriate conceptual interpretation – and that means pushing such interpretation to its very limits. Otherwise the inconceivability remains, as it were, mute. Yet this interpretation of faithful existence is the task of theology. And so, why philosophy? Whatever is discloses itself only on the grounds of a preliminary (although not explicitly known), preconceptual understanding of what and how such a being is. Every ontic interpretation operates on the basis, at first and for the most part concealed, of an ontology. But can such things as the cross, sin, etc., which manifestly belong to the ontological context of Christianness, be understood specifically as to what they are and how they are, except through faith? How does one ontologically disclose the what (the essence) and the how (the mode of being) underlying these fundamental concepts that are constitutive of Christianness? Is faith to become the criterion of knowledge for an ontological-philosophical explication? Are not the basic theological concepts completely withdrawn from philosophical-ontological reflection?

Of course one should not lose sight here of something essential: the explication of basic concepts, insofar as it proceeds correctly, is never accomplished by explicating and defining isolated concepts with reference to themselves alone and then operating with them here and there as if they were playing chips. Rather, all such explication must take pains to envision and hold constantly in view in its original totality the primary, self-contained ontological context to which all the basic concepts refer. What does this mean for the explication of basic theological concepts?

We characterized faith as the essential constitutive element of Christianness: faith is rebirth. Though faith does not bring itself about, and though what is revealed in faith can never be founded by way of a rational knowing as exercised by autonomously functioning reason, nevertheless the sense of the Christian occurrence as rebirth is that Dasein's prefaithful, i.e., unbelieving, existence is sublated [*aufgehoben*] therein. Sublated does not mean done away with, but raised up, kept, and preserved in the new creation. One's pre-Christian existence is indeed existentielly, ontically, overcome in faith. But this existentiell overcoming of one's pre-Christian existence (which belongs to faith as rebirth) means precisely that one's overcome pre-Christian Dasein is existentially, ontologically included within faithful existence. To overcome does not mean to dispose of, but to have at one's disposition in a new way. Hence we can say that precisely because all basic theological concepts, considered in their full regional context, include a content that is indeed existentielly powerless, i.e., *ontically* sublated, they are *ontologically* determined by a content that is pre-Christian and that can thus be grasped purely rationally. All theological concepts necessarily contain *that* understanding of being that is constitutive of human Dasein as such, insofar as it exists at all.[2] Thus, for example, sin is manifest only in faith, and only the believer can factically exist as a sinner. But if sin, which is the counterphenomenon to faith as rebirth and hence a phenomenon of existence, is to be interpreted in theological concepts, then the *content* of the concept *itself*, and not just any philosophical preference of the theologian, calls for a return to the concept of guilt. But guilt is an original ontological determination of the existence of Dasein.[3] The more originally and appropriately the basic constitution of Dasein is brought to light in a genuine ontological manner and the more originally, for example, the concept of guilt is grasped, the more clearly it can function as a guide for the theological explication of sin.

But if one takes the ontological concept of guilt as a guide, then it seems that it is primarily philosophy that decides about theological concepts. And, then, is not theology being led on the leash by philosophy? Not at all. For sin, in its essence, is not to be deduced rationally from the concept of guilt. Even less so should or can the basic fact of sin be rationally demonstrated, in whatever manner, by way of this orientation to the ontological concept of guilt. Not even the factical possibility of sin is in the least bit evidenced in this way. Only one thing is accomplished by this orientation; but that one thing is indispensable for theology as a science: The theological concept of sin as a concept of existence acquires that correction (i.e., co-direction) that is necessary for it insofar as the concept of existence has pre-Christian content. But the primary direction (derivation), the source of its Christian content, is given only by faith. *Therefore ontology functions only as a corrective to the ontic, and in particular pre-Christian, content of basic theological concepts.*

Here one must note, however, that this correction does not found any-thing, in the way, for example, that the basic concepts of physics acquire from an ontology of nature their original foundation, the demonstration of all their inner possibilities, and hence their higher truth. Rather, this correction is only formally indicative; that is to say, the ontological concept of guilt as such is never a theme of theology. Also the concept of sin is not simply built up upon the ontological concept of guilt. Nevertheless, the latter is determinative in one respect, in that it formally indicates the ontological character of *that* region of being in which the concept of sin *as a concept of existence* must necessarily maintain itself.

In thus formally indicating the ontological region, there lies the direc-tive not to calculate philosophically the specific theological content of the concept but rather to allow it to arise out of, and to present itself within, the specific existential dimension of faith thereby indicated. Thus, formally indicating the ontological concept does not serve to bind but, on the con-trary, to release and point to the specific, i.e., credal source of the disclosure of theological concepts. The function of ontology here is not to direct, but only, in "co-directing," to correct.

Philosophy is the formally indicative ontological corrective of the ontic and, in particular, of the pre-Christian content of basic theological concepts.

But it is not of the essence of philosophy, and it can never be estab-lished by philosophy itself or for its own purpose, that it must have such a corrective function for theology. On the other hand, it can be shown that philosophy, as the free questioning of purely self-reliant Dasein, does of its essence have the task of directing all other nontheological, positive sciences with respect to their ontological foundation. As ontology, philosophy does provide the *possibility* of being employed by theology as a corrective, in the sense we have discussed, if indeed theology is to be factical with respect to the facticity of faith. The demand, however, that it *must* be so employed is not made by philosophy as such but rather by theology, insofar as it understands itself to be a science. In summary, then, the precise formulation is:

Philosophy is the possible, formally indicative ontological corrective of the ontic and, in particular, of the pre-Christian content of basic theological concepts. But philosophy can be what it is without functioning factically as this corrective.

This peculiar relationship does not exclude but rather includes the fact that *faith*, as a specific possibility of existence, is in its innermost core the mortal enemy of the *form of existence* that is an essential part of *philosophy* and that is factically ever-changing.[4] Faith is so absolutely the mortal enemy that philosophy does not even begin to want in any way to do battle with it. This *existentiell opposition* between faithfulness and the free appropriation of one's whole Dasein is not first brought about by the sciences of theology and philosophy but is *prior* to them. Furthermore, it is precisely this *opposition* that must bear the *possibility of a community of the sciences* of theology and philosophy, if indeed they are to communicate in a genuine way, free from illusions and weak attempts at mediation. Accordingly, there is no such thing as a Christian philosophy; that is an absolute "square circle." On the other hand, there is likewise no such thing as a neo-Kantian, or axiological, or phenomenological theology, just as there is no phenomenological mathematics. Phenomenology is always only the name for the procedure of ontology, a procedure that essentially distinguishes itself from that of all other, positive sciences.

It is true that someone engaged in research can master, in addition to his own positive science, phenomenology as well, or at least follow its steps and investigations. But philosophical knowledge can become genuinely relevant and fertile for his own positive science *only when*, within the problematic that stems from such positive deliberation on the ontic correlations in his field, he comes upon the basic concepts of his science and, furthermore, questions the suitability of traditional fundamental concepts with respect to those beings that are the theme of his science. Then, proceeding from the demands of his science and from the horizon of his own scientific inquiry, which lies, so to speak, on the frontiers of his basic concepts, he can search back for the original ontological constitution of those beings that are to remain and *become* anew the object of his science. The questions that arise in this way methodically thrust beyond themselves insofar as that *about which* they are asking is accessible and determinable only ontologically. To be sure, scientific communication between researchers in the positive sciences and philosophy cannot be tied down to definite rules, especially since the clarity, certainty, and originality of critiques by scientists of the foundations of their own positive sciences change as often and are as varied as the stage reached and maintained by philosophy at any point in clarifying its own essence. This communication becomes and remains genuine, lively, and fruitful only when the respective positive-ontic and transcendental-ontological inquiries are guided by an instinct for the issues and by the certainty of scientific good sense, and when all the questions about dominance, preeminence, and validity of the sciences recede behind the inner necessities of the scientific problem itself.

APPENDIX

The Theological Discussion of "The Problem of a Nonobjectifying Thinking and Speaking in Today's Theology" – Some Pointers to Its Major Aspects

Freiburg im Breisgau, March 11, 1964

What is it that is worth questioning in this problem? As far as I see, there are *three themes* that must be thought through.

(1) Above all else one must determine *what* theology, as a mode of thinking and speaking, is to place in discussion. That is the Christian faith, and what is believed therein. Only if this is kept clearly in view can one inquire how thinking and speaking are to be formulated so that together they correspond to the proper sense and claim of faith and thus avoid projecting into faith ideas that are alien to it.

(2) *Prior* to a discussion of *non*objectifying thinking and speaking, it is ineluctable that one state what is intended by *objectifying* thinking and speaking. Here the question arises whether or not all thinking and speaking are objectifying by their very nature.

Should it prove evident that thinking and speaking are by no means in themselves already objectifying, then this leads to a third theme.

(3) One must decide to what extent the problem of a nonobjectifying thinking and speaking is a genuine problem at all, whether one is not inquiring here about something in such a way that only circumvents the matter, diverts from the theme of theology and unnecessarily confounds it. In this case the convened theological dialogue would have the task of clearly seeing that it was on a path leading nowhere with its problem. This would – so it seems – be a merely negative result of the dialogue. But it only seems that way. For in truth this would necessitate that theology once and for all get clear about the requisite of its major task not to borrow the categories of its thinking and the form of its speech from philosophy or the sciences, but to think and speak out of faith for faith with fidelity to its subject matter. If this faith by the power of its own conviction concerns the human being as human being in his very nature, then genuine theological thinking and speaking have no need of any special preparation in order to reach people and find a hearing among them.

These three themes have to be placed in discussion in more detail. I for my part, proceeding from philosophy, can give some pointers only with regard to the second topic. For it is the task of theology to place in discussion the first theme, which necessarily underlies the entire dialogue if it is not to remain up in the air.

The third theme comprises the theological consequences of the first and second, when they are treated sufficiently.

I shall now attempt to give some pointers for treating the *second* theme – but this again only in the form of a few questions. One should avoid the impression that dogmatic theses are being stated in terms of a Heideggerian philosophy, when there is no such thing.

SOME POINTERS WITH REGARD TO
THE SECOND THEME

Prior to placing in discussion the question of a *non*objectifying thinking and speaking in theology, it is necessary to reflect on what one understands by an *objectifying* thinking and speaking, as this problem has been put to the theological dialogue. This reflection necessitates that we ask:

Is objectifying thinking and speaking a particular kind of thinking and speaking, or does all thinking as thinking, all speaking as speaking, necessarily have to be objectifying?

This question can be decided only if beforehand the following questions are clarified and answered:

(a) What does objectifying mean?

(b) What does thinking mean?

(c) What does speaking mean?

(d) Is all thinking in itself a speaking, and all speaking in itself a thinking?

(e) In what sense are thinking and speaking objectifying, and in what sense are they not?

It is of the nature of the matter that these questions interpenetrate when we place them in discussion. The entire weight of these questions, however, lies at the basis of the problem of your theological dialogue. Moreover, these same questions – when more or less clearly and adequately unfolded – form the still hidden center of those endeavors toward which the "philosophy" of our day, from its most extreme counterpositions (Carnap → Heidegger), tends. One calls these positions today: the technical-scientistic view of language and the speculative-hermeneutical experience of language.

Both positions are determined by tasks profoundly different from one another. The first position desires to subjugate all thinking and speaking, including that of philosophy, to a sign-system that can be constructed logically or technically, that is, to secure them as an instrument of science. The other position has arisen from the question: what is it that is to be experienced as the proper matter of philosophical thinking, and how is this matter (being as being) to be said?

Hence neither position is concerned with a philosophy of language as a separate province (in the way we have a philosophy of nature or of art). Rather, both positions recognize language as the realm within which the thinking of philosophy and every kind of thinking and saying move and reside. Insofar as the Western tradition has tended to determine the essence of man as that living being that "has language," as ζῷον λόγον ἔχον (even man as an acting being is such only as one that "has language"), the debate between the two positions has nothing less at stake than the question of human existence and its determination.

It is up to theology to decide in what manner and to what extent it can and should enter into this debate.

We preface the following brief elucidation of questions (a) to (e) with an observation that presumably led to the occasion for proposing the "problem of a nonobjectifying thinking and speaking in today's theology." I mean the widespread, uncritically accepted opinion that all thinking, as representing, and all speaking, as vocalization, are already "objectifying." It is not possible here to trace this opinion in detail back to its origins. The determining factor has been the distinction, set forth in an unclarified manner long ago, between the rational and the irrational. This distinction in turn is brought to bear in the jurisdiction of a reasonable but itself unclarified thinking.

Recently, however, the teachings of Nietzsche, Bergson, and the life-philosophers set the standard for this claim concerning the objectifying character of all thinking and speaking. To the extent that, in speaking,[a] we say "is" everywhere, whether expressly or not, yet being means presence, which in modern times has been interpreted as objectivity – to that extent thinking as re-presenting and speaking as vocalization have inevitably entailed a solidifying of the intrinsic flow of the "life-stream," and thus a falsifying thereof. On the other hand, such a consolidation of what is permanent, even though it falsifies, is indispensable for the preservation and continuance of human life. The following text from Nietzsche's *Will to Power*, no. 715 (1887/88), may suffice to document this variously modified opinion: "The means of expression in language cannot be used to express 'becoming'; to posit continually a more crude world of what is permanent, of things, etc. [i.e., of objects] is part of our *irredeemable need for preservation*."

The following pointers[b] to questions (a) through (e) are themselves to be understood and thought through as questions. For the phenomenon most worthy of thought and questioning remains the mystery of language – wherein our entire reflection has to gather itself – above all when it dawns on us that language is not a work of human beings: language speaks. Humans speak only insofar as they co-respond to language. These statements are not the offspring of some fantastic "mysticism." Language is a primal phenomenon which, in what is proper to it, is not amenable to factual proof but can be caught sight of only in an unprejudiced experience of language. Humans may be able to invent artificial speech constructions and signs, but they are able to do so only in reference to and from out of an already spoken language. Thinking remains critical also with respect to primal phenomena. For to think critically means to distinguish (κρίνειν) constantly between that which requires proof for its justification and that which, to confirm its truth, demands a simple catching sight of and taking in. It is invariably easier to set forth a proof in a given case than, in a differently presented case, to venture into catching sight of and holding in view.

(a) What does it mean to objectify? To make an object of something, to posit it as object and represent it only as such. And what does object mean? In the Middle Ages *obiectum* signified that which is thrown before, held

---

[a] First edition, 1970: Inadequate; instead: as those who dwell (i.e., interpret our abode in the world).

[b] First edition, 1970: The pointers deliberately leave the ontological difference unheeded.

over and against our perceiving, imagination, judging, wishing, and intuiting. *Subiectum*, on the other hand, signified the ὑποχείμενον, that which lies present before us from out of itself (not brought before us by representation), whatever is present, e.g., things. The signification of the words *subiectum* and *obiectum* is precisely the reverse of what subject and object usually mean today: *subiectum* is what exists independently (objectively), and *obiectum* is what is merely (subjectively) represented.

As a consequence of Descartes's reformulation of the concept of *subiectum* (cf. *Holzwege*, pp. 98ff.), the concept of object [*Objekt*] also ends up with a changed signification. For Kant object means what exists as standing over against [*Gegenstand*] the experience of the natural sciences. Every object stands over against, but not everything standing over against (e.g., the thing-in-itself) is a possible object. The categorical imperative, moral obligation, and duty are not objects of natural-scientific experience. When they are thought about, when they are intended in our actions, they are not thereby objectified.

Our everyday experience of things, in the wider sense of the word, is neither objectifying nor a placing over against. When, for example, we sit in the garden and take delight in a blossoming rose, we do not make an object of the rose, nor do we even make it something standing over against us in the sense of something represented thematically. When in tacit saying [*Sagen*] we are enthralled with the lucid red of the rose and muse on the redness of the rose, then this redness is neither an object nor a thing nor something standing over against us like the blossoming rose. The rose stands in the garden, perhaps sways to and fro in the wind. But the redness of the rose neither stands in the garden nor can it sway to and fro in the wind. All the same we think it and tell of it by naming it. There is accordingly a thinking and saying that in no manner objectifies or places things over against us.

The statue of Apollo in the museum at Olympia we can indeed regard as an object of natural-scientific representation; we can calculate the physical weight of the marble; we can investigate its chemical composition. But this objectifying thinking and speaking does not catch sight of the Apollo who shows forth his beauty and so appears as the visage of the god.

(b) What does it mean to think? If we heed what has just been set forth, it will be clear that thinking and speaking are not exhausted by theoretical and natural-scientific representation and statement. Thinking rather is that comportment that lets itself be given, by whatever shows itself in whatever way it shows itself, what it has to say of that which appears. Thinking is not necessarily a representing of something as an object. Only the thinking and speaking of the natural sciences is objectifying. If all thinking as such were objectifying, then it would be meaningless to fashion works of art, for they could never show themselves to anyone: one would immediately make an object of that which appears and thus would prevent the artwork from appearing.

The assertion that all thinking as thinking is objectifying is without foundation. It rests on a disregard of phenomena and belies a lack of critique.

(c) What does it mean to speak? Does language consist only in converting what is thought into vocables, which one then perceives only as tones and sounds that can be identified objectively? Or is the vocalization of speech (in a dialogue) something entirely different from a series of acoustically objectifiable sounds furnished with a signification by means of which objects are spoken about? Is not speaking, in what is most proper to it, a saying, a manifold showing of that which hearing, i.e., an obedient heeding of what appears, lets be said? Can one, if we keep only this carefully in view, still assert uncritically that speaking, as speaking, is always already objectifying? When we speak condolence to a sick person and speak to him heart to heart, do we make an object of this person? Is language only an instrument that we employ to manipulate objects? Is language at all within the human being's power of disposal? Is language only a work of humans? Is the human being that being that has language in its possession? Or is it language that "has" human beings, insofar as they belong to, pay heed to language, which first opens up the world to them and at the same time thereby their dwelling in the world?

(d) Is all thinking a form of speaking and all speaking a form of thinking?

The questions placed in discussion up to now direct us to surmise that thinking and speaking belong together (form an identity). This identity was testified to long ago, insofar as λόγος and λέγειν simultaneously signify talking and thinking. But this identity has still not been adequately placed in discussion and commensurately experienced. One principal hindrance is concealed in the fact that the Greek explication of language, that is to say the grammatical interpretation, is oriented to stating something about things. Later, modern metaphysics reinterpreted things to mean objects. This suggested the erroneous opinion that thinking and speaking refer to objects and only to objects.

If, on the other hand, we keep in view the decisive matter at stake, namely, that thinking is in each case a letting be said of what shows itself, and accordingly a co-responding (saying) to that which shows itself, then it will become evident to what extent poetizing too is a pensive saying. And the proper nature of this saying, it will be admitted, cannot be determined by means of the traditional logic of statements about objects.

It is this insight into the interrelation of thinking and saying that lets us see that the thesis that thinking and speaking as such necessarily objectify is untenable and arbitrary.

(e) In what sense do thinking and speaking objectify, and in what sense do they not? Thinking and speaking objectify, i.e., posit as an object something given, in the field of natural-scientific and technical representation. Here they are of necessity objectifying, because scientific-technological knowing must establish its theme in advance as a calculable, causally explicable *Gegenstand*, i.e., as an object as Kant defined the word. Outside this field thinking and speaking are by no means objectifying.

But today there is a growing danger that the scientific-technological manner of thinking will spread to all realms of life. And this magnifies the deceptive appearance that makes all thinking and speaking seem objectifying. The thesis that asserts this dogmatically and without foundation promotes and supports for its part a portentous tendency: to represent everything henceforth only technologically-scientifically as an object of possible control and manipulation. This process of unrestrained technological objectification naturally also affects language itself and its determination. Language is deformed into an instrument of reportage and calculable information. It is treated like a manipulable object, to which our manner of thinking must conform. And yet the saying of language is not necessarily an expressing of propositions *about* objects. Language, in what is most proper to it, is a saying *of* that which reveals itself to human beings in manifold ways and which addresses itself to human beings insofar as they do not, under the dominion of objectifying thinking, confine themselves to the latter and close themselves off from what shows itself.

That thinking and speaking are objectifying only in a derivative and limited sense can never be deduced by way of scientific proof. Insight into the proper nature of thinking and saying comes only by holding phenomena in view without prejudice.

Hence it just might be erroneous to suppose that only that which can be objectively calculated and proven technically and scientifically as an object is capable of being.

This erroneous opinion is oblivious of something said long ago that Aristotle wrote down: ἔστι γὰρ ἀπαιδευσία τὸ μὴ γιγνώσκειν τίνων δεῖ ζητεῖν ἀπόδειξιν καὶ τίνων οὐ δεῖ. "It is the mark of not being properly brought up, not to see in relationship to what it is necessary to seek proofs and when this is not necessary" (*Metaphysics*, 1006 a6ff.).

Now that we have given these pointers we may turn to the third theme – the decision whether and to what extent the theme of the dialogue is a genuine problem – and say the following:

On the basis of our deliberations on the *second* theme, the problem put by the dialogue must be expressed less equivocally. It must, in a purposely pointed formulation, read: "the problem of a nontechnological, non-natural-scientific thinking and speaking in today's theology." From this more commensurate reformulation, it is very clear that the problem as stated is not a genuine problem insofar as it is geared to a presupposition whose nonsense is evident to anyone. Theology is not a natural science.

Yet the problem as stated conceals the positive task for theology. That task is for theology to place in discussion, within its own realm of the Christian faith and out of the proper nature of that faith, what theology has to think and how it has to speak. This task also includes the question whether theology can still be a science – because presumably it should not be a science at all.

ADDITION TO THE POINTERS

An example of an outstanding nonobjectifying thinking and speaking is poetry.

In the third of the *Sonnets to Orpheus*, Rilke says in poetic speech by what means poetic thinking and saying is determined. "*Gesang ist Dasein*" – "Song is existence" (cf. *Holzwege*, pp. 292ff.). Song, the singing saying of the poet, is "not coveting," "not soliciting" that which is ultimately accomplished by humans as an effect.

Poetic saying is "Dasein," existence. This word, "Dasein," is used here in the traditional metaphysical sense. It signifies: presence.

Poetic thinking is being in the presence of... and for the god. Presence means: simple willingness that wills nothing, counts on no successful outcome. Being in the presence of...: purely letting the god's presence be said.

Such saying does not posit and represent anything as standing over against us or as object. There is nothing here that could be placed before a grasping or comprehending representation.

"A breath for nothing." "Breath" stands for a breathing in and out, for a letting be said that responds to the word given us. There is no need for an extensive discussion in order to show that underlying the question of a thinking and saying commensurate to the matter at stake is the question of the being of whatever is and shows itself in each instance.

Being as presence can show itself in various modes of presence. What is present does not have to stand over against us; what stands over against us does not have to be empirically perceived as an object. (Cf. Heidegger, *Nietzsche*, vol. II, sections VIII and IX.)

From the Last Marburg Lecture Course

Translated by Michael Heim[1]

[373] In the summer semester of 1928 this lecture course set itself the task of attempting a confrontation with Leibniz. This intent was guided by its perspective on the ecstatic being-in-the-world of human beings granted by a look into the question of being.

The first Marburg semester of 1923/24 had ventured a corresponding confrontation with Descartes, one which then became part of *Being and Time* (§§19–21).

These and other interpretations were shaped by the insight that in our philosophical thought we are a dialogue with the thinkers of previous times. Such a dialogue means something other than completing a system of philosophy through a historiographical presentation of philosophy's history. Nor should it be compared to that unique identity that Hegel attained for the thinking of his thought or of the history of thinking.

In keeping with tradition, the metaphysics that Leibniz develops is an interpretation of the substantiality of substance.

The following text, which has been excerpted and revised from the said lecture course, attempts to show the projection and guiding thread on the basis of which Leibniz determines the being of beings.

The word Leibniz chooses to designate the substantiality of substance is already indicative. Substance is monad. The Greek word μονάς means the simple, unity, the one. But it means also: the individual, the solitary. Leibniz uses the word monad only after he had developed his metaphysics of substance, after 1696. All the fundamental Greek meanings are contained, as it were, in what Leibniz intends by this word. The essence of [374] substance resides in its being a monad. Beings proper have the character of the simple unity of the individual, of what stands by itself. To anticipate, the monad is that which simply and originarily unifies and which individuates in advance.

63

Three things are therefore to be kept in mind if we are to adequately define the monad:

(1) The monads, the units or points, are not themselves in need of unification but rather are that which gives unity. They make something possible.

(2) The units that confer unity are themselves primordially unifying, in a certain sense active. Therefore Leibniz designates these points *vis primitiva*, *force primitive*, primordially simple force.

(3) This conception of the monad has metaphysical-ontological intent. Thus Leibniz also calls the points *points metaphysiques*, "metaphysical points," and not mathematical points (G. IV, 482; E. 126).² They are further called "formal atoms," not material atoms. That is, they are not ultimate, elemental pieces of ὕλη, of *materia*, but they are the primordial, indivisible principle of formation, of the *forma*, the εἶδος.

Every independent being is constituted as monad. Leibniz states, "ipsum persistens... primitivam vim habet": Every independent being is endowed with force (G. II, 262).

Understanding the metaphysical meaning of the doctrine of monads depends on correctly understanding the concept of *vis primitiva*.

The problem of the substantiality of substance should be solved positively, and for Leibniz this problem is a problem of unity, of the monad. Everything said about force and its metaphysical function must be understood from the perspective of the problem of defining the unity of substance in a positive way. The nature of force must be understood by way of the problem of unity as it is inherent in substantiality. Leibniz delineates his concept of force, of *vis activa*, against the Scholastic [375] conception of *potentia activa* [active power]. *Vis activa* and *potentia activa* seem literally to say the same. But:

Differt enim vis activa a potentia nuda vulgo scholis cognita, quod potentia activa Scholasticorum, seu facultas, nihil aliud est quam propinqua agendi possibilitas, quae tamen aliena excitatione et velut stimulo indiget, ut in actum transferatur.

Vis activa differs from the mere power to act familiar to the Schools, for the active power or faculty of the Scholastics is nothing but a proximate possibility of acting, of accomplishing, which needs an external excitation or stimulus, as it were, to be transferred into action. (G. IV, 469)

The *potentia activa* of the Scholastics is merely a disposition to act, a disposition that is about to act but does not yet act. It is a present-at-hand capacity in something present at hand, a capacity that has not yet come into play.

Sed vis activa actum quendam sive ἐντελέχειαν continet, atque inter facultatem agendi actionemque ipsam media est, et conatum involvit.

But *vis activa* contains a certain acting that is already actual, an entelechy, and is thus midway between a merely static capacity for acting and the act itself and involves an intrinsic *conatus*, a seeking. (Ibid.)

The *vis activa* is accordingly a certain activity and, nevertheless, not activity in its real accomplishment. It is a capacity, but not a capacity at rest. We call what Leibniz means here "to tend toward..." or, better yet, in order to bring out the specific, already somewhat actual moment of activity: to press or drive toward, *drive* [Drang]. Neither a disposition nor a process is meant, rather a letting something be taken on (namely, taken upon oneself), a being set on oneself (as in the idiom "he is set on it"), a taking it on oneself.

Of itself, drive characteristically leads into activity, not just occasionally but [376] essentially. This leading into requires no prior external stimulus. Drive is the impulse that in its very essence is self-propulsive. The phenomenon of drive not only brings along with it, as it were, the cause, in the sense of release, but drive is as such always already released. It is triggered, however, in such a way that it is still always tensed. Drive can indeed be inhibited in its thrust, but even as inhibited it is not the same as a static capacity for acting. Eliminating whatever inhibits it can nevertheless first allow the thrust to become free. The disappearance of whatever inhibits it, or, to use Max Scheler's felicitous expression, disinhibition [*Enthemmung*], is something other than an additional cause coming from outside. Leibniz says: "Atque ita per se ipsam in operationem fertur; nec auxiliis indiget, sed sola sublatione impedimenti" [It is thus carried into action by itself and needs no help, but only the removal of an impediment] (ibid.). The image of a bent bow illustrates his meaning. The expression "force" can therefore easily lead us astray, because it suggests the idea of a static property.

After this clarification of *vis activa* as drive, Leibniz arrives at the essential definition: "Et hanc agendi virtutem omni substantiae inesse ajo, semperque aliquam ex ea actionem nasci": I say that this power of acting inheres in every substance (constitutes its substantiality) and that some action always arises from it (ibid., 470). In other words, it is drive and is productive. *Producere* means: to lead something forth, to let it come out of itself and to maintain this outcome in itself. This applies also to corporeal substances.

When bodies impact on one another, the drive only becomes variously limited and restricted. Those (the Cartesians) overlooked this "qui essentiam eius (substantiam corporis) in sola extensione collocaverunt" [who located the essence (of corporeal substance) in extension alone] (ibid.).

Every being has this character of drive and is defined, in its being, as having drive. This is the monad's fundamental metaphysical feature, though the structure of drive has not yet been explicitly determined.

[377] Implied here is a metaphysical statement of the greatest importance, which we must now anticipate. For, as universal, this interpretation of what properly is must also explain the possibility of beings as a whole. What does the fundamental claim of the monadology imply about the way the various beings are present together in the universe as a whole?

If the essence of substance is interpreted as monad, and the monads are interpreted as *vis primitiva*, as drive, *conatus, nisus prae-existens*, as originarily driving and bearing within them that which completely unifies, then the following questions arise with respect to this interpretation of beings and its important consequences:

(1) To what extent is drive as such that which unifies in an originary and simple manner?

(2) How, on the basis of the monadic character of substances, are we to interpret their unity and togetherness in the universe?

If each being, each monad, has its own drive, that means it brings along with it the essentials of its being, the goal and manner of its drive. All the concomitant drives operative in the other monads are, in their possible relation to each individual monad, essentially negative. No substance can confer its drive, which is its essential being, on other substances. It can merely inhibit or disinhibit, and even this negative function it can exercise only indirectly. The relation one substance has to another is solely restrictive and hence negative in nature.

Leibniz is very clear on this point:

Apparebit etiam ex nostris meditationibus, substantiam creatam ab alia substantia creata non ipsam vim agendi, sed praeexistentis iam nisus sui, sive virtutis agendi, limites tantummodo ac determinationem accipere.

[It will be apparent from our meditations that one created substance receives from another created substance, not the force of acting itself but only the limits and the determination of its own preexistent striving or power of action.]

This *nisus praeexistens* is decisive. Leibniz concludes by saying: "Ut alia nunc taceam ad solvendum illud problema difficile, de substantiarum operatione in se invicem, profutura." [Not to speak now of other matters, I shall leave the solution of the difficult problem of the mutual action of substances upon each other for the future.]

[378] N.B. Leibniz describes *vis activa* also as ἐντελέχεια, with reference to Aristotle (cf., for instance, the *New System*, §3). In the *Monadology* (§18) he adds the explanation for this designation: "car elles ont en elles une certaine perfection (ἔχουσι τὸ ἐντελές)": for they have in them a certain perfection, in a certain manner they carry within them a completeness, insofar as each monad (as will be shown later) brings its positive content already with it, and brings it in such a way that this content is potentially the universe itself.

This construal of ἐντελέχεια does not conform to Aristotle's real intention. On the other hand, by giving it new meaning, Leibniz claims this very term for his monadology.

Already in the Renaissance ἐντελέχεια was translated in the Leibnizian sense with *perfectihabia*; the *Monadology*, in §48, names Hermolaus Barbarus the translator of the term. In the Renaissance, Hermolaus Barbarus translated and commented on Aristotle and on the commentary of Themistius (320–390), and he did so in order to restore the Greek Aristotle against medieval Scholasticism. Naturally his task harbored considerable difficulties. The story goes that, compelled by his perplexity over the philosophical meaning of the term ἐντελέχεια, he invoked the Devil to provide him with instruction.

At this point we have explained, in general, the concept of *vis activa*: (1) *vis activa* means "drive." (2) This drive is supposed to be inherent in every substance as substance. (3) Some accomplishing or carrying out continually arises from drive.

But now we are just coming to the real metaphysical problem of substantiality, to the question about the unity of substance as that which primarily is. Leibniz calls that which is not substance a "phenomenon," something derivative, a surplus.

The unity belonging to the monads is not the result of an accumulation, a subsequent addition; rather, the unity is to be found in that which confers unity in advance. Unity as the conferral of unity is active, [379] *vis activa*, drive as the *primum constitutivum* of the unity of substance. Herein lies the central problem of the monadology, the problem of *drive* and of *substantiality*.

The fundamental character of this activity has now come into view. It remains to be seen how drive should itself be unity-conferring. A further question of decisive importance is: On the basis of this intrinsically unitary monad, how does the universe as a whole constitute itself in its interconnectedness?

We first need to interpose another consideration. We emphasized several times that we can find the metaphysical meaning of the monadology only when we venture to construct essential connections and perspectives, and when we do so by following that which directed Leibniz himself in projecting the monadology.

The monadology tries to clarify the being of beings. Hence a paradigmatic idea of being must be obtained somewhere. Such an idea has been found where something like being manifests itself immediately to the one asking philosophical questions. We comport ourselves toward beings, become involved with and lose ourselves in them; we are overwhelmed and captivated by beings. Yet not only do we relate to beings, but we are likewise ourselves beings. This we each are, and we are so, not indifferently, but in such a way that our very own being is a concern for us. Aside from other reasons, one's own being as that of the questioner is therefore in a certain way always the guiding thread: so too in projecting the monadology. What is thereby seen in advance, however, remains uninterrogated ontologically.

Constant regard for our own existence [*Dasein*], for the ontological constitution and manner of being of one's own "I," provides Leibniz with the model of the unity he attributes to every being. This becomes clear in many passages. Clarity about this guiding thread is of decisive importance for understanding the monadology.

De plus, par le moyen de l'âme ou forme, il y a une véritable unité qui répond à ce qu'on appelle MOI en nous; ce qui ne [380] sauroit avoir lieu ni dans les machines de l'art, ni dans la simple masse de la matière, quelque organisée qu'elle puisse être; qu'on ne peut considérer que comme une armée ou un troupeau, ou comme un étang plein de poissons, ou comme une montre composée de ressorts et de roues.

By means of regarding the "soul" or the "form" there results the idea of a true unity corresponding to what in us is called the "I"; such a unity could not occur in artificial machines or in a simple mass of matter as such, however organized (formed) it may be. It can only be compared, then, to an army or a herd, or to a pond full of fish, or a watch composed of springs and wheels. (*New System*, §11)

Substantiam ipsam potentia activa et passiva primitivis praeditam, veluti τὸ Ego vel simile, pro indivisibili seu perfecta monade habeo, non vires illas derivatas quae continue aliae atque aliae reperientur.

I regard substance itself, if indeed it has originarily the character of drive, as an indivisible and perfect monad – comparable to our ego.... (Letter to the Cartesian de Volder, philosopher at the University of Leyden, June 20, 1703; G. II, 251; B. II, 325)

Operae autem pretium est considerare, in hoc principio Actionis plurimum inesse intelligibilitatis, quia in eo est analogum aliquod ei quod inest nobis, nempe perceptio et appetitio, ...

It can be further suggested that this principle of activity (drive) is intelligible to us in the highest degree because it forms to some extent an analogue to what is intrinsic to ourselves, namely, representing and striving. (Letter to de Volder, June 30, 1704; G. II, 270; B. II, 347)

Here it is especially evident, first, that the analogy with the "I" is essential and, second, that precisely this origin results in the highest degree of intelligibility.

Ego vero nihil aliud ubique et per omnia pono quam quod in nostra anima in multis casibus admittimus omnes, nempe mutationes [381] internas spontaneas, atque ita uno mentis ictu totam rerum summam exhaurio.

I, on the contrary, presuppose everywhere only that which all of us have to admit happens frequently enough in our soul, that is, intrinsic self-activated changes, and with this single presupposition of thought I exhaust the entire sum of things. (Letter to de Volder, 1705; G. II, 276; B. II, 350)

So the only presupposition, the proper content of the metaphysical projection, is this idea of being that is taken from the experience of the self, from the self-activated change perceptible in the ego, from the activity of drive.

"If we conceive substantial forms (*vis primitiva*) as something analogous to souls, then one may doubt whether they have been repudiated rightfully" (letter to Johann Bernoulli, July 29, 1698; G. Math. Schr.[3] III, 521; B. II, 366). This does not mean substantial forms are simply souls, that they are new things and small particles, but they rather correspond to the soul. The latter merely serves as incentive for projecting the basic structure of the monad.

... et c'est ainsi, qu'en pensant à nous, nous pensons à l'Etre, à la substance, au simple ou au composé, à l'immatériel et à Dieu même, en concevant que ce qui est borné en nous, est en lui sans bornes.

It is thus, as we think of ourselves, that we think of being, of substance, of the simple and the compound, of the immaterial, and of God himself, conceiving of that which is limited in us as being without limits in him. (via eminentiae.) (*Monadology*, §30)

From where, then, does Leibniz take the guiding thread for determining the being of beings? Being is interpreted by analogy with soul, life, and spirit. The guiding thread is the "I."

That concepts themselves and truth do not come from the senses, but arise in the "I" and the understanding, is shown by a letter to Queen Sophia Charlotte of Prussia: *Lettre* [382] *touchant ce qui est indépendant des Sens et de la Matière*, "On What Is Independent of Sense and Matter" (1702; G. VI, 499ff.; B. II, 410ff.).

For the entire problem concerning the guiding thread of self-reflection and self-consciousness in general this letter is of great importance. In it Leibniz says:

Cette pensée de *moy*, qui m'apperçois des objets sensibles, et de ma propre action qui en resulte, adjoute quelque chose aux objets des sens. Penser à quelque couleur et considerer qu'on y pense, ce sont deux pensées tres differentes, autant que la couleur même differe de moy qui y pense. Et comme je conçois que d'autres Estres peuvent aussi avoir le droit de dire *moy*, ou qu'on pourroit le dire pour eux, c'est par là que je conçois ce qu'on appelle *la substance* en general, et c'est aussi la consideration de moy même, qui me fournit d'autres notions de *metaphysique*, comme de cause, effect, action, similitude etc., et même celles de la *Logique* et de la *Morale*.

This thought of *myself*, who perceives sensible objects, and of my own action which results from it, adds something to the objects of sense. To think of some color and to consider that I think of it – these two thoughts are very different, just as much as color itself differs from the *ego* who thinks of it. And since I conceive that there are other beings who also have the right to say "I" or for whom this can be said, it is by this that I conceive what is called *substance* in general. It is the consideration of myself which provides me also with other metaphysical concepts, such as those of cause, effect, action, similarity, etc., and even with those of *logic* and *ethics*. (G. VI, 502; B. II, 414)

"*L'Estre* même et *la Verité* ne s'apprend pas tout à fait par les sens": *Being itself* and *truth* are not understood completely through the senses (ibid.).

"Cette conception de *l'Estre et de la Verité* se trouve donc dans ce Moy, et dans l'Entendement plustost que dans les sens externes [383] et dans la perception des objets exterieurs": This conception *of being and of truth* is thus found in the ego and in the understanding rather than in the external senses and the perception of exterior objects (G. VI, 503; B. II, 415).

Regarding knowledge of being in general, Leibniz says: "Et je voudrois bien savoir, comment nous pourrions avoir l'idee de l'estre, si nous n'estions des Estres nous mêmes, et ne trouvions ainsi l'estre en nous" (*New Essays* I, 1, §23; cf. also §21 and *Monadology*, §30). Here, too, being and subjectivity are brought together, albeit in a way that can be misunderstood: We could not have the idea of being if we were not ourselves beings and found beings in ourselves.

Certainly we must be – as Leibniz indicates – in order to have the idea of being. It is, to speak metaphysically, our very essence that we cannot be what we are without the idea of being. An understanding of being is constitutive for Dasein (*Discourse on Metaphysics*, §27).

But from this it does not follow that we obtain the idea of being by recourse to ourselves as beings.

We ourselves are the source of the idea of being. But this source must be understood as the *transcendence* of *Dasein* as ecstatic. Only on the ground of transcendence is there the articulation of the various ways of being. Determining the idea of being as such is, however, a difficult and ultimate problem.

Because an understanding of being belongs to the subject as Dasein in its transcendence, the idea of being can be drawn from the subject.

What is the result of all this? First, that Leibniz – for all his differences with Descartes – like Descartes maintains the self-certainty of the "I" as the primary certainty. Like Descartes, he sees in the "I," in the *ego cogito*, the dimension out of which all fundamental metaphysical concepts must be drawn. The attempt is made to solve the problem of being as the fundamental problem of metaphysics by recourse to the subject. And yet [384] in Leibniz too, just as in his predecessors and successors, this recourse to the "I" remains ambiguous, because the "I" is not grasped in its essential structure and specific manner of being.

The function of the *ego* as guiding thread is equivocal in many respects. On the one hand, the subject is the exemplary being with regard to the problem of being. The subject itself, as a being, in its being provides the idea of being in general. On the other hand, however, the subject *is* as a subject that understands being; as a being of a particular kind, it has, *in* its being, an understanding of being, where being does not only mean existing Dasein.

Despite a highlighting of genuine ontic phenomena, the concept of the subject itself remains unclarified ontologically.

This is why, precisely with Leibniz, the impression must arise that the monadological interpretation of beings is simply anthropomorphism, some universal animism by analogy with the "I." But this would be a superficial and arbitrary reading. Leibniz himself tries to ground this analogical consideration metaphysically: "... cum rerum natura sit uniformis nec ab aliis substantiis simplicibus ex quibus totum consistit Universum, nostra infinite differre possit": For since the nature of things is uniform, our own nature cannot differ infinitely from the other simple substances of which the whole universe consists (letter to de Volder, June 30, 1704; G. II, 270; B. II, 347). Of course the general ontological principle Leibniz cites in order to ground his observation here would itself still have to be grounded.

Instead of being satisfied with a crude confirmation of anthropomorphism, we must ask conversely: Which structures of our own Dasein are supposed to become relevant for the interpretation of the being of substance? How are these structures modified so as to have the prerogative of making intelligible monadologically every being and all levels of being?

[385] The central problem that must be raised once more is: How does the drive that distinguishes substance as such confer unity? How must drive itself be defined?

If drive, or what is defined as that which is as drive, is supposed to confer unity insofar as it is as drive, then it must itself be simple. It must have no parts in the sense of an aggregate, a collection. The *primum constitutivum* (G. II, 342) must be an indivisible unity.

"Quae res in plura (actu iam existentia) dividi potest, ex pluribus est aggregata, et res quae ex pluribus aggregata est, non est unum nisi mente nec habet realitatem nisi a contentis mutuatam" [Whatever can be divided into many (actually existing) is an aggregate of many, and something that is an aggregate of many is not one, except mentally, nor does it have reality except by borrowing it from its contents] (letter to de Volder, G. II, 267). That which is divisible has only a borrowed content.

"Hinc jam inferebam, ergo dantur in rebus unitates indivisibiles, quia alioqui nulla erit in rebus unitas vera, nec realitas non mutuata. Quod est absurdum" [From this I now inferred that there are indivisible unities in things because otherwise there will be no true unity in things nor a reality that is not borrowed. And that is absurd] (ibid.).

La Monade dont nous parlerons ici, n'est autre chose, qu'une substance simple, qui entre dans les composés; *simple*, c'est à dire, sans parties.

The monad we are to discuss here is nothing but a simple substance that enters into compounds. It is simple, i.e., it has no parts. (*Monadology*, §1)

If, however, substance is simply unifying, there must already be something manifold that it unifies. For otherwise the problem of unification would be senseless and superfluous. That which unifies and whose essence is to unify must therefore essentially have a relation to the manifold. There must be a manifold precisely in the monad as simply unifying. The monad as essentially unifying must as such predelineate the possibility of a manifold.

Drive as simply unifying and as executing this drive must at the same time carry within itself something manifold, must *be* something manifold. In that case, however, the manifold too must have the character of active drive [*Drängen*], of something pressed upon [*Be-drängte*] and driven [*Gedrängte*], of movement in general. Something manifold in motion is something changeable, [386] that which changes. Yet in drive, it is drive itself that is pressed upon. The change in drive, that which changes within the active drive itself, is that which is driven [*das Ge-drängte*].

Drive, as *primum constitutivum*, should be simply unifying and both origin and mode of being of the changeable.

"Simply unifying" means that the unity should not be the subsequent assembling of a collection, but the original organizing unification. The constitutive principle of unification must be prior to that which is subject to possible unification. What unifies must anticipate by reaching *ahead* toward something from which every manifold has already received its unity. That which is simply unifying must be originally a reaching out and, as reaching out, must embrace in advance in such a way that every manifold is in each case already made manifold within the grasp of such embrace. As reaching out and grasping in its embrace it already surpasses in advance, it is *substantia prae-eminens* (letter to de Volder, G. II, 252; S. II, 35).

Drive, *vis primitiva* as *primum constitutivum* of original unification, must therefore be a reaching out and embracing. Leibniz expresses this by saying that *the monad is in its essence fundamentally pre-hensive, re-presenting* [vorstellend, re-präsentierend].[4]

The deepest metaphysical motive for the monad's characteristic prehension is the ontological unifying function of drive. This motive remained concealed from Leibniz himself. Yet according to the very nature of the matter, this can be the only motive, and not the following reasoning: The monad is, as force, something living, and living things have a soul, and the soul, in turn, has apprehension [*Vorstellen*]. This form of reasoning would remain a superficial application of the psychic to beings in general.

Because drive is supposed to be that which originarily and simply unifies, it must be a reaching out and embracing; it must be *"pre-hensive"* ["vor-stellend"]. Pre-hension [*Vor-stellen*] is to be understood here ontologically, structurally, and not as a particular faculty of the soul. Thus, in its metaphysical essence, the monad is not soul but, conversely, *soul is one possible modification of the monad*. Drive [387] is not a process that occasionally also prehends or even produces prehensions, but is essentially prehensive. The structure of the drive process is itself a reaching out, it is ecstatic. Prehension is not a pure staring, but is an anticipatory reaching that directs itself toward the manifold and unifies it in the simple. In *Principles of Nature and of Grace* (§2) Leibniz states: "... les actions internes ... ne peuvent être autre chose que ses *perceptions*, (c'est à dire les représentations du composé, ou de ce qui est dehors, dans le simple). ..." [... internal actions ... can be nothing other than its *perceptions* (that is to say, representations of the composite, or of what is outside, in the simple).] To des Bosses he writes: "Perceptio nihil aliud quam multorum in uno expressio" [Perception is nothing other than the expression of many in one] (G. II, 311), and: "Nunquam versatur perceptio circa objectum in quo non sit aliqua varietas seu multitudo" [Perception never turns to an object in which there is not some variety or multiplicity] (ibid., 317).

Along with "apprehension" ["*Vorstellen*"] there is also a "striving" that belongs to the structure of drive (νόησις – ὄρεξις). In addition to *perceptio* (*repraesentatio*), Leibniz expressly mentions a second faculty, *appetitus* [appetition]. He has to give special emphasis to *appetitus* only because he has not himself immediately grasped the essence of *vis activa* with sufficient radicality – despite his clearly contrasting it with *potentia activa* and *actio*. Force apparently remains itself still something substantial, a core that is then endowed with apprehending and striving, whereas in fact drive is in itself already an apprehending striving or a striving apprehending. To be sure, the characteristic of *appetitus* has itself a special meaning and does not mean the same as drive. *Appetitus* refers to a particular, essential, constitutive moment of drive, as does *perceptio*.

Drive as originarily unifying must already anticipate every possible manifold. It must be able to deal with every manifold in its possibility; that is, drive must have already surpassed and exceeded such manifoldness. Drive must in a certain way bear manifoldness within itself and allow it to be born in its activity of driving. The task is to see the essential source of manifoldness within drive as such.

Let us remember that drive, as surpassing in advance, is the primordially unifying unity; i.e., the monad is *substantia*. "Substantiae non tota sunt quae contineant partes formaliter, [388] sed res totales quae partiales continent eminenter" [Substances are not such wholes that contain parts formally but they are total realities that contain particulars eminently] (letter to de Volder, January 21, 1704; G. II, 263).

Drive is the nature, i.e., the essence, of substance. As drive it is in a certain way active, but as active it is always primordially pre-hensive (*Principles of*

Nature and of Grace, §2; S. II, 122). In the letter to de Volder cited above, Leibniz continues:

Si nihil sua natura activum est, nihil omnino activum erit; quae enim tandem ratio actionis si non in natura rei? Limitationem tamen adjicis, *ut res sua natura activa esse possit, si actio semper se habeat eodem modo.* Sed cum omnis actio mutationem contineat, ergo habemus quae negare videaris, tendentiam ad mutationem internam, et temporale sequens ex rei natura.

[If nothing is active by its own nature, there will be nothing active at all, for what reason for activity can there be if not in the nature of a thing? Yet you add the restriction that "a thing can be active by its own nature, if its action always maintains itself in the same mode." But since every action contains change, we must have in it precisely what you would seem to deny it, namely, a tendency toward internal change and a temporal succession following from the nature of the thing.]

Here it is stated clearly that the activity of the monad as drive is in itself drive toward change.

Drive, of its very nature, drives on to something else; it is self-surpassing drive. This means that a manifold arises in the driving thing itself, as driving. Substance is given over to *successioni obnoxia*, successiveness. As drive, drive delivers itself to succession, not as if to something other than itself, but as to that which belongs to it. That which drive seeks to press upon submits itself to temporal succession. The manifold is not something alien to it; rather, drive is this manifold itself.

In drive itself there resides a tendency toward transition from something to something. This tendency toward transition is what Leibniz means by *appetitus*. *Appetitus* and *perceptio*, in the sense characterized, are equiprimordial features of the monad. The tendency is itself pre-hending. This means that it unifies from a unity that surpasses in advance, unifying the transitions from prehension to prehension, transitions that are driven on in the drive and that drive themselves on. "Imo rem accurate considerando dicendum est nihil in rebus esse nisi substantias simplices et in his perceptionem atque appetitum" [Indeed, considering the matter carefully, it may be said that there is nothing in the world except simple substances and, in them, perception and appetite] (letter to de Volder, G. II, 270).

Revera igitur (principium mutationis) est internum omnibus substantiis simplicibus, cum ratio non sit cur uni magis quam [389] alteri, consistitque in progressu perceptionum Monadis cuiusque, nec quicquam ultra habet tota rerum natura.

[(The principle of change) is therefore truly internal to all simple substances, since there is no reason why it should be in one rather than in another, and it consists in the progress of the perceptions of each monad, the entire nature of things containing nothing besides.] (Ibid., 271)

The *progressus perceptionum* is what is primordial in the monad; it is the prehensive transition tendency, the drive.

Porro ultra haec progredi et quaerere cur sit in substantiis simplicibus perceptio et appetitus, est quaerere aliquid ultramundanum ut ita dicam, et Deum ad rationes vocare cur aliquid eorum esse voluerit quae a nobis concipiuntur.

[To go beyond these principles and ask why there is perception and appetite in simple substances is to inquire about something ultramundane, so to speak, and to demand reasons of God why he has willed things to be such as we conceive them to be.] (Ibid., 271)

The following passage from the first draft of the letter of January 19, 1706, to de Volder is illuminating on the genesis of the doctrine of drive and the transition tendency:

Mihi tamen sufficit sumere quod concedi solet, esse quandam vim in percipiente sibi formandi ex prioribus novas perceptiones, quod idem est ac si dicas, ex priore aliqua perceptione sequi interdum novam. Hoc quod agnosci solet alicubi a philosophis veteribus et recentioribus, nempe in voluntariis animae operationibus, id ego semper et ubique locum habere censeo, et omnibus phaenomenis sufficere, magna et uniformitate rerum et simplicitate.

[But it is enough for me to accept what is usually granted, that there is a certain force in the percipient's forming for itself new perceptions from previous ones, which is the same as if you were also to say that a new perception at times follows from some previous perception. What is usually recognized by philosophers everywhere, both ancient and more recent, in the voluntary activities of the soul, I judge to have always and everywhere a place and to be sufficient for all phenomena in both the great regularity and simplicity of things.] (G. II, 282, note; S. II, 54f., note)

To what extent is drive as drive unifying? The answer to this question requires that we attain an insight into the essential structure of drive.

(1) Drive is primordially unifying: it is not unifying thanks to that which it unifies or to the conglomeration thereof. Rather, it unifies in reaching ahead and embracing, as *perceptio*.

(2) This *percipere* [Latin, to take, grasp] is embracing; it is oriented toward a manifold that is itself already involved in drive and originates from it. Drive is self-surpassing, pressing on. This belongs to the monadic structure, which itself always remains prehensive.

(3) Drive as *progressus perceptionum* drives to surpass itself; it is *appetitus*. The transition tendency is *tendentia interna ad mutationem* [an internal tendency to change].

The monad is originarily unifying, simply and in advance, and indeed in such a way that this unifying precisely individuates. The inner [390] possibility of individuation, its essence, lies within the monad as such. The essence of the monad is drive.

Let us quickly recall what was said about the substantiality of substance. Substance is that which constitutes the unity of a being. What unifies is drive, and it does so taken in the precise sense we have just now elaborated: pre-hension as the tendency to transition that develops the manifold in itself.

As what unifies, drive is the nature of a being. Every monad has its "propre constitution originale." The latter is given along with Creation.

What then makes each monad ultimately just this particular monad? How is individuation itself constituted? Recourse to the Creation is only the dogmatic explanation of the origin of what is individuated, and not the clarification of individuation itself. What makes up the latter? The answer to this question must explicate the essence of the monad even further.

Obviously individuation must take place in that which basically constitutes the essence of the monad, in drive. What essential character in the structure of drive makes a particular individuation possible and thus grounds the peculiar uniqueness of each monad? To what extent is that which primordially unifies a self-individuating in its very unifying?

When we previously set aside the connection with Creation, we did so only inasmuch as it is a dogmatic explanation. Nevertheless, the metaphysical sense expressed in describing the monad as created is its *finitude*. Considered formally, finitude means restrictedness. To what extent can drive be restricted?

If finitude as restrictedness belongs to the essence of drive, then finitude must be defined within the fundamental metaphysical feature of drive. But this fundamental feature is unification, and unification as pre-hending, as surpassing in advance. In this prehensive unifying there lies a possession of unity in advance [391] to which drive looks, as prehending and tending toward transition. In drive as prehending *appetitus* there is a point, as it were, upon which attention is directed in advance. This point is the unity itself, starting from which the drive unifies. This attention point or *point de vue* [point of view], this view-point, is constitutive for drive.

What is in advance apprehended in this viewpoint is also that which regulates in advance the entire drive activity itself. Such activity is not extrinsically prompted; rather, as prehensive motion, that which moves freely is always what is pre-hended in advance. *Perceptio* and *appetitus* are therefore determined in their activity of drive primarily in terms of the viewpoint.

Yet herein lies something that has not yet been conceived explicitly: Something that, like drive, is in itself a reaching out – and indeed in such a way that it is and maintains itself in this very reaching out – has in itself the possibility of grasping itself. In driving toward, that which drives always traverses a dimension. That is, that which drives traverses itself and is in this way open to itself, and is able to be so by its very essence.

Because of this dimensional self-openness, that which drives can therefore expressly grasp its own self; i.e., in addition to perceiving, it can also present itself at the same time along with its perceiving. It can perceive itself concomitantly (*ad*): it can *apperceive*. In *Principles of Nature and of Grace*, §4, Leibniz writes:

Ainsi il est bon de faire distinction entre la *Perception* qui est l'état interieur de la Monade representant les choses externes, et *l'Apperception* qui est la *Conscience*, ou la connaissance reflexive de cet état interieur, laquelle n'est point donnée à toutes les Ames, ny tousjours à la même Ame.

[So it is well to make a distinction between *perception*, which is the inner state of the monad representing external things, and *apperception*, which is *consciousness* or the reflective knowledge of this inner state itself and which is not given to all souls nor to the same soul all the time.] (G. VI, 600; cf. *Monadology*, §21ff.)

In this viewpoint the whole universe is, as it were, held in view – in a particular perspective of beings and of the possible in each case. But the view is refracted in a particular way, namely, in each case according to the monad's stage of drive. That is, it is refracted in each case according to the monad's possibility for unifying itself in its manifoldness. From this it becomes clear [392] that a certain co-presentation of itself is found in the monad as prehensive drive.

This unveiling of self can have various degrees, from full transparency to insensibility and captivated distraction. No monad lacks *perceptio* and *appetitus* and thus a certain accompanying openness to itself (though this need not be full self-apprehension), if only of the lowest degree. Accordingly, the particular viewpoint, and the correlative possibility of unification, its unity, is that which individuates each and every monad.

Inasmuch as it unifies – and that is its essence – the monad individuates itself. Yet, in individuation, in the drive from its own particular perspective, the monad unifies the universe prehended in advance only according to the possibility of its own perspective. Each monad is thus in itself a *mundus concentratus*. Every drive concentrates in itself, in its driving, the world in each case after its own fashion.

But because each monad, in a way of its own, is the world insofar as it presents the world, every drive is in *consensus* with the universe. Because of the consonance [*Einstimmigkeit*] every prehensive drive has with the universe, the monads themselves are also interconnected with one another. The idea of the monad as prehensive drive tending toward transition implies that the world belongs in each case to the monad in a perspectival refraction, that all monads as units of drive are thus oriented in advance toward a predisposed harmony of the totality of beings: *harmonia praestabilita*.

As the fundamental structure of the actual world, of the *actualia*, however, *harmonia praestabilita* is that which, as the goal of drive [*das Erdrängte*], stands opposite the central monad, God. God's drive is his will. But the correlate of divine will is the *optimum*, "distinguendum enim inter ea, quae Deus potest, et quae vult: potest omnia, vult optima. Actualia nihil aliud sunt, quam possibilium (omnibus comparatis) optima; Possibilia sunt quae non implicant contradictionem" [we must distinguish between the things that God can do and those that he wills to do; he can do all things, but he wills the best. Actual things are nothing but the best of possibles, all things considered. Possible things are those that do not imply a contradiction] (letter to Johann Bernoulli, February 21, 1699; S. II, 11).

[393] In every monad the whole universe is potentially present. The individuation that takes place in drive as unifying is thus always essentially the individuating of a being that belongs, as monad, to the world. Monads are not isolated pieces producing the world by being added together. Each monad, as the drive we have characterized, is in each case and in its own way the universe itself. Drive is pre-hensive drive that in each case presents the world from a viewpoint. Every monad is a little world, a microcosm. This way of speaking does not touch the essential, inasmuch as each monad is the universe in such a way that, in its driving, it in each case apprehends the *whole world* in its unity, although it never comprehends it totally. Each monad is, according to its particular level of awakeness, a world history that presents the world. Thus the universe is, in a certain sense, multiplied by as many times as there are monads, just as the same

city is variously represented by each of the various situations of individual observers (*Discourse on Metaphysics*, §9).

From what has been said we can now elucidate the image Leibniz frequently likes to use to describe the entire essence of the monad. The monad is *a living mirror of the universe.*

One of the most important passages is contained in the letter to de Volder from June 20, 1703:

Entelechias differre necesse est, seu non esse penitus similes inter se, imo principia esse diversitatis, nam aliae aliter exprimunt universum ad suum quaeque spectandi modum, idque ipsarum officium est ut sint totidem specula vitalia rerum seu totidem Mundi concentrati.

It is necessary that the entelechies (monads) differ from one another or not be completely similar to each other. In fact, they (themselves as such) must be the principles of diversity, for each expresses the universe differently in accordance with its own way of seeing (pre-hending). And precisely this is their most proper task, that they should be so many living mirrors of that which is, or so many concentrated worlds. (G. II, 251/52)

[394] This statement contains several points:

(1) The differentiation of monads is necessary; it belongs to their essence. In unifying, each unifies from its own viewpoint, and thus they individuate themselves.

(2) On account of their way of seeing, *perceptio – appetitus*, monads are thus themselves the origin of their diversity in each case.

(3) This unifying presentation [*Dar-stellen*] of the universe in each individuation is precisely what concerns each monad as such in its being (its drive).

(4) Monads are each the universe in concentrated form. The center of concentration is drive determined from a particular viewpoint in each instance: *concentrationes universi* (G. II, 278).

(5) The monad is *speculum vitale* [a living mirror] (cf. *Principles of Nature and of Grace*, §3; *Monadology*, §§63 and 77; and the letter to Rémond, G. III, 623). Mirror, *speculum*, means a letting-be-seen: *miroir actif indivisible* (G. IV, 557; S. I, 146), an actively driving, indivisible, simple mirroring. This letting-be-seen first comes about in the manner of the monad's being, whereby a particular unveiling of world transpires. Mirroring is not a fixed copying, but itself drives as such toward new predelineated possibilities of itself. The mirror is *simple* because it possesses in advance the one universe within a single viewpoint from which the manifold first becomes visible.

From this we can grasp more sharply the essence of finite substance from an aspect we have not yet considered. Leibniz says in his letter to de

Volder of June 20, 1703 (G. II, 249): "omnis substantia est activa, et omnis substantia finita est passiva, passioni autem connexa resistentia est." [Every substance is active and every finite substance is passive, and connected with this passivity is resistance.] What is this supposed to mean?

Insofar as the monad is always the whole within a *single* viewpoint, the grounds of its finitude lie precisely in its being related to the order of the universe in this way. The monad relates to a resistance, to something it is not but could well be. Drive is indeed active, yet in every finite drive occurring in a particular [395] perspective, there is always and necessarily something resistant, something that opposes the drive as such. For insofar as it is driving from a particular viewpoint toward the whole universe in each case, there are many things that the drive is not. The drive is modified by the viewpoint. We must heed the fact that drive as an active driving is related to resistance precisely because such drive can be the whole universe potentially but in fact is not. This passivity, in the sense of what the drive does not attain in its driving [*erdrängt*], belongs to the finitude of drive.

This negative aspect, purely as a structural moment of finite drive, characterizes the nature of what Leibniz understands by *materia prima*. He writes to des Bosses:

Materia prima cuilibet Entelechiae est essentialis, neque unquam ab ea separatur, cum eam compleat et sit ipsa potentia passiva totius substantiae completae. Neque enim materia prima in mole seu impenetrabilitate et extensione consistit . . .

[Prime matter is essential for any entelechy, nor can it ever be separated from it since it completes the entelechy and is the passive power itself of the total complete substance. For prime matter does not consist in mass nor in impenetrability and extension . . .] (G. II, 324)

Because of this essential primordial passivity, the monad has the intrinsic possibility of *nexus* with *materia secunda*, i.e., with *massa*, with definite resistance in the sense of material mass and weight. (Cf. on this Leibniz's correspondence with the mathematician Bernoulli and with the Jesuit des Bosses, professor of philosophy and theology at the Jesuit college in Hildesheim.)

This structural moment of passivity provides Leibniz with the foundation for making metaphysically intelligible the *nexus* of the monad with a material body (*materia secunda, massa*) and for demonstrating positively why *extensio* cannot constitute the essence of material substance as Descartes had taught. We cannot pursue this here, however, nor can we go into the further development of the monadology or the metaphysical principles connected with it.

What Is Metaphysics?

Translated by David Farrell Krell[1]

[1] "What is metaphysics?" The question awakens expectations of a discussion about metaphysics. This we will forgo. Instead we will take up a particular metaphysical question. In this way it seems we will let ourselves be transposed directly into metaphysics. Only in this way will we provide metaphysics the proper occasion to introduce itself.

Our plan begins with the unfolding of a metaphysical inquiry, then tries to elaborate the question, and concludes by answering it.

THE UNFOLDING OF A METAPHYSICAL INQUIRY

From the point of view of sound common sense, philosophy is in Hegel's words "the inverted world." Hence the peculiar nature of our undertaking requires a preliminary sketch. The sketch will develop out of a twofold character of metaphysical interrogation.

First, every metaphysical question always encompasses the whole range of metaphysical problems. Each question is itself always the whole. Therefore, second, every metaphysical question can be asked only in such a way that the questioner as such is also there within the question, that is, is placed in question. From this we conclude that metaphysical inquiry must be posed as a whole and from the essential position of the existence [*Dasein*] that questions. We are questioning, here and now, for ourselves. Our existence – in the community of researchers, teachers, and students – is determined by science. What is happening to us, essentially, in the grounds of our existence, when science has become our passion?

[2] The scientific fields are quite diverse. The ways they treat their objects of inquiry differ fundamentally. Today only the technical organization of universities and faculties consolidates this multiplicity of dispersed

disciplines; the practical establishment of goals by each discipline provides the only meaningful source of unity. Nonetheless, the rootedness of the sciences in their essential ground has atrophied.

Yet when we follow their most proper intention, in all the sciences we adopt a stance toward beings themselves. Precisely from the point of view of the sciences, no field takes precedence over another, neither nature over history nor vice versa. No particular way of treating objects of inquiry dominates the others. Mathematical knowledge is no more rigorous than philological-historical knowledge. It merely has the character of "exactness," which does not coincide with rigor. To demand exactness in the study of history is to violate the idea of the specific rigor of the humanities. The relation to the world that pervades all the sciences as such lets them seek beings themselves in order to make them objects of investigation and to determine their grounds – in each case according to their particular content and manner of being. According to the idea behind them, in the sciences we approach what is essential in all things.

This distinctive relation to the world in which we turn toward beings themselves is supported and guided by a freely chosen stance of human existence. To be sure, man's prescientific and extrascientific activities also are related to beings. But science is exceptional in that, in a way peculiar to it, it gives the matter itself explicitly and solely the first and last word. In such impartiality of inquiring, determining, and grounding, a peculiarly delineated submission to beings themselves obtains, such that beings are allowed to reveal themselves. This position of service in research and theory evolves in such a way as to become the ground of the possibility [3] of a proper though limited leadership in the whole of human existence. The special relation science sustains to the world and the human stance that guides it can of course be fully grasped only when we see and comprehend what happens in the relation to the world thus attained. The human being – one being among others – "pursues science." In this "pursuit" nothing less transpires than the irruption by one being called "the human being" into the whole of beings, indeed in such a way that in and through this irruption beings break open and show what they are and how they are. The irruption that breaks open, in its way, helps beings to themselves for the first time.

This trinity – relation to the world, stance, and irruption – in its radical unity brings a luminous simplicity and aptness of Da-sein to scientific existence. If we are to take explicit possession of the Dasein illuminated in this way for ourselves, then we must say:

That to which the relation to the world refers are beings themselves – and nothing besides.[a]

That from which every stance takes its guidance are beings themselves – and nothing further.

That with which the scientific confrontation in the irruption occurs are beings themselves – and beyond that, nothing.

But what is remarkable is that, precisely in the way scientific man secures to himself what is most properly his, he speaks, whether explicitly or not,[2] of something different. What should be examined are beings only, and besides that – nothing; beings alone, and further – nothing; solely beings, and beyond that – nothing.

What about this nothing? Is it an accident that we talk this way so automatically? Is it only a manner of speaking – and nothing besides?

However, why do we trouble ourselves with this nothing? The nothing is rejected precisely by science, given up as a nullity. But when we give up the nothing in such a way do we not concede it? Can we, however, speak of concession when we concede nothing? But perhaps [4] our confused talk already degenerates into an empty squabble over words. Against it, science must now reassert its seriousness and soberness of mind, insisting that it is concerned solely with beings. The nothing – what else can it be for science but an outrage and a phantasm? If science is right, then only one thing is sure: science wishes to know nothing of the nothing. Ultimately this is the scientifically rigorous conception of the nothing. We know it, the nothing, in that we wish to know nothing about it.

Science wants to know nothing about the nothing. But even so it is certain that when science tries to express its own proper essence[b] it calls upon the nothing for help. It has recourse to what it rejects. What duplicitous[c] state of affairs reveals itself here?

With this reflection on our existence at this moment as an existence determined by science we find ourselves enmeshed in a controversy. In the course of this controversy a question has already unfolded. It only requires explicit formulation: How is it with the nothing?

---

[a] First edition, 1929: People have passed off this additional remark following the dash as arbitrary and contrived, without knowing that Taine, who may be taken as the representative and sign of an entire era, the one that still prevails, knowingly employs this formula to characterize his fundamental position and intent.

[b] Fifth edition, 1949: Its positive and exclusive stance toward beings.

[c] Third edition, 1931: Ontological difference.
Fifth edition, 1949: Nothing as "being."

THE ELABORATION OF THE QUESTION

The elaboration of the question of the nothing must bring us to the point where an answer becomes possible or the impossibility of any answer becomes clear. The nothing is conceded. With a studied indifference science abandons it as what "there is not."

All the same, we shall try to ask about the nothing. What is the nothing? Our very first approach to this question has something unusual about it. In our asking we posit the nothing in advance as something that "is" such and such; we posit it as a being. But that is exactly what it is distinguished from.[a] Interrogating the nothing – asking what and how it, the nothing, [5] is – turns what is interrogated into its opposite. The question deprives itself of its own object.

Accordingly, every answer to this question is also impossible from the start. For it necessarily assumes the form: the nothing "is" this or that. With regard to the nothing, question and answer alike are inherently absurd.

But it is not science's rejection that first of all teaches us this. The commonly cited ground rule of all thinking, the proposition that contradiction is to be avoided, universal "logic" itself, lays low this question. For thinking, which is always essentially thinking about something, must act in a way contrary to its own essence when it thinks of the nothing.

Since it remains wholly impossible for us to make the nothing into an object, have we not already come to the end of our inquiry into the nothing – assuming that in this question "logic"[b] is of supreme importance, that the intellect is the means, and thought the way, to conceive the nothing originally and to decide about its possible unveiling?

But are we allowed to tamper with the rule of "logic"? Is not intellect the taskmaster in this question of the nothing? Only with its help can we at all define the nothing and pose it as a problem – which, it is true, only devours itself. For the nothing is the negation of the totality of beings; it is nonbeing pure and simple. But with that we bring the nothing under the higher determination of the negative, viewing it, it seems,[3] as the negated. However, according to the reigning and never-challenged doctrine of "logic," negation is a specific act of the intellect. How then can we in our question of the nothing, indeed in the question of its questionability, wish to brush the intellect aside? Yet are we altogether sure about what we are presupposing in this matter? Do the "not," negatedness, and thereby

[a] Fifth edition, 1949: The distinction, the difference.
[b] First edition, 1929: I.e., logic in the usual sense, what one takes to be logic.

85

negation too represent the higher determination under which the nothing falls as a particular kind of negated matter? Is the nothing given only because the "not," i.e., negation, is [6] given? Or is it the other way around? Are negation and the "not" given only because the nothing is given? That has not been decided; it has not even been raised expressly as a question. We assert that the nothing is more originary[a] than the "not" and negation.

If this thesis is right, then the possibility of negation as an act of the intellect, and thereby the intellect itself, are somehow dependent upon the nothing. Then how can the intellect hope to decide about the nothing? Does the ostensible absurdity of question and answer with respect to the nothing in the end rest solely in a blind conceit[b] of the far-ranging intellect?

But if we do not let ourselves be misled by the formal impossibility of the question of the nothing, if we pose the question in spite of this, then we must at least satisfy what remains the basic demand for the possible advancing of every question. If the nothing itself is to be questioned as we have been questioning it, then it must be given beforehand. We must be able to encounter it.

Where shall we seek the nothing? Where will we find the nothing? In order to find something must we not already know in general that it is there? Indeed! At first and for the most part human beings can seek only when they have anticipated the being at hand of what they are looking for. Now, the nothing is what we are seeking. Is there ultimately such a thing as a search without that anticipation, a search to which pure discovery belongs?

Whatever we may make of it, we are acquainted with the nothing, if only as a word we rattle off every day. For this common nothing that glides so inconspicuously through our chatter, blanched with the anemic pallor of the obvious, we can without hesitation furnish even a "definition":

The nothing is the complete negation of the totality of beings.

Does not this characterization of the nothing ultimately provide an indication of the direction from which alone the nothing can come to meet us?

[7] The totality of beings must be given in advance so as to be able to fall prey straightway to negation – in which the nothing itself would then be manifest.

But even if we ignore the questionableness of the relation between negation and the nothing, how should we who are essentially finite make the whole of beings totally accessible in itself and also for us? We can of course think the whole of beings in an "idea," then negate what we have imagined

---

[a] Fifth edition, 1949: Ordering in terms of origin.
[b] Fifth edition, 1949: The blind conceit: the *certitudo* of the *ego cogito*, subjectivity.

in our thought, and thus "think" it negated. In this way we do attain the formal concept of the imagined nothing but never the nothing itself. But the nothing is nothing, and if the nothing represents total indistinguishability no distinction can obtain between the imagined and the "proper" nothing. And the "proper" nothing itself – is not this the camouflaged but absurd concept of a nothing that is? For the last time now the objections of the intellect would call a halt to our search, whose legitimacy, however, can be demonstrated only on the basis of a fundamental experience of the nothing.

As surely as we can never comprehend absolutely the whole of beings in themselves we certainly do find ourselves stationed in the midst of beings that are unveiled somehow as a whole. In the end an essential distinction prevails between comprehending the whole of beings in themselves and finding oneself [Sichbefinden] in the midst of beings as a whole. The former is impossible in principle. The latter happens all the time in our Dasein. It does seem as though we cling to this or that particular being, precisely in our everyday preoccupations, as though we were completely lost in this or that region of beings. No matter how fragmented our everyday existence may appear to be, however, it always deals with beings in a unity of the "whole," if only in a shadowy way. Even and precisely when we are not actually busy with things or ourselves, this "as a whole" comes over us – for example, in authentic boredom. Such boredom is still distant when it is only this book [8] or that play, that business or this idleness, that drags on and on. It irrupts when "one is bored." Profound boredom, drifting here and there in the abysses of our existence like a muffling fog, removes all things and human beings and oneself along with them into a remarkable indifference. This boredom manifests beings as a whole.

Another possibility of such manifestation is concealed in our joy in the presence of the Dasein – and not simply of the person – of a human being whom we love.

Such being attuned, in which we "are" one way or another and which determines us through and through, lets us find ourselves among beings as a whole. Finding ourselves attuned not only unveils beings as a whole in various ways, but this unveiling – far from being merely incidental – is also the fundamental occurrence of our Da-sein.

What we call a "feeling" is neither a transitory epiphenomenon of our thinking and willing comportment, nor simply an impulse that provokes such comportment, nor merely a present condition we have to find some way of coping with.

But just when moods of this sort bring us face to face with beings as a whole they conceal from us the nothing we are seeking. We will now come to share even less in the opinion that the negation of beings as a whole that are manifest to us in attunement places us before the nothing. Such a thing could happen only in a correspondingly originary attunement that in the most proper sense of unveiling makes manifest the nothing.

Does such an attunement, in which man is brought before the nothing itself, occur in human existence?

It can and does occur, although rarely enough and only for a moment, in the fundamental mood of anxiety. By such anxiety we do not mean the quite common anxiousness, ultimately reducible to fearfulness, which all too readily comes over us. Anxiety is fundamentally different from fear. We become afraid always in the face of this or that [9] particular being that threatens us in this or that particular respect. Fear in the face of something is also in each case a fear concerning something in particular. Because fear possesses this trait of being "fear in the face of" and "fear concerning," he who fears and is afraid is captive to the mood in which he finds himself. Striving to rescue himself from this particular thing, he becomes unsure of everything else and completely "loses his head."

Anxiety does not let such confusion arise. Much to the contrary, a peculiar calm pervades it. Anxiety is indeed anxiety in the face of . . . , but not in the face of this or that thing. Anxiety in the face of . . . is always anxiety concerning . . . , but not concerning this or that. The indeterminateness of that in the face of which and concerning which we become anxious is no mere lack of determination but rather the essential impossibility of determining it. In the following familiar phrase[4] this indeterminateness comes to the fore.

In anxiety, we say, "one feels uncanny." What is "it" that makes "one" feel uncanny? We cannot say what it is before which one feels uncanny. As a whole it is so for one. All things and we ourselves sink into indifference.[a] This, however, not in the sense of mere disappearance. Rather, in their very receding, things turn toward us. The receding of beings as a whole, closing in on us in anxiety, oppresses us. We can get no hold on things. In the slipping away of beings only this "no hold on things" comes over us and remains.

Anxiety makes manifest the nothing.

We "hover" in anxiety. More precisely, anxiety leaves us hanging, because it induces the slipping away of beings as a whole. This implies that we ourselves – we humans who are in being[b] – in the midst of beings slip

---

[a] Fifth edition, 1949: Beings no longer speak to us.

[b] Fifth edition, 1949: But not the human being as the being human "of" Da-sein.

away from ourselves. At bottom therefore it is not as though "you" or "I" feel uncanny; rather, it is this way for some "one." In the altogether unsettling experience of this hovering where there is nothing to hold on to, pure Da-sein[a] is all that is still there.

Anxiety robs us of speech. Because beings as a whole slip away, so that precisely the nothing crowds around, all utterance of the "is" falls silent in the face of the nothing. That in the uncanniness [10] of anxiety we often try to shatter the vacant stillness with compulsive talk only proves the presence of the nothing. That anxiety unveils the nothing is immediately demonstrated by human beings themselves when anxiety has dissolved. In the lucid vision sustained by fresh remembrance we must say that that in the face of which and concerning which we were anxious was "properly" – nothing. Indeed, the nothing itself – as such – was there.[b]

→ *copula*

With the fundamental attunement of anxiety we have arrived at that occurrence in Dasein in which the nothing is manifest and from which it must be interrogated.

How is it with the nothing?

THE RESPONSE TO THE QUESTION

We have already won the answer that for our purposes is at least at first the only essential one when we take heed that the question of the nothing remains actually posed. This requires that we actively complete the transformation of the human being[c] into the Da-sein that every instance of anxiety occasions in us, in order to get a grip on the nothing announced[d] there as it makes itself known. At the same time this demands that we expressly hold at a distance those designations of the nothing that do not result from its claims.

The nothing unveils itself in anxiety – but not as a being. Just as little is it given as an object. Anxiety is no kind of grasping of the nothing. All the same, the nothing becomes manifest in and through anxiety, although, to repeat, not in such a way that the nothing becomes manifest in our uncanniness[e] quite "apart from" beings as a whole. Rather, we said that in

[a] Fifth edition, 1949: The Da-sein "in" the human being.
[b] Fifth edition, 1949: Which means: it unveiled itself; revealing and attunement.
[c] Fifth edition, 1949: As subject! But Da-sein is already experienced thoughtfully here in a preliminary way, and only for this reason has it become possible to pose the question "What is metaphysics?" here.
[d] Fifth edition, 1949: Revealing.
[e] Fifth edition, 1949: Uncanniness and unconcealment.

anxiety the nothing is encountered at one with beings as a whole. What does this "at one with" mean?[a]

In anxiety beings as a whole become superfluous. In what sense does this happen? Beings are not annihilated by anxiety, so that nothing is left. How [11] could they be, when anxiety finds itself precisely in utter impotence with regard to beings as a whole? Rather, the nothing makes itself known with beings and in beings expressly as a slipping away of the whole.

No kind of annihilation of the whole of beings in themselves takes place in anxiety; just as little do we produce a negation of beings as a whole in order to attain the nothing for the first time. Apart from the consideration that the explicit enactment of a negating assertion remains foreign to anxiety as such, we also come always too late with such a negation that should produce the nothing. The nothing rises to meet us already before that. We said it is encountered "at one with" beings that are slipping away as a whole.

In anxiety there occurs a shrinking back before ... that is surely not any sort of flight but rather a kind of entranced calm. This "back before" takes its departure from the nothing. The nothing itself does not attract; it is essentially repelling. But this repulsion is itself as such a parting gesture toward beings that are submerging as a whole. This wholly repelling gesture[b] toward beings that are slipping away as a whole, which is the action of the nothing that closes in on Dasein in anxiety, is the essence of the nothing: nihilation. It is neither an annihilation of beings nor does it spring from a negation. Nihilation will not submit to calculation in terms of annihilation and negation. The nothing itself nihilates.[c]

Nihilation is not some fortuitous incident. Rather, as the repelling gesture toward beings as a whole in their slipping away, it manifests these beings in their full but heretofore concealed strangeness as what is radically other – with respect to the nothing.

In the clear night of the nothing of anxiety the original openness of beings as such arises: that they are beings – and not nothing. But this "and not nothing" we add in our talk is not some kind of appended [12] clarification. Rather, it makes possible in advance[d] the manifestness of beings in general. The essence of the originally nihilating nothing lies in this, that it brings Da-sein for the first time before[e] beings as such.

---

[a] Fifth edition, 1949: The distinction.

[b] Fifth edition, 1949: Repelling: beings by themselves; gesturing toward: the *being* of beings.

[c] Fifth edition, 1949: Prevails essentially, endures as nihilation, grants the nothing.

[d] Fifth edition, 1949: I.e., being.

[e] Fifth edition, 1949: Specifically before the being of beings, before the distinction.

Only on the ground of the original manifestness of the nothing can human Dasein approach and penetrate beings. But since Dasein in its essence adopts a stance toward beings – those which it is not and that which it is – it emerges as such existence in each case from the nothing already manifest.

Da-sein means[a]: being held out into the nothing. ⋇

Holding itself out into[b] the nothing, Dasein is in each case already beyond beings as a whole. Such being beyond beings we call *transcendence*. If in the ground of its essence Dasein were not transcending, which now means, if it were not in advance holding itself out into the nothing, then it could never adopt a stance toward beings[c] nor even toward itself.

Without the original manifestness of the nothing, no selfhood and no freedom.[d]

With that the answer to the question of the nothing is gained. The nothing is neither an object nor any being at all. The nothing comes forward neither for itself nor next to beings, to which it would, as it were, adhere. For[e] human Dasein, the nothing makes possible the manifestness of beings as such. [The nothing does not merely serve as the counterconcept of beings; rather, it originally belongs to their essential unfolding[f] as such. In the being of beings the nihilation of the nothing occurs.]

But now a suspicion we have been suppressing for too long must finally find expression. If Dasein can adopt a stance toward beings only by holding itself out into the nothing and can exist only thus, and if the nothing is originally manifest only in anxiety, then must we not hover in this anxiety constantly in order to be able to exist at all? And have we not ourselves confessed that this original anxiety is rare? But above all else, we all do exist and comport ourselves toward beings [13] that we may or may not be – without this anxiety. Is this not an arbitrary invention and the nothing attributed to it a flight of fancy?

Yet what does it mean that this original anxiety occurs only in rare moments? Nothing else than that the nothing is at first and for the most part distorted with respect to its originary character. How, then? In this way: We usually lose ourselves altogether among beings in a certain way. The

[a] First edition, 1929: (1) inter alia, not only, (2) the consequence is not: therefore everything is nothing, but the reverse: taking over and apprehending beings, being and finitude.
[b] Fifth edition, 1949: Who holds originarily?
[c] Fifth edition, 1949: I.e., nothing and being the Same.
[d] Fifth edition, 1949: Freedom and truth in the lecture "On the Essence of Truth."
[e] Fifth edition, 1949: Not "through."
[f] Fifth edition, 1949: Essence: verbally; essential unfolding of being.

more we turn toward beings in our preoccupations the less we let beings as a whole slip away as such and the more we turn away from the nothing. Just as surely do we hasten into the public superficies of our existence.

And yet this constant if ambiguous turning away from the nothing accords, within certain limits, with the most proper significance of the nothing. In its nihilation the nothing directs us precisely toward beings.[a] The nothing nihilates incessantly without our properly knowing of this occurrence in the manner of our everyday knowledge.

What testifies to the constant and widespread though distorted manifestness of the nothing in our existence more compellingly than negation? But negation does not conjure the "not" out of itself as a means for making distinctions and oppositions in whatever is given, inserting itself, as it were, in between what is given. How could negation produce the "not" from itself when it can negate only if something negatable is already granted to it? But how could the negatable and what is to be negated be viewed as something susceptible to the "not" unless all thinking as such has already caught sight of the "not"? But the "not" can become manifest only when its origin, the nihilation of the nothing in general, and therewith the nothing itself, is disengaged from concealment. The "not" does not originate through negation; rather, negation is grounded in the "not"[b] that springs from the nihilation of the nothing. But negation is also only one way of nihilating, that is, only one sort of comportment that has been grounded beforehand in the nihilation of the nothing.

[14] In this way the above thesis in its main features has been proven: the nothing is the origin of negation, not vice versa. If the power of the intellect in the field of inquiry into the nothing and into being is thus shattered, then the destiny of the reign of "logic"[c] in philosophy is thereby decided. The idea of "logic" itself disintegrates in the turbulence of a more originary questioning.

No matter how much or in how many ways negation, expressed or implied, permeates all thought, it is by no means the sole authoritative witness of the manifestness of the nothing belonging essentially to Dasein. For negation cannot claim to be either the sole or the leading kind of nihilative comportment in which Dasein remains shaken by the nihilation of the nothing. Unyielding antagonism and stinging rebuke have a more abysmal source than the measured negation of thought. Galling failure and

[a] Fifth edition, 1949: Because *into* the being of beings.
[b] First edition, 1929: And yet here – as elsewhere in the case of assertion – negation is conceived in too retrospective and extrinsic a manner.
[c] First edition, 1929: "Logic," i.e., the *traditional* interpretation of thinking.

merciless prohibition require some deeper answer. Bitter privation is more burdensome.

These possibilities of nihilative comportment – forces in which Dasein bears its thrownness without mastering it – are not types of mere negation. That does not prevent them, however, from speaking out in the "no" and in negation. Indeed, here for the first time the barrenness and range of negation betray themselves. The saturation of Dasein by nihilative comportment testifies to the constant though doubtlessly obscured manifestation of the nothing that only anxiety originally unveils. But this implies that the originary anxiety in Dasein is usually repressed. Anxiety is there. It is only sleeping. Its breath quivers perpetually through Dasein, only slightly in what makes us "jittery," imperceptibly in the "Oh, yes" and the "Oh, no" of men of affairs; but most readily in the reserved, and most assuredly in those who are basically daring. But those daring ones are sustained by that on which they expend themselves – in order thus to preserve the ultimate grandeur of Dasein.

[15] The anxiety of those who are daring cannot be opposed to joy or even to the comfortable enjoyment of tranquilized bustle. It stands – outside all such opposition – in secret alliance with the cheerfulness and gentleness of creative longing.

Originary anxiety can awaken in Dasein at any moment. It needs no unusual event to rouse it. Its sway is as thoroughgoing as its possible occasionings are trivial. It is always ready, though it only seldom springs, and we are snatched away and left hanging.

Being held out into the nothing – as Dasein is – on the ground of concealed anxiety makes the human being a lieutenant of the nothing. We are so finite that we cannot even bring ourselves originally before the nothing through our own decision and will. So abyssally does the process of finitude entrench itself in Dasein that our most proper and deepest finitude refuses to yield to our freedom.

Being held out into the nothing – as Dasein is – on the ground of concealed anxiety is its surpassing of beings as a whole. It is transcendence.

Our inquiry concerning the nothing is to bring us face to face with metaphysics itself. The name "metaphysics" derives from the Greek μετὰ τὰ φυσικά. This peculiar title was later interpreted as characterizing the questioning that extends μετά or *trans* – "over" – beings as such.

Metaphysics is inquiry beyond or over beings that aims to recover them as such and as a whole for our grasp.

In the question concerning the nothing such an inquiry beyond or over beings, beings as a whole, takes place. It proves thereby to be a "metaphysical" question. At the outset we attributed a twofold character to such questions: first, each metaphysical question always encompasses the whole of metaphysics; second, every metaphysical question in each case implicates the questioning Dasein in the question.

[16] To what extent does the question concerning the nothing permeate and embrace the whole of metaphysics?

For a long time metaphysics has expressed the nothing in a proposition clearly susceptible of more than one meaning: *ex nihilo nihil fit* – from nothing, nothing comes to be. Although in discussions of the proposition the nothing itself never becomes a problem in its own right, the respective views of the nothing nevertheless express the guiding fundamental conception of beings. Ancient metaphysics conceives the nothing in the sense of nonbeing, that is, unformed matter, matter that cannot take form as an in-formed being that would offer an outward aspect (εἶδος). To be in being is to be a self-forming form that exhibits itself as such in an image (as something envisaged). The origins, legitimacy, and limits of this conception of being are as little discussed as the nothing itself. On the other hand, Christian dogma denies the truth of the proposition *ex nihilo nihil fit* and thereby bestows on the nothing a transformed significance, the sense of the complete absence of beings apart from God: *ex nihilo fit – ens creatum* [From nothing comes – created being]. Now the nothing becomes the counterconcept to that which properly is, the *summum ens*, God as *ens increatum*. Here too the interpretation of the nothing indicates the fundamental conception of beings. But the metaphysical discussion of beings stays on the same level as the question of the nothing. The questions of being and of the nothing as such are not posed. Therefore no one is bothered by the difficulty that if God creates out of nothing precisely he must be able to comport himself to the nothing. But if God is God, he cannot know the nothing, assuming that the "Absolute" excludes all nothingness.

This cursory historical recollection shows the nothing as the counterconcept to that which properly is, i.e., as its negation. But if the nothing somehow does become a problem, then this opposition does not merely undergo a somewhat clearer determination; rather, it awakens for the first time the proper formulation of the metaphysical question concerning the being of beings. The nothing does not remain [17] the indeterminate opposite of beings but unveils itself as belonging to the being of beings.

"Pure Being and pure Nothing are therefore the same." This proposition of Hegel's (*Science of Logic*, Book I: *Werke*, vol. III, p. 74) is correct. Being and the nothing do belong together, not because both – from the point of view of the Hegelian concept of thought – agree in their indeterminateness and immediacy, but rather because being itself is essentially finite and manifests itself only in the transcendence of a Dasein that is held out into the nothing.

Assuming that the question of being as such is the encompassing question of metaphysics, the question of the nothing proves to be such that it embraces the whole of metaphysics. But the question of the nothing pervades the whole of metaphysics since it forces us to face the problem of the origin of negation, that is, ultimately, to face up to a decision concerning the legitimacy of the dominion of "logic"[a] in metaphysics.

The old proposition *ex nihilo nihil fit* is therefore found to contain another sense, one appropriate to the problem of being itself, which runs: *ex nihilo omne ens qua ens fit* [From the nothing all beings as beings come to be]. Only in the nothing of Dasein do beings as a whole, in accord with their most proper possibility – that is, in a finite way – come to themselves. To what extent then has the question of the nothing, if it is a metaphysical question, implicated our questioning Dasein? We have characterized our Dasein, experienced here and now, as essentially determined by science. If our Dasein thus defined is implicated in the question of the nothing, then it must have become questionable through this question.

Scientific existence possesses its simplicity and aptness in that it comports itself toward beings themselves in a distinctive way, and only to them. Science would like to dismiss the nothing with a lordly wave of the hand. But in our inquiry concerning the nothing it has by now become manifest that such scientific existence is possible only if in advance it [18] holds itself out into the nothing. It understands itself for what it is only when it does not surrender the nothing. The presumed soberness of mind and superiority of science become laughable when it does not take the nothing seriously. Only because the nothing is manifest can science make beings themselves objects of investigation. Only if science exists on the basis of metaphysics can it fulfill in ever-renewed ways its essential task, which is not to amass and classify bits of knowledge, but to disclose in ever-renewed fashion the entire expanse of truth in nature and history.

Only because the nothing is manifest in the ground of Dasein can the total strangeness of beings overwhelm us. Only when the strangeness of beings oppresses us does it arouse and evoke wonder. Only on the ground of wonder – the manifestness of the nothing – does the "why?" loom before us. Only because the "why" is possible as such can we in a definite way inquire into grounds and ground things. Only because we can question and

[a] First edition, 1929: I.e., always of traditional logic and its *logos* as origin of the categories.

ground things is the destiny of our existence placed in the hands of the researcher.

The question of the nothing puts us, the questioners, ourselves in question. It is a metaphysical question.

Human Dasein can comport itself toward beings only if it holds itself out into the nothing. Going beyond beings occurs in the essence of Dasein. But this going beyond is metaphysics itself. This implies that metaphysics belongs to the "nature of the human being." It is neither a division of academic philosophy nor a field of arbitrary notions. Metaphysics is the fundamental occurrence in our Dasein. It is that Dasein itself. Because the truth of metaphysics dwells in this abyssal ground it stands in closest proximity to the constantly lurking possibility of deepest error. For this reason no amount of scientific rigor attains to the seriousness of metaphysics. Philosophy can never be measured by the standard of the idea of science.

[19] If the question of the nothing unfolded here has actually questioned us, then we have not simply brought metaphysics before us in an extrinsic manner. Nor have we merely been "transposed" into it. We cannot be transposed into it at all, because insofar as we exist we are always already within it. Φύσει γάρ, ὦ φίλε, ἔνεστί τις φιλοσοφία τῇ τοῦ ἀνδρὸς διανοίᾳ ["For by nature, my friend, a human being's thinking dwells in philosophy"] (Plato, *Phaedrus*, 279a). As long as human beings exist, philosophizing of some sort occurs. Philosophy – what we call philosophy – is the getting under way of metaphysics, in which it comes to itself and to its explicit tasks.[a] Philosophy gets under way only by a peculiar insertion of our own existence into the fundamental possibilities of Dasein as a whole. For this insertion it is of decisive importance, first, that we allow space for beings as a whole; second, that we release ourselves into the nothing, that is to say, that we liberate ourselves from those idols everyone has and to which they are wont to go cringing; and finally, that we let the sweep of our suspense take its full course, so that it swings back into the fundamental question of metaphysics that the nothing itself compels: Why are there beings at all, and why not far rather Nothing?

---

[a] *Wegmarken*, first edition, 1967: Two things are said: "essence" of metaphysics and its own history in terms of the destining of being; both are later named in the "recovery" ["*Verwindung*"].

On the Essence of Ground [a]

Translated by William McNeill[1]

PREFACE TO THE THIRD EDITION (1949)

[21] The treatise "On the Essence of Ground" was written in 1928 at the same time as the lecture "What Is Metaphysics?" The lecture ponders the nothing, while the treatise names the ontological difference.

The nothing is the "not" of beings, and is thus being, experienced from the perspective of beings. The ontological difference is the "not" between beings and being. Yet just as being, as the "not" in relation to beings, is by no means a nothing in the sense of a *nihil negativum*, so too the difference, as the "not" between beings and being, is in no way merely the figment of a distinction made by our understanding (*ens rationis*).

That nihilative "not" of the nothing and this nihilative "not" of the difference are indeed not identical, yet they are the Same in the sense of belonging together in the essential prevailing of the being of beings. [b] The two essays – which were intentionally kept separate – attempt to determine more closely this Same as what is worthy of thought, without being equal to this task.

What if those who reflect on such matters were to begin at last to enter thoughtfully into this same issue that has been waiting for two decades?

❧

---

[a] *Wegmarken*, first edition, 1967: Cf. the self-critique of this treatise in *Der Satz vom Grund* (1957), pp. 82ff. [Translated as *The Principle of Reason* by Reginald Lilly (Bloomington: Indiana University Press, 1991).]

[b] Third edition, 1949: Within this genitive.

Aristotle sums up his analysis of the manifold meanings of the word ἀρχή[a] in the following way: πασῶν μὲν οὖν κοινὸν τῶν ἀρχῶν τὸ πρῶτον εἶναι ὅθεν ἢ ἔστιν ἢ γίγνεται ἢ γιγνώσκεται.[2] Here the variations in what we are accustomed to call "ground" are identified: the ground of what-being, of that-being, and of being true. In addition, [22] however, there is the endeavor to grasp that wherein these "grounds" agree as such. Their κοινόν [what they have in common] is τὸ πρῶτον ὅθεν, the First, starting from which... Besides this threefold articulation of the foremost "beginnings" we also find a fourfold division of αἴτιον ("cause") into ὑποχείμενον, τὸ τί ἦν εἶναι, ἀρχὴ τῆς μεταβολῆς and οὗ ἕνεκα.[3] This division has remained the predominant one in the subsequent history of "metaphysics" and "logic." Although πάντα τὰ αἴτια [all the causes] are recognized as ἀρχαί, the intrinsic connection between the divisions, and their principle in each case, remain obscure. And there must be some doubt as to whether the essence of ground can be found by way of characterizing what is "common" to the "kinds" of ground, even though there is an unmistakable orientation toward illuminating ground in general in an originary manner. Indeed, Aristotle was not content merely to list the "four causes" alongside one another, but was concerned with understanding their interconnection and the grounding of this fourfold division. This is shown both by his detailed analysis in Book II of the *Physics* and especially by the way in which the question of the "four causes" is discussed in terms of the "history of the problem" in *Metaphysics* Book I, chapters 3–7. Aristotle concludes this discussion by noting: ὅτι μὲν οὖν ὀρθῶς διώρισται περὶ τῶν αἰτίων καὶ πόσα καὶ ποῖα, μαρτυρεῖν ἐοίκασιν ἡμῖν καὶ οὗτοι πάντες, οὐ δυνάμενοι θιγεῖν ἄλλης αἰτίας, πρὸς δὲ τούτοις ὅτι ζητητέαι αἱ ἀρχαὶ ἢ οὕτως ἅπασαι ἢ τινὰ τρόπον τοιοῦτον, δῆλον. [It appears, then, that all these thinkers, since they are unable to arrive at any other cause, testify that we have

---

[a] First edition, 1929: ἀρχή (1) in general in its guiding meaning of the "First, starting from which," is already comprehended in terms of being qua presencing of something constant; (2) unfolded in its multiple articulation (the intrinsic connection between the threefold and fourfold division of αἴτια, the grounds for the absence of any grounding of this diverse articulation), but especially in terms of conducting the interpretation of beingness in accordance with what-being, that-being, and being true.

ἀρχή is not a guiding concept for being, but has itself sprung from the originary Greek determination of being.

The question concerning the essence of ground is therefore the question concerning the *truth of beyng* [Seyn] itself.

correctly classified the causes, both how many they are and of what kind they are. In addition, it is clear that in seeking the causes, either all must be sought thus, or they must be sought in one of these ways.]⁴ Here we shall have to omit the history of the problem of ground both prior to and after Aristotle. With respect to the way we plan to approach the problem, however, we may recall the following. Through Leibniz we are familiar with the problem of ground in the form of the question concerning the *principium rationis sufficientis*. The "principle of reason" [*"Satz vom Grunde"*]⁵ was treated for the first time in a monograph by Christian A. Crusius in his *Philosophical Dissertation concerning the Use and Limits of the Principle of Determinative and Commonly Sufficient Reason* (1743),⁶ and finally by Schopenhauer [23] in his dissertation *Concerning the Fourfold Root of the Principle of Sufficient Reason* (1813).⁷ Yet if the problem of ground is in general bound up with the central questions of metaphysics, then it must also be at issue even where it is not dealt with explicitly in its familiar form. Thus Kant apparently showed little interest in the "principle of reason," even though he explicitly discusses it both at the beginning⁸ and toward the end⁹ of his philosophizing. And yet it stands at the center of his *Critique of Pure Reason.*¹⁰ Of no lesser significance for the problem are Schelling's *Philosophical Investigations concerning the Essence of Human Freedom and Related Matters* (1809).¹¹ The very reference to Kant and Schelling makes it questionable as to whether the problem of ground is equivalent to that of the "principle of reason" and whether it is even raised at all in that principle. If not, then the problem of ground must first be awakened. This, however, does not exclude the possibility that a discussion of the "principle of reason" might give rise to such an awakening and provide an initial pointer. The exposition of the problem, however, is equivalent to attaining and designating the distinctive *domain* within which we may treat *of* the essence of ground without any claim to make visible that essence at a stroke. This domain is shown to be *transcendence*. This means at the same time that transcendence itself is first determined more originarily and more comprehensively via the problem of ground. Any illumination of essence that is a *philosophizing* one, i.e., an intrinsically *finite* endeavor, must also necessarily always testify to that *nonessence* that drives *human* knowledge in its entire essence. Accordingly, the structure of what follows is stipulated: I. The [24] Problem of Ground; II. Transcendence as the Domain of the Question concerning the Essence of Ground; III. On the Essence of Ground.

I. THE PROBLEM OF GROUND[a]

The "principle of reason" as a "supreme principle" seems to preclude from the very outset anything like a *problem* of ground. Yet is the "principle of reason" an assertion *about* ground as such? As a supreme principle, does it reveal at all the essence of ground? The usual,[12] abbreviated version of the principle states: *nihil est sine ratione*, nothing is without reason.[b] Transcribing it positively, this states: *omne ens habet rationem*, every being has a reason. The principle makes an assertion *about beings*, and does so with regard to something like "ground."[c] Yet what constitutes the essence of ground is not determined *in* this principle. It is presupposed *for* this principle as a self-evident "idea." However, the "supreme" principle of reason makes use of the *unclarified* essence of ground in yet another way; for the specific character of principle belonging to this principle as a "grounding" principle, the character of principle belonging to this *principium grande* (Leibniz) can after all be delimited originarily only with regard to the essence of ground.

The "principle of reason" is thus worthy of question both in the way it is posed and in terms of the "content" it posits, if the essence of ground is indeed now able to become a problem over and above some indeterminate general "idea."[d]

Even though the principle of reason sheds no immediate light on ground as such, it can nevertheless serve as a point of departure for characterizing the problem of ground. The principle is indeed subject to many kinds of interpretation and appraisal, quite irrespective of those points worthy of question that we have indicated. Yet for our present purposes it seems

[a] First edition, 1929: The approach in terms of the truth of beyng is undertaken here still entirely within the framework of traditional metaphysics and in a straightforward retrieval corresponding to the truth of beings, the unconcealment of beings, and the unveiledness pertaining to beingness. Beingness as ἰδέα is itself unveiledness. Here *one* path toward overcoming "ontology" as such is broached (cf. Part III), but the overcoming is not accomplished or constructed in an originary manner from out of what has been attained.

[b] First edition, 1929: Wherever and whenever there are beyings [*Seyendes*], there there is ground; thus, there is *grounding* wherever there is beyng. What is the essence of beyng, such that grounding belongs to it; what does grounding mean here; how is this "belonging" to be understood, and how does it change in accordance with the particular way of being? (Cf. Part III.) Where does the necessity lie for grounding? In abyss of ground and in non-ground. And where is this? In Da-sein.

[c] First edition, 1929: Here there lies a specific interpretation of beyng: (1) being asserted (being true); (2) being produced from (what something is made of, φύσις); (3) (1 and 2) presence – constant.

[d] First edition, 1929: This "idea" of ground is not only universally accepted in an indeterminate manner, but behind this indeterminacy there lies the determinacy of a quite limited provenance. Λόγος – (*ratio*) – ὑποκείμενον as οὐσία – τί ἐστιν, that which is most constant, present. Cf. the "origin" of the four causes.

pertinent to adopt the principle in the version and role first explicitly assigned to it by Leibniz. However, precisely here there is dispute [25] as to whether the *principium rationis* is a "logical" or a "metaphysical" principle for Leibniz, or indeed both. Of course so long as we admit that we really know nothing of either the concept of "logic" or that of "metaphysics," or indeed of the "relation" between them, these disputes in the historical interpretation of Leibniz remain without any secure guideline and are therefore philosophically unfruitful. In no case can they compromise what will be drawn from Leibniz in what follows concerning the *principium rationis*. It will be sufficient to quote one major section from the tractatus *Primae Veritates*:[13]

Semper igitur praedicatum seu consequens inest subjecto seu antecedenti; et in hoc ipso consistit natura veritatis in universum seu connexio inter terminos enuntiationis, ut etiam Aristoteles observavit. Et in identicis quidem connexio illa atque comprehensio praedicati in subjecto est expressa, in reliquis omnibus implicata, ac per analysin notionum ostendenda, in qua demonstratio a priori sita est.

[Thus a predicate, or consequent, is always present in a subject, or antecedent; and in this fact consists the universal nature of truth, or the connection between the terms of the assertion, as Aristotle has also observed. This connection and inclusion of the predicate in the subject is explicit in relations of identity. In all other relations it is implicit and is revealed through an analysis of notions, upon which a priori demonstration is based.]

Hoc autem verum est in omni veritate affirmativa universali aut singulari, necessaria aut contingente, et in denominatione tam intrinseca quam extrinseca. Et latet hic arcanum mirabile a quo natura contingentiae seu essentiale discrimen veritatum necessariarum et contingentium continetur et difficultas de fatali rerum etiam liberarum necessitate tollitur.

[The above holds true for every affirmative truth, whether universal or singular, necessary or contingent, as well as for both intrinsic and extrinsic denomination. This wondrous secret goes unnoticed, this secret that reveals the nature of contingency, or the essential distinction between necessary and contingent truths, and which even removes the difficulty regarding the inevitable necessity of free beings.]

[26] Ex his propter nimiam facilitatem suam non satis consideratis multa consequuntur magni momenti. Statim enim hinc nascitur axioma receptum, *nihil esse sine ratione*, seu *nullum effectum esse absque causa*. Alioqui veritas daretur, quae non potest probari a priori, seu quae non resolveretur in identicas, quod est contra naturam veritatis, quae semper vel expresse vel implicite identica est.

[From these things, which have not been adequately considered due to their great simplicity, there follow many other things of great importance. Indeed, from them there at once arises the familiar axiom: "Nothing is without reason," or "there is no effect without a cause." If the axiom did not hold, there might be a truth that could not be proved a priori, i.e., which could not be resolved into relations of identity; and this is contrary to the nature of truth, which is always identical, whether explicitly or implicitly.]

Leibniz, in a manner typical for him, here provides, *together* with a characterization of the "*first* truths," a determination of what truth is *in the first instance* and in general, and does so with the intent of showing the "birth" of the *principium rationis* from the *natura veritatis*. And precisely in undertaking this he considers it necessary to point out that the apparent self-evidence of concepts such as "truth" and "identity" forestalls any clarification of them that would suffice to demonstrate the origin of the *principium rationis* and the other axioms. What is at issue in the present inquiry, however, is not the derivation of the *principium rationis*, but an analysis of the problem of ground. To what extent does this passage from Leibniz provide us with a guideline?

The *principium rationis* persists, because without its persistence there would be beings that would have to be without ground. For Leibniz this means: There would be true things that would resist being resolved into identities, there would be truths that would contravene the "nature" of truth in general. Since this is impossible, however, and truth persists, the *principium rationis*, since it springs from the essence of truth, also persists. The essence of truth, however, is to be found in the *connexio* (συμπλοχή) of subject and predicate. Leibniz thus conceives of truth from the outset – explicitly, though not entirely legitimately, appealing to Aristotle – as truth of assertion (proposition). He determines the *nexus* as the "*inesse*" of P in S, and the "*inesse*" as "*idem esse*." Identity as the essence of propositional truth here evidently does not mean the empty sameness of something with itself, but unity in the sense of the original unitary agreement of that which belongs together. [27] Truth thus means a unitary accord [*Einstimmigkeit*], which for its part can be such only as an overarching accordance [*Übereinstimmung*] with whatever is announced as unitary in the identity. In keeping with their nature, "truths" – true assertions – assume a relation to something *on whose grounds* they are able to be in accord. That linking which is a taking apart within every truth in each case always is what it is on the grounds of..., that is, as self-"grounding." In its very essence, *truth* thus houses a relation to something like "*ground*." In that case, however, the problem of truth necessarily brings us into a "proximity" to the problem of ground. Therefore the more originarily we master the essence of truth, the more pressing the problem of ground must become.

However, can anything more originary be brought to bear beyond the delimitation of the essence of truth as a characteristic of the assertion?

Nothing less than the insight that this determination of the essence of truth – however it may be conceived in its details – is indeed an uncircumventable one, yet nevertheless derivative.[14] The overarching accordance of the *nexus with* beings, and their consequent accord, do not *as such* primarily make beings accessible. Rather beings, as the concern of any predicative determination, must already be manifest *before* such predication and *for* it. For it to be possible, predication must be able to take up residence in a making-manifest that is *not predicative* in character. Propositional truth is rooted in a *more originary* truth (unconcealment), in the pre-predicative manifestness *of beings*, which may be called *ontic truth*. In keeping with the different kinds and domains of beings, the character of their possible manifestness and of the accompanying ways of interpretively determining them changes. Thus, for example, the truth of what is present at hand (for example, material things) as *discoveredness* [28] is specifically distinct from the truth of those beings that we ourselves are, from the *disclosedness* of existing Dasein.[15] Yet however multifaceted the distinctions between these two kinds of ontic truth may be, it remains valid for all pre-predicative manifestness that making manifest never *primarily* has the character of a mere presenting [*Vorstellen*] (intuiting), not even in "aesthetic" contemplation. The characterization of pre-predicative truth as intuition[a] readily suggests itself *because* ontic truth – supposedly truth proper – is in the first place defined as propositional truth, i.e., as a "*connection of presentations.*" That which is more simple by contrast to truth *thus defined* is then taken to be a straightforward presenting, free of any such connection. Such presentation indeed has its own function in the task of *objectifying* beings, which are of course always already and necessarily manifest. Ontic manifestation, however, occurs in our finding ourselves [*Sichbefinden*],[16] in accordance with our attunement and drives, in the midst of beings and in those ways of comporting ourselves toward beings in accordance with our striving and willing that are also grounded therein.[b] Yet even such kinds of comportment, whether they are interpreted as pre-predicative or as predicative, would be incapable of making beings accessible in themselves if their making manifest were not always illuminated and guided in advance by an understanding of the being (the ontological constitution: what-being and how-being) of beings. *Unveiledness of being first makes possible the manifestness of beings.* This

---

[a] First edition, 1929: Note here the historical origin from φύσις: [the connection] νοεῖν – εἶναι is essential.

[b] First edition, 1929: Here with respect to the openness of that which is closed as the rounding (εὐχυχλέος, Parmenides) of Da-sein; clearing [*Lichtung*] of the Da, not in terms of psychology; rather these abilities are first possible on the grounds of Da-sein.

unveiledness, as the truth concerning being, is termed *ontological truth*.[a] Certainly, the terms "ontology" and "ontological" are ambivalent, indeed in such a way that the problem peculiar to any ontology is precisely concealed. Λόγος of the ὄν means: the addressing (λέγειν) of beings as beings, yet at the same time it signifies that *with respect to which* beings are addressed (λεγόμενον). Addressing something *as* something, however, does not yet necessarily entail *comprehending in its essence* whatever is thus addressed. The *understanding* [29] of being (λόγος in a quite broad sense)[b] that guides and illuminates in advance all comportment toward beings is neither a grasping of being[c] as such, nor is it a conceptual comprehending of what is thus grasped (λόγος in its narrowest sense = "ontological" concept). We therefore call this understanding of being that has not yet been brought to a concept a pre-ontological understanding, or ontological in the broader sense. A conceptual comprehending of being presupposes that our understanding of being has developed itself, and that being as understood, projected in general, and somehow unveiled in such understanding, has expressly been made thematic and problematic. Between preontological understanding of being and the explicit problematic of conceptually comprehending being there are many different levels. One characteristic level, for example, is that projection of the ontological constitution of beings that simultaneously marks out a determinate field (nature, history) as a region for possible objectification through scientific knowledge. The prior determination of the being (what-being and how-being) of nature in general is anchored in the "fundamental concepts" [*Grundbegriffe*] of the relevant science. In such concepts, space, place, time, motion, mass, force, and velocity are delimited, for example, and yet the essence of time or motion does not become an explicit problem. The understanding of the being of a being that is present at hand is here brought to a concept, yet the conceptual determination of time and place, etc., the definitions, are, in their approach and range, governed solely by the fundamental manner of questioning directed toward beings in the relevant *science*. The fundamental concepts of contemporary

---

[a] First edition, 1929: Unclear! Ontological truth is unveiling of beingness – via the categories – but beingness as such is already *one* particular truth of beyng, one way in which its essential prevailing is cleared. This distinction between "ontic and ontological truth" is only a doubling of unconcealment and initially remains ensconced within the Platonic approach. Thus what has been said hitherto only points the direction of an overcoming, but no overcoming is accomplished or grounded in terms of its own proper ground.

[b] First edition, 1929: Here the erroneous procedure of merely extending ontological-metaphysical thinking to the question concerning the truth of beyng.

[c] First edition, 1929: Grasping of being: (a) in categorial-metaphysical terms, or (b) in a quite different manner, as projection of the essential prevailing of the truth of beyng.

science neither contain the "proper" ontological concepts of the being of those beings concerned, nor can such concepts be attained merely through a "suitable" extension of these fundamental concepts. Rather, the originary ontological concepts must be attained *prior* to any scientific definition of fundamental concepts. For it is from those ontological concepts that it first becomes possible to assess the restrictive way – which in each case delimits from a particular perspective – in which the fundamental concepts of the sciences correlate with being, which can be grasped in these purely onto-logical concepts. The "fact" of the sciences, [30] i.e., the factical subsistence of an understanding of being, which is necessarily contained in them as in all comportment toward beings, can neither be the authority that grounds their apriori, nor can it be the source for knowledge of that apriori. Rather, it can only be one possible occasion for pointing us toward the originary ontological constitution of, for example, history or nature. Such a pointer must itself remain subject to a constant critique that has already taken its guidelines from the fundamental problematic of all questioning concerning the being of beings.

The possible levels and variations of ontological truth in the broader sense at the same time betray the wealth of originary truth lying at the ground of all ontic truth.[17] Unconcealment of being, however, is always truth of the being *of* beings, whether such beings are actual or not. Con-versely, in the unconcealment of beings there already lies in each case an unconcealment of their being. Ontic and ontological truth each concern, in different ways, *beings in* their being, and *being of* beings. They belong essentially together on the grounds of their relation to the *distinction between being and beings*[a] (ontological difference).[b] The essence of truth in general, which is thus necessarily forked in terms of the ontic and the ontological,[c]

---

[a] First edition, 1929: The ambiguous nature of this distinction: in terms of what has gone before, a step toward its overcoming, and yet a fateful link back to it that obstructs every path toward the originary "unity" and hence also to the truth of the distinction.

[b] First edition, 1929: On this, cf. the lecture course of summer semester 1927 "The Basic Problems of Phenomenology," §22, where the term is first conveyed publicly. The con-clusion corresponds to the beginning where Kant's thesis concerning "being" (the "is"), namely, that it is not a real predicate, is discussed. The discussion occurs with the intent of first getting a view of the ontological difference *as such*, and of doing so in coming from ontology, ontology itself, however, being experienced in terms of fundamental ontology. This lecture course as a whole belongs to *Being and Time*, Part I, Division Three, "Time and Being."

[c] First edition, 1929: Here the essence of truth is conceived as "forked" in terms of the "distinction" as a fixed reference point, instead of the contrary approach *of overcoming* the "distinction" from out of the essence of the truth of beyng, or of first thinking the "distinc-tion" as beyng itself and therein the *beyings of beyng* [*das* Seyende des Seyns] – no longer as the being *of beings.*

is possible only together with the irruption of this distinction. And if what is [31] distinctive about Dasein indeed lies in the fact that in understanding being it comports itself toward beings, then *that* potential for distinguishing in which the ontological difference becomes factical must have sunk the roots of its own possibility in the ground of the essence of Dasein. By way of anticipation, we shall call this ground of the ontological difference the *transcendence* of Dasein.

If one characterizes all *comportment* toward beings as intentional, then *intentionality* is possible only *on the grounds of transcendence*. Intentionality, however, is neither identical with transcendence, nor, conversely, does it itself make transcendence possible.[18]

Our task hitherto has merely been to show, in a few essential steps, that the essence of truth must be sought more originarily than the traditional characterization of truth in the sense of a property of assertions would admit. Yet if the essence of ground has an intrinsic relation to the essence of truth, then the *problem* of ground too can be housed only where the essence of truth draws its inner possibility, namely, in the essence of transcendence. The question concerning the essence of ground becomes the *problem of transcendence*.

If this conjunction of truth, ground, and transcendence is originarily a unitary one, then a chain of corresponding problems must come to light wherever the question of "ground" – if only in the form of an explicit discussion of the principle of reason – is taken hold of in a more resolute fashion.

The statement cited from Leibniz already betrays the relatedness between the problem of "ground" and that of being. *Verum esse* means *inesse qua idem esse*. For Leibniz, however, *verum esse* – being *true*, at the same time means *being* "in truth" – *esse* pure and simple. The idea of being in general is then interpreted by *inesse qua idem esse*. What constitutes an *ens* as an *ens* is "identity," unity correctly understood that, as simple unity, originarily unifies and simultaneously individuates in such unifying. [32] That unifying, however, that individuates originarily (in advance) and simply, and which constitutes the essence of beings as such, is the essence of the "subjectivity" of the *subjectum* (substantiality of substance) understood monadologically. Leibniz's derivation of the *principium rationis* from the essence of propositional truth tells us that it is grounded upon a quite specific idea of being in general, an idea in whose light alone that "deduction" becomes possible. We see the connection between "ground" and "being" above all in Kant's metaphysics. It is certainly the case that one commonly finds a lack of any explicit treatment of the "principle of reason" in his "critical" writings, unless one allows the proof of the second analogy to count as a substitute for this almost incomprehensible shortcoming. Yet Kant did indeed consider the principle of reason, and did so at a distinctive place in his *Critique of Pure Reason* under the title of the "supreme grounding principle [*Grundsatz*] of all synthetic judgments." This "principle" analyzes *what in general* – within the sphere, and at the level of Kant's ontological inquiry – belongs *to the being* of beings as accessible in experience. He provides a definition concerning the reality of transcendental truth; i.e., he determines its intrinsic possibility via the unity of time, imagination, and "I think."[19] When Kant says concerning the Leibnizian principle of sufficient reason that it is "a notable pointer to investigations that have yet to be undertaken in metaphysics,"[20] then this is also true of his own highest principle of all synthetic knowledge to the extent that the *problem* of the essential connection between being, truth, and ground is *concealed* therein. The question of the original relationship between [33] transcendental and formal logic and the legitimacy of such a distinction in general is one that can then first be derived from here.

This brief exposition of the Leibnizian derivation of the principle of reason from the essence of truth was intended to clarify the connection between the problem of ground and the question concerning the inner possibility of ontological truth, i.e., ultimately the *more* originary and accordingly more comprehensive question concerning the essence of transcendence. *Transcendence* is thus the *domain* within which the problem of ground must allow itself to be encountered. Our task is to make visible this domain in terms of several of its main traits.

II. TRANSCENDENCE AS THE DOMAIN OF THE QUESTION CONCERNING THE ESSENCE OF GROUND

A preliminary remark on terminology must guide our use of the word "transcendence" and prepare our definition of the phenomenon to which this word refers. Transcendence means surpassing [*Überstieg*]. That which accomplishes such surpassing and dwells in this surpassing is transcendent (transcending). As an occurrence, this surpassing pertains to something that is. Formally speaking, surpassing may be grasped as a "relation" that passes "from" something "to" something. To surpassing there thus belongs that *toward which* such surpassing occurs, that which is usually, though inaccurately, called the "transcendent." And finally, there is in each case *something* that is surpassed in this surpassing. These moments are taken from a "spatial" occurrence to which the expression "transcendence" initially refers.

Transcendence in the terminological sense to be clarified and demonstrated means something that properly pertains to *human Dasein*, and does so not merely as one kind of comportment among other possible kinds that are undertaken from time to time. Rather, it belongs to human Dasein as the *fundamental constitution of this being, one that occurs prior to all comportment*. Certainly, human Dasein as existing "spatially" has the possibility, among others, [34] of spatially "surpassing" a spatial boundary or gap. Transcendence, however, is that surpassing that makes possible such a thing as existence in general, thereby also making it possible to move "oneself" in space.

If one chooses the title of "subject" for that being that we ourselves in each case are and that we understand as "Dasein," then we may say that transcendence designates the essence of the subject, that it is the fundamental structure of subjectivity. The subject never exists beforehand as a "subject," in order then, *if* there are objects at hand, *also* to transcend. Rather, to *be* a subject means to be a being in and as transcendence. The problem of transcendence can never be worked out by seeking a decision as to whether or not transcendence might pertain to a subject; rather, an understanding of transcendence is already a decision about whether we are able to conceptualize such a thing as "subjectivity" at all, or merely import a truncated subject, as it were.

Certainly a characterization of transcendence as the fundamental structure of "subjectivity" initially accomplishes little with respect to our penetrating into this constitution of Dasein. On the contrary, because we have now specifically warded off in general any explicit, or usually inexplicit, approach via the concept of a subject, transcendence may also no longer be determined as a "subject-object relation." In that case, transcendent Dasein (already a tautological expression) surpasses neither a "boundary" placed before the subject, forcing it in advance to remain inside (immanence), nor a "gap" separating it from the object. Yet nor are objects – the beings that are objectified – that *toward which* a surpassing occurs. *What* is surpassed is precisely and solely *beings themselves*, indeed every being that can be or become unconcealed for Dasein, thus *including precisely* that being as which "it itself" exists.

In this surpassing Dasein for the first time comes toward that being that *it* is, and comes toward it *as* it "itself." Transcendence constitutes [35] selfhood. Yet once again, it never in the first instance constitutes only selfhood; rather, the surpassing in each case intrinsically concerns also beings that Dasein "itself" is *not*. More precisely, in and through this surpassing it first becomes possible to distinguish among beings and to decide who and in what way a "self" is, and what is not a "self." Yet insofar – and only insofar – as Dasein exists as a self, it can comport "itself" *toward* beings, which prior to this must have been surpassed. Although it exists in the midst of beings and embraced by them, Dasein as existing has always already surpassed nature.

Whatever the beings that have on each particular occasion been surpassed in any Dasein, they are not simply a random aggregate; rather, beings, however they may be individually determined and structured, are surpassed in advance as a whole. This whole may remain unrecognized as such, even though – for reasons we shall not discuss now – it is always interpreted starting from beings and usually with respect to a prominent domain of beings, and is therefore at least familiar to us.

Surpassing occurs as a whole and never merely at certain times and not at other times. It does not, for instance, occur merely or in the first place as a theoretical grasping of objects. Rather, with the fact of Da-sein, such surpassing is there.

Yet if beings are *not* that *toward which* this surpassing proceeds, how then must we determine, or indeed even search for, this "toward which"? We name *world* that *toward which* Dasein as such transcends, and shall now determine transcendence as *being-in-the-world*. World co-constitutes the unitary structure of transcendence; as belonging to this structure, the concept of world may be called *transcendental*. This term names all that belongs essentially to transcendence and bears its intrinsic possibility thanks to such transcendence. And it is for this reason that an elucidation and interpretation of transcendence may be called a "transcendental" exposition. What "transcendental" means, however, is not to be taken from a philosophy to which one attributes the "standpoint" [36] of the "transcendental" or even of being "epistemological." This does not preclude our observing that precisely Kant came to recognize the "transcendental" as a problem concerning the intrinsic possibility of ontology in general, even though the "transcendental" for him still retains an essentially "critical" significance. For Kant the transcendental has to do with the "possibility" of (that which makes possible) that knowledge that *does not illegitimately* "soar beyond" our experience, i.e., is not "transcendent," but is experience itself. The transcendental thus provides the restrictive, yet thereby simultaneously positive, delimitation (definition) of the essence of nontranscendent ontic knowledge – i.e., knowledge that is possible for human beings as such. A more radical and more universal conception of the essence of transcendence, however, necessarily entails a more originary elaboration of the idea of ontology and thus of metaphysics.

The expression "being-in-the-world" that characterizes transcendence names a "state of affairs," indeed one that is purportedly readily understood. Yet what the expression means depends on whether the concept of *world* is taken in a prephilosophical, ordinary sense, or in its transcendental signif-icance. This can be elucidated by the discussion of a twofold signification of the talk of being-in-the-world.

Transcendence, conceived as being-in-the-world, is supposed to pertain to human Dasein. But this is in the end the emptiest and most trivial thing that can be said: Dasein, the human being that exists,[21] crops up among other beings and can therefore be encountered as such. Transcendence then means: belonging among the other beings that are already present at hand, or among those beings that we can always multiply to the point where they become unsurveyable. World is then the term for everything that is, for totality as the unity that determines "everything" only in terms of its being taken together, and no further. If we take this concept of world as underlying the talk of being-in-the-world, then we must indeed ascribe "transcendence" to *every* being *as present at hand.* Beings that are present at hand, that is, that crop up before us among other beings, *"are in the world."* If "transcendent" [37] means nothing more than "belonging among other beings," then it is obviously impossible to attribute transcendence to human *Dasein* as the constitution *distinctive* of its essence. Then the statement: To the essence of human Dasein belongs being-in-the-world, is even obviously false. For it is not essentially necessary that a being such as human Dasein factically exist. It can also *not* be.

Yet if, on the other hand, being-in-the-world is attributed legitimately and exclusively to Dasein, indeed as its essential constitution, then this expression cannot have the aforementioned meaning. In which case world also signifies something other than the totality of those beings that are present at hand.

To attribute being-in-the-world to Dasein as its essential constitution means to state something about its essence (its ownmost, intrinsic possibility as Dasein). In so doing, we may precisely *not* regard as our decisive criterion *whether* Dasein factically exists or not in a particular case, or *which* Dasein does so. The talk of being-in-the-world is not an observation concerning the factical appearing of Dasein; it is not an ontic statement at all. It concerns an essential state of affairs that determines Dasein in general and thus has the character of an ontological thesis. It is therefore the case that Dasein is a being-in-the-world not because, or only because, it factically exists, but the converse: it *can be* as existing, i.e., as Dasein, only *because* its essential constitution lies in being-in-the-world.

The statement: Factical Dasein is in a world (appears among other beings), betrays itself as a tautology that tells us nothing. The assertion: It belongs to the essence of Dasein to be in the world (necessarily to appear as well "alongside" other beings), proves to be false. The thesis: To the essence of Dasein as such belongs being-in-the-world, contains the *problem* of transcendence.

This thesis is an originary and simple one. This does not entail that it is simple to unveil, even though we can in each case come to understand being-in-the-world – in a preparatory manner that must once again be completed conceptually (albeit always relatively) [38] – only in *a single projection*, one that is transparent in varying degrees.

With the characterization of being-in-the-world that we have provided, the transcendence of Dasein has at first been determined only in a prohibitive manner. To transcendence there belongs world as that toward which surpassing occurs. The positive problem of what world is to be understood as, and of how the "relation" of Dasein to world is to be determined, i.e., of how being-in-the-world as the originary and unitary constitution of Dasein is to be comprehended conceptually, is to be discussed here only in the direction of, and within the limits demanded by, our guiding problem of ground. To this end we shall attempt an interpretation of the *phenomenon of world*, which is to serve the illumination of transcendence as such.

In order to orient us concerning this transcendental phenomenon of world, we shall first provide a characterization of the chief meanings that come to the fore in the history of the concept of world, although our characterization necessarily has certain gaps. In the case of such elementary concepts, the ordinary meaning is usually not the originary and essential one. The latter is repeatedly covered over, and attains its conceptual articulation only rarely and with difficulty.

Something essential shows itself already in the decisive commencements of ancient philosophy.[22] Κόσμος does not refer to this or that particular being, to those beings that press upon us and oppress us; yet nor does it refer to all these beings taken together. Rather, it means a "state of affairs," i.e., *how* beings, and indeed beings *as a whole*, are. Κόσμος οὗτος does not, therefore, designate this domain of beings as delimited from another, but this world of beings as distinct from another world *of the same* beings, the ἐόν itself χατὰ χόσμον.[23] The world as this "how as a whole" already underlies every possible fragmentation [39] of beings; such fragmentation does not annihilate the world, but rather always *requires* it. Whatever is ἐν τῷ ἑνὶ κόσμῳ²⁴ did not form the latter by first being stuck together, but is in advance governed through and through by the world. Heraclitus recognizes a further essential trait of κόσμος:²⁵ ὁ Ἡράκλειτός φησι τοῖς ἐγρηγορόσιν ἕνα καὶ κοινὸν κόσμον εἶναι, τῶν δὲ κοιμωμένων ἕκαστον εἰς ἴδιον ἀποστρέφεσθαι: To those who are awake there belongs a single and therefore common world, whereas whoever is asleep turns toward a world of his own. Here we find the world being related to fundamental ways in which human Dasein factically exists. When awake, beings show themselves in a thoroughly concordant way that is accessible to everyone in an average manner. In sleep, the world of beings is individuated exclusively with respect to each particular Dasein.

Several points are already visible from these brief hints: (1) World refers to a *"how" of being* of beings, rather than to these beings themselves. (2) This "how" determines beings *as a whole*. In its grounds it is the possibility of every "how" in general as limit and measure. (3) This "how" as a whole is in a certain manner *prior*. (4) This prior "how" as a whole is itself *relative to* human *Dasein*. The world thus belongs precisely to human Dasein, even though it embraces in its whole all beings, including Dasein.

Certain though it is that this rather inexplicit and somewhat dawning understanding of κόσμος may be compressed into the above meanings, it is also incontestable that this word often merely names those beings themselves that are experienced in such a "how."

It is no accident, however, that in connection with the new ontic understanding of existence that irrupted in Christianity the relation between κόσμος and human Dasein, and thereby the concept of world in general, became sharper and clearer. The relation is experienced in such an originary manner [40] that κόσμος now comes to be used directly as a term for a particular fundamental kind of human existence. Κόσμος οὗτος in Saint Paul (cf. I Corinthians and Galatians) means not only and not primarily the state of the "cosmic," but the state and situation of the *human being*, the kind of stance he takes *toward* the cosmos, his esteem for things. Κόσμος means being human in the manner of a way of thinking that has turned away from God (ἡ σοφία τοῦ κόσμου). Κόσμος οὗτος refers to human Dasein in a particular "historical" existence, distinguished from another one that has already dawned (αἰὼν ὁ μέλλων).

The Gospel according to Saint John employs the concept κόσμος unusually frequently – above all in relation to the Synoptics – and does so in a sense that is quite central.²⁶ World designates the fundamental form of human Dasein removed from God, the *character of being human* pure and simple. Consequently, world is also a regional term for all human beings together, without any distinction between the wise and the foolish, the just and the sinners, the Jews and the Gentiles. The central meaning of this completely anthropological concept of world is expressed in the fact that it functions as the opposing concept to that of Jesus son of God, which filiation is conceived as life (ζωή), truth (ἀλήθεια), light (φῶς).

This coining of the meaning of κόσμος that begins in the New Testament then appears unmistakably, for example, in Augustine and Thomas Aquinas. According to Augustine, *mundus* on the one hand means the whole of created beings. But just as often *mundus* stands for *mundi habitatores*. This term again has the specifically existentiell sense of the *dilectores mundi, impii, carnales* [those who delight in the world, the impious, the carnal]. *Mundus non dicuntur iusti*, quia licet carne in eo habitent, *corde* cum deo sunt [The *just* are *not* called the world, since, though they may dwell in the world in flesh, *in heart* they are with God].[27] Augustine might well have drawn this concept of world [41] – which then helped to determine the history of the Western spirit – just as much from Saint Paul as from the Gospel of Saint John. The following excerpt from the Prologue to the Gospel according to Saint John may provide evidence for this: ἐν τῷ κόσμῳ ἦν, καὶ ὁ κόσμος δι᾽ αὐτοῦ ἐγένετο· καὶ ὁ κόσμος αὐτὸν οὐκ ἔγνω [He was in the world, and the world was made by him, and the world knew him not] (John 1:10). In this context, Augustine provides an interpretation of *mundus* in which he shows the *two* uses of *mundus*, in *"mundus per ipsum factus est"* and *"mundus eum non cognovit,"* to imply a *twofold* usage. In its first meaning *mundus* means as much as *ens creatum*. In the second, *mundus* means *habitare corde in mundo* [dwelling in the world in heart] as *amare mundum* [loving the world], which is equivalent to *non cognoscere Deum* [not knowing God]. In context, the excerpt reads:

Quid est, *mundus factus est per ipsum?* Coelum, terra, mare et omnia quae in eis sunt, mundus dicitur. Iterum alia significatione, dilectores mundi mundus dicuntur. *Mundus per ipsum factus est, et mundus eum non cognovit.* Num enim coeli non cognoverunt Creatorem suum, aut angeli non cognoverunt Creatorem suum, aut non cognoverunt Creatorem suum sidera, quem confitentur daemonia? Omnia undique testimonium perhibuerunt. Sed qui non cognoverunt? Qui amando mundum dicti sunt mundus. Amando enim habitamus corde: amando autem, hoc appellari meruerunt quod ille, ubi habitabant. Quomodo dicimus, mala est illa domus, aut, bona est illa domus, non in illa quam dicimus malam, parietes accusamus, aut in illa, quam dicimus bonam, parietes laudamus, sed malam domum: inhabitantes malos, et bonam domum: inhabitantes bonos. Sic et mundum, qui inhabitant amando mundum. Qui sunt? Qui diligunt mundum, ipsi enim corde habitant in mundo. Nam qui non diligunt mundum, carne versantur in mundo, sed corde inhabitant coelum.[28]

[What does it mean to say: "The world was made by him"? Heaven and Earth, sea, and all things which are in them are called the world. Yet in another sense, those who delight in the world are called the world. "The world was made by him, and the world knew him not." But did the heavens not know their creator, did the angels not know their creator, did the stars not know their creator, whom even the devils acknowledged? Everywhere, all things bore witness to him. Who did not know him? Those who, because they love the world, are called the world. For, when we love a place, we dwell there in heart. And, if we love the place where we live, we deserve to be called what it is called. When we say this house is bad or that house is good, we do not find fault with the walls of the house we call bad, nor do we praise the walls of the house we call good. Rather, what we mean by "bad house" is "bad inhabitants" and, by "good house," "good inhabitants." In the same way, by "world" we mean those who dwell in the world by virtue of loving the world. Who are they? Those who delight in the world, since these same dwell in the world in their hearts. For those who do not delight in the world are engaged in the world in their flesh, but in their hearts they dwell in heaven.]

Accordingly, world means: beings as a whole, namely, as the decisive "how" in accordance with which human Dasein assumes a stance and maintains itself in relation to beings. Thomas Aquinas [42] likewise on occasion uses *mundus* as synonymous with *universum* [universe], *universitas creaturarum* [the whole world of creatures], but also as meaning *saeculum* (worldly way of thinking), *quod mundi nomine amatores mundi significantur. Mundanus (saecularis)* is the opposing concept to *spiritualis*.[29]

Without going into detail about the concept of world in Leibniz, let us mention the determination of world in Scholastic metaphysics. Baumgarten's definition is: *mundus (universum, πᾶν) est series (multitudo, totum) actualium finitorum, quae non est pars alterius* [The world (*universum*, πᾶν) is that series (*multitudo, totum*) of actually existing, finite things that is not equivalent to anything else].[30] Here world is equated with the totality of what is present at hand, namely, in the sense of *ens creatum*. This entails, however, that our conception of the concept of world is dependent upon an understanding of the essence and possibility of proofs of God. This becomes especially clear in Christian A. Crusius, who defines the concept of a world thus: "a *world* means that kind of real association of finite things that is not itself in turn part of another one to which it would belong by means of a real association."[31] World is accordingly set over and against God himself. But it is also distinguished from an "*individual* creature," and no less from "*several simultaneously existing* creatures" that "stand *in no* association *whatsoever.*" Finally, world is also distinguished from any comprehensive concept of creatures "that is *only a part* of another such concept with which it stands in real association."[32]

The essential determinations belonging to such a world may be derived from a twofold source. What must be present in any world is on the one hand "whatever follows from the general essence of things." In addition, everything that "in the positing of certain creatures may be recognized as necessary from the essential properties [43] of God."[33] Within metaphysics as a whole, the "doctrine of world" is therefore subordinate to ontology (the doctrine of the essence of, and most universal distinctions between things in general) and to "theoretical natural theology." World is accordingly the regional term for the highest unity of association in the totality of created beings.

If the concept of world thus functions as a fundamental concept of metaphysics (of rational cosmology as a discipline of *metaphysica specialis*), and if Kant's *Critique of Pure Reason* presents a laying of the ground for metaphysics as a whole,[34] then the problem of the concept of world must, corresponding to a transformation in the idea of metaphysics, attain an altered form in Kant. In this respect, however, it is all the more necessary to provide a pointer, albeit a rather concise one, since in addition to the "cosmological" meaning of "world" in Kant's anthropology, the existentiell meaning emerges once more, although without its specifically Christian hue.

Already in the "Dissertation of 1770," where the introductory characterization of the concept *mundus* in part still transpires entirely within the orbit of the traditional ontic metaphysics,[35] Kant touches on a difficulty in the concept of world that later becomes sharpened and expanded into a major problem in the *Critique of Pure Reason*. Kant begins his discussion of the concept of world in the "Dissertation" by giving a formal determination of what is understood by "world": world as a *"terminus"* is essentially related to "synthesis": In composito substantiali, quemadmodum Analysis non terminatur nisi parte quae non est totum, h.e. *Simplici,* ita synthesis non nisi toto quod non est pars, i.e. *Mundo.* [Just as, in dealing with a complex of substances, analysis ends only with a part that is not a whole, i.e., with the *simple;* so synthesis ends only with a whole that is not a part, i.e., with the *world.*] In §2 he characterizes those "moments" that are essential for a definition of the concept of world: (1) *Materia* (in sensu transcendentali) h.e. *partes,* quae hic [44] sumuntur esse *substantiae.* [*Matter* (in a transcendental sense), i.e., the *parts,* which are here assumed to be *substances.*] (2) *Forma,* quae consistit in substantiarum *coordinatione,* non subordinatione. [*Form,* which consists in the *coordination*, not in the subordination, of substances.] (3) *Universitas*, quae est omnitudo compartium *absoluta*. [*Entirety*, which is the absolute totality of conjoined parts.] In relation to this third moment, Kant notes: *Totalitas* haec absoluta, quanquam conceptus quotidiani et facile obvii speciem prae se ferat, praesertim cum negative enuntiatur, sicuti fit in definitione, tamen penitius perpensa crucem figere philosopho videtur. [This absolute *totality* appears to be an ordinary, easily understandable concept, especially when it is negatively expressed as in our original definition. But, when more closely considered, it is seen to confront the philosopher with a crucial problem (cross).]

This "cross" weighs upon Kant in the next decade, for in the *Critique of Pure Reason* precisely this *"universitas mundi"* becomes a problem, and indeed in several respects. What must be clarified is: (1) *To what* does the totality represented under the title "world" relate, and to what alone can it relate? (2) *What* is accordingly represented in the concept of world? (3) What *character* does this *representing* of such totality have; i.e., what is the conceptual structure of the *concept* of world as such? Kant's answers to these questions, which he himself does not pose explicitly in this manner, bring about a complete change in the problem of world. Kant's concept of world indeed continues to relate the totality represented in it to *finite* things that are present at hand. However, this relation to finitude – a relation essential to the content of the concept of world – receives a new sense. The finitude of things present at hand is not determined by way of an ontic demonstration of their having been created by God, but is interpreted with regard to the fact that these things exist for a finite knowing, and with regard to the extent to which they are possible objects for such knowing, i.e., for a knowing that must first of all let them be *given* to it as things that are already present at hand. Kant names these beings themselves, which with respect to their accessibility are referred to a receptive apprehending (finite intuition), "appearances," i.e., "things in their appearance." *The same beings*, understood, however, as possible "objects" of an absolute, i.e., creative intuition, he calls "things in themselves." The unity of the connection of appearances, i.e., the constitution of the being of those beings accessible in finite knowledge, is determined by ontological [45] principles of ground, i.e., the system of synthetic knowledge a priori. The substantive content represented a priori in these "synthetic" principles, their "reality" in the old meaning – precisely retained by Kant – of substantiveness, may be presented free of experience and by way of intuition from out of the objects, i.e., from out of that which is necessarily intuited a priori along with such objects, namely, the pure intuition of "time." The reality of the synthetic principles is objective; it can be presented from the objects. And yet the *unity of appearances*, because it is necessarily referred to a factically contingent being-given, is at all times *conditioned* and in principle fundamentally incomplete. If this unity of a manifold of appearances is represented as complete, then the representation of a comprehensive concept arises whose content (reality) in principle cannot be projected in an image, i.e., in something that can be intuited. Such a representation is "transcendent." Yet to the extent that this representation of a completeness is nevertheless necessary a priori, even though it is transcendent it does have *transcendental reality*. Representations of this kind Kant calls *"ideas."* They "contain a certain completeness that no possible empirical knowledge can attain, and here reason has only a systematic unity in mind, which it tries to make our empirically possible unity approach, without it ever being fully attained."[36] "By a system, however, I understand the unity of manifold knowledge under an idea. The latter is reason's concept of the form of a whole."[37] Because the unity and wholeness represented in the ideas "can never be projected in an image,"[38] it can never relate immediately to anything intuitable either. As a higher unity, it therefore only ever concerns the unity of synthesis of the understanding. These ideas, however, "are not arbitrarily dreamt up, but given to us by the nature of reason itself, and therefore necessarily relate to the entire employment of our understanding."[39] As pure concepts of reason [46], they spring not from the reflection of the understanding, which still relates to something given, but rather from the pure procedure of reason as inferential. Kant thus calls the ideas "inferred" concepts, as distinct from the "reflective" concepts of of the understanding.[40] In its inferential activity, reason is concerned with attaining something unconditioned in relation to the conditions. The ideas as reason's pure concepts of totality are therefore representations of the unconditioned. "Thus the transcendental concept of reason is none other than a concept of the *totality of conditions* for something given and conditioned. And since the *unconditioned* alone makes possible the totality of conditions, and conversely, the totality of conditions is itself at all times unconditioned, a pure concept of reason in general can be explained by the concept of the unconditioned insofar as it contains a ground for the synthesis of the conditioned."[41]

As representations of the unconditioned totality of a realm of beings, ideas are necessary representations. And insofar as a threefold relation of representations to something is possible, namely, to the subject and to the object, and to the object in two ways, one finite (appearances) and the other absolute (things in themselves), there arise three classes of ideas, to which we may assign the three disciplines of traditional *metaphysica specialis*. The concept of world is accordingly that idea in which the absolute totality of those objects accessible in finite knowledge is represented a priori. World thus means as much as "the sum-total [*Inbegriff*] of all appearances,"[42] or "sum-total of all objects of possible experience."[43] "I name all [47] transcendental ideas, insofar as they concern absolute totality in the synthesis of appearances, concepts of world [*Weltbegriffe*]."[44] Yet since those beings accessible to finite knowledge may be viewed ontologically with respect to both their what-being (*essentia*) and their "existence" (*existentia*) – or in Kant's formulation of this distinction, in accordance with which he also divides the categories and principles of the transcendental analytic, "*mathematically*" and "*dynamically*"[45] – there thus results a division of the concepts of world into mathematical and dynamic. The mathematical concepts of world are the concepts of world "in their more restricted meaning," as distinguished from the dynamical concepts, which he also calls "transcendent concepts of nature."[46] Yet Kant considers it "quite fitting" to call these ideas "as a whole" concepts of world, "because by world we understand the sum-total of all appearances, and our ideas too are directed only toward the unconditioned in appearances; in part also because the word world, understood transcendentally, means the absolute totality of the sum-total of existing things, and we are directing our attention solely to the completeness of synthesis (albeit really only in regression to the conditions)."[47]

[48] Not only the connection between Kant's concept of world and that of traditional metaphysics comes to light in this remark, but with equal clarity the transformation accomplished in the *Critique of Pure Reason*, i.e., the more originary ontological interpretation of the concept of world. This interpretation, by way of a concise response to our three questions above, may be characterized as follows: (1) The concept of world is not an ontic association of things in themselves, but a transcendental (ontological) concept of the sum-total of things as appearances. (2) In the concept of world we are not presented with a "coordination" of substances, but precisely with a subordination, namely, the "increasing series" of conditions of synthesis, up to the unconditioned. (3) The concept of world is not a "rational" representation whose conceptuality is undetermined; rather, it is determined as an idea, i.e., as a pure synthetic concept of reason, and is distinguished from concepts of the understanding.

The character of *universitas* (totality) that was earlier attributed to it is thus now removed from the concept *mundus* and reserved for a still higher class of transcendental ideas that the concept of world itself points toward, and that Kant calls the "transcendental ideal."[48]

At this point we must forgo an interpretation of this highest point of Kantian speculative metaphysics. Only one thing needs to be mentioned so as to let the essential character of the concept of world, namely, finitude, emerge more clearly.

As an idea the concept of world is the representation of an *unconditioned* totality. And yet it does not represent that which is altogether and "properly" unconditioned, insofar as the totality thought in this concept remains related to appearances, to the possible object of *finite* knowledge. World as an idea is indeed transcendent, it *surpasses* appearances, and in such a way that as *their* totality it precisely *relates back* to them. But transcendence in the Kantian [49] sense of surpassing experience is ambivalent. On the one hand, it can mean: *within* experience, exceeding that which is given *within it* as such, namely, the manifold of appearances. This is the case for the represention "world." But transcendence also means: stepping *out* of experience as finite knowledge altogether and representing the possible whole of all things as the "object" of an *intuitus originarius*. In such transcendence there arises the transcendental ideal, compared to which world constitutes a *restriction* and becomes a term for finite, *human* knowledge in its totality. The concept of world stands, as it were, *between* the "possibility of experience" and the "transcendental ideal," and thus in its core means the totality of the finitude that is *human* in essence.

From here, an insight opens up into a possible second, specifically existentiell meaning that, in addition to the "cosmological" one, pertains to the concept of world in Kant.

"The most important object in the world, to which man can apply all progress in culture, is *man*, because he is his own ultimate end. – To recognize him, therefore, in accordance with his species as an earthly being endowed with reason, especially deserves to be called *worldly knowledge*, even though he comprises only one part of the creatures of this earth."[49] Knowledge of *man*, and indeed precisely with respect "to what *he* makes, or can and ought to make of himself as a freely acting being," i.e., *precisely not* knowledge of man in a "physiological" respect, is here termed knowledge of the *world*. Knowledge of the world is synonymous with pragmatic *anthropology* (knowledge of the human being). "Such an anthropology, considered . . . as *worldly knowledge*, is then not yet properly called *pragmatic* when it contains an extensive knowledge of *matters* in the world, e.g., of animals, plants, and minerals in various lands and climates, but when it contains knowledge of man as *citizen of the world*."[50]

[50] The fact that "world" means precisely human existence in historical being with one another, and not the appearance of the human being in the

cosmos as a species of living being, becomes especially clear from the turns of phrase that Kant has recourse to in clarifying this existentiell concept of world: "knowing the world" and "having class [world]." Although they both refer to the existence of human beings, the two expressions each mean something different, "for the first (the human being who knows the world) merely *understands* the game as a spectator, whereas the second has *played along with it.*"[51] Here world is the term for the "game" of everyday Dasein, for the latter itself.

Commensurate with this, Kant distinguishes "worldly erudition" from "private erudition." "The first refers to the skillfulness of one human being in exercising influence upon others, in order to use them for his own ends."[52] Furthermore: "A history is composed in a pragmatic manner whenever it makes one *erudite*, i.e., instructs the world as to how it may procure its advantage better or at least just as well as the previous world."[53]

From this "worldly knowledge" in the sense of "life-experience" and understanding of existence Kant distinguishes "Scholastic knowledge."[54] Along the guideline of this distinction he then develops the concept of philosophy in accordance with its "Scholastic concept" and its "worldly concept."[55] Philosophy in the Scholastic sense remains an affair of the mere "artificer of reason." Philosophy in accordance with its worldly concept is the concern of the "teacher in the ideal," i.e., of the one [51] who aims for the "divine human being in us."[56] "The concept of world here means that concept which concerns what is necessarily of interest to everyone."[57]

In this whole context world is the designation for human Dasein in the core of its essence. This concept of world corresponds entirely to the existentiell concept of Augustine, except that the specifically Christian evaluation of "worldly" existence, of the *amatores mundi*, is omitted and world has the positive significance of the "participators" in the game of life.

This *existentiell* meaning of the concept of world cited from Kant prefigures the more recent appearance of the expression *"Weltanschauung."*[58] Yet expressions like "man of the world" and "the aristocratic world" show a similar meaning of the concept of world. Here again "world" is not a mere regional title used to designate the human community as distinct from the totality of natural things; rather, world refers precisely to human beings *in their relations* to beings as a whole; town houses and mews, for example, also belong to the "aristocratic world."

It is therefore equally erroneous to appeal to the expression world either as a designation for the totality of natural things (the natural concept of world), or as a term for the community of human beings (the personal concept of world).⁵⁹ Rather, what is metaphysically [52] essential in the more or less clearly highlighted meaning of κόσμος, *mundus*, world, lies in the fact that it is directed toward an interpretation of human existence [*Dasein*] *in its relation to beings as a whole*. Yet for reasons that we cannot discuss here, the development of the concept of world first encounters *that* meaning according to which it characterizes the "how" of beings as a whole, and in such a way that their *relation to* Dasein is at first understood only in an indeterminate manner. World belongs to a *relational* structure distinctive of Dasein as such, a structure that we called being-in-the-world. This employment of the concept of world – as our historiographical references were intended to indicate – is so far from being arbitrary that it precisely attempts to raise to a level of explicitness and to sharpen into a *problem* a phenomenon of Dasein that is constantly already familiar to us, yet not ontologically grasped in its unity.

Human Dasein – a being that finds itself situated *in the midst* of beings, comporting itself *toward* beings – in so doing exists in such a way that beings are always manifest as a whole. Here it is not necessary that this wholeness be expressly conceptualized; its belonging to Dasein can be veiled, the expanse of this whole is changeable. This [53] wholeness is understood without the whole of those beings that are manifest being explicitly grasped or indeed "completely" investigated in their specific connections, domains, and layers. Yet the understanding of this wholeness, an understanding that in each case reaches ahead and embraces it, is a surpassing in the direction of world. The task now is to attempt a more concrete interpretation of the phenomenon of world. This may unfold through our response to the following questions: (1) What is the fundamental character of the wholeness we have described? (2) To what extent does this characterization of world make it possible for us to illuminate the essence of Dasein's relation to world, i.e., to shed light upon the intrinsic possibility of being-in-the-world (transcendence)?

World as a wholeness "is" not a being, but that from out of which Dasein *gives itself the signification* of whatever beings it *is able* to comport itself toward in whatever way. That Dasein gives "*itself*" such signification from out of "*its*" world then means: In this coming toward itself from out of the world Dasein gives rise to itself [*zeitigt sich*]⁶⁰ as a *self*, i.e., as a being entrusted with having *to be*. In the being of this being *what is at issue is its potentiality for being*. Dasein is in such a way that it exists *for the sake of itself*. If, however, it is a surpassing in the direction of world that first gives rise to selfhood, then world shows itself to be that for the sake of which Dasein exists. World has the fundamental character of the "for the sake of …," and indeed in the originary sense that it first provides the intrinsic possibility for every factically self-determining "for your sake," "for his sake," "for the sake of that," etc. Yet that for the sake of which Dasein exists is it itself. To selfhood there belongs world; world is essentially related to Dasein.

Before we attempt to inquire into the essence of this relation and thus to interpret being-in-the-world starting from the "for the sake of" as the primary character of world, we need to ward off several misinterpretations that may suggest themselves with regard to what has been said.

The statement: *Dasein exists for the sake of itself,* does not contain the positing of an egoistic or ontic end for some blind narcissism on the part of the factical human being in each case. It cannot, therefore, be "refuted," for instance, by pointing out that many human beings [54] sacrifice themselves *for others* and that in general human beings do not merely exist alone on their own, but in community. The statement in question contains neither a solipsistic isolation of Dasein nor an egoistic intensification thereof. By contrast, it presumably gives the condition of possibility of the human being's being able to comport "himself" *either* "egoistically" *or* "altruistically." Only because Dasein as such is determined by selfhood can an I-self comport itself toward a you-self. Selfhood is the presupposition for the possibility of being an "I," the latter only ever being disclosed in the "you." Never, however, is selfhood relative to a "you," but rather – because it first makes all this possible – is neutral with respect to being an "I" and being a "you," and above all with respect to such things as "sexuality." All statements of essence in an ontological analytic of the Dasein in the human being take this being from the outset in such neutrality.

How then is Dasein's relation to world to be determined? Since world is not a being, and supposedly belongs to Dasein, this relation is evidently not to be thought as a relation between Dasein as one being and world as another. Yet if this is the case, does not world then get taken into Dasein (the subject) and declared as something purely "subjective"? Yet the task is to gain, through an illumination of transcendence, one possibility for determining what is meant by "subject" and "subjective." In the end, the concept of world must be conceived in such a way that world is indeed subjective, i.e., belongs to Dasein,[61] but precisely on this account does not fall, as a being, into the inner sphere of a "subjective" subject. For the same reason, however, world is not merely objective either, if "objective" means: belonging among beings as objects.

As the respective wholeness of that for the sake of which Dasein exists in each case, world is brought before Dasein through Dasein itself. This bringing world before itself is the originary projection of the possibilities of Dasein, insofar as, in the midst of beings, it is to be able to comport itself toward such beings. Yet just as it does not explicitly grasp that which has been projected, this projection of world [55] also always *casts* the projected world *over* beings. This prior casting-over [*Überwurf*] first makes it possible for beings as such to manifest themselves. This occurrence of a projective casting-over, in which the being of Dasein is temporalized, is being-in-the-world. "Dasein transcends" means: in the essence of its being it is *world-forming*, "forming" [*bildend*] in the multiple sense that it lets world occur, and through the world gives itself an original view (form [*Bild*]) that is not explicitly grasped, yet functions precisely as a paradigmatic form [*Vor-bild*] for all manifest beings, among which each respective Dasein itself belongs.

Beings, such as nature in the broadest sense, could in no way become manifest unless they found *occasion* to enter into a world. This is why we speak of their possible and occasional *entry into world*. Entry into world is not some process that transpires in those beings that enter it, but is something that "happens" "with" beings. And such occurrence is the existing of Dasein, which as existing transcends.[a] Only if, amid beings in their totality, beings come to be "more in being" in the manner of the temporalizing of Dasein are there the hours and days of beings' entry into world. And only if this primordial history, namely, transcendence, occurs, i.e., only if beings having the character of being-in-the-world irrupt into beings, is there the possibility of beings manifesting themselves.[62] [b]

Our elucidation of transcendence thus far already lets us understand that, if it is indeed in transcendence alone that beings can come to light as beings, transcendence comprises an *exceptional domain* for the elaboration of all questions that concern beings as such, i.e., in their being. Before we dissect our guiding problem of ground within the domain of transcendence, and thereby [56] sharpen the problem of transcendence in one particular respect, we should become better acquainted with the transcendence of Dasein via a further historical recollection.

---

[a] First edition, 1929: But Dasein and beyng itself? Not yet thought, not until *Being and Time*, Part II. Da-sein belongs to beyng itself as the simple onefold of beings and being; the essence of the "occurrence" – temporalizing of Temporality [*Temporalität*] as a preliminary name for the truth of beyng.

[b] First edition, 1929: Yet here the erroneous determination of the relationship between "distinguishing" and transcendence. Transcendence prevails in essence in the distinguishing – the latter is the carrying through [*Austrag*] of the distinction. Here the preparation of the quite other commencement; everything still mixed and confused; contorted into phenomenological-existential and transcendental "research"; occurrence not as "leap," and the latter? Comes into its own in the event of appropriation.

Transcendence is specifically expressed in Plato's ἐπέκεινα τῆς οὐσίας.[63] [a]
Yet may we interpret the ἀγαθόν as the transcendence of *Dasein?* Even a
fleeting glance at the context in which Plato discusses the question of the
ἀγαθόν must dispel such doubts. The problem of the ἀγαθόν is merely the
culmination of the central and concrete question concerning the chief and
fundamental possibility of the *existence of Dasein* in the polis. Even though
the task of an ontological projection of Dasein upon its fundamental metaphysical constitution is not explicitly posed or even developed, the threefold
characterization of the ἀγαθόν undertaken with constant reference to the
"sun" impels us toward the question of the possibility of truth, understanding, and being – i.e., taking these phenomena together, toward the question
concerning the originary and unitary ground of possibility of the truth of
our understanding of being. Such understanding, however – as an unveiling projecting of being – is the primordial activity of human existence, in
which all existing in the midst of beings must be rooted. For the ἀγαθόν is
that ἕξις (sovereign power) that is sovereign with respect to the possibility
(in the sense of the enabling)[64] of truth, understanding, and even being,
and indeed of all three together in their unity.

It is not by accident that the ἀγαθόν is indeterminate with respect to its
content, so that all definitions and interpretations in this respect must fail.
Rationalistic explanations fall short, as does the "irrationalist" recourse that
takes flight in the "mystery." The illumination of the ἀγαθόν, in keeping
with the pointer that Plato himself provides, must stick to the task of interpreting the essence of the connection between truth, understanding, and
being. Inquiry back into the intrinsic possibility of this connection sees
itself "compelled" to accomplish *explicitly* [57] the surpassing that occurs
necessarily in every Dasein as such, yet mostly in a concealed manner. The
essence of the ἀγαθόν lies in its sovereignty over itself as οὗ ἕνεκα – as the
"for the sake of . . . ," it is the source of possibility as such. And because the
possible indeed lies higher than the actual, ἡ τοῦ ἀγαθοῦ ἕξις, the essential
source of possibility, is even μειζόνως τιμητέον.[65]

Certainly the relation of the "for the sake of" to Dasein becomes problematic precisely here. Yet this problem does not come to light. Rather,
according to the doctrine that has become traditional, the ideas remain in a
ὑπερουράνιος τόπος; the task is merely to secure them as the most objective
of objects, as that which *is* in beings, without the "for the sake of" showing itself as the primary character of world so that the originary content

---

[a] Second edition, 1931: No! Da-sein not at all comprehended, and not experienced. ἐπέκεινα
not transcendence either, but ἀγαθόν as αἰτία.

of the ἐπέκεινα might come to the fore as the transcendence of Dasein. Indeed there later awakens the converse tendency, already prefigured in Plato's "recollective" "dialogue of the soul with itself," to conceive of the ideas as innate to the "subject." Both attempts testify that the world is both held before Dasein (beyond it), and yet also forms itself within Dasein. The history of the problem of the ideas shows how transcendence always already comes to light, yet at the same time oscillates to and fro between two poles of possible interpretation, poles that are themselves inadequately grounded and determined. The ideas count as more objective than the objects and at the same time as more subjective than the subject. Just as an exceptional domain of everlasting beings takes the place of the unrecognized phenomenon of world, so too the *relation* to world in the sense of a particular comportment toward this being comes to be interpreted as νοεῖν, *intuitus*, as an apprehending that is no longer mediated, as "reason." The "transcendental ideal" goes together with the *intuitus originarius*.

In this fleeting recollection of the still concealed history of the original problem of transcendence we must have the growing insight [58] that transcendence cannot be unveiled or grasped by a flight into the objective, but solely through an ontological interpretation of the subjectivity of the subject, an interpretation that must constantly be renewed and that actively opposes "subjectivism" in the same way that it refuses to follow "objectivism."[66]

III. ON THE ESSENCE OF GROUND[a]

[59] Our discussion of the "principle of reason" referred the problem of reason or ground to the domain of transcendence (I). Transcendence has, by way of an analysis of the concept of world, been determined as the being-in-the-world of Dasein (II). The task now is to illuminate the essence of ground from out of the transcendence of Dasein.

To what extent does there lie in transcendence the intrinsic possibility of something like ground in general? World gives itself to Dasein in each case as the respective whole of its "for the sake of itself," i.e., for the sake of a being that is equioriginarily being alongside . . . what is present at hand, being

---

[a] First edition, 1929: In keeping with the essence of ground, bring to the fore the originary *fathoming of ground* [Ergründen]. Fathoming of ground prior to all grounding of something. Fathoming of ground in philosophy and art, but not in religion. In III, an approach to the destructuring of I, i.e., of the ontological difference; ontic-ontological truth. In III the step into a realm that compels the destruction of what has gone before and makes a complete overturning necessary. In III the essence of willing as Da-sein, superseding and overcoming of all capacities.

with ... the Dasein of others, and being toward ... itself. Dasein is able to be in relation to itself as itself in this manner only if it surpasses "itself" in this "for the sake of" [*Umwillen*]. This surpassing that occurs "for the sake of" does so only in a "will" [*"Willen"*] that as such projects itself upon possibilities of itself. This will that essentially casts the "for the sake of itself" over and thereby before Dasein cannot therefore be a particular willing, an "act of will" as distinct from other forms of comportment (such as representing, judging, or enjoyment). All forms of comportment are rooted in transcendence. The "will" in question, however, must first "form" the "for-the-sake-of" itself as and in a surpassing. Yet whatever, in accordance with its essence, casts something like the "for the sake of" projectively before it, rather than simply producing it as an occasional and additional accomplishment, is that which we call *freedom*. Surpassing in the direction of world is freedom itself. Accordingly, transcendence does not merely come upon the "for the sake of" as anything like a value or end that would be present at hand in itself; rather, freedom holds the "for the sake of" *toward* itself, *and does so as freedom*. In this transcending that holds the "for the sake of" toward itself there occurs the Dasein in human beings,[a] such that in the essence of their existence they can be obligated to themselves, i.e., be free selves. In this, however, freedom simultaneously unveils itself as making possible [60] something binding, indeed obligation in general. *Freedom alone can let a world prevail and let it world for Dasein.* World never *is*, but *worlds*.

In this interpretation of freedom arrived at in terms of transcendence there ultimately lies a more originary characterization of the essence of freedom than that which determines it as spontaneity, i.e., as a kind of causality. The beginning of something by itself provides only the negative characterization of freedom according to which there is no determinative cause lying further back. This characterization, however, overlooks above all the fact that it speaks in an ontologically undifferentiated manner of "beginnings" and "occurrences," without explicitly characterizing what it means to be a cause in terms of the specific manner of being pertaining to the being that is in *this* way, namely, Dasein. Accordingly, if spontaneity ("beginning by oneself") is to be capable of serving as an essential characterization of the "subject," then two things are first required: (1) Selfhood must be clarified ontologically for any possible appropriate conception of what is meant by this "by oneself"; (2) precisely the same clarification of selfhood must provide us in advance with an indication of the way in which

---

[a] First edition, 1929: The reverse: Dasein withstands the prevailing [*Walten*], or better the essential unfolding [*Wesen*], of truth and thus grounds the possibility of being human as being human *in* Dasein!

a self *occurs*, so as to be able to determine the kind of movement that pertains to "beginning." *The selfhood of that self that already lies at the grounds of all spontaneity, however, lies in transcendence.* Letting world prevail in projectively casting it over us is freedom. Only because transcendence consists in freedom can freedom make itself known as a distinctive kind of causality in existing Dasein. Yet the interpretation of freedom as "causality" above all already moves within a particular understanding of ground. Freedom as transcendence, however, is not only a unique "kind" of ground, but the *origin of ground in general. Freedom is freedom for ground.*

We shall name the originary relation of freedom to ground a *grounding* [Gründen]. In grounding, freedom *gives* and *takes* ground.[a] This grounding that is rooted in transcendence is, however, *strewn* into manifold ways. There are three such ways: (1) grounding as establishing [*Stiften*]; (2) grounding as taking up a basis [*Bodennehmen*]; [61] (3) grounding as the grounding *of* something [*Begründen*]. If these ways of grounding belong to transcendence, then the expressions "establishing" and "taking a basis" evidently cannot have an ordinary, ontic meaning, but must have a *transcendental* meaning. Yet to what extent is Dasein's transcending a grounding in the said ways?

As the "first" of these ways we deliberately cite "establishing," though not because the others derive from it. Nor is it that manner of grounding initially familiar to us, or that we come to know first. And yet precisely this manner of grounding has a priority, one that shows itself in the fact that the illumination of transcendence provided above was unable to avoid it. This "first" form of grounding is nothing other than *the projection of the "for the sake of."* If such freely letting world prevail was determined as transcendence, and if the other ways of grounding also necessarily belong to the projection of world as grounding, then this implies that neither transcendence nor freedom has as yet been fully determined. It indeed always pertains to Dasein's projection of world that in and through its surpassing Dasein comes back to beings as such. The "for the sake of" that is projectively cast before us points back to the entirety of those beings that can be unveiled within this horizon of world. To such beings, in whatever levels of prominence or degrees of explicitness, there also always belong in each case both beings as Dasein and beings that do not have the character of Dasein. Yet in the projection of world, such beings are not yet manifest in themselves. Indeed, they would have to remain concealed, were it not for the fact that Dasein in its projecting is, *as projecting*, also already *in the midst* of such beings. Yet this

[a] First edition, 1929: Places into the ground-less (abyss of ground), non-ground.

"in the midst of . . ." refers neither to a cropping up among other beings, nor even to a specific self-directedness *toward* this particular being in *comporting* oneself *toward* it. Rather, this being in the midst of . . . belongs to transcendence. That which surpasses, in passing *over and beyond* and thus elevating itself, must *find itself* [sich befinden] as such among beings. As finding itself, Dasein is *absorbed* by beings in such a way that, in its belonging to beings, it *is thoroughly attuned* by them. *Transcendence means projection of world* [62] *in such a way that those beings that are surpassed also already pervade and attune that which projects.* With this *absorption* by beings that belongs to transcendence, Dasein has taken up a basis within beings, gained "ground." This "second" form of grounding does not arise *after* the "first," but is "simultaneous" with it. This does not mean to say that the two are present at hand within the same "now"; rather, projection of world and absorption by beings, as ways of grounding, belong in each case to a *single* temporality insofar as they co-constitute its temporalizing. Yet just as the future precedes "in" time, yet temporalizes only insofar as having-been and present also – as intrinsic to time – temporalize in the specific unity of time, so too those ways of grounding that spring from transcendence display this connection. Such correspondence is to be found, however, because transcendence is rooted in the *essence* of time, i.e., in its ecstatic-horizonal constitution.[67]

Dasein would be unable to be pervasively attuned by beings as the being that it is,[68] and thus would be unable, for example, to be embraced, captivated, or permeated by them; it would be altogether deprived of any leeway for this, were it not for the fact that an irruption of world, and be it only a glimmer of world, accompanies such being absorbed by beings. In this, the world that is unveiled may be scarcely or not at all transparent conceptually; world may even be interpreted as *one* particular being among others; any explicit knowledge of Dasein's transcending may be absent; the freedom of Dasein that brings along with it the projection of world may be barely awake – and yet only *as* being-in-the-world is Dasein absorbed by beings. Dasein grounds (establishes) world only as grounding itself in the midst of beings.

This grounding that establishes, as the projection of *possibilities of itself,*[69] entails, however, that in this process Dasein in each case [63] *exceeds* itself. In accordance with its essence, the projection of possibilities is in each case richer than the possession of them by the one projecting. The ready possession of possibilities belongs to Dasein, however, because, as projective, it finds itself in the midst of beings. Certain other possibilities are thereby already *withdrawn* from Dasein, and indeed merely through its own facticity. Yet precisely this *withdrawal* of certain possibilities pertaining to its potentiality for being-in-the-world – a withdrawal entailed in its being absorbed by beings – first brings those possibilities of world-projection that can "actually" be seized upon *toward* Dasein as its world. Such withdrawal lends precisely the binding character of what remains projected before us the power to prevail within the realm of Dasein's existence. *Corresponding to these two ways of grounding, transcendence at once exceeds and withdraws.* The fact that the ever-excessive projection of world attains its power and becomes our possession only in such withdrawal is at the same time a transcendental testimony to the *finitude* of Dasein's freedom. And does not the *finite* essence of freedom in general thereby announce itself?

For the interpretation of the manifold grounding of freedom, what is essential initially is to see the *unity* of the two ways of grounding we have so far discussed, the unity that comes to light in the way in which excess and withdrawal become transcendentally attuned to one another.

Yet Dasein is a being that not only finds itself in the midst of beings, but also *comports itself toward* beings and thus also toward itself. Such comportment toward beings is at first and for the most part even equated with transcendence. If this is indeed a failure to recognize the essence of transcendence, then the transcendental possibility of intentional comportment must become a *problem*. And if intentionality is indeed distinctive of the constitution of Dasein's existence, then an illumination of transcendence cannot pass it over.

The *projection of world* indeed makes possible – although we cannot show this here – a prior understanding of the being of beings, [64] yet is not itself a relation of Dasein to *beings*. And our *being absorbed*, which lets Dasein find itself in the midst of beings and pervasively attuned by them (though never without the unveiling of world), is likewise not a *comportment* toward beings. Yet presumably *both* – in their unity as characterized – make intentionality possible transcendentally, and in such a way that, as ways of grounding, they co-temporalize a *third* manner of grounding: *grounding as the grounding of something.* In this form of grounding, the transcendence of Dasein assumes the role of making possible the manifestation of beings in themselves, the possibility of ontic truth.

"The grounding of something" should here be taken not in the restricted and derivative sense of proving ontic or theoretical propositions, but in a fundamentally originary meaning. According to this meaning, grounding something means *making possible the why-question in general.* To make visible the originarily grounding character proper to the grounding of something means, therefore, to illuminate the transcendental origin of the "why" as such. We are not therefore seeking, for instance, something that occasions the factical irruption of the why-question in Dasein, but are inquiring concerning the *transcendental* possibility of the "why" in general. For this reason, we must interrogate transcendence itself insofar as we have determined it via the two ways of grounding discussed thus far. Grounding as establishing sets forth possibilities of existence in its projection of world. Existing always means: comporting oneself toward beings – toward those not having the character of Dasein, and toward oneself and those like oneself – in finding oneself in the midst of beings, and doing so in such a way that in this comportment in which one finds oneself, the potentiality for being of Dasein itself is at stake. In the projection of world an excess of possibility is given with respect to which, in our being pervaded by those (actual) beings that press around us as we find ourselves, the "why" springs forth.

Yet because the first two ways of grounding *belong together* in transcendence, the springing forth of the "why" is transcendentally necessary. The "why" even becomes manifold at its very origin. Its [65] fundamental forms are: Why *in this way* and not otherwise? Why this and not that? *Why something at all and not nothing?* In this "why," in whatever manner it is expressed, there also lies already a preunderstanding, albeit a preconceptual one, of what-being, how-being, and being (nothing) in general. This understanding of being first makes possible the "why." This means, however, that it already contains the ultimate and primordial originary answer[a] to all questioning. As altogether the most antecedent *answer,* our understanding of being provides the ultimate and primary *grounding of things.* In such understanding of being, transcendence as such grounds things. Because being and the constitution of being are unveiled therein, the transcendental grounding of something may be called *ontological truth.*

Such grounding of things lies "at the ground" of all comportment toward beings, and in such a way that only in the illumination granted by our understanding of being can beings become manifest in themselves (i.e., *as* the beings they are and in the way they are). Yet because such *grounding of something* prevails transcendentally from the outset throughout all becoming-manifest of beings (ontic truth), all ontic discovery and disclosing must in its way be a "grounding of something"; i.e., it must *account for* itself. In such accounting, what occurs is the *referral to a being* that then makes itself known, for example, as "cause" or as the "motivational grounds" (motive) for an already manifest nexus of beings. This referral is in each case demanded by the what-being and how-being of the relevant

---

[a] First edition, 1929: The essence of this answer: The relation of beyng, as beyng, to the human essence. The extent to which the proper thinking of beyng is *not a questioning*.

beings and by the *manner of unveiling* (truth) belonging to them. Because the transcendence of Dasein, as projectively finding itself, and as forming the development of an understanding of being, is a grounding of things; and because *this* way of grounding is equioriginary with the first two ways within the unity of transcendence, i.e., springs forth from the finite freedom of Dasein; for this reason Dasein *can*, in its factical accounting and justifications, cast "grounds" aside, suppress any demand for them, pervert them, and cover them over. As a consequence of this origin of grounding things and thus also of accounting for them, it is in each case left to the freedom in Dasein how far to extend such grounding [66] and whether indeed it understands how to attain an authentic grounding of things, i.e., an unveiling of the transcendental possibility of such grounding. Even though being is always unveiled in transcendence, this does not require any conceptual ontological grasp. Thus it is altogether possible for transcendence to remain concealed *as such* and be familiar only in an "indirect" interpretation. Yet even then it is unveiled, because it lets there be precisely beings that have irrupted with the fundamental constitution of being-in-the-world, and in this the self-unveiling of transcendence makes itself known. Transcendence explicitly unveils itself as the origin of grounding, however, when such grounding is brought to *spring forth* in its threefold character. In accordance with this, ground means: *possibility, basis, account*. Strewn in this threefold manner, the grounding that is transcendence first brings about in an originarily unifying manner that whole within which a Dasein must be able to exist in each case. Freedom in this threefold manner is freedom for ground. The occurrence of transcendence as grounding is the forming of a leeway into which there can irrupt the factical *self-maintaining* of factical Dasein in each case in the midst of beings as a whole.

Are we then restricting to three the four grounds discovered by the tradition, or are these three ways of grounding equivalent to the three kinds of πρῶτον ὅθεν in Aristotle? The comparison cannot be made in such a superficial manner; for what is peculiar to the first discovery of the "four grounds" is that it does not yet distinguish in principle between transcendental grounds and specifically ontic causes. The transcendental grounds appear merely as the "more universal" in relation to the ontic. The originary character of the transcendental grounds and their specific character of *ground* remain covered over beneath the formal characterization of "first" and "highest" beginnings. And for this reason they also lack unity. Such unity can consist only in the equioriginary character of the transcendental origin of the threefold grounding. The essence "of" ground cannot even be sought, let alone found, by asking after a universal genus that is supposed to result by way of [67] an "abstraction." *The essence of ground is the transcendental springing forth of grounding, strewn threefold into projection of world, absorption within beings, and ontological grounding of beings.*

And it is for this reason alone that even the earliest questioning concerning the essence of *ground* shows itself to be entwined with the task of shedding light upon the essence of *being* and *truth*.

Yet may we not still inquire as to why these three determinative components of transcendence that belong together may be designated by the same term "grounding"? Is it simply a matter of a contrived similarity based on wordplay? Or are the three ways of grounding after all identical in *one* respect, although in a different way in each case? We must indeed respond in the affirmative to this question. At the "level" of our present appraisal, however, we cannot undertake to illuminate the meaning of that *particular* respect in which these three inseparable ways of grounding correspond to one another in a unitary and yet strewn manner. By way of indication it must suffice to point out that establishing, taking up a basis, and legitimation each in their own way *spring forth from a care for steadfastness and subsistence*, a care that in turn is itself possible only as temporality.[a]

Deliberately turning away from this domain of the problem, and instead looking back to the point of departure of our investigation, we shall now discuss briefly whether anything, and if so, what, has been attained with regard to the problem of the "principle of reason" through our attempt at shedding light upon the "essence" of ground. The principle means: every being has its reason [ground]. The exposition we have given first of all illuminates *why* this is so. Because being, as understood in advance, "intrinsically" *grounds* things in an originary manner, every being as a being in its own way announces "grounds," whether these are specifically grasped and determined in an appropriate way or not. Because "ground" is a transcendental characteristic of the essence of *being in general*, the principle of reason [ground] is valid for *beings*. Ground, however, belongs to the essence of being because being (not beings) [68] is given only in transcendence as a grounding that finds itself in a projecting of world.

Furthermore, it has become clear with respect to the principle of reason [ground] that the "birthplace" of this principle lies neither in the essence of proposition nor in propositional truth, but in ontological truth, i.e., in transcendence itself. *Freedom is the origin of the principle of reason [ground];* for in freedom, in the unity of excess and withdrawal, the grounding of things that develops and forms itself as ontological truth is grounded.

---

[a] First edition, 1929: And the latter in time as Temporality [*Temporalität*].

Coming from this origin we not only understand this principle in its intrinsic possibility, but we also gain an eye for something noteworthy and hitherto unelucidated concerning the way it has been conceived, something that is, however, suppressed in the way the principle is ordinarily formulated. In Leibniz we indeed find the principle coined in ways that lend expression to an apparently insignificant moment of its content. These may be schematically brought together as follows: ratio est cur hoc *potius* existit quam aliud; ratio est cur sic *potius* existit quam aliter; ratio est cur aliquid *potius* existit quam nihil. [A reason is why this exists *rather* than something else; a reason is why something exists in this way *rather* than in another way; a reason is why anything exists *rather* than nothing.] The *"cur"* ["why"] is expressed as *"cur potius quam"* ["why rather than"]. Here again the first problem is not that of the ways and means by which these questions, in each case posed factically in ontic ways of comportment, are to be decided. Rather, what needs to be clarified is why it is that the *"cur"* ["why"] could associate itself with the *"potius quam"* ["rather than"] at all.

Every accounting for things must move within a sphere of what is *possible*, because as a manner of intentional comportment toward beings with respect to their possibility it is already compliant with the explicit or implicit (ontological) grounding of something. In accordance with its essence, such grounding always necessarily provides a given *range* of what is possible – here the character of possibility changes according to how the being of those beings to be unveiled is constituted – and it does so because being (the constitution of being), in grounding something, is, as transcendentally binding for Dasein, rooted in Dasein's *freedom*. The reflection of *this* origin of the essence of ground in the grounding that pertains to finite freedom shows itself in the [69] *"potius quam"* found in these formulations of the principle of reason. But once again, shedding light upon the concrete, transcendental connections between "ground" and the "rather than" presses us to clarify the idea of being in general (what-being and how-being, something, nothing and nothingness).

In its traditional form and role, the principle of reason has remained stuck in a trivialized form that necessarily entails that we first of all illuminate everything that has the character of a "grounding principle." For even declaring this principle to be a "grounding principle" and, for instance, placing it together with the principle of identity and principle of noncontradiction, or even deriving it from these, does not lead us into the origin, but is equivalent to cutting off all further questioning. Here we should observe, moreover, that even the principles of identity and noncontradiction are not only *also transcendental*, but point back to something more originary that does not have the character of a proposition, but rather belongs to the occurrence of transcendence as such (temporality).

Thus the principle of reason too lets its non-essence interfere with the essence of ground, and in the sanctioned form of a grounding principle suppresses a problematic that would first open up this very principle. Yet this "non-essence" cannot simply be attributed to the supposed "superficiality" of individual philosophers, and nor can it therefore be overcome by supposedly more radical "progress." Ground has its non-essence because it springs from finite freedom. This freedom is itself unable to withdraw from whatever springs forth from it in this way. The ground that springs forth in transcending folds back upon freedom itself, and freedom *as origin* itself becomes "ground." *Freedom is the ground of ground.* Yet not simply in the sense of a formal, endless "iteration." Freedom's being a ground does not – as we are always tempted to think – have the character of *one* of the ways of grounding, but determines itself as the grounding unity of the transcendental strewal of grounding. As *this* ground, however, freedom is the *abyss of ground* [Ab-grund] in Dasein. Not that our individual, [70] free comportment is groundless; rather, in its essence as transcendence, freedom places Dasein, as potentiality for being, in possibilities that gape open before its finite choice, i.e., within its destiny.[a]

Yet in its world-projective surpassing of beings, Dasein must surpass itself so as to be able to first of all understand *itself* as an abyss of ground from out of this elevation. And the character of this abyssal ground of Dasein is in turn nothing that lends itself to a dialectic, or to psychological dissection. The irruption of this abyssal ground in transcendence as grounding is rather the primordial movement that freedom accomplishes with us ourselves and thereby "gives us to understand," i.e., proffers as the originary content of world, that this content, the more originarily it is grounded, concerns all the more directly the heart of Dasein, its selfhood in action. Accordingly, the non-essence of ground is "overcome" only in factical existing, but never eliminated.

If, however, transcendence in the sense of freedom for ground is understood in the first and last instance as an abyss of ground, then the essence of what was called Dasein's *absorption* in and by beings also thereby becomes sharper. Dasein – although finding itself in the midst of beings and pervasively attuned by them – is, *as free* potentiality for being, *thrown* among beings. The fact *that* it has the possibility of being a self, and has this

---

[a] First edition, 1929: Still the futile attempt to think Da-sein while shielding the truth of beyng in its turning.

factically in keeping with its freedom in each case; the fact *that* transcendence temporalizes itself as a primordial occurrence, does not stand in the power of this freedom itself. Yet such impotence (thrownness) is not first the result of beings forcing themselves upon Dasein, but rather determines Dasein's being as such. All projection of world is therefore *thrown*. Clarifying the *essence of finitude* in Dasein from out of the constitution of its being[a] must precede all "self-evident" assumptions concerning the finite "nature" of the human being, all description of properties that first ensue from finitude, and above all any overhasty "explanation" of the ontic provenance of such properties.

[71] The essence of the finitude of Dasein is, however, unveiled in *transcendence as freedom for ground*.[b]

And so the human being, existing as a transcendence that exceeds in the direction of possibilities, is a *creature of distance*. Only through originary distances that he forms for himself in his transcendence with respect to all beings does a true nearness to things begin to arise in him. And only being able to listen into the distance awakens Dasein as a self to the response of the other Dasein in whose company [*Mitsein*] it can surrender its I-ness so as to attain itself as an authentic self.

---

[a] First edition, 1929: The leap [*Sprung*] into the origin [*Ursprung*]! (Da-sein) origin – freedom – temporality; finitude of Dasein not identical with the finitude of the human being, to be grasped otherwise: character of origin!

[b] First edition, 1929: But freedom has nothing in common with grounding or with ground, just as little as with cause [*Ursache*] or causation [*Ver-ursachen*] or any kind of "substance" or "making" [*"sachen"* und *"machen"*].

On the Essence of Truth

Translated by John Sallis[1]

[73] Our topic is the *essence*[a] of truth. The question regarding the essence of truth is not concerned with whether truth is a truth of practical experience or of economic calculation, the truth of a technical consideration or of political sagacity, or, in particular, a truth of scientific research or of artistic composition, or even the truth of thoughtful reflection or of cultic belief. The question of essence disregards all this and attends to the one thing that in general distinguishes every "truth" as truth.

Yet with this question concerning essence do we not soar too high into the void of generality that deprives all thinking of breath? Does not the extravagance of such questioning bring to light the groundlessness of all philosophy? A radical thinking that turns to what is actual must surely from the first insist bluntly on establishing the actual truth that today gives us a measure and a stand against the confusion of opinions and reckonings. In the face of this actual need, what use is the question concerning the essence of truth, this "abstract" question that disregards everything actual? Is not the question of essence the most unessential and superfluous that could be asked?

No one can evade the evident certainty of these considerations. None can lightly neglect their compelling seriousness. But what is it that speaks in these considerations? "Sound" common sense. It harps on the demand for palpable utility and inveighs against knowledge of the essence of beings, which essential knowledge has long been called "philosophy."[2]

[74] Common sense has its own necessity; it asserts its rights with the weapon peculiarly suitable to it, namely, appeal to the "obviousness" of its claims and considerations. However, philosophy can never refute common

---

[a] Third edition, 1954: Essence: (1) *quidditas* – the "what" – κοινόν; (2) enabling – condition of possibility; (3) ground of enabling.

sense, for the latter is deaf to the language of philosophy. Nor may it[3] even wish to do so, since common sense is blind to what philosophy sets before its essential vision.

Moreover, we ourselves remain within the sensibleness of common sense to the extent that we suppose ourselves to be secure in those multiform "truths" of practical experience and action, of research, composition, and belief. We ourselves intensify that resistance which the "obvious" has to every demand made by what is questionable.

Therefore even if some questioning concerning truth is necessary, what we then demand is an answer to the question as to where we stand today. We want to know what our situation is today. We call for the goal that should be posited for human beings in and for their history. We want the actual "truth." Well then – truth!

But in calling for the actual "truth" we must already know what truth as such means. Or do we know this only by "feeling" and "in a general way"? But is not such vague "knowing" and our indifference regarding it more desolate than sheer ignorance of the essence of truth?

1. THE USUAL CONCEPT OF TRUTH

What do we ordinarily understand by "truth"? This elevated yet at the same time worn and almost dulled word "truth"[a] means what makes[b] a true thing true. What is a true thing? We say, for example, "It is a true joy to cooperate in the accomplishment of this task." [75] We mean that it is purely and actually a joy. The true is the actual. Accordingly, we speak of true gold in distinction from false. False gold is not actually what it appears to be. It is merely a "semblance" and thus is not actual. What is not actual is taken to be the opposite of the actual. But what merely seems to be gold is nevertheless something actual. Accordingly, we say more precisely: actual gold is genuine gold. Yet both are "actual," the circulating counterfeit no less than the genuine gold. What is true about genuine gold thus cannot be demonstrated merely by its actuality. The question recurs: what do "genuine" and "true" mean here? Genuine gold is that actual gold the actuality of which is in accordance [in der Übereinstimmung steht] with what, always and in advance, we "properly" mean by "gold." Conversely, wherever we suspect false gold, we say: "Here something is not in accord"

[a] First edition, 1943, and third edition, 1954: Truth, Wahr-heit, -heit: die Heitere (das Heiternde) [the bright (that which brightens)], that which clears [das Lichtende].
[b] First edition, 1943, and third edition, 1954: Making – setting forth – letting emerge into the clearing.

[*stimmt nicht*]. On the other hand, we say of whatever is "as it should be": "It is in accord." The *matter* is in accord [*Die* Sache *stimmt*].

However, we call true not only an actual joy, genuine gold, and all beings of such kind, but also and above all we call true or false our statements about beings, which can themselves be genuine or not with regard to their kind, which can be thus or otherwise in their actuality. A statement is true if what it means and says is in accordance with the matter about which the statement is made. Here too we say, "It is in accord." Now, though, it is not the matter that is in accord but rather the *proposition*.

The true, whether it be a matter or a proposition, is what accords, the accordant [*das Stimmende*]. Being true and truth here signify accord, and that in a double sense: on the one hand, the consonance [*Einstimmigkeit*] of a matter with what is supposed in advance regarding it and, on the other hand, the accordance of what is meant in the statement with the matter.

This dual character of the accord is brought to light by the traditional definition of truth: *veritas est adaequatio rei et intellectus*. This can be taken to mean: truth is the correspondence [*Angleichung*] of the matter to knowledge. But it can [76] also be taken as saying: truth is the correspondence of knowledge to the matter. Admittedly, the above definition is usually stated only in the formula *veritas est adaequatio intellectus ad rem* [truth is the adequation of intellect to thing]. Yet truth so conceived, propositional truth, is possible only on the basis of material truth [*Sachwahrheit*], of *adaequatio rei ad intellectum* [adequation of thing to intellect]. Both concepts of the essence of *veritas* have continually in view a conforming to . . . [*Sichrichten nach* . . .], and hence think truth as *correctness* [Richtigkeit].

Nonetheless, the one is not the mere inversion of the other. On the contrary, in each case *intellectus* and *res* are thought differently. In order to recognize this we must trace the usual formula for the ordinary concept of truth back to its most recent (i.e., the medieval) origin. *Veritas* as *adaequatio rei ad intellectum* does not imply the later transcendental conception of Kant – possible only on the basis of the subjectivity of the human essence – that "objects conform to our knowledge." Rather, it implies the Christian theological belief that, with respect to what it is and whether it is, a matter, as created (*ens creatum*), is only insofar as it corresponds to the *idea* preconceived in the *intellectus divinus*, i.e., in the mind of God, and thus measures up to the idea (is correct) and in this sense is "true." The *intellectus humanus* too is an *ens creatum*. As a capacity bestowed upon human beings by God, it must satisfy its *idea*. But the understanding measures up to the idea only by accomplishing in its propositions the correspondence of what is thought to the matter, which in its turn must be in conformity with the *idea*. If all beings are "created," the possibility of the truth of human knowledge is grounded in the fact that matter and proposition measure up to the idea in the same way and therefore are fitted to each other on the basis of the unity of the divine plan of creation. *Veritas* as *adaequatio rei (creandae) ad intellectum (divinum)* guarantees *veritas* as *adaequatio intellectus (humani) ad rem (creatam)*. Throughout, *veritas* essentially implies *convenientia*, the coming of beings themselves, as created, [77] into agreement with the Creator, an "accord" with regard to the way they are determined in the order of creation.[a]

But this order, detached from the notion of creation, can also be represented in a general and indefinite way as a world-order. The theologically conceived order of creation is replaced by the capacity of all objects to be planned by means of a worldly reason [*Weltvernunft*] that supplies the law for itself and thus also claims that its procedure is immediately intelligible (what is considered "logical"). That the essence of propositional truth consists in the correctness of statements is thought to need no further special proof.[4] Even where an effort is made – with a conspicuous lack of success – to explain how correctness is to occur, it is already presupposed as being the essence of truth. Likewise, material truth always signifies the consonance of something at hand with the "rational" concept of its essence. The impression arises that this definition of the essence of truth is independent of the interpretation of the essence of the Being of all beings, which always includes a corresponding interpretation of the essence of the human being as the bearer and executor of *intellectus*. Thus the formula for the essence of truth (*veritas est adaequatio intellectus et rei*) comes to have its general validity as something immediately evident to everyone. Under the domination of the obviousness that this concept of truth seems to have, but that is hardly attended to as regards its essential grounds, it is considered equally obvious that truth[5] has an opposite, and that there is untruth. The untruth of the proposition (incorrectness) is the nonaccordance of the statement with the matter. The untruth of the matter (nongenuineness) signifies nonagreement of a being with its essence. In each case untruth is conceived as a nonaccord. The latter falls outside the essence of truth. Therefore when it is a question of comprehending the pure essence of truth, untruth, as such an opposite of truth, can be put aside.

[a] First edition, 1943: Not a double coming into agreement, but *one*, yet multiply articulated: Because of agreement with the Creator, there is also agreement [of beings] *among one another* (since what is created is in a certain way divine); "correspondence" in a more essential sense than that intended by the crude, unthought *analogia entis* adopted from Aristotle by the Scholastics.

[78] But then is there any further need at all for a special unveiling of the essence of truth? Is not the pure essence of truth already adequately represented in the generally accepted concept, which is upset by no theory and is secured by its obviousness? Moreover, if we take the tracing back of propositional truth to material truth to be what in the first instance it shows itself to be, namely, a theological explanation, and if we then keep the philosophical definition completely pure of all admixture of theology and limit the concept of truth to propositional truth, then we encounter an old – though not the oldest – tradition of thinking, according to which truth is the accordance (ὁμοίωσις) of a statement (λόγος) with a matter (πρᾶγμα). What is it about statements that here remains still worthy of question – granted that we know what is meant by accordance of a statement with the matter? Do we know that?

2. THE INNER POSSIBILITY OF ACCORDANCE

We speak of accordance in various senses. We say, for example, considering two five-mark coins lying on the table: they are in accordance with one another. They come into accord in the oneness of their outward appearance. Hence they have the latter in common, and thus they are in this regard alike. Furthermore, we speak of accordance whenever, for example, we state regarding one of the five-mark coins: this coin is round. Here the statement is in accordance with the thing. Now the relation obtains, not between thing and thing, but rather between a statement and a thing. But wherein are the thing and the statement supposed to be in accordance, considering that the relata are manifestly different in their outward appearance? The coin is made of metal. The statement is not material at all. The coin is round. The statement has nothing [79] at all spatial about it. With the coin something can be purchased. The statement about it is never a means of payment. But in spite of all their dissimilarity the above statement, as true, is in accordance with the coin. And according to the usual concept of truth this accord is supposed to be a correspondence. How can what is completely dissimilar, the statement, correspond to the coin? It would have to become the coin and in this way relinquish itself entirely. The statement never succeeds in doing that. The moment it did, it would no longer be able as a statement to be in accordance with the thing. In the correspondence the statement must[6] remain – indeed even first become – what it is. In what does its essence, so thoroughly different from every thing, consist? How is the statement able to correspond to something else, the thing, precisely by persisting in its own essence?

Correspondence here cannot signify a thing-like approximation between dissimilar kinds of things. The essence of the correspondence is determined rather by the kind of relation that obtains between the statement and the thing. As long as this "relation" remains undetermined and is not grounded in its essence, all dispute over the possibility and impossibility, over the nature and degree, of the correspondence loses its way in a void. But the statement regarding the coin relates "itself" to this thing in that it presents [vor-stellt] it and says of what is presented how, according to the particular perspective that guides it, it is disposed. What is stated by the presentative statement is said of the presented thing in just such manner as that thing, as presented, is. The "such-as" has to do with the presenting and what it presents. Disregarding all "psychological" preconceptions as well as those of any "theory of consciousness," to present here means to let the thing stand opposed as object. As thus placed, what stands opposed must traverse an open field of opposedness [Entgegen][a] and nevertheless must maintain its stand as a thing and show itself as something withstanding [ein Ständiges]. This appearing of the thing in traversing a field of opposedness takes place within an open region, the openness of which [80] is not first created by the presenting but rather is only entered into and taken over as a domain of relatedness. The relation of the presentative statement to the thing is the accomplishment of that *bearing* [Verhältnis] that originarily and always comes to prevail as a comportment [*Verhalten*].[b] But all comportment is distinguished by the fact that, standing in the open region, it in each case adheres to something opened up *as such*.[7] What is thus opened up, solely in this strict sense, was experienced early in Western thinking as "what is present" and for a long time has been named "being."

Comportment stands open[c] to beings. Every open relatedness is a comportment. Man's open stance varies depending on the kind of beings and the way of comportment. All working and achieving, all action and calculation, keep within an open region within which beings, with regard to what they are and how they are, can properly take their stand[d] and become capable of being said. This can occur only if beings present themselves along with the presentative statement so that the latter subordinates itself to the directive that it speak of beings *such-as* they are. In following such a directive the statement conforms to beings. Speech that directs

[a] Third edition, 1954: The openness of a field of opposedness.
[b] Third edition, 1954: Comportment: abiding [sich aufhalten] in the clearing (standing in [inständig in] the clearing) of the presence of that which is present.
[c] Third edition, 1954: As standing in the openness.
[d] Third edition, 1954: Show, come into place, come to the fore, presence.

itself accordingly is correct (true). What is thus said is the correct (the true).

A statement is invested with its correctness by the openness[a] of comportment; for only through the latter can what is opened up really become the standard for the presentative correspondence. Open comportment must let itself be assigned this standard. This means that it must take over a pregiven standard for all presenting. This belongs to the openness of comportment. But if the correctness (truth) of statements becomes possible only through this openness of comportment, then what first makes correctness possible must with more original legitimacy be taken as the essence of truth.

Thus the traditional assignment of truth exclusively to statements as the sole essential locus of truth falls away. [81] Truth does not originally reside in the proposition. But at the same time the question arises as to the ground of the inner possibility of the open comportment that pregives a standard, which possibility alone lends to propositional correctness the appearance of fulfilling the essence of truth at all.

3. THE GROUND OF THE POSSIBILITY OF CORRECTNESS

Whence does the presentative statement receive the directive to conform to the object and to accord by way of correctness? Why is this accord involved in determining the essence of truth? How can something like the accomplishment of a pregiven directedness occur? And how can the initiation into an accord occur? Only if this pregiving has already entered freely into an open region for something opened up that prevails there and that binds every presenting. To free oneself for a binding directedness is possible only by *being free* for what is opened up in an open region. Such being free points to the heretofore uncomprehended essence of freedom. The openness of comportment as the inner condition of the possibility of correctness is grounded in freedom. *The essence of truth, as the correctness of a statement,*[8] *is freedom.*

But does not this proposition regarding the essence of correctness substitute one obvious item for another? In order to be able to carry out any act and therefore one of presentative stating and even of according or not according with a "truth," the actor must of course be free, i.e., unimpeded.[9] However, the proposition in question does not really mean that an unconstrained act belongs to the execution of the statement, to its

---

[a] Third edition, 1954: And this within the clearing.

pronouncement and reception; rather the proposition says that freedom[a] is the *essence* of truth itself. In this connection "essence" is understood as the ground of the inner possibility of what is initially and generally admitted as known. Nevertheless in the concept of freedom we do not think truth, and certainly not at all its essence. The proposition that the essence [82] of truth (correctness of statements) is freedom must consequently seem strange.

To place the essence of truth in freedom – does not this mean to submit truth to human caprice? Can truth be any more radically undermined than by being surrendered to the arbitrariness of this "wavering reed"? What forced itself upon sound judgment again and again in the previous discussion now all the more clearly comes to light: truth is here driven back to the subjectivity of the human subject. Even if an objectivity is also accessible to this subject, such objectivity, along with subjectivity, still remains something human and at human disposal.

Certainly deceit and dissimulation, lies and deception, illusion and semblance – in short, all kinds of untruth – are ascribed to human beings. But of course untruth is also the opposite of truth. For this reason, as the nonessence of truth, it is appropriately excluded from the sphere of the question concerning the pure essence of truth. This human origin of untruth indeed only serves to confirm by contrast the essence of truth "in itself" as holding sway "beyond" the human being. Metaphysics regards such truth as the imperishable and eternal, which can never be founded on the transitoriness and fragility that belong to the human essence. How then can the essence of truth still have its subsistence and its ground in human freedom?

Resistance to the proposition that the essence of truth is freedom is based on preconceptions, the most obstinate of which is that freedom is a property of the human being. The essence of freedom neither needs nor allows any further questioning. Everyone knows what the human being is.

4. THE ESSENCE OF FREEDOM

[83] However, indication of the essential connection between truth as correctness and freedom uproots those preconceptions – granted of course that we are prepared for a transformation of thinking. Consideration of the essential connection between truth and freedom leads us to pursue the question of the human essence in a regard that assures us an experience of a concealed essential ground of the human being (of Dasein), and in such

---

[a] Third edition, 1954: Freedom and clearing of self-concealing sheltering (event of appropriation).

a manner that the experience transposes us in advance into the originarily essential domain of truth. But here it becomes evident also that freedom is the ground of the inner possibility of correctness only because it receives its own essence from the more originary essence of uniquely essential truth. Freedom was initially determined as freedom for what is opened up in an open region. How is this essence of freedom to be thought? That which is opened up, that to which a presentative statement as correct corresponds, are beings opened up in an open comportment. Freedom for what is opened up in an open region lets beings be the beings they are. Freedom now reveals itself as letting beings be.[a]

Ordinarily we speak of letting be whenever, for example, we forgo some enterprise that has been planned. "We let something be" means we do not touch it again, we have nothing more to do with it. To let something be has here the negative sense of letting it alone, of renouncing it, of indifference and even neglect.

However, the phrase required now – to let beings be – does not refer to neglect and indifference but rather the opposite. To let be is to engage oneself with beings.[b] On the other hand, to be sure, this is not to be understood only as the mere management, [84] preservation, tending, and planning of the beings in each case encountered or sought out. To let be – that is, to let beings be as the beings that they are – means to engage oneself with the open region and its openness into which every being comes to stand, bringing that openness, as it were, along with itself. Western thinking in its beginning conceived this open region as τὰ ἀληθέα, the unconcealed. If we translate ἀλήθεια as "unconcealment" rather than "truth," this translation is not merely "more literal"; it contains the directive to rethink the ordinary concept of truth in the sense of the correctness of statements and to think it back to that still uncomprehended disclosedness and disclosure of beings. To engage oneself with the disclosedness of beings is not to lose oneself in them; rather, such engagement withdraws in the face of beings in order that they might reveal themselves with respect to what and how they are, and in order that presentative correspondence might take its standard from them. As this letting-be it exposes itself to beings as such and transposes all comportment into the open region. Letting-be, i.e., freedom, is intrinsically exposing, ek-sistent.[10] Considered in regard to the

---

[a] First edition, 1943: Letting be: (1) not in the negative sense, but granting – preservation; (2) not as an ontically oriented effecting. Heeding, taking heed of being as beyng.

[b] First edition, 1943: Leaving that which is present its presencing, and not importing anything else into it in addition.

essence of truth, the essence of freedom manifests itself as exposure to the disclosedness of beings.

Freedom is not merely what common sense is content to let pass under this name: the caprice, turning up occasionally in our choosing, of inclining in this or that direction. Freedom is not mere absence of constraint with respect to what we can or cannot do. Nor is it on the other hand mere readiness for what is required and necessary (and so somehow a being). Prior to all this ("negative" and "positive" freedom), freedom is engagement in the disclosure of beings as such. Disclosedness itself is conserved in ek-sistent engagement, through which the openness of the open region, i.e., the "there" ["*Da*"], is what it is.

In Da-sein the essential ground, long ungrounded, on the basis of which human beings are able to ek-sist, is preserved for them. [85] Here "existence" does not mean *existentia* in the sense of occurring or being at hand. Nor on the other hand does it mean, in an "existentiell" fashion, the moral endeavor of the human being on behalf of his "self," based on his psychophysical constitution. Ek-sistence, rooted in truth as freedom, is exposure to the disclosedness of beings as such. Still uncomprehended, indeed, not even in need of an essential grounding, the ek-sistence of historical human beings begins at that moment when the first thinker takes a questioning stand with regard to the unconcealment of beings by asking: what are beings? In this question unconcealment is experienced for the first time. Beings as a whole reveal themselves as φύσις, "nature," which here does not yet mean a particular sphere of beings but rather beings as such as a whole, specifically in the sense of upsurgent presencing [*aufgehendes Anwesen*]. History begins only when beings themselves are expressly drawn up into their unconcealment and conserved in it, only when this conservation is conceived on the basis of questioning regarding beings as such. The originary disclosure of beings as a whole, the question concerning beings as such, and the beginning of Western history are the same; they occur together in a "time" which, itself unmeasurable, first opens up the open region[11] for every measure.

But if ek-sistent Da-sein, which lets beings be, sets the human being free for his "freedom" by first offering to his choice something possible (a being) and by imposing on him something necessary (a being), human caprice does not then have freedom at its disposal. The human being does not "possess" freedom as a property. At best, the converse holds: freedom, ek-sistent, disclosive Da-sein, possesses the human being – so originarily that only *it* secures for humanity that distinctive relatedness to beings as a whole as such which first founds all history. Only the ek-sistent human being is historical.[a] "Nature" has no history.

[86] Freedom, understood as letting beings be, is the fulfillment and consummation of the essence of truth in the sense of the disclosure of beings. "Truth" is not a feature of correct propositions that are asserted of an "object" by a human "subject" and then "are valid" somewhere, in what sphere we know not; rather, truth is disclosure of beings through which an openness essentially unfolds [west]. All human comportment and bearing are exposed in its open region. Therefore the human being *is* in the manner of ek-sistence.

Because every mode of human comportment is in its own way open and plies itself to that toward which it comports itself, the restraint of letting-be, i.e., freedom, must have granted it its endowment of that inner directive for correspondence of presentation to beings in each instance. That the human being ek-sists now means that for historical humanity the history of its essential possibilities is conserved in the disclosure of beings as a whole. The rare and the simple decisions of history arise from the way the originary essence of truth essentially unfolds.

However, because truth is in essence freedom, historical human beings can, in letting beings be, also *not* let beings be the beings that they are and as they are. Then beings are covered up and distorted. Semblance comes to power. In it the nonessence of truth comes to the fore. However, because ek-sistent freedom as the essence of truth is not a property of human beings; because on the contrary humans ek-sist and so become capable of history only as the property of this freedom; the nonessence of truth cannot first arise subsequently from mere human incapacity and negligence. Rather, untruth must derive from the essence of truth. Only because truth and untruth are, *in essence, not* irrelevant to one another, but rather belong together, is it possible for a true proposition to enter into pointed opposition to the corresponding untrue proposition. The question concerning the essence of truth thus first reaches [87] the originary domain of what is at issue when, on the basis of a prior glimpse of the full essence of truth, it has included a consideration of untruth in its unveiling of that essence. Discussion of the nonessence of truth is not the subsequent filling of a gap but rather the decisive step toward an adequate posing of the *question* concerning the essence of truth. Yet how are we to comprehend the nonessence in the essence of truth? If the essence of truth is not exhausted

---

[a] First edition, 1943: Inadequate; essence of history in terms of history as event of appropriation [*Ereignis*].

by the correctness of statements, then neither can untruth be equated with the incorrectness of judgments.

5. THE ESSENCE OF TRUTH

The essence of truth reveals itself as freedom. The latter is ek-sistent, disclosive letting beings be. Every mode of open comportment flourishes in letting beings be and in each case is a comportment to this or that being. As engagement in the disclosure of beings as a whole as such, freedom has already attuned all comportment to beings as a whole. However, being attuned (attunement)[12] can never be understood as "experience" and "feeling," because it is thereby simply deprived of its essence. For here it is interpreted on the basis of something ("life" and "soul") that can maintain the semblance of the title of essence only as long as it bears in itself the distortion and misinterpretation of being attuned. Being attuned, i.e., ek-sistent exposedness to beings as a whole, can be "experienced" and "felt" only because the "human being who experiences," without being aware of the essence of the attunement, is always engaged in being attuned in a way that discloses beings as a whole. Every mode of comportment on the part of historical human beings – whether accentuated or not, whether understood or not – is attuned, and by this attunement is drawn up into [88] beings as a whole. The openedness of beings as a whole does not coincide with the sum of all immediately familiar beings. On the contrary: where beings are not very familiar to humans and are scarcely and only roughly known by science, the openedness of beings as a whole can prevail more essentially than it can where the familiar and well known has become boundless, and nothing is any longer able to withstand the business of knowing, since technical mastery over things bears itself without limit. Precisely in the leveling and planing of this omniscience, this mere knowing, the openedness of beings gets flattened out into the apparent nothingness of what is no longer even a matter of indifference, but rather is simply forgotten.

Letting beings be, which is an attuning, a bringing into accord, prevails throughout and anticipates all the open comportment that flourishes in it. Human comportment is brought into definite accord throughout by the openedness of beings as a whole. However, from the point of view of everyday calculations and preoccupations this "as a whole" appears to be incalculable and incomprehensible. It cannot be understood on the basis of the beings opened up in any given case, whether they belong to nature or to history. Although it ceaselessly brings everything into definite accord, still it remains indefinite, indeterminable; it then coincides for the most part with what is most fleeting and most unconsidered. However, what brings into accord is not nothing, but rather a concealing of beings as a whole. Precisely because letting-be always lets beings be in a particular comportment that relates to them and thus discloses them, it conceals beings as a whole. Letting-be is intrinsically at the same time a concealing. In the ek-sistent freedom of Da-sein a concealing of beings as a whole comes to pass [ereignet sich]. Here there *is* concealment.[a]

6. UNTRUTH AS CONCEALING

[89] Concealment deprives ἀλήθεια of disclosure yet does not render it στέρησις (privation); rather, concealment preserves what is most proper to ἀλήθεια as its own. Considered with respect to truth as disclosedness, concealment is then un-disclosedness and accordingly the un-truth that is most proper to the essence of truth. The concealment of beings as a whole does not first show up subsequently as a consequence of the fact that knowledge of beings is always fragmentary. The concealment of beings as a whole, un-truth proper, is older than every openedness of this or that being. It is older even than letting-be itself, which in disclosing already holds concealed and comports itself toward concealing. What conserves letting-be in this relatedness to concealing? Nothing less than the concealing of what is concealed as a whole, of beings as such, i.e., the mystery; not a particular mystery regarding this or that, but rather the one mystery – that, in general, mystery (the concealing of what is concealed) as such holds sway throughout the Da-sein of human beings.

In letting beings as a whole be, which discloses and at the same time conceals, it happens that concealing appears as what is first of all concealed. Insofar as it ek-sists, Da-sein conserves the first and broadest un-disclosedness, un-truth proper. The proper non-essence of truth is the mystery. Here non-essence does not yet have the sense of inferiority to essence in the sense of what is general (χοινόν, γένος), its *possibilitas* and the ground of its possibility. Non-essence is here what in such a sense would be a pre-essential essence. But "nonessence" means at first and for the most part the deformation of that already inferior essence. Indeed, in each of these significations the non-essence remains always in its own way essential to the essence and never becomes unessential in the sense of irrelevant. [90] But to speak of nonessence and untruth in this manner goes very much

---

[a] First edition, 1943: Between 5. and 6. the leap into the turning (whose essence unfolds in the event of appropriation).

against the grain of ordinary opinion and looks like a dragging up of forcibly contrived "*paradoxa.*" Because it is difficult to eliminate this impression, such a way of speaking, paradoxical only for ordinary *doxa* (opinion), is to be renounced. But surely for those who know about such matters the "non-" of the originary non-essence of truth, as un-truth, points to the still unexperienced domain of the truth of Being (not merely of beings).

As letting beings be, freedom is intrinsically the resolutely open bearing that does not close up in itself.[13] All comportment [*Verhalten*] is grounded in this bearing [*Verhältnis*] and receives from it directedness toward beings and disclosure of them. Nevertheless, this bearing toward concealing conceals itself in letting a forgottenness of the mystery take precedence and disappearing in such forgottenness. Certainly the human being takes his bearings [*verhält sich*] constantly in his comportment toward beings; but for the most part he acquiesces in this or that being and its particular openedness. Humans cling to what is readily available and controllable even where ultimate matters are concerned. And if the human being sets out to extend, change, newly assimilate, or secure the openedness of the beings pertaining to the most various domains of his activity and interest, then he still takes his directives from the sphere of readily available intentions and needs.

However, to reside in what is readily available is intrinsically not to let the concealing of what is concealed hold sway. Certainly, among readily familiar things there are also some that are puzzling, unexplained, undecided, questionable. But these self-certain questions are merely transitional, intermediate points in our movement within the readily familiar and thus not essential. Wherever the concealment of beings as a whole is conceded only as a limit that occasionally announces itself, concealing as a fundamental occurrence has sunk into forgottenness.

[91] But the forgotten mystery of Dasein is not eliminated by the forgottenness; rather, the forgottenness bestows on the apparent disappearance of what is forgotten a peculiar presence [*Gegenwart*]. By disavowing itself in and for forgottenness, the mystery leaves historical human beings in the sphere of what is readily available to them, leaves them to their own resources. Thus left, humanity replenishes its "world" on the basis of the latest needs and aims, and fills out that world by means of proposing and planning. From these human beings then take their standards, forgetting beings as a whole. Humans persist in these standards and continually supply themselves with new standards, yet without considering either the ground for taking up standards or the essence of what gives the standard. In spite of their advance to new standards and goals, human beings go wrong as regards the essential genuineness of their standards. Human beings are all

the more mistaken the more exclusively they take themselves, as subject, to be the standard for all beings. The inordinate forgetfulness of humanity persists in securing itself by means of what is readily available and always accessible. This persistence has its unwitting support in that *bearing* by which Dasein not only ek-sists but also at the same time *in-sists*, i.e., holds fast to what is offered by beings, as if they were open of and in themselves.

As ek-sistent, Dasein is insistent. Even in insistent existence the mystery holds sway, but as the forgotten and hence "unessential" essence of truth.

7. UN-TRUTH AS ERRANCY

As insistent, the human being is turned toward the most readily available beings. But he insists only by being already ek-sistent, since, after all, he takes beings as his standard. However, in taking its standard, humanity is turned away from the mystery. The insistent turning toward what is readily available [92] and the ek-sistent turning away from the mystery belong together. They are one and the same. Yet turning toward and away from is based on a peculiar turning to and fro proper to Dasein. The human being's flight from the mystery toward what is readily available, onward from one current thing to the next, passing the mystery by – this is *erring*.[14]

Humans err. Human beings do not merely stray into errancy. They are always astray in errancy, because as ek-sistent they in-sist and so already stand within errancy. The errancy through which human beings stray is not something that, as it were, extends alongside them like a ditch into which they occasionally stumble; rather, errancy belongs to the inner constitution of the Da-sein into which historical human beings are admitted. Errancy is the free space for that turning in which in-sistent ek-sistence adroitly forgets and mistakes itself constantly anew. The concealing of concealed beings as a whole holds sway in that disclosure of specific beings, which, as forgottenness of concealment, becomes errancy.

Errancy is the essential counteressence to the originary essence of truth. Errancy opens itself up as the open region for every counterplay to essential truth. Errancy is the open site for and ground of *error*. Error is not merely an isolated mistake but the kingdom (the dominion) of the history of those entanglements in which all kinds of erring get interwoven.

In conformity with its openness and its relatedness to beings as a whole, every mode of comportment has its manner of erring. Error extends from the most ordinary wasting of time, making a mistake, and miscalculating, to going astray and venturing too far in one's essential attitudes and de-cisions. However, what is ordinarily and even according to the teachings of philosophy recognized as error, namely, incorrectness of judgments and falsity of knowledge, is only one mode of erring and, moreover, the most superficial one. The errancy in which any given segment of historical humanity must proceed for its course to be errant is essentially connected with the openness of Dasein. [93] By leading them astray, errancy dominates human beings through and through. But, as leading astray, errancy at the same time contributes to a possibility that humans are capable of drawing up from their ek-sistence – the possibility that, by experiencing errancy itself and by not mistaking the mystery of Da-sein, they *not* let themselves be led astray.

Because the human being's in-sistent ek-sistence proceeds in errancy, and because errancy as leading astray always oppresses in some manner or other and is formidable on the basis of this oppression of the mystery, specifically as something forgotten, in the ek-sistence of his Dasein the human being is subjected to the rule of the mystery and *at the same time* to the oppression of errancy. He is in the *needful condition of being constrained* by the one and the other. The full essence of truth, including its most proper nonessence, keeps Dasein in need by this perpetual turning to and fro. Dasein is a turning into need. From the Da-sein of human beings and from it alone arises the disclosure of necessity and, as a result, the possibility of being transposed into what is inevitable.

The disclosure of beings as such is simultaneously and intrinsically the concealing of beings as a whole. In the simultaneity of disclosure and concealing, errancy holds sway. Errancy and the concealing of what is concealed belong to the originary essence of truth. Freedom, conceived on the basis of the in-sistent ek-sistence of Dasein, is the essence of truth (in the sense of the correctness of presenting), only because freedom itself originates from the originary essence of truth, the rule of the mystery in errancy. Letting beings be takes its course in open comportment. However, letting beings as such be as a whole occurs in a way befitting its essence only when from time to time it gets taken up in its originary essence. Then resolute openness toward the mystery [*die Ent-schlossenheit zum Geheimnis*] is under way into errancy as such. Then the question of the essence of truth gets asked more originally. Then the ground of the intertwining of the essence of truth with the truth of essence reveals itself. The glimpse into the mystery [94] out of errancy is a questioning – in the sense of that unique question of what beings as such are as a whole. This questioning thinks the question of the *Being* of beings, a question that is essentially misleading and thus in its manifold meaning is still not mastered. The thinking of Being, from which such questioning originarily stems, has since Plato been understood as "philosophy," and later received the title "metaphysics."

8. PHILOSOPHY AND THE QUESTION OF TRUTH

In the thinking of Being the liberation of human beings for ek-sistence, the liberation that grounds history, is put into words. These are not merely the "expression" of an opinion but always already the ably conserved articulation of the truth of beings as a whole. How many have ears for these words matters not. Who those are that can hear them determines the human being's standpoint in history. However, in the same period in which the beginning of philosophy takes place, the *marked* domination of common sense (sophistry) also begins.

The latter appeals to the unquestionable character of the beings that are opened up and interprets all thoughtful questioning as an attack on, an unfortunate irritation of, sound common sense.

However, what philosophy is according to the estimation of common sense, which is quite justified in its own domain, does not touch on the essence of philosophy, which can be determined only on the basis of relatedness to the original truth of beings as such as a whole. But because the full essence of truth contains the nonessence and above all holds sway as concealing, philosophy as a questioning into this truth is intrinsically discordant. Philosophical thinking is gentle releasement that does not renounce the concealment of beings as a whole. Philosophical thinking is especially the stern and resolute openness that does not disrupt the concealing [95] but entreats its unbroken essence into the open region of understanding and thus into its own truth.

In the gentle sternness and stern gentleness with which it lets beings as such be as a whole, philosophy becomes a questioning that does not cling solely to beings yet that also can allow no externally imposed decree. Kant presaged this innermost need that thinking has. For he says of philosophy:

Here philosophy is seen in fact to be placed in a precarious position, which is supposed to be stable – although neither in heaven nor on earth is there anything on which it depends or on which it is based. It is here that it has to prove its integrity as the keeper of its laws [*Selbsthalterin ihrer Gesetze*], not as the mouthpiece of laws secretly communicated to it by some implanted sense or by who knows what tutelary nature. (*Grundlegung zur Metaphysik der Sitten. Werke*, Akademieausgabe vol. IV, p. 425)

With this essential interpretation of philosophy, Kant, whose work introduces the final turning of Western metaphysics, envisages a domain that to be sure he could understand only on the basis of his fundamental metaphysical position, founded on subjectivity, and which he had to understand as the keeping of its laws. This essential view of the determination of philosophy nevertheless goes far enough to renounce every subjugation of philosophical thinking, the most destitute kind of which lets philosophy still be of value as an "expression" of "culture" (Spengler) and as an ornament of productive humankind.

However, whether philosophy as "keeper of its laws" fulfills the essence originarily decided for it, or whether it is not itself first of all kept and appointed to its task as keeper by the truth of that to which its laws in each case pertain – this depends on the primordiality with which the original essence of truth becomes essential for thoughtful questioning.

The present undertaking takes the question of the essence of truth beyond the confines of the ordinary definition provided in the usual concept of essence and helps us to [96] consider whether the question of the essence of truth must not be, at the same time and even first of all, the question concerning the truth of essence. But in the concept of "essence" philosophy thinks Being. In tracing the inner possibility of the correctness of statements back to the ek-sistent freedom of letting-be as its "ground," and likewise in pointing to the essential beginning of this ground in concealing and in errancy, we want to show that the essence of truth is not the empty "generality" of an "abstract" universality but rather that which, self-concealing, is unique in the unremitting history of the disclosure of the "meaning" of what we call Being – what we for a long time have been accustomed to considering only as beings as a whole.

9. NOTE

The question of the essence of truth arises from the question of the truth of essence. In the former question essence is understood initially in the sense of whatness (*quidditas*) or material content (*realitas*), whereas truth is understood as a characteristic of knowledge. In the question of the truth of essence, essence is understood verbally; in this word, remaining still within metaphysical presentation, Beyng is thought as the difference that holds sway between Being and beings. Truth signifies sheltering that clears [*lichtendes Bergen*] as the fundamental trait of Being. The question of the essence of truth finds its answer in the proposition *the essence of truth is the truth of essence*. After our explanation it can easily be seen that the proposition does not merely reverse the word order so as to conjure the specter of paradox. The subject of the proposition – if this unfortunate grammatical category may still be used at all – is the truth of essence. Sheltering that clears is – i.e., lets essentially unfold – accordance between knowledge and beings. The proposition is [97] not dialectical. It is no proposition at all in the sense of a statement. The answer to the question of the essence of truth is the saying of a turning [*die Sage einer Kehre*] within the history of Beyng. Because sheltering that clears belongs to it, Beyng appears originarily in the light of concealing withdrawal. The name of this clearing [*Lichtung*] is ἀλήθεια.

Already in the original project, the lecture "On the Essence of Truth" was to have been completed by a second lecture, "On the Truth of Essence." The latter failed for reasons that are now indicated in the "Letter on Humanism."

The decisive question (in *Being and Time*, 1927) of the meaning, i.e., of the project-domain (see *Being and Time*, p. 151), i.e., of the openness, i.e., of the truth of Being and not merely of beings, remains intentionally undeveloped. Our thinking apparently remains on the path of metaphysics. Nevertheless, in its decisive steps, which lead from truth as correctness to ek-sistent freedom, and from the latter to truth as concealing and as errancy, it accomplishes a change in the questioning that belongs to the overcoming of metaphysics. The thinking attempted in the lecture comes to fulfillment in the essential experience that a nearness to the truth of Being is first prepared for historical human beings on the basis of the Da-sein into which human beings can enter. Every kind of anthropology and all subjectivity of the human being as subject is not merely left behind – as it was already in *Being and Time* – and the truth of Being sought as the ground of a transformed historical position; rather, the movement of the lecture is such that it sets out to think from this other ground (Da-sein). The course of the questioning is intrinsically the path of a thinking that, instead of furnishing representations and concepts, experiences and tests itself as a transformation of its relatedness to Being.

Plato's Doctrine of Truth

Translated by Thomas Sheehan[1]

[109] The knowledge that comes from the sciences usually is expressed in propositions and is laid before us in the form of conclusions that we can grasp and put to use. But the "doctrine" of a thinker is that which, within what is said, remains unsaid, that to which we are exposed so that we might expend ourselves on it.

In order to experience and to know for the future what a thinker left unsaid, whatever that might be, we have to consider what he said. To properly satisfy this demand would entail examining all of Plato's "dialogues" in their interrelationship. Since this is impossible, we must let a different path guide us to the unsaid in Plato's thinking.

What remains unsaid in Plato's thinking is a change in what determines the essence of truth. The fact that this change does take place, what it consists in, and what gets grounded through this transformation of the essence of truth – all of that can be clarified by an interpretation of the "allegory of the cave."

The "allegory of the cave" is presented at the beginning of the seventh book of the "dialogue" on the essence of the πόλις (*Republic*, VII, 514 a2 to 517 a7). The "allegory" tells a story. The tale unfolds in the conversation between Socrates and Glaucon. Socrates presents the story, Glaucon shows his awakening astonishment. The translation that we provide for the text includes phrases that go beyond the Greek in an effort to elucidate it; these we have put in parentheses.[2]

❧

ἰδὲ γὰρ ἀνθρώπους οἷον ἐν καταγείῳ οἰκήσει σπηλαιώδει, ἀναπεπταμένην πρὸς τὸ φῶς τὴν εἴσοδον ἐχούσῃ μακρὰν παρὰ πᾶν τὸ σπήλαιον, ἐν ταύτῃ ἐκ παίδων ὄντας ἐν δεσμοῖς καὶ τὰ σκέλη καὶ τοὺς αὐχένας, ὥστε μένειν τε αὐτοὺς εἴς τε τὸ πρόσθεν μόνον ὁρᾶν, κύκλῳ δὲ τὰς κεφαλὰς ὑπὸ τοῦ δεσμοῦ ἀδυνάτους περιάγειν, φῶς δὲ αὐτοῖς πυρὸς ἄνωθεν καὶ πόρρωθεν καόμενον ὄπισθεν αὐτῶν, μεταξὺ δὲ τοῦ πυρὸς καὶ τῶν δεσμωτῶν ἐπάνω ὁδόν, παρ' ἣν ἰδὲ τειχίον παρῳκοδομημένον, ὥσπερ τοῖς θαυματοποιοῖς πρὸ τῶν ἀνθρώπων πρόκειται τὰ παραφράγματα, ὑπὲρ ὧν τὰ θαύματα δεικνύασιν. – ὁρῶ, ἔφη. –

ὅρα τοίνυν παρὰ τοῦτο τὸ τειχίον φέροντας ἀνθρώπους σκεύη τε παντοδαπὰ ὑπερέχοντα τοῦ τειχίου καὶ ἀνδριάντας καὶ ἄλλα ζῷα λίθινά τε καὶ ξύλινα καὶ παντοῖα εἰργασμένα, οἷον εἰκὸς τοὺς μὲν φθεγγομένους, τοὺς δὲ σιγῶντας τῶν παραφερόντων.

ἄτοπον, ἔφη, λέγεις εἰκόνα καὶ δεσμώτας ἀτόπους. – ὁμοίους ἡμῖν, ἦν δ' ἐγώ· τοὺς γὰρ τοιούτους πρῶτον μὲν ἑαυτῶν τε καὶ ἀλλήλων οἴει ἄν τι ἑωρακέναι ἄλλο πλὴν τὰς σκιὰς τὰς ὑπὸ τοῦ πυρὸς εἰς τὸ καταντικρὺ αὐτῶν τοῦ σπηλαίου προσπιπτούσας;

– πῶς γάρ, ἔφη, εἰ ἀκινήτους γε τὰς κεφαλὰς ἔχειν ἠναγκασμένοι εἶεν διὰ βίου; –

– τί δὲ τῶν παραφερομένων; οὐ ταὐτὸν τοῦτο; – τί μήν; –

– εἰ οὖν διαλέγεσθαι οἷοί τ' εἶεν πρὸς ἀλλήλους, οὐ ταῦτα ἡγῇ ἂν τὰ ὄντα αὐτοὺς νομίζειν ἅπερ ὁρῷεν; – ἀνάγκη. –

[111] "Imagine this: People live under the earth in a cavelike dwelling. Stretching a long way up toward the daylight is its entrance, toward which the entire cave is gathered. The people have been in this dwelling since childhood, shackled by the legs and neck. For this reason they also stay in the same place so that the only thing for them to look at is whatever they encounter in front of their faces. But because they are shackled, they are unable to turn their heads around. Some light, of course, is allowed them, namely, from a fire that casts its glow toward them from behind them, being above and at some distance. Between the fire and those who are shackled (therefore, behind their backs) there runs a walkway at a certain height. Imagine that a low wall has been built the length of the walkway, like the low curtain that puppeteers put up, over which they show their puppets." "I see," he said.

"So now imagine that along this low wall people are carrying all sorts of things that reach up higher than the wall: statues and other carvings made of stone or wood and many other artifacts that people have made. As you would expect, some of the people carrying things talk to each other (as they walk along) and some are silent."

"This is an unusual picture that you are presenting here, and these are unusual prisoners." "They are very much like us humans," I responded. "What do you think? From the beginning these people have never gotten to see, whether on their own or with the help of others, anything besides the shadows that the glow of the fire (continually) projects on the wall in front of them."

"How could it be otherwise," he said, "since they are forced to keep their heads immobile for their entire lives?"

[113] "And what do they see of the things that are being carried along (behind them)? Do they not see just these (namely the shadows)?" "Certainly."

"Now if they were able to say something about what they saw and to talk it over, do you not think that they would regard that which they saw on the wall as beings?" "They would have to."

τί δ᾽ εἰ καὶ ἠχὼ τὸ δεσμωτήριον ἐκ τοῦ καταντικρὺ ἔχοι; ὁπότε τις τῶν παριόντων φθέγξαιτο, οἴει ἂν ἄλλο τι αὐτοὺς ἡγεῖσθαι τὸ φθεγγόμενον ἢ τὴν παριοῦσαν σκιάν; – μὰ Δί᾽ οὐκ ἔγωγ᾽, ἔφη. – παντάπασι δή, ἦν δ᾽ ἐγώ, οἱ τοιοῦτοι οὐκ ἂν ἄλλο τι νομίζοιεν τὸ ἀληθὲς ἢ τὰς τῶν σκευαστῶν σκιάς. – πολλὴ ἀνάγκη, ἔφη. –

– σκόπει δή, ἦν δ᾽ ἐγώ, αὐτῶν λύσιν τε καὶ ἴασιν τῶν τε δεσμῶν καὶ τῆς ἀφροσύνης, οἷα τις ἂν εἴη φύσει, εἰ τοιάδε συμβαίνοι αὐτοῖς. ὁπότε τις λυθείη καὶ ἀναγκάζοιτο ἐξαίφνης ἀνίστασθαί τε καὶ περιάγειν τὸν αὐχένα καὶ βαδίζειν καὶ πρὸς τὸ φῶς ἀναβλέπειν, πάντα δὲ ταῦτα ποιῶν ἀλγοῖ τε καὶ διὰ τὰς μαρμαρυγὰς ἀδυνατοῖ καθορᾶν ἐκεῖνα ὧν τότε τὰς σκιὰς ἑώρα, τί ἂν οἴει αὐτὸν εἰπεῖν, εἴ τις αὐτῷ λέγοι ὅτι τότε μὲν ἑώρα φλυαρίας, νῦν δὲ μᾶλλόν τι ἐγγυτέρω τοῦ ὄντος καὶ πρὸς μᾶλλον ὄντα τετραμμένος ὀρθότερον βλέποι, καὶ δὴ καὶ ἕκαστον τῶν παριόντων δεικνὺς αὐτῷ ἀναγκάζοι ἐρωτῶν ἀποκρίνεσθαι ὅτι ἔστιν; οὐκ οἴει αὐτὸν ἀπορεῖν τε ἂν καὶ ἡγεῖσθαι τὰ τότε ὁρώμενα ἀληθέστερα ἢ τὰ νῦν δεικνύμενα; – πολύ γ᾽, ἔφη. –

Οὐκοῦν κἂν εἰ πρὸς αὐτὸ τὸ φῶς ἀναγκάζοι αὐτὸν βλέπειν, ἀλγεῖν τε ἂν τὰ ὄμματα καὶ φεύγειν ἀποστρεφόμενον πρὸς ἐκεῖνα ἃ δύναται καθορᾶν, καὶ νομίζειν ταῦτα τῷ ὄντι σαφέστερα τῶν δεικνυμένων; – οὕτως, ἔφη.

εἰ δέ, ἦν δ᾽ ἐγώ, ἐντεῦθεν ἕλκοι τις αὐτὸν βίᾳ διὰ τραχείας τῆς ἀναβάσεως καὶ ἀνάντους, καὶ μὴ ἀνείη πρὶν ἐξελκύσειεν εἰς τὸ τοῦ ἡλίου φῶς, ἆρα οὐχὶ ὀδυνᾶσθαί τε ἂν καὶ ἀγανακτεῖν ἑλκόμενον, καὶ ἐπειδὴ πρὸς τὸ φῶς ἔλθοι, αὐγῆς ἂν ἔχοντα τὰ ὄμματα μεστὰ ὁρᾶν οὐδ᾽ ἂν ἓν δύνασθαι τῶν νῦν λεγομένων ἀληθῶν;

"And now what if this prison also had an echo reverberating off the wall in front of them (the one that they always and only look at)? Whenever one of the people walking behind those in chains (and carrying the things) would make a sound, do you think the prisoners would imagine that the speaker were anyone other than the shadow passing in front of them?" "Nothing else, by Zeus!" he said.[3] "All in all," I responded, "those who were chained would consider nothing besides the shadows of the artifacts to be the unhidden." "That would absolutely have to be," he said.

"So now," I replied, "watch the process whereby the prisoners are set free from their chains and, along with that, cured of their lack of insight,[4] and likewise consider what kind of lack of insight this must be if the following were to happen to those who are chained. Whenever any of them was unchained and was forced to stand up suddenly, to turn around,[5] to walk, and to look up toward the light, in each case the person would be able to do this only with pain, and because of the flickering brightness he would be unable to look at those things whose shadows he saw before. (If all this were to happen to the prisoner), what do you think he would say if someone were to inform him that what he saw before were (mere) trifles but that now he is much nearer to beings; and that, as a consequence of now being turned toward what is more in being, he also sees more correctly? And if someone were (then) to show him any of the things that are passing by and were to force him to answer the question about what it is, do you [115] not think that he would be at wits' end and also would consider that what he saw before (with his own eyes) is more unhidden than what is now being shown (to him by someone else)?" "Yes, absolutely," he said.

"And if someone even forced him to look into the glare of the fire, would his eyes not hurt him, and would he not then turn away and flee (back) to that which he is capable of looking at? And would he not decide that (what he could see before without any help) is in fact clearer than what is now being shown to him?" "Precisely," he said.

"Now, however, if someone, using force, were to drag him (who had been freed from his chains) away from there and to pull him up the cave's rough and steep ascent and not let go of him until he had dragged him out into the light of the sun, would not the one who had been dragged like this feel, in the process, pain and rage? And when he got into the sunlight, would not his eyes be filled with the glare, and would he not thus be unable to see any of the things that are now revealed to him as the unhidden?"

– οὐ γὰρ ἄν, ἔφη, ἐξαίφνης γε. –

συνηθείας δὴ οἶμαι δέοιτ᾽ ἂν, εἰ μέλλοι τὰ ἄνω ὄψεσθαι. καὶ πρῶτον μὲν τὰς σκιὰς ἂν ῥᾷστα καθορῷ, καὶ μετὰ τοῦτο ἐν τοῖς ὕδασι τά τε τῶν ἀνθρώπων καὶ τὰ τῶν ἄλλων εἴδωλα, ὕστερον δὲ αὐτά· ἐκ δὲ τούτων τὰ ἐν τῷ οὐρανῷ καὶ αὐτὸν τὸν οὐρανὸν νύκτωρ ἂν ῥᾶον θεάσαιτο, προσβλέπων τὸ τῶν ἄστρων τε καὶ σελήνης φῶς, ἢ μεθ᾽ ἡμέραν τὸν ἥλιόν τε καὶ τὸ τοῦ ἡλίου. – πῶς δ᾽ οὔ;

τελευταῖον δὴ οἶμαι τὸν ἥλιον, οὐκ ἐν ὕδασιν οὐδ᾽ ἐν ἀλλοτρίᾳ ἕδρᾳ φαντάσματα αὐτοῦ, ἀλλ᾽ αὐτὸν καθ᾽ αὑτὸν ἐν τῇ αὑτοῦ χώρᾳ δύναιτ᾽ ἂν κατιδεῖν καὶ θεάσασθαι οἷός ἐστιν. – ἀναγκαῖον, ἔφη. –

καὶ μετὰ ταῦτ᾽ ἂν ἤδη συλλογίζοιτο περὶ αὐτοῦ ὅτι οὗτος ὁ τάς τε ὥρας παρέχων καὶ ἐνιαυτοὺς καὶ πάντα ἐπιτροπεύων τὰ ἐν τῷ ὁρωμένῳ τόπῳ, καὶ ἐκείνων ὧν σφεῖς ἑώρων τρόπον τινὰ πάντων αἴτιος.

δῆλον, ἔφη, ὅτι ἐπὶ ταῦτα ἂν μετ᾽ ἐκεῖνα ἔλθοι. –

τί οὖν; ἀναμιμνησκόμενον αὐτὸν τῆς πρώτης οἰκήσεως καὶ τῆς ἐκεῖ σοφίας καὶ τῶν τότε συνδεσμωτῶν οὐκ ἂν οἴει αὐτὸν μὲν εὐδαιμονίζειν τῆς μεταβολῆς, τοὺς δὲ ἐλεεῖν; – καὶ μάλα. –

"He would not be able to do that at all," he said, "at least not right away."

"It would obviously take some getting accustomed, I think, if it is a matter of grasping with one's eyes that which is up there (outside the cave, in the light of the sun). And (in this process of getting accustomed) he would first and most easily be able to look at shadows, and thereafter at the images of people and of other things as they are reflected in water. Later, however, he would be able to view the things themselves (the beings, instead of the dim reflections). But within the range of such things, it might be easier for him to contemplate whatever there is in the heavenly vault, and the vault itself, by doing so at night, by looking at the light of the stars and the moon, (easier, that is to say,) than by looking at the sun and its glare during the day." "Certainly."

[117] "But I think that finally he would be in a condition to look at the sun itself, not just at its reflection whether in water or wherever else it might appear, but at the sun itself, as it is in and of itself and in the place proper to it, and to contemplate of what sort it is." "It would necessarily happen this way," he said.

"And having done all that, by this time he would also be able to gather the following about it (the sun): that it is that which grants both the seasons and the years and that which governs whatever there is in the (now) visible region (of sunlight), and moreover that it (the sun) is also the cause of all those things that the people (who dwell below in the cave) in some way have before their eyes."

"It is obvious," he said, "that he would get to these (the sun and whatever stands in its light) after he had gone out beyond those (that are merely reflections and shadows)."

"And then what? If he again recalled his first dwelling, and the 'knowing' that passes as the norm there, and those with whom he once was chained,[6] do you not think he would consider himself lucky because of the transformation (that had happened) and by contrast feel sorry for them?" "Very much so."

τιμαὶ δὲ καὶ ἔπαινοι εἴ τινες αὐτοῖς ἦσαν τότε παρ᾽ ἀλλήλων καὶ γέρα τῷ ὀξύτατα καθορῶντι τὰ παριόντα, καὶ μνημονεύοντι μάλιστα ὅσα τε πρότερα αὐτῶν καὶ ὕστερα εἰώθει καὶ ἅμα πορεύεσθαι, καὶ ἐκ τούτων δὴ δυνατώτατα ἀπομαντευομένῳ τὸ μέλλον ἥξειν, δοκεῖς ἂν αὐτὸν ἐπιθυμητικῶς αὐτῶν ἔχειν καὶ ζηλοῦν τοὺς παρ᾽ ἐκείνοις τιμωμένους τε καὶ ἐνδυναστεύοντας, ἢ τὸ τοῦ Ὁμήρου ἂν πεπονθέναι καὶ σφόδρα βούλεσθαι "ἐπάρουρον ἐόντα θητευέμεν ἄλλῳ ἀνδρὶ παρ᾽ ἀκλήρῳ" καὶ ὁτιοῦν ἂν πεπονθέναι μᾶλλον ἢ ᾽κεῖνά τε δοξάζειν καὶ ἐκείνως ζῆν;

– οὕτως, ἔφη ἔγωγε οἶμαι, πᾶν μᾶλλον πεπονθέναι ἂν δέξασθαι ἢ ζῆν ἐκείνως. –

καὶ τόδε δὴ ἐννόησον, ἦν δ᾽ ἐγώ. εἰ πάλιν ὁ τοιοῦτος καταβὰς εἰς τὸν αὐτὸν θᾶκον καθίζοιτο, ἆρ᾽ οὐ σκότους ἀνάπλεως σχοίη τοὺς ὀφθαλμούς, ἐξαίφνης ἥκων ἐκ τοῦ ἡλίου; – καὶ μάλα γ᾽, ἔφη. –

τὰς δὲ δὴ σκιὰς ἐκείνας πάλιν εἰ δέοι αὐτὸν γνωματεύοντα διαμιλλᾶσθαι τοῖς ἀεὶ δεσμώταις ἐκείνοις, ἐν ᾧ ἀμβλυώττει, πρὶν καταστῆναι τὰ ὄμματα, οὗτος δ᾽ ὁ χρόνος μὴ πάνυ ὀλίγος εἴη τῆς συνηθείας, ἆρ᾽ οὐ γέλωτ᾽ ἂν παράσχοι, καὶ λέγοιτο ἂν περὶ αὐτοῦ ὡς ἀναβὰς ἄνω διεφθαρμένος ἥκει τὰ ὄμματα καὶ ὅτι οὐκ ἄξιον οὐδὲ πειρᾶσθαι ἄνω ἰέναι; καὶ τὸν ἐπιχειροῦντα λύειν τε καὶ ἀνάγειν, εἴ πως ἐν ταῖς χερσὶ δύναιντο λαβεῖν καὶ ἀποκτείνειν, ἀποκτεινύναι ἄν;

σφόδρα γ᾽, ἔφη. –

"However, if (among the people) in the previous dwelling place (namely, in the cave) certain honors and commendations were established for whoever most clearly catches sight of what passes by (the things that happen every day) and also best remembers which of them normally is brought by first, which ones later, and which ones at the same time, and for whoever (then) could most easily foresee which ones might come by next – do you think that he (the one who had gotten out of the cave) would (now still) envy those (in the cave) and want to compete with those (there) who are esteemed and who have power? Or would he not much rather wish upon himself the condition Homer speaks of: 'Living on the land (above ground) as the [119] paid menial of another destitute peasant'? And will he not prefer to put up with absolutely anything else rather than associate himself with those opinions (that hold in the cave) and be that kind of human being?"

"I think," he said, "that he would prefer to endure everything rather than be that kind (the cave-dwelling kind) of human being."

"And now," I responded, "consider this: If this person who had gotten out of the cave were to go back down again and sit in the same place as before, would he not find in that case, coming suddenly out of the sunlight, that his eyes were filled with darkness?" "Yes, very much so," he said.

"If he now once more had to engage himself with those who had remained shackled there in the business of asserting and maintaining opinions about the shadows – while his eyes are still weak and before they have readjusted, an adjustment that would require quite a bit of time – would he not then be exposed to ridicule down there? And would they not let him know that he had gone up but only in order to come back (into the cave) with his eyes ruined, and so too it certainly does not pay to go up? And if they can get hold of this person who takes it in hand to free them from their chains and to lead them up, and if they could kill him, will they not actually kill him?"

"They certainly will," he said.

❧

What does this story mean? Plato himself provides the answer: he has the interpretation immediately follow the story (517 a8 to 518 d7).

The cavelike abode is the "image" for τὴν ... δι᾽ ὄψεως φαινομένην ἕδραν, "the place of our dwelling which (in an everyday way) is revealed to sight as we look around." The fire in the cave, which burns above those who dwell there, is the "image" for the sun. The vault of the cave represents the dome of the heavens. People live under this dome, assigned to the earth and bound to it. What surrounds and concerns them there [120] is, for them, "the real" ["*das Wirkliche*"], i.e., that which is. In this cavelike dwelling they feel that they are "in the world" and "at home" and here they find what they can rely on.

On the other hand, the things that the "allegory" mentions as visible outside the cave are the image for what the proper being of beings [*das eigentlich Seiende des Seienden*] consists in. This, according to Plato, is that whereby beings show up in their "visible form." Plato does not regard this "visible form" as a mere "aspect." For him the "visible form" has in addition something of a "stepping forth" whereby a thing "presents" itself.[a] Standing in its "visible form" the being itself shows itself. In Greek, "visible form" is εἶδος or ἰδέα. In the "allegory" the things that are visible in the daylight outside the cave, where sight is free to look at everything, are a concrete illustration of the "ideas." According to Plato, if people did not have these "ideas" in view, that is to say, the respective "appearance" of things – living beings, humans, numbers, gods – they would never be able to perceive this or that as a house, as a tree, as a god. Usually they think they see this house and that tree directly, and the same with every being. Generally they never suspect that it is always and only in the light of the "ideas" that they see everything that passes so easily and familiarly for the "real." According to Plato, what they presume to be exclusively and properly the real – what they can immediately see, hear, grasp, compute – always remains a mere adumbration of the idea, and consequently a shadow. That which is nearest, even though it has the consistency of shadows, holds humans captive day after day. They live in a prison and leave all "ideas" behind them. And since in no way do they recognize this prison for what it is, they consider that this everyday region under the dome of the heavens is the arena of the experience and judgment that provide the sole standard for all things and relations and fix the only rules of their disposition and arrangement.

[a] Offprint from *Geistige Überlieferung*, 1942: Being present, i.e., being near [*An-, d.h. herzu -wesen*].

Now if human beings, considered in the terms of the "allegory," were suddenly, while still within the cave, to glance back at the fire whose radiance [121] produces the shadows of the things being carried back and forth, they would immediately experience this unaccustomed turning around of their gaze as a disruption of customary behavior and of current opinion. In fact, the mere suggestion of such a strange stance, to be adopted while still within the cave, is rejected, for there in the cave one is in clear and complete possession of the real. The people in the cave are so passionately attached to their "view" that they are incapable of even suspecting the possibility that what they take for the real might have the consistency of mere shadows. But how could they know about shadows when they do not even want to be aware of the fire in the cave and its light, even though this fire is merely something "man-made" and hence should be familiar to human beings? In contrast, the sunlight outside the cave is in no way a product of human making. In its brightness things that have grown and are present show themselves immediately without needing adumbrations to represent them. In the "allegory" the things that show themselves are the "image" for the "ideas." But the sun in the "allegory" is the "image" for that which makes all ideas visible. It is the "image" for the idea of all ideas. This latter, according to Plato, is called ἡ τοῦ ἀγαθοῦ ἰδέα, which one translates with the "literal" but quite misleading phrase "the idea of the good."

The allegorical correspondences that we have just now enumerated – between the shadows and reality as experienced every day, between the radiance of the cave fire and the light in which the habitual and closest "reality" stands, between the things outside the cave and the ideas, between the sun and the highest idea – these correspondences do not exhaust the content of the "allegory." In fact, the proper dimension of it has not even come into our grasp yet. The "allegory" recounts a series of movements rather than just reporting on the dwelling places and conditions of people inside and outside the cave. In fact, the movements that it recounts are movements of passage out of the cave into the daylight and then back out of the daylight into the cave.

[122] What happens in these movements of passage? What makes these events possible? From what do they derive their necessity? What issue is at stake in these passages?

The movements of passing out of the cave into the daylight and then back from there into the cave require in each case that the eyes accustom themselves to the change from darkness to brightness and from brightness back to darkness. Each time, in so doing, the eyes experience confusion, indeed for opposite reasons in each case: διτταὶ καὶ ἀπὸ διττῶν γίγνονται ἐπιταράξεις ὄμμασιν (518 a2). "Two kinds of confusion come about for the eyes, and for two reasons."

This means that there are two possibilities. On the one hand people can leave their hardly noticed ignorance and get to where beings show themselves to them more essentially, but where initially they are not adequate to the essential. On the other hand people can fall out of the stance of essential knowing and be forced back into the region where common reality reigns supreme, but without their being able to recognize what is common and customary there as being the real.

And just as the physical eye must accustom itself, slowly and steadily at first, either to the light or to the dark, so likewise the soul, patiently and through an appropriate series of steps, has to accustom itself to the region of beings to which it is exposed. But this process of getting accustomed requires that before all else the soul in its entirety be turned around as regards the fundamental direction of its striving, in the same way as the eye can look comfortably in whatever direction only when the whole body has first assumed the appropriate position.

But why does this process of getting accustomed to each region have to be slow and steady? The reason is that the turning around has to do with one's being and thus takes place in the very ground of one's essence. This means that the normative bearing that is to result from this turning around must unfold from a relation that already sustains our essence and develop into a stable comportment. This process whereby the human essence is reoriented and accustomed to the region assigned to it at each point is the essence of what Plato [123] calls παιδεία. The word does not lend itself to being translated. As Plato defines its essence, παιδεία means the περιαγωγὴ ὅλης τῆς ψυχῆς, leading the whole human being in the turning around of his or her essence. Hence παιδεία is essentially a movement of passage, namely, from ἀπαιδευσία into παιδεία. In keeping with its character as a movement of passage, παιδεία remains always related to ἀπαιδευσία. The German word *Bildung* ["education," literally "formation"] comes closest to capturing the word παιδεία, but not entirely. In this case, of course, we need to restore to *Bildung* its original power as a word, and we have to forget the misinterpretation to which it fell victim in the late nineteenth century. *Bildung* ["formation"] means two things. On the one hand formation means forming someone in the sense of impressing on him a character that unfolds. But at the same time this "forming" of someone "forms" (or impresses a character on) someone by antecedently taking measure in terms of some paradigmatic image, which for that reason is called the proto-type [*Vorbild*]. Thus at one and the same time "formation" means impressing a character on someone and guiding someone by a paradigm. The contrary of παιδεία is ἀπαιδευσία, lack of formation, where no fundamental bearing is awakened and unfolded, and where no normative proto-type is put forth.

The "allegory of the cave" concentrates its explanatory power on making us able to see and know the essence of παιδεία by means of the concrete images recounted in the story. At the same time Plato seeks to avoid false interpretations; he wants to show that the essence of παιδεία does not consist in merely pouring knowledge into the unprepared soul as if it were some container held out empty and waiting. On the contrary real education lays hold of the soul itself and transforms it in its entirety by first of all leading us to the place of our essential being and accustoming us to it. That the "allegory of the cave" is meant to illustrate the essence of παιδεία is stated clearly enough in the very sentence with which Plato introduces the story at the beginning of Book Seven: Μετὰ ταῦτα δή, εἶπον, ἀπείχασον τοιούτῳ πάθει τὴν ἡμετέραν φύσιν παιδείας τε πέρι χαὶ ἀπαιδευσίας. "And after that, try to conjure up for yourself from the kind of experience (to be presented in the following story) a view (of the essence) both of 'education' and of the lack of education, [124] both of which (as belonging together) concern the very foundation of our being as humans."

Plato's assertion is clear: The "allegory of the cave" illustrates the essence of "education." By contrast, the interpretation of the "allegory" that we are now going to attempt means to point out the Platonic "doctrine" of truth. Are we not then burdening the "allegory" with something foreign to it? The interpretation threatens to degenerate into a reinterpretation that does violence to the text. Let this appearance stand until we have confirmed our insight that Plato's thinking subjects itself to a transformation in the essence of truth that becomes the hidden law governing what the thinker says. According to our interpretation, which is made necessary from out of a future need, the "allegory" not only illustrates the essence of education but at the same time opens our eyes to a transformation in the essence of "truth." If the "allegory" can show both, must it not be the case that an essential relation holds between "education" and "truth"? This relation does, in fact, obtain. And it consists in the fact that the essence of truth and the sort of transformation it undergoes here first make possible "education" in its basic structures.

But what is it that links "education" and "truth" together into an original and essential unity?

Παιδεία means turning around the whole human being. It means removing human beings from the region where they first encounter things and transferring and accustoming them to another realm where beings appear.

This transfer is possible only by the fact that everything that has been heretofore manifest to human beings, as well as the way in which it has been manifest, gets transformed. Whatever has been unhidden to human beings at any given time, as well as the manner of its unhiddenness, has to be transformed. In Greek, unhiddenness is called ἀλήθεια, a word that we translate as "truth." And for a long time now in Western thinking, truth has meant the agreement of the representation in thought with the thing itself: *adaequatio intellectus et rei*.

But if we are not satisfied with simply translating the words παιδεία and ἀλήθεια "literally," if instead we attempt [125] to think through the issue according to the Greek way of knowing and to ponder the essential matter that is at stake in these translations, then straightaway "education" and "truth" come together into an essential unity. If we take seriously the essential content of what the word ἀλήθεια names, then we must ask: From what perspective does Plato approach his determination of the essence of unhiddenness? For the answer to this question we are referred to the proper content of the "allegory of the cave." The answer will show both the fact that and the way in which the "allegory" deals with the essence of truth.

The unhidden and its unhiddenness designate at each point what is present and manifest in the region where human beings happen to dwell. But the "allegory" recounts a story of passages from one dwelling place to another. Thus this story is divided in a general way into a series of four different dwelling places in specific gradations of up and down. The distinctions between the dwelling places and stages within the movement of passage are grounded in the different kinds of ἀληθές normative at each level, that is, the different kinds of "truth" that are dominant at each stage. For that reason, in one way or another we have to think out and designate what the ἀληθές, the unhidden, is at each stage.

In stage one, people live chained inside the cave, engrossed in what they immediately encounter. The description of this dwelling place ends with the emphatic sentence: παντάπασι δὴ ... οἱ τοιοῦτοι οὐκ ἂν ἄλλο τι νομίζοιεν τὸ ἀληθὲς ἢ τὰς τῶν σκευαστῶν σκιάς (515 c1-2). "In no way, then, would those who are chained like this ever consider anything else to be the unhidden except the shadows cast by the artifacts."

Stage two tells about the removal of the chains. Although still confined to the cave, those imprisoned are now free in a certain sense. Now they can turn around in every direction. It becomes possible to see the very things that were previously carried along behind them. Those who before looked only at shadows now come μᾶλλόν [126] τι ἐγγυτέρω τοῦ ὄντος (515 d2), "a little nearer to what is." The things themselves offer their visible form in a certain way, namely, in the glow of the man-made fire of the cave, and they are no longer hidden by the shadows they project. As long as one encounters nothing but shadows, these hold one's gaze captive and thus insinuate themselves in place of the things themselves. But when one's gaze is freed from its captivity to shadows, it becomes possible for the person who has been freed to enter the sphere of what is ἀληθέστερα (515 d6), "more unhidden." And yet it must be said of him who has been freed: ἡγεῖσθαι τὰ τότε ὁρώμενα ἀληθέστερα ἢ τὰ νῦν δεικνύμενα (ibid.). "He will consider that (the shadows) that were previously seen (without any help) are more unhidden than what is now (expressly) being shown (to him by others)."

Why is this so? The glow of the fire, to which their eyes are not accustomed, blinds those who have been liberated. This blinding hinders them from seeing the fire itself and from apprehending how its glow illuminates the things and thus lets these things appear for the first time. That is why those who have been blinded cannot comprehend that what they previously saw were merely shadows of those things, cast by the light from this very fire. Certainly those who have been liberated now see other things besides the shadows, but all these appear only in confusion. By contrast, what they see in the reflected light of the still unseen and unknown fire, namely, the shadows, appears in sharp outline. Because it can be seen without confusion, this consistency with which the shadows appear must strike those who have been freed as being "more unhidden." Therefore the word ἀληθές occurs again at the end of the description of stage two, and now in the comparative degree: ἀληθέστερα, the "more unhidden." The more proper "truth" is to be found in the shadows. So even those who have been freed from their chains still assess wrongly in what they posit as true, because they lack the prior condition for "assessing," namely, freedom. Certainly removing the chains brings a sort of liberation, but being let loose is not yet real freedom.

[127] Real freedom is attained only in stage three. Here someone who has been unshackled is at the same time conveyed outside the cave "into the open." There above ground all things are manifest. The looks that show what things are now no longer appear merely in the man-made and confusing glow of the fire within the cave. The things themselves stand there in the binding force and validity of their own visible form. The open into which the freed prisoner has now been placed does not mean the unboundedness of some wide-open space; rather, the open sets boundaries to things and is the binding power characteristic of the brightness radiating from the sunlight, which we also see. The looks that show what things

themselves are, the εἴδη (ideas), constitute the essence in whose light each individual being shows itself as this or that, and only in this self-showing does the appearing thing become unhidden and accessible.

The level of dwelling that has now been reached is, like the others, defined in terms of what is normatively and properly unhidden at this level. Therefore right at the beginning of his description of stage three Plato speaks of τῶν νῦν λεγομένων ἀληθῶν (516 a3), "of what is now addressed as the unhidden." This unhidden is ἀληθέστερον, even more unhidden than the things illuminated by the man-made fire in the cave were in distinction to the shadows. The unhidden that has now been reached is the most unhidden of all: τὰ ἀληθέστατα. While it is true that Plato does not use that word at this point in the text, he does mention τὸ ἀληθέστατον, the most unhidden, in the corresponding and equally important discussion at the beginning of Book VI of the *Republic*. There (484 c5ff.) he mentions οἱ ... εἰς τὸ ἀληθέστατον ἀποβλέποντες, "those who gaze upon the most unhidden." The most unhidden shows itself in each case in the whatness of a being. Without such a self-showing of the whatness (i.e., the ideas), each and every specific thing – in fact, absolutely everything – would remain hidden. "The most unhidden" is so called because it is what appears antecedently in everything that appears, and it makes whatever appears be accessible.

[128] Already within the cave, to shift one's gaze from the shadows to the glow of the fire and to focus on the things that show themselves in the firelight was a difficult task that proved unsuccessful; but now being freed into the open that is outside of the cave requires fully every bit of endurance and effort. Liberation does not come about by the simple removal of the chains, and it does not consist in unbridled license; rather, it first begins as the continuous effort at accustoming one's gaze to be fixed on the firm limits of things that stand fast in their visible form. Authentic liberation is the steadiness of being oriented toward that which appears in its visible form and which is the most unhidden in this appearing. Freedom exists only as the orientation that is structured in this way. But what is more, this orientation as a turning toward ... alone fulfills the essence of παιδεία as a turning around. Thus the fulfillment of the essence of "education" can be achieved only in the region of, and on the basis of, the most unhidden, i.e., the ἀληθέστατον, i.e., the truest, i.e., truth in the proper sense. The essence of "education" is grounded in the essence of "truth."

But because the essence of παιδεία consists in the περιαγωγὴ ὅλης τῆς ψυχῆς, then insofar as it is such a turning around, it constantly remains an overcoming of ἀπαιδευσία. Παιδεία includes within itself an essential relation to lack of education. And if, according to Plato's own interpretation, the "allegory of the cave" is supposed to clarify the essence of παιδεία, then this clarification must also make manifest precisely this essential factor, the constant overcoming of lack of education. Hence the telling of the story does not end, as is often supposed, with the description of the highest level attained in the ascent out of the cave. On the contrary, the "allegory" includes the story of the descent of the freed person back into the cave, back to those who are still in chains. The one who has been freed is supposed to lead these people too away from what is unhidden for them and to bring them face to face with the most unhidden. But the would-be liberator no longer knows his or her way around the cave and risks the danger of succumbing to the overwhelming power of the kind of truth that is normative there, the danger of being overcome by the claim of the common "reality" [129] to be the only reality. The liberator is threatened with the possibility of being put to death, a possibility that became a reality in the fate of Socrates, who was Plato's "teacher."

The return to the cave and the battle waged within the cave between the liberator and the prisoners who resist all liberation, of itself makes up stage four of the "allegory," where the story comes to a conclusion. Admittedly the word ἀληθές is no longer used in this part of the story. Nonetheless this stage also has to deal with the unhidden that conditions the area of the cave that the freed person now visits once again. But was not the "unhidden" that is normative in the cave – the shadows – already mentioned in stage one? Yes, it was. But two factors are essential to the unhidden: not only does it in some way or other render accessible whatever appears and keep it revealed in its appearing, but it also constantly overcomes a hiddenness of the hidden. The unhidden must be torn away from a hiddenness; it must in a sense be stolen from hiddenness. Originally for the Greeks[a] hiddenness, as an act of self-hiding, permeated the essence of being and thus also determined beings in their presentness and accessibility ("truth"); and that is why the Greek word for what the Romans call "*veritas*" and for what we call "truth" was distinguished by the alpha-privative (ἀ-λήθεια). Truth[b] originally means what has been wrested from hiddenness.[c] Truth is thus a wresting away in each case, in the form of a revealing. The hiddenness can be of various kinds: closing off, hiding away, disguising, covering over, masking, dissembling. Since, according to Plato's "allegory," the supremely unhidden must be wrested from a base and stubborn hiding, for this reason one's movement out of the cave into the open and into the light of day is

---

[a] Offprint from *Geistige Überlieferung*, 1942: Heraclitus, fragment 123.
[b] Offprint from *Geistige Überlieferung*, 1942: In the sense of that which is true.
[c] Offprint from *Geistige Überlieferung*, 1942: [from a] hiding.

a life-and-death struggle. Stage four of the "allegory" gives us a special glimpse [130] into how "privation" – attaining the unhidden by wresting it away – belongs to the essence of truth. Therefore, like each of the three previous stages of the "allegory of the cave," stage four also deals with ἀλήθεια.

This "allegory" can have the structure of a cave image at all only because it is antecedently co-determined by the fundamental experience of ἀλήθεια, the unhiddenness of beings, which was something self-evident for the Greeks. For what else is the underground cave except something open in itself that remains at the same time covered by a vault and, despite the entrance, walled off and enclosed by the surrounding earth? This cave-like enclosure that is open within itself, and that which it surrounds and therefore hides, both refer at the same time to an outside, the unhidden that is spread out in the light above ground. Only the essence of truth understood in the original Greek sense of ἀλήθεια – the unhiddenness that is related to the hidden (to something dissembled and disguised) – has an essential relation to this image of an underground cave. Wherever truth has another essence, wherever it is not unhiddenness or at least is not co-determined by unhiddenness, there an "allegory of the cave" has no basis as an illustration.

And yet, even though ἀλήθεια is properly experienced in the "allegory of the cave" and is mentioned in it at important points, nonetheless in place of unhiddenness another essence of truth pushes to the fore. However, this also implies that unhiddenness still maintains a certain priority.

The presentation of the "allegory," along with Plato's own interpretation of it, understands the underground cave and the area outside almost self-evidently as the region within which the story's events get played out. But in all this what are essential are the movements of passage, both the ascent from the realm of the light of the man-made fire into the brightness of the sunlight as well as the descent from the source of all light back into the darkness of the cave. The illustrative power of the "allegory of the cave" does not come from the image of the closedness of the subterranean vault and the imprisonment of people within its confines, [131] nor does it come from the sight of the open space outside the cave. For Plato, rather, the expository power behind the images of the "allegory" is concentrated on the role played by the fire, the fire's glow and the shadows it casts, the brightness of day, the sunlight and the sun. Everything depends on the shining forth of whatever appears and on making its visibility possible. Certainly unhiddenness is mentioned in its various stages, but it is considered simply in terms of how it makes whatever appears be accessible in its visible form (εἶδος) and in terms of how it makes this visible form, as that which shows itself (ἰδέα), be visible. The reflection proper focuses on the visible form's appearing, which is imparted in the very brightness of its shining. The visible form provides a view of that as which any given being is present. The reflection proper aims at the ἰδέα. The "idea" is the visible form that offers a view of what is present. The ἰδέα is pure shining in the sense of the phrase "the sun shines." The "idea" does not first let something else (behind it) "shine in its appearance" [*"erscheinen"*]; it itself is what shines, it is concerned only with the shining of itself. The ἰδέα is that which can shine [*das Scheinsame*]. The essence of the idea consists in its ability to shine and be seen [*Schein- und Sichtsamkeit*]. This is what brings about presencing, specifically the coming to presence of what a being is in any given instance. A being becomes present in each case in its whatness. But after all, coming to presence is the essence of being. That is why for Plato the proper essence of being consists in whatness. Even later terminology shows this: *quidditas*, and not *existentia*, is true *esse*, i.e., *essentia*. What the idea, in its shining forth, brings into view and thereby lets us see is – for the gaze focused on that idea – the unhidden of that as which the idea appears. This unhidden is grasped antecedently and by itself as that which is apprehended in apprehending the ἰδέα, as that which is known (γιγνωσχόμενον) in the act of knowing (γιγνώσχειν). Only in this Platonic revolution do νοεῖν and νοῦς (apprehending) first get referred essentially to the "idea." The adoption of this orientation to the ideas henceforth determines the essence of apprehension [*Vernehmung*] and subsequently the essence of "reason" [*"Vernunft"*].

[132] "Unhiddenness" now means: the unhidden always as what is accessible thanks to the idea's ability to shine. But insofar as the access is necessarily carried out through "seeing," unhiddenness is yoked into a "relation" with seeing, it becomes "relative" to seeing. Thus toward the end of Book VI of the *Republic* Plato develops the question: What makes the thing seen and the act of seeing be what they are in their relation? What spans the space between them? What yoke (ζυγόν, 508 a1) holds the two together? The "allegory of the cave" was written in order to illustrate the answer, which is set forth in an image: The sun as source of light lends visibility to whatever is seen. But seeing sees what is visible only insofar as the eye is ἡλιοειδές, "sunlike" by having the power to participate in the sun's kind of essence, that is, its shining. The eye itself "emits light" and devotes itself to the shining and in this way is able to receive and apprehend whatever appears. In terms of what is at stake, the image signifies a relationship that Plato expresses as follows (VI, 508 e1 ff.): τοῦτο τοίνυν τὸ τὴν ἀλήθειαν παρέχον τοῖς γιγνωσχομένοις καὶ τῷ γιγνώσχοντι τὴν δύναμιν ἀποδιδὸν τὴν τοῦ ἀγαθοῦ ἰδέαν φάθι εἶναι. "Thus what provides unhiddenness to

the thing known and also gives the power (of knowing) to the knower, this, I say, is the idea of the good."

The "allegory" mentions the sun as the image for the idea of the good. What does the essence of this idea consist in? As ἰδέα the good is something that shines, thus something that provides vision, thus in turn something visible and hence knowable, in fact: ἐν τῷ γνωστῷ τελευταία ἡ τοῦ ἀγαθοῦ ἰδέα καὶ μόγις ὁρᾶσθαι (517 b8). "In the sphere of what can be known, the idea of the good is the power of visibility that accomplishes all shining forth and that therefore is properly seen only last, in fact it is hardly (only with great pains) really seen at all."

We translate τὸ ἀγαθόν[a] with the apparently understandable term "the good." Most often we think of this as the "moral good," which is so called because it is in conformity with the moral law. [133] This interpretation falls outside Greek thought, even though Plato's interpretation of the ἀγαθόν as idea offers the occasion for thinking of "the good" "morally" and ultimately for reckoning it to be a "value." The notion of value that came into fashion in the nineteenth century in the wake of the modern conception of "truth" is the last and at the same time the weakest offspring of ἀγαθόν. Insofar as "value" and interpretation in terms of "values" are what sustains Nietzsche's metaphysics – in the absolute form of a "revaluation of all values" – and since for him all knowledge takes its departure from the metaphysical origin of "value," to that extent Nietzsche is the most unrestrained Platonist in the history of Western metaphysics. However, insofar as he understands value as the condition of the possibility of "life," a condition posited by "life itself," Nietzsche has held on to the essence of ἀγαθόν with much less prejudice than those who go chasing after the absurdity of "intrinsically valid values."

Moreover if we follow modern philosophy and think the essence of the "idea" as *perceptio* ("subjective representation"), then we find in the "idea of the good" a "value" present somewhere in itself, of which in addition we have an "idea." This "idea" must naturally be the highest because what matters is that everything run its course in the "good" (in the well-being of prosperity or in the orderliness of an order). Within this modern way of thinking there is absolutely nothing more to grasp of the original essence of Plato's ἰδέα τοῦ ἀγαθοῦ.

In Greek thought τὸ ἀγαθόν means that which is capable of something and enables another to be capable of something. Every ἰδέα, the visible form of something, provides a look at what a being is in each case. Thus

---

[a] First edition, 1947: The ἀγαθόν certainly is an ἰδέα, but no longer present, and therefore hardly visible.

in Greek thinking the "ideas" enable something to appear in its whatness and thus be present in its constancy. The ideas are what is in everything that is. Therefore, what makes every idea be capable as an idea – in Plato's expression: the idea of all ideas – consists in making possible the appearing, in all its visibility, of everything present. [134] The essence of every idea certainly consists in making possible and enabling the shining that allows a view of the visible form. Therefore the idea of ideas is that-which-enables as such, τὸ ἀγαθόν. It brings about the shining of everything that can shine, and accordingly is itself that which properly appears by shining, that which is most able to shine in its shining. For this reason Plato calls the ἀγαθόν also τοῦ ὄντος τὸ φανότατον (518 c9), "that which most shines (the most able to shine) of beings."

The expression "the idea of the good" – which is all too misleading for modern thinking – is the name for that distinctive idea which, as the idea of ideas, is what enables everything else. This idea, which alone can be called "the good," remains ἰδέα τελευταία, because in it the essence of the idea comes to its fulfillment, i.e., begins to be, so that from it there also first arises the possibility of all other ideas. The good may be called the "highest idea" in a double sense: It is the highest in the hierarchy of making possible; and seeing it is a very arduous task of looking straight upward. Despite the difficulty of properly grasping it, this idea that, granted the essence of idea, must be called "the good" in the Greek sense, somehow always constantly stands in view wherever any beings at all show themselves. Even where people see only the shadows, whose essence still lies hidden, there too the fire's glow must already be shining, even though people do not properly grasp this shining and experience it as coming from the fire, and even though here, above all, they are still unaware that this fire is only an offspring (ἔκγονον, VI, 507 a3) of the sun. Within the cave the sun remains invisible, and yet even the shadows live off its light. But the fire in the cave, which makes possible an apprehending of the shadows that is unaware of its own essence, is the image for the unrecognized ground of any experiencing of beings that intends them without knowing them as such. Nevertheless, by its shining the sun bestows brightness upon everything that appears, and along with that brightness visibility and thus "unhiddenness." But not just that. At the same time its shining [135] radiates warmth and by this glowing enables everything that "comes to be" to go forth into the visibility of its stable duration (509 b).

However, once the sun itself is truly seen (ὀφθεῖσα δέ) – or, to drop the metaphor, once the highest idea is caught sight of – then συλλογιστέα εἶναι ὡς ἄρα πᾶσι πάντων αὕτη ὀρθῶν τε καὶ καλῶν αἰτία (517 c), "then one may draw the conclusion – gathered together (from the highest idea itself) – that obviously for all people this [idea of the good] is the original source [Ur-sache] both of all that is right (in their comportment) and of all that is beautiful" – that is, of that which manifests itself to comportment in such a way as to bring the shining of its visible form to appearance. The highest idea is the origin, i.e., the original source [Ur-sache] of all "things" ["Sachen"] and their thingness [Sachheit]. "The good" grants the appearing of the visible form in which whatever is present has its stability in that which it is. Through this granting, the being is held within being and thus is "saved."

As regards all forms of prudential insight that inform practical activity, it follows from the essence of the highest idea ὅτι δεῖ ταύτην ἰδεῖν τὸν μέλλοντα ἐμφρόνως πράξειν ἢ ἰδίᾳ ἢ δημοσίᾳ (517 c4/5), "that anyone who is concerned to act with prudential insight, either in personal matters or in public affairs, must have this in view (namely, the idea that, insofar as it is the enabling of the essence of idea, is called the good)." Whoever wants to act and has to act in a world determined by "the ideas" needs, before all else, a view of the ideas. And thus the very essence of παιδεία consists in making the human being free and strong for the clarity and constancy of insight into essence. Now since, according to Plato's own interpretation, the "allegory of the cave" is supposed to provide a concrete image of the essence of παιδεία, it also must recount the ascent to the vision of the highest idea.

But is it not the case that the "allegory of the cave" deals specifically with ἀλήθεια? Absolutely not. And yet the fact remains that this "allegory" contains Plato's "doctrine" of truth, for the "allegory" is grounded in the unspoken event whereby ἰδέα gains dominance over ἀλήθεια. The "allegory" puts into images [136] what Plato says about ἰδέα τοῦ ἀγαθοῦ, namely, that αὐτὴ κυρία ἀλήθειαν καὶ νοῦν παρασχομένη (517 c4), "she herself is mistress in that she bestows unhiddenness (on what shows itself) and at the same time imparts apprehension (of what is unhidden)." Ἀλήθεια comes under the yoke of the ἰδέα. When Plato says of the ἰδέα that she is the mistress that allows unhiddenness, he points to something unsaid, namely, that henceforth the essence of truth does not, as the essence of unhiddenness, unfold from its proper and essential fullness but rather shifts to the essence of the ἰδέα. The essence of truth gives up its fundamental trait of unhiddenness.

If our comportment with beings is always and everywhere a matter of the ἰδεῖν of the ἰδέα, the seeing of the "visible form," then all our efforts must be concentrated above all on making such seeing possible. And that requires the correct vision. Already within the cave, when those who have been liberated turn away from the shadows and turn toward the things, they direct their gaze to that which, in comparison with the mere shadows, "is more in being": πρὸς μᾶλλον ὄντα τετραμμένος ὀρθότερον βλέποι (515 d3/4), "and thus turned to what is more in being, they should certainly see more correctly." The movement of passage from one place to the other consists in the process whereby the gaze becomes more correct. Everything depends on the ὀρθότης, the correctness of the gaze. Through this correctness, seeing or knowing becomes something correct so that in the end it looks directly at the highest idea and fixes itself in this "direct alignment." In so directing itself, apprehending conforms itself to what is to be seen: the "visible form" of the being. What results from this conforming of apprehension, as an ἰδεῖν, to the ἰδέα is a ὁμοίωσις, an agreement of the act of knowing with the thing itself. Thus, the priority of ἰδέα and ἰδεῖν over ἀλήθεια results in a transformation in the essence of truth. Truth becomes ὀρθότης, the correctness of apprehending and asserting.

With this transformation of the essence of truth there takes place at the same time a change of the locus of truth. As unhiddenness, truth is still a fundamental trait of beings themselves. But as the correctness [137] of the "gaze," it becomes a characteristic of human comportment toward beings.

Nevertheless in a certain way Plato has to hold on to "truth" as still a characteristic of beings, because a being, as something present, has being precisely by appearing, and being brings unhiddenness with it. But at the same time, the inquiry into what is unhidden shifts in the direction of the appearing of the visible form, and consequently toward the act of seeing that is ordered to this visible form, and toward what is correct and toward the correctness of seeing. For this reason there is a necessary ambiguity in Plato's doctrine. This is precisely what attests to the heretofore unsaid but now sayable change in the essence of truth. The ambiguity is quite clearly manifested in the fact that whereas ἀλήθεια is what is named and discussed, it is ὀρθότης that is meant and that is posited as normative – and all this in a single train of thought.

The ambiguity in the determination of the essence of truth can be seen in a single sentence taken from the section that contains Plato's own interpretation of the "allegory of the cave" (517 b7 to c5). The guiding thought is that the highest idea yokes together the act of knowing and what it knows. But this relation is understood in two ways. First of all, and therefore normatively, Plato says: ἡ τοῦ ἀγαθοῦ ἰδέα [the idea of the good] is πάντων ὀρθῶν τε καὶ καλῶν αἰτία, "the original source (i.e., the enabling of the essence) of everything correct as well as of everything beautiful." But then it is said that the idea of the good is κυρία ἀλήθειαν καὶ νοῦν παρασχομένη, "the mistress who bestows unhiddenness as well as apprehension." These two assertions do not run parallel to each other, such that ἀλήθεια would correspond to the ὀρθά (what is correct) and νοῦς (apprehending) would correspond to the χαλά (what is beautiful). Rather the correspondence works in crisscross fashion. Corresponding to the ὀρθά, what is correct and its correctness, there is correct apprehension, and corresponding to what is beautiful there is the unhidden; for the essence of the beautiful lies in being ἐκφανέστατον (cf. *Phaedrus*), that which, as most of all and most purely shining of and from itself, shows the visible form and thus is unhidden. Both sentences [138] speak of the primacy of the idea of the good as enabling both the correctness of knowing and the unhiddenness of the known. Here truth still is, at one and the same time, unhiddenness and correctness, although unhiddenness already stands under the yoke of the ἰδέα. The same ambiguity in the determination of the essence of truth still prevails in Aristotle as well. In the closing chapter of Book IX of the *Metaphysics* (*Metaphysics* Θ, 10, 1051 a34ff.) where Aristotelian thinking on the being of beings reaches its peak, unhiddenness is the all-controlling fundamental trait of beings. But Aristotle can also say οὐ γάρ ἐστι τὸ ψεῦδος χαὶ τὸ ἀληθὲς ἐν τοῖς πράγμασιν ... ἀλλ᾽ ἐν διανοίᾳ (*Metaphysics* E, 4, 1027 b25ff.). "In fact, the false and the true are not in things (themselves) ... but in the intellect."

The assertion of a judgment made by the intellect is the place of truth and falsehood and of the difference between them. The assertion is called true insofar as it conforms to the state of affairs and thus is a ὁμοίωσις. This determination of the essence of truth no longer contains an appeal to ἀλήθεια in the sense of unhiddenness; on the contrary ἀλήθεια, now taken as the opposite of ψεῦδος (i.e., of the false in the sense of the incorrect), is thought of as correctness. From now on this characterization of the essence of truth as the correctness of both representation and assertion becomes normative for the whole of Western thinking. As evidence of that, let it suffice to cite the guiding theses that typify the characterizations of the essence of truth in the main epochs of metaphysics.

For medieval Scholasticism, Thomas Aquinas's thesis holds good: veritae proprie invenitur in intellectu humano vel divino (*Quaestiones de Veritate*, quaestio I, articulus 4, responsio): "Truth is properly encountered in the human or in the divine intellect." The intellect is where truth has its essential locus. In this text truth is no longer ἀλήθεια but ὁμοίωσις (*adaequatio*).

At the beginning of modern times Descartes sharpens the previous thesis by saying: veritatem proprie vel falsitatem non nisi in [139] solo intellectu esse posse (*Regulae ad directionem ingenii, Regula VIII, Opuscula*

178

posthuma X, 396). "Truth or falsehood in the proper sense can be nowhere else but in the intellect alone."

And in the age when the modern era enters its fulfillment Nietzsche sharpens the previous thesis still further when he says, "*Truth is the kind of error* without which a certain kind of living being could not live. In the final analysis, the value for *life* is what is decisive." (Note from the year 1885, *The Will to Power*, number 493.) If for Nietzsche truth is a kind of error, then its essence consists in a way of thinking that always, indeed necessarily, falsifies the real, specifically insofar as every act of representing halts the continual "becoming" and, in erecting its established facts against the flow of "becoming," sets up as the supposedly real something that does not correspond – i.e., something incorrect and thus erroneous.

Nietzsche's determination of truth as the incorrectness of thinking is in agreement with the traditional essence of truth as the correctness of assertion (λόγος). Nietzsche's concept of truth displays the last glimmer of the most extreme consequence of the change of truth from the unhiddenness of beings to the correctness of the gaze. The change itself is brought about in the determination of the being of beings (in Greek: the being present of what is present) as ἰδέα.

As a consequence of this interpretation of beings, being present is no longer what it was in the beginning of Western thinking: the emergence of the hidden into unhiddenness, where unhiddenness itself, as revealing, constitutes the fundamental trait of being present. Plato conceives being present (οὐσία) as ἰδέα. However, ἰδέα is not subordinate to unhiddenness in the sense of serving what is unhidden by bringing it to appearance. Rather, the opposite is the case: it is the shining (the self-showing) that, within its essence and in a singular self-relatedness, may yet be called unhiddenness. The ἰδέα is not [140] some foreground that ἀλήθεια puts out there to present things;[7] rather, the ἰδέα is the ground that makes ἀλήθεια possible. But even as such the ἰδέα still lays claim to something of the original but unacknowledged essence of ἀλήθεια.

Truth is no longer, as it was qua unhiddenness, the fundamental trait of being itself. Instead, as a consequence of getting yoked under the idea, truth has become correctness, and henceforth it will be a characteristic of the knowing of beings.

Ever since, there has been a striving for "truth" in the sense of the correctness of the gaze and the correctness of its direction. Ever since, what matters in all our fundamental orientations toward beings is the achieving of a correct view of the ideas. The reflection on παιδεία and the change in the essence of ἀλήθεια belong together and belong within the same tale of the passage from one abode to another, the tale that is recounted in the "allegory of the cave."

The difference between the two abodes, the one inside and the one outside the cave, is a difference of σοφία. In general this word means being astute about something, being skilled at something. Properly speaking σοφία means being astute about that which is present as the unhidden and which, as present, perdures.[a] Astuteness is not the equivalent of merely possessing knowledge. It means inhering within an abode that everywhere and primarily has a hold in what perdures.

The kind of astuteness that is normative down there in the cave – ἡ ἐχεῖ σοφία (516 c5) – is surpassed by another σοφία. This latter strives solely and above all else to glimpse the being of beings in the "ideas." This σοφία, in contrast to the one in the cave, is distinguished by the desire to reach out beyond what is immediately present and to acquire a basis in that which, in showing itself, perdures. In itself this σοφία is a predilection for and friendship with (φιλία) the "ideas," which bestow the unhidden. Outside the cave σοφία is φιλοσοφία. The Greek language already knew this word before the time of Plato and used it in general [141] to name the predilection for correct astuteness. Plato first appropriated the word as a name for the specific astuteness about beings that at the same time defines the being of beings as idea. Since Plato, thinking about the being of beings has become – "philosophy," because it is a matter of gazing up at the "ideas." But the "philosophy" that begins with Plato has, from that point on, the distinguishing mark of what is later called "metaphysics." Plato himself concretely illustrates the basic outline of metaphysics in the story recounted in the "allegory of the cave." In fact, the coining of the word "metaphysics" is already prefigured in Plato's presentation. In the passage (516) that depicts the adaptation of the gaze to the ideas, Plato says (516 c3): Thinking goes μετ᾽ἐχεῖνα, "beyond" those things that are experienced in the form of mere shadows and images, and goes εἰς ταῦτα, "out toward" these things, namely, the "ideas." These are the suprasensuous, seen with a nonsensuous gaze; they are the being of beings, which cannot be grasped with our bodily organs. And the highest in the region of the suprasensuous is that idea which, as the idea of all ideas, remains the cause of the subsistence and the appearing of all beings. Because this "idea" is thereby the cause of everything, it is also "the idea" that is called "the good." This highest and first cause is named by Plato and correspondingly by Aristotle τὸ θεῖον, the

---

[a] Offprint from *Geistige Überlieferung*, 1942: Cf. Heraclitus, fragment 112.

divine. Ever since being got interpreted as ἰδέα, thinking about the being of beings has been metaphysical, and metaphysics has been theological. In this case theology means the interpretation of the "cause" of beings as God and the transferring of being onto this cause, which contains being in itself and dispenses being from out of itself, because it is the being-est of beings.

This same interpretation of being as ἰδέα, which owes its primacy to a change in the essence of ἀλήθεια, requires that viewing the ideas be accorded high distinction. Corresponding to this distinction is παιδεία, the "education" of human beings. Concern with human being and with the position of humans amidst beings entirely dominates metaphysics.

[142] The beginning of metaphysics in the thought of Plato is at the same time the beginning of "humanism." Here the word must be thought in its essence and therefore in its broadest sense. In that regard "humanism" means the process that is implicated in the beginning, in the unfolding, and in the end of metaphysics, whereby human beings, in differing respects but always deliberately, move into a central place among beings, of course without thereby being the highest being. Here "human being" sometimes means humanity or humankind, sometimes the individual or the community, and sometimes the people [das Volk] or a group of peoples. What is always at stake is this: to take "human beings," who within the sphere of a fundamental, metaphysically established system of beings are defined as *animal rationale*, and to lead them, within that sphere, to the liberation of their possibilities, to the certitude of their destiny, and to the securing of their "life." This takes place as the shaping of their "moral" behavior, as the salvation of their immortal souls, as the unfolding of their creative powers, as the development of their reason, as the nourishing of their personalities, as the awakening of their civic sense, as the cultivation of their bodies, or as an appropriate combination of some or all of these "humanisms." What takes place in each instance is a metaphysically determined revolving around the human being, whether in narrower or wider orbits. With the fulfillment of metaphysics, "humanism" (or in "Greek" terms: anthropology) also presses on to the most extreme – and likewise unconditioned – "positions."

Plato's thinking follows the change in the essence of truth, a change that becomes the history of metaphysics, which in Nietzsche's thinking has entered upon its unconditioned fulfillment. Thus Plato's doctrine of "truth" is not something that is past. It is historically "present," not just in the sense that his teachings have a "later effect" that historians can calculate, nor as a reawakening or imitation of antiquity, not even as the mere preservation of what has been handed down. Rather, this change in the essence of truth is present as the all-dominating fundamental reality – long established and thus still in place – [143] of the ever-advancing world history of the planet in this most modern of modern times.

Whatever happens with historical human beings always derives from a decision about the essence of truth that was taken long ago and is never up to humans alone. Through this decision the lines are always already drawn regarding what, in the light of the established essence of truth, is sought after and established as true and likewise what is thrown away and passed over as untrue.

The story recounted in the "allegory of the cave" provides a glimpse of what is really happening in the history of Western humanity, both now and in the future: Taking the essence of truth as the correctness of the representation, one thinks of all beings according to "ideas" and evaluates all reality according to "values." That which alone and first of all is decisive is not which ideas and which values are posited, but rather the fact that the real is interpreted according to "ideas" at all, that the "world" is weighed according to "values" at all.

Meanwhile we have recollected the original essence of truth. Unhiddenness[a] reveals itself to this recollection as the fundamental trait of beings themselves.[b] Nonetheless, recollection of the original essence of truth must think this essence more originally. Therefore, such recollection can never take over unhiddenness merely in Plato's sense, namely, as yoked under the ἰδέα. As Plato conceives it, unhiddenness remains harnessed in a relation to looking, apprehending, thinking, and asserting. To follow this relation means to relinquish the essence of unhiddenness. No attempt to ground the essence of unhiddenness in "reason," "spirit," "thinking," "*logos,*" or in any kind of "subjectivity," can ever rescue the essence of unhiddenness. In all such attempts, what is to be grounded – the essence of hiddenness itself – is not yet adequately sought out. What always gets "clarified" is merely some essential consequence of the uncomprehended essence of unhiddenness.

[144]What is first required is an appreciation of the "positive" in the "privative" essence of ἀλήθεια. The positive must first be experienced as the fundamental trait of being itself. First of all what must break in upon us is that exigency whereby we are compelled to question not just beings in their being but first of all being itself (that is, the difference). Because this exigency[c] stands before us, the original essence of truth still lies in its hidden origin.

---

[a] First edition, 1947: Ἀλήθεια is a name for *esse*, not for *veritas*.

[b] First edition, 1947: That is, as beyng [*Seyn*].

[c] First edition, 1947: The exigency of the lack of exigency [*Die Not der Notlosigkeit*]: the fact that we are unaffected by being itself, that being is forgotten. In this exigency, the forgottenness of being does not leave us.

On the Essence and Concept of Φύσις in Aristotle's Physics B, 1

Translated by Thomas Sheehan[1]

[309] The Romans translated φύσις by the word *natura*. *Natura* comes from *nasci*, "to be born, to originate..." as in the Greek root γεν–. *Natura* means "that which lets something originate from itself."

Since those times "nature" has become the fundamental word that designates essential relations that Western historical humanity has to beings, both to itself and to beings other than itself. This fact is shown by a rough list of dichotomies that have become prevalent: nature and grace (i.e., super-nature), nature and art, nature and history, nature and spirit. But we likewise speak of the "nature" of spirit, the "nature" of history, and the "nature" of the human being. By this last phrase we mean not just one's body or even the species "human," but one's whole essence. Therefore generally when we speak of the "nature of things," we mean *what* things are in their "possibility" and *how* they are, regardless of whether and to what degree they "actually" are.

In Christian thought, the human being's "natural state" means what is bestowed upon humans in creation and turned over to their freedom. Left to itself, *this* "nature," through the passions, brings about the total destruction of the human being. For this reason "nature" must be *suppressed*. It is in a certain sense what should not be.

In another interpretation, it is precisely the unleashing of the drives and passions that is natural for human beings. According to Nietzsche, *homo naturae* is someone who makes the "body" the key to the interpretation of the world and who thus secures a new and harmonious relation to the "sensible" in general, to the "elements" (fire, water, earth, light), to the passions and drives and whatever is conditioned by them. And at the same time, in virtue of this new relation these people bring "the elemental" into their power [310] and by this power make themselves capable of the mastery of the world in the sense of a systematic world-domination.

183

And finally "nature" becomes the word for what is not only above every-thing "elemental" and everything human, but even above the gods. Thus Hölderlin says in the hymn, "As when on feast day..." (third verse):

> Now breaks the day! I yearned for it and saw it come.
> And my word for what I saw shall be the Holy.
> For nature herself, more ancient than the ages
> And above the gods of East and West,
> Has awakened with the clang of a warrior's arms.
> And from aether on high to abyss below
> By unswerving law as once from frightful Chaos born,
> She feels herself again renewed,
> The Inspirer, the All-creating.

(Here "nature" becomes the name for what is *above* the gods and "more ancient than the ages" in which beings always come to be. "Nature" be-comes the word for "being": being is prior to all beings, for they owe what they are to being. And the gods likewise: to the degree that they *are*, and however they are, they too all stand *under* "being.")

Here beings as a whole are not misinterpreted "naturalistically" and reduced to "nature" in the sense of matter endowed with force, nor is this whole "mystically" obscured and dissolved into indeterminacy.

Whatever range has been attributed to the word "nature" in the various ages of Western history, in each case the word contains an interpretation of beings as a whole, even when "nature" seems to be meant as only one term in a dichotomy. In all such dichotomies, "nature" is not just one of two equal terms but "essentially" holds the position of priority, inasmuch as the other terms are always and primarily differentiated by contrast with – and therefore are determined by – *nature*. (For example, when "nature" is taken in a one-sided and superficial manner as "stuff," "matter," element, or the unformed, [311] then "spirit" is taken correspondingly as the "non-material," the "spiritual," the "creative," or that which gives form.)

[But the perspective within which the distinction itself is made is "being."][2]

Therefore in our thinking, even the distinction between nature and his-tory must be pushed back into the underlying area that sustains the di-chotomy, the area where nature and history *are*. Even if we disregard or leave open the question about whether and how "history" rests upon "nature," even if we understand history in terms of human "subjectivity" and conceive of history as "spirit" and therefore let nature be determined by spirit, even then we are in essence *still* and *already* thinking about the *subiectum*, the ὑποχείμενον, and therefore about φύσις. The impossibility of getting around φύσις is shown in *that* name which we use to designate the kind of knowledge that, up until now, Westerners have had about beings as a whole. The systematic articulation of the truth at any given time "about" beings as a whole is called "metaphysics." It makes no difference whether or not this metaphysics is given expression in propositions, whether or not the expressions are formed into an explicit system. Metaphysics is that knowledge wherein Western historical humanity preserves the truth of its relations to beings as a whole and the truth about those beings themselves. In a quite essential sense, meta-physics is "physics," i.e., knowledge of φύσις (ἐπιστήμη φυσική).

At first blush our question about the essence and concept of φύσις might seem to be simply an inquiry, out of curiosity, into the origin of past and present interpretations of "nature." But if we consider that this fundamental word of Western metaphysics harbors within itself decisions about the truth of beings; if we recall that today the truth about beings as a whole has become entirely questionable; moreover, if we suspect that the essence of truth therefore remains thoroughly in dispute; and finally if we know that all this is grounded in the history of the interpretations of the essence of φύσις, then we stand outside the [312] merely historical interests that philosophy might have in the "history of a concept." Then we experience, although from afar, the nearness of future decisions.

[For the world is shifting out of joint – if indeed it ever was *in* joint – and the question arises whether modern humanity's planning, even if it be worldwide, can ever bring about the ordering of world.]

The first coherent and thoughtful discussion ("first" because of its way of questioning) of the essence of φύσις comes down to us from the time when Greek philosophy reached its fulfillment. It stems from Aristotle and is preserved in his φυσικὴ ἀκρόασις (Lectures given – or better, "Lectures heard" – on φύσις).

Aristotle's Physics *is the hidden, and therefore never adequately studied, foundational book of Western philosophy.*

Probably the eight books of the *Physics* were not projected as a unity and did not come into existence all at once. Such questions have no importance here. In general it makes little sense to say that the *Physics* precedes the *Metaphysics*, because metaphysics is just as much "physics" as physics is "metaphysics." For reasons based on the work itself, as well as on historical grounds, we can take it that around 347 B.C. (Plato's death) the second book was already composed. (Cf. also Jaeger, *Aristotle: Fundamentals of the History of His Development*, p. 296, originally published in 1923. For all its erudition, this book has the single fault of thinking through Aristotle's philosophy in the modern Scholastic neo-Kantian manner that is entirely *foreign to Greek thought*. Much of Jaeger's *Entstehungsgeschichte der Metaphysik des Aristoteles*, 1912, is more accurate because less concerned with "content.")

But even so, this first thoughtful and unified conceptualization of φύσις is already the last echo of the original (and thus supreme) thoughtful *projection* of the essence of φύσις that we still have preserved for us in the fragments of Anaximander, Heraclitus, and Parmenides.

[313] In Book Two, chapter one, of the eight books of the *Physics* (*Physics* B, 1, 192 b8–193 b21), Aristotle gives the interpretation of φύσις that sustains and guides all succeeding interpretations of the essence of "nature." Here too are hidden the roots of that later determination of the essence of *nature* wherein it is distinguished from spirit and determined through the "spirit." In saying this we mean to intimate that the differentiation of "nature and spirit" is simply *foreign to the Greeks*.

Before we follow the individual steps of Aristotle's determination of the essence of φύσις, let us look at *two sentences* that Aristotle pronounces in the first and introductory book (A):

ἡμῖν δ᾽ ὑποκείσθω τὰ φύσει ἢ πάντα ἢ ἔνια κινούμενα εἶναι δῆλον δ᾽ ἐκ τῆς ἐπαγωγῆς.

"But from the outset it should be (a settled issue) for us that those beings that are by φύσις, whether all of them or some of them [those not in rest], are moving beings (i.e., determined by movedness). But this is evident from an immediate 'leading toward' (that leads *toward* these beings and *over* and beyond them to their 'being')." (A, 2, 185 a12ff.)

Here Aristotle explicitly emphasizes what he perceives to be decisive for the projection of the essence of φύσις, namely, κίνησις, the state of movedness. And therefore the key issue in the question about "physics" becomes one of defining the essence of movement. For us today it is merely a truism to say that the processes of nature are processes of movement – in fact, it is a tautology. We have no inkling of the importance of Aristotle's sentences just cited, nor of his interpretation of φύσις, unless we know that it was through and for Aristotle that what we take for a truism first entered the formative essential insight of Western humanity. Certainly the Greeks before Aristotle had already experienced the fact that sky and sea, plants and animals are in movement, and certainly thinkers before him had already attempted to say what movement was. But it was Aristotle who first [314] attained – and thus, first created – that level of questioning where (movement is not considered as something merely given along with other things, but rather where) *being-moved* is explicitly questioned and understood as the fundamental mode of being. (But this means that defining the essence of being is impossible without an essential insight into movedness as such. Of course this is not at all to say that being is understood "as movement" [or as rest], for such thinking would be *foreign to the Greeks* and, in fact, absolutely unphilosophical [inasmuch as movedness is not "nothing," and only being, in essence, rules over the nothing and over beings and over their modes].)

According to Aristotle, the fact that all beings from φύσις are in motion or at rest is evident: δῆλον ἐκ τῆς ἐπαγωγῆς. We usually translate the word ἐπαγωγή as "induction" and, taken literally, the translation is almost adequate. But with regard to the issue, i.e., as an interpretation, it is totally erroneous. Ἐπαγωγή does not mean running through individual facts and series of facts in order to conclude something common and "general" from their similar properties. Ἐπαγωγή means "leading toward" what comes into view insofar as we have previously looked *away*, over and *beyond* individual beings. At what? At being. For example, only if we already have treeness in view can we identify individual trees. Ἐπαγωγή is seeing and making visible what already stands in view – for example, treeness. Ἐπαγωγή is "constituting" in the double sense of, first, bringing something up into view and then likewise establishing what has been seen. Ἐπαγωγή is what immediately becomes suspect to those caught up in scientific thinking and mostly remains foreign to them. These people see in it an inadmissible *petitio principii*, i.e., an "offense" against "empirical thinking," whereas the *petere principium*, the reaching out to the supporting ground, is the only move philosophy makes. It is the "offensive" that breaks open the territory within whose borders a science can first settle down.

[315] If we directly experience and intend φύσει-beings, we already have in view both the "moved" and its movedness. But what stands in view here is not yet "constituted" as what it is and how it is present.

Therefore the question about φύσις must inquire into the movedness of these beings and try to see what φύσις is in relation to this movedness. But first, in order to establish clearly the direction of our inquiry, we must delineate, within the whole of beings, the region that we can say comprises beings that *are* because they are determined by φύσις, namely, τὰ φύσει ὄντα.

Physics B, 1 begins with this delineation. (In the following pages we give a "translation" that is divided into *appropriate* sections. Since this "translation" is already the *interpretation* proper, only an explanation of the "translation" is called for. This is certainly not a "trans-lation" in the sense of a "carrying over" of the Greek words into the *proper force and weight of our language*. It is not intended to *replace* the Greek but only to place us *into* the Greek and in so doing to disappear in it. This is why it lacks all the character and fullness that come from the depths of our own language, and why it is neither pleasing nor "polished.")³

I. "Of beings (as a whole) some are from φύσις, whereas others are by other 'causes.' By φύσις, as we say, are animals as well as their members (parts), likewise plants and the simple elements of bodies, like earth and fire and water and air." (192 b8–11)

The other beings, which are not yet expressly mentioned, *are* by other "causes," but the first group, the ones "named," are by φύσις. Thus from the outset φύσις is taken as cause (αἴτιον – αἰτία) in the sense of the "origin" ["*Ur-sache*"]. The word and concept "cause" makes us think almost automatically of "causality" [*Kausalität*], that is, the manner and mode in which one thing "acts on" another. Αἴτιον, for which Aristotle will soon introduce a more precise definition, means in the present context: that which is responsible for the fact that a being is *what* it is. This [316] responsibility does not have the character of causation in the sense of a "causally" efficient actualizing. Thus, for example, spatiality belongs to the very character of materiality, but space does not efficiently cause matter. Cause as the origin [*Ur-sache*] must be understood here literally as the originary [*Ur-tümliche*], that which constitutes the thingness of a thing. "Causality" is only a derivative way of being an origin.

By simply mentioning animals, plants, earth, fire, water, and air, Aristotle points to the region in which the question about φύσις has to be lodged.

II. "But all the aforementioned appear as different from whatever has *not* composed itself by φύσις into a stand and a stability." (192 b12–13)

Συνεστῶτα is here used for ὄντα (cf. 193 a36, τοῖς φύσει συνισταμένοις). From this we infer what "being" meant for the Greeks. They address beings as the "stable" [*das "Ständige"*]. "The stable" means two things. On the one hand, it means whatever, of and by itself, stands on its own, that which stands "there"; and at the same time "the stable" means the enduring, the lasting. We would certainly not be thinking like the Greeks if we were to conceive of the stable as what "stands *over against*" in the sense of the objective. Something "standing over against" [*Gegenstand*] is the "translation" of the word "object." But beings can be experienced as objects only where human beings have become subjects, those who experience their fundamental relation to beings as the objectification – understood as mastery – of what is encountered. For the Greeks, human beings are never subjects, and therefore non-human beings can never have the character of objects (things that stand-over-against). Φύσις is what is responsible for the fact that the stable has a unique kind of standing-on-its-own. Φύσις is more clearly delineated in the following sentence:

III. "Indeed each of these beings [that are *what* they are and *how* they are from φύσις] has in itself the originating ordering (ἀρχή) of its movedness and its standing still (rest), where movedness and rest are meant sometimes with regard to place, [317] sometimes with regard to growth and diminution, other times with regard to alteration (change)." (192 b13–15)

Here in place of αἴτιον and αἰτία we find explicitly the word ἀρχή. The Greeks ordinarily hear two meanings in this word. On the one hand ἀρχή means that from which something has its origin and beginning; on the other hand it means that which, *as* this origin and beginning, likewise keeps rein *over,* i.e., restrains and therefore dominates, something else that emerges from it. Ἀρχή means, at one and the same time, beginning and control. On a broader and therefore lower scale we can say: origin and ordering. In order to express the unity that oscillates between the two, we can translate ἀρχή as originating ordering and as ordering origin. The unity of these two is *essential.* And this concept of ἀρχή gives a more definite content to the word αἴτιον (cause) used above. (Probably the *concept* ἀρχή is not an "archaic" concept, but one that later was read back into the origins of Greek philosophy, first by Aristotle and then subsequently by the "doxographers.")

Φύσις is ἀρχή, i.e., the origin and ordering of movedness and rest, specifically in a moving being that has this ἀρχή in itself. We do not say "in *its* self" because we want to indicate that a being of this kind does not have the ἀρχή *"for itself"* by explicitly *knowing* it, insofar as it does not "possess" *"itself"* as a self at all. Plants and animals are *in* movedness even when they stand still and rest. Rest is a kind of movement; only that which is able to move can rest. It is absurd to speak of the number 3 as "resting." Because plants and animals are *in* movement regardless of whether they rest or move, for this reason not only are they in *movement*; they *are* in movedness. This means: they are not, in the first instance, beings for themselves and among others, beings that then occasionally happen to slip into states of movement. Rather, they *are* beings only insofar as they have their essential abode and ontological footing in movedness. However, their being-moved is *such* [318] that the ἀρχή, the origin and ordering of their movedness, rules from within those beings themselves.

Here where Aristotle defines φύσις as ἀρχή κινήσεως, he does not fail to point out various kinds of movement: growth and diminution, alteration and change of place (locomotion). These kinds are merely enumerated, i.e., they are not differentiated according to any explicit respect, nor grounded in any such differentiation (cf. *Physics* E 1, 224 b35–225 b9). In fact, this mere enumeration is not even complete. In fact, the kind of movement that is *not* mentioned is precisely the one that will be crucial for determining the essence of φύσις. Nevertheless, mentioning various kinds of movement at this point has its own significance. It indicates that Aristotle understands κίνησις, movedness, in a very *broad* sense – but not "broad" in the sense of "extended," "approximate," and superficial, but rather in the sense of the essential and of a grounding fullness.

Today, with the predominance of the mechanistic thinking of the modern natural sciences, we are inclined both to hold that the basic form of movement is movedness in the sense of motion from one position in space to another; and then to "explain" everything that is moved in terms of it. That kind of movedness – κίνησις κατὰ τόπον, movedness in terms of place or location – is for Aristotle only *one* kind of movedness among others, but it in no way counts *as movement pure and simple*.

What is more, we should note that in a certain sense what Aristotle means by "change of place" is something different from the modern conception of the change of location of some mass in space. Τόπος is the ποῦ, the place where a specific body belongs. What is fiery belongs above, what is earthly belongs below. The places themselves – above, below (heaven, earth) – are special: by way of them are determined distances and relations, i.e., what we call "space," something for which the Greeks had neither a word nor a concept. For us today space is not determined by way of [319] place; rather, all places, as constellations of points, are determined by infinite space that is everywhere homogeneous and nowhere distinctive. When movedness is taken as change of place, there is a corresponding kind of rest, namely, remaining in the same place. But something that continues to occupy the same place and thus is *not* moved in the sense of change of place, can nonetheless be in a process of movedness. For example, a plant that is rooted "in place" grows (increases) or withers (decreases) [αὔξησις – φθίσις]. And conversely, something that moves insofar as it changes its place can still "rest" by remaining as it was constituted. The running fox is at rest in that it keeps the same color; this is the rest of nonalteration, rest without ἀλλοίωσις. Or something can be moved in the sense of withering and yet at the same time be moved in still another way, namely, by being altered: on the withering tree the leaves dry up, the green becomes yellow. The tree that is moved in this twofold sense of φθίσις and ἀλλοίωσις is simultaneously *at rest* insofar as it is the tree that *stands* there.

If we perceive all these overlapping "appearances" as types of movedness, we gain an insight into their fundamental character, which Aristotle fixes in the word and the concept μεταβολή. Every instance of movedness is a change from something (ἔκ τινος) into something (εἴς τι). When we speak of a change in the weather or a change of mood, what we have in mind is an "alteration." We also speak of "exchange points" where commercial goods change hands in business transactions. But the essential core of what the *Greeks* meant in thinking μεταβολή is attained only by observing that in a change [*Umschlag*]⁴ something heretofore hidden and absent comes into appearance. (In German: *"Aus-schlag"* [the breaking out of, e.g., a blossom] and *"Durchschlag"* [breaking through so as to appear on the other side].)

(We of today must do two things: first, free ourselves from the notion that movement is *primarily* change of place; and second, learn to see how for the Greeks movement as a mode of *being* has the character of emerging into presencing.)

[320] Φύσις is ἀρχὴ κινήσεως, origin and ordering of change, such that each thing that changes has this ordering within itself. At the very beginning of the chapter, φύσει-beings were contrasted with other beings, but the second group were not expressly named and characterized. There now follows an explicit and definite, and yet curiously narrow, delineation:

IV. "However, a couch (bedstead) and a robe and any other kind (of such things) that there is *insofar as* it is cited and grasped according to a given way of addressing it (e.g., as a robe) and inasmuch as it comes from a productive know-how, (such a thing) has *absolutely no* impulse to change arising from itself. *However, insofar as* it also pertains to such things (in a given instance) to be made of stone or of earth or of a mixture of the two, they *do have* in themselves an impulse to change, but they have it only to this extent." (192 b16–20)

Here, such beings as "plants," animals, earth, and air are now contrasted with beings such as bedsteads, robes, shields, wagons, ships, and houses. The first group are "growing things" [*"Gewächse"*] in the same broad sense that we employ when we speak of a "field under growth." The second group are "artifacts" (ποιούμενα), in German, *Gemächte*, although this last term must be stripped of any derogatory connotations. The contrast achieves its

191

purpose – to further highlight the proper essence of φύσει ὄντα and φύσις – only if it stays within the parameters of the guiding perspective, that of an inquiry into moving beings and their movedness and into the ἀρχή of that movedness.

But are bedsteads and garments, shields and houses moving things? Indeed they are, but usually we encounter them in the kind of movement that typifies things at rest and therefore is hard to perceive. Their "rest" has the character of having-been-completed, having-been-produced, and, on the basis of *these* determinations, as standing "there" and lying present before us. Today we easily overlook this special kind of rest and so too the movedness that corresponds to it, or at least [321] we do not take it essentially enough as the proper and distinguishing characteristic of the being of these beings. And why? Because under the spell of our modern way of being, we are addicted to thinking of beings as *objects* and allowing the being of beings to be exhausted in the objectivity of the object. But for Aristotle, the issue here is to show that artifacts *are what* they are and *how* they are precisely in the movedness of production and thus in the rest of having-been-produced. Above all he wants to show that this movedness has another ἀρχή and that beings that are moved in this other way are related to their ἀρχή in a different manner. (There is no reason to read ἀρχή in place of ὁρμή in this text, as Simplicius does, for ὁρμή, "impulse," illustrates well the essence of ἀρχή.)

The ἀρχή of artifacts is τέχνη. Τέχνη does not mean "technique" in the sense of methods and acts of production, nor does it mean "art" in the wider sense of an ability to produce something. Rather, τέχνη is a form of knowledge; it means: know-how in, i.e., familiarity with, what grounds every act of making and producing. It means knowing what the production of, e.g., a bedstead, must come to, where it must achieve its end and be completed. In Greek, this "end" is called τέλος. That whereat an act of producing "ceases" is the table as finished – but finished precisely *as* table, as what a table is and how a table looks. The εἶδος must stand in view beforehand, and this antecedently envisioned appearance, εἶδος προαιρετόν, is the end, τέλος, that about which τέχνη has its know-how. Only *for this reason* does τέχνη also come to be defined as the kind and manner of procedure that we call "technique." But again, the essence of τέχνη is not movement in the sense of the activity of manipulating things; rather, it is know-how in dealing with things. And τέλος does not mean "goal" or "purpose," but "end" in the sense of the finite perfectedness that determines the essence of something; *only for this reason* can it be taken as a goal and posited as a purpose. However, the τέλος, the antecedently envisioned appearance of the bedstead, is what is known by the person with the know-how, and it exists in *that person*. Only in this way is it the origin of the idea of the thing and the ordering of its manufacture. [322] The εἶδος in itself is not the ἀρχή of the artifact. Rather, the εἶδος προαιρετόν, i.e., the προαίρεσις, i.e., the τέχνη, is the ἀρχή of the artifact.

In the case of artifacts, therefore, the ἀρχή of their movedness – and thus of the rest that characterizes their being-completed and being-made – is *not* in the artifacts themselves but in something else, in the ἀρχιτέκτων, the one who controls the τέχνη as ἀρχή. This would seem to complete the contrast of artifacts with φύσει ὄντα, for these latter are called φύσει ὄντα precisely because they have the ἀρχή of their movedness *not* in another being but in the beings that they themselves are (to the degree that they are these beings). But according to Aristotle's explanation, the difference between artifacts and growing things is not at all so simple. Even the structure of the section we are considering gives a hint: ἦ μὲν – ἦ δέ: "insofar as artifacts are seen in this way...insofar as they are seen in another way..." We can consider the ποιούμενα from two perspectives. In the *first perspective* we consider the produced thing insofar as it is cited and grasped according to a given way of addressing it: κατηγορία.

Here we run across a use of κατηγορία that goes back *prior* to its establishment as a philosophical "term." It was Aristotle, in fact, who established the term, but he did so on the basis of the common usage that is operative in the present text. We translate κατηγορία as the "addressing" of something [*Ansprechung*], but even then we hardly capture the full meaning in the Greek. Κατὰ-ἀγορεύειν means: to accuse someone to his face in the ἀγορά, the public court, of being "the very one who..." From this comes the broader meaning: to address something as this or that, so that, in and through our addressing it, the addressed thing is put forth into the public view, into the open, as manifest. Κατηγορία is the naming of what something is: house, tree, sky, sea, hard, red, healthy. On the other hand, "category" as a philosophical "term" means a *special* kind of addressing. We are able to address a present thing *as* a house or a tree only insofar as we have already beforehand, and without words, addressed what we encounter – i.e., have brought it into our open field of "vision" – as something standing-on-its-own, a thing. Likewise, [323] we can address a garment as "red" only if from the outset and without words it has already been addressed in terms of something like quality. Standing-on-its-own ("substance") and quality ("of-what-sort-ness") and the like constitute the being (beingness) of beings. Therefore the "categories" are special ways of addressing things – χατηγορίαι in an emphatic sense – for they sustain all our habitual and everyday ways of addressing things; they underlie those everyday statements, which in turn get developed into assertions, "judgments." *Conversely*, only for this reason can one discover the "categories" by using the assertion, the λόγος, as a clue. This is why Kant has to "derive" the table of categories from the table of *judgments*. Thus, knowledge of categories as determinations of the being of beings – what people call metaphysics – is, in an essential sense, knowledge of λόγος – i.e., *"logic."* Therefore, metaphysics receives this name at the stage where it comes to the *full* (as full as is possible for it) *consciousness of itself*, in *Hegel*. [The *Science of Logic* is absolute knowledge of the knowable as something known or represented. (In modern philosophy, the state of being represented is beingness or being.)]

In the text we are considering, χατηγορία is used in a *pre*terminological sense. Inasmuch as we consider something produced – e.g., a bedstead – within the horizon opened up by the everyday way of addressing and naming, we take such a being according to its appearance as something of use. In this capacity it does *not* have the ἀρχὴ χινήσεως in itself. But we can consider it from a *second perspective:* we can take this very same being, the bedstead, as something made out of wood, hence as a piece of wood. As wood, it is part of a tree trunk, a growing thing. This tree has the ἀρχὴ χινήσεως in itself. The bedstead, on the other hand, is not wood as such, but merely wooden, made *out of* wood. Only what is something other than wood can be wooden. This is why we never call a tree trunk wooden, but we do say a person's bearing is "wooden," and in German one can say an apple is "wooden." What the bedstead is when taken according to the χατηγορία, namely, a usable thing that looks thus and so, has no absolutely necessary relation to wood. It could [324] just as well be made out of stone or steel. Its woodenness is συμβεβηχός, that is to say: in reference to what the bed "really" and properly is, woodenness *appears only incidentally*. Insofar – but *only* insofar – as it is just wood, a bedstead certainly does have the ἀρχὴ χινήσεως in itself, for wood is the what-has-grown of a growing thing.

On the basis of this contrast between artifacts and growing things Aristotle can summarize what he has said up to now and thus establish an initial outline of the essence of φύσις:

V. "Accordingly, φύσις is something like origin and ordering and therefore originary [source] of the self-moving and resting of something in which it antecedently (ὑπό) exercises originating and ordering power (ἄρχει) primarily in itself and from itself *and toward itself* and thus *never* in such a way that the ἀρχή would appear (in the being) only incidentally." (192 b20–23)

Here, simply and almost severely, Aristotle sketches the essential outline: φύσις is not just the origin and ordering of the movedness of a moving being, but also belongs to this moving being itself in such a way that this being, in itself and from itself and toward itself, orders its own movedness. Hence the ἀρχή is not like the starting point of a push, which pushes the thing away and leaves it to itself. Rather, something determined by φύσις not only stays with itself in its movedness but precisely goes back into itself even as it unfolds in accordance with the movedness (the change).

We can illustrate the kind of essence that is meant here by the example of "growing things" in the narrower sense ("plants"). While the "plant" sprouts, emerges, and expands into the open, it simultaneously goes back into its roots, insofar as it plants them firmly in the closed ground and thus takes its stand. The act of self-unfolding emergence is inherently a going-back-into-itself. This kind of becoming present is φύσις. But it must not be thought of as a kind of built-in "motor" that drives something, nor as an "organizer" on hand somewhere, directing the thing. [325] Nonetheless, we might be tempted to fall back on the notion that φύσει-determined beings could be a kind that *make themselves.* So easily and spontaneously does this idea suggest itself that it has become normative for the interpretation of living nature in particular, as is shown by the fact that ever since modern thinking became dominant, a living being has been understood as an "organism." No doubt a good deal of time has yet to pass before we learn to see that the idea of "organism" and of the "organic" is a purely modern, mechanistic-technological concept, according to which "growing things" are interpreted as artifacts that make themselves. Even the word and concept "plant" takes what grows as something "planted," something sown and cultivated. And it is part of the essential illogicality of language that in German we nonetheless speak of greenhouses as *Gewächshäusern* (houses for what grows) instead of as *Pflanzenhäusern* (houses for what has been planted).

In the case of every artifact, however, the origin of the making is "outside" the thing made. Viewed from the perspective of the artifact, the ἀρχή always and only appears as something "in addition." In order to avoid misunderstanding φύσις as a kind of *self-producing* and the φύσει ὄντα merely as a special kind of artifact, Aristotle clarifies the καθ᾽ αὐτό by adding καὶ μὴ κατὰ συμβεβηκός. The καὶ here has the meaning of "and that is to say..."

This phrase seeks to ward off an error, and Aristotle explains its meaning by an example:

VI. "But I add the phrase 'not like something appearing in addition' because someone, entirely of and by himself, might become the (originating and ordering) source of 'health' for himself, and could at the same time be a doctor. He has the medical know-how *in himself*, but not insofar as he regains his health. Rather in this case, being a doctor and regaining health happen to have come together in one and the same person. But for this very reason the two also remain separated from each other, each on its own." (192 b23–27)

Aristotle, a doctor's son, likes to use examples drawn from medical "πρᾶξις," and he does so in other contexts as well. [326] Here he gives us the case of a doctor who treats himself and thereby regains his health. Two kinds of movedness are interwoven here in a peculiar way: ἰάτρευσις, the practicing of medicine as a τέχνη, and ὑγίαισις, the regaining of health as "φύσις." In the present case, that of a doctor who treats himself, both movements are found in one and the same being, in this specific person. The same holds for the respective ἀρχή of each of the two "movements." The "doctor" has the ἀρχή of regaining his health ἐν ἑαυτῷ, *in* himself, but not καθ αὑτόν, not according to himself, not insofar as he is a *doctor.* The origin and ordering of regaining health is not being a doctor but being human, and this only insofar as the human being is a ζῷον, a living being that lives only inasmuch as it *"is a body"* ["*leibt*"]. As even we say, a healthy "nature," capable of resistance, is the real origin and ordering of regaining health. Without this αρχή, all medical practice is in vain. But on the other hand, the doctor has the ἀρχή of practicing medicine in himself: being a doctor is the origin and ordering of the treatment. But this ἀρχή, namely, this know-how and *antecedent view* (τέχνη) of what health is and what pertains to keeping and regaining it (the εἶδος τῆς ὑγιείας) – this ἀρχή is not in the human being qua human but is something in addition, attained by someone only through studying and learning. Consequently, in relation to regaining health, τέχνη itself is always merely something that can appear in addition. Doctors and the practice of medicine do not grow the way trees do. Of course, we do speak of a "born" doctor, by which we mean that a person brings with him or her the talent for recognizing diseases and treating the sick. But these talents are never, in the manner of φύσις, the ἀρχή for being a doctor, inasmuch as they do not unfold *from out of themselves* toward the end of being a doctor.

Nonetheless, at this point the following objection could be raised. Say two doctors suffer from the same disease under the same conditions, and each one treats herself. However, between the two cases of illness there lies a period of [327] five hundred years, during which the "progress" of modern medicine has taken place. The doctor of today has at her disposal a "better" technique, and she regains her health, whereas the one who lived earlier dies of her disease. So apparently the ἀρχή of the cure of today's doctor *is precisely* the τέχνη. However, there is something further to consider here. For one thing, the fact of not dying, in the sense of prolonging one's life, is not yet necessarily the recovery of health. The fact that people live longer today is no proof that they are healthier; one might even conclude the contrary. But even supposing that the modern doctor, beneficiary of the progress of medicine, not only escapes death for a while but also recovers her health, even then the art of medicine has only better supported and guided φύσις. Τέχνη can merely cooperate with φύσις, can more or less expedite the cure; but as τέχνη it can never replace φύσις and in its stead become the ἀρχή of *health* as such. This could happen only if life as such were to become a "technically" producible artifact. However, at that very moment there would also no longer be such a thing as health, any more than there would be birth and death. Sometimes it seems as if modern humanity is rushing headlong toward this goal of *producing itself technologically*. If humanity achieves this, it will have exploded itself, i.e., *its essence* qua *subjectivity*, into thin air, into a region where the absolutely meaningless is valued as the one and only "meaning" and where preserving this value appears as the human "domination" of the globe. "Subjectivity" is not overcome in this way but merely "tranquilized" in the "eternal progress" of a Chinese-like *"constancy"* ["Konstanz"]. This is the most extreme nonessence [*Unwesen*] in relation to φύσις-οὐσία.

Aristotle also uses this example, in which two different kinds of movedness interweave, as an occasion for determining more clearly the mode and manner in which the ποιούμενα (artifacts) stand in relation to their ἀρχή:

VII. "And the same holds for everything else that belongs among things made. That is to say, none of them has in itself the origin and ordering of its being-made. [328] Rather, some have their ἀρχή in another being and thus have it from the outside, such as, for example, a house and anything else made by hand. Others, however, do indeed have the ἀρχή in themselves, but not inasmuch as they are themselves. To this latter group belong all things that can be 'causes' for themselves in an incidental way." (192 b27–32)

A house has the origin and ordering of its being a house, i.e., something constructed, in the constructor's prior intention to build, which is given concrete form in the architect's blueprint. This blueprint – in Greek terms, the house's *appearance as envisioned beforehand* or, literally, the ἰδέα – orders each step of the actual constructing and governs the choice and use of materials. Even when the house "is standing," it stands on the foundation that has been *laid* for it; however, it never stands *from out of* itself, but always as a mere *construction*. As long as it stands there – in Greek terms, as long as it stands forth into the open and unhidden – the *house*, due to its way of standing, can never place itself back into its ἀρχή. It will never take root in the earth but will always remain merely placed on the earth, built upon it.

But let us take an example: What if someone were to hit himself in the eye and injure the eye by a clumsy movement of his own hand? Certainly both the injury and the movement of the hand are ἐν ταὐτῷ, "in" the same being. However, they do not belong together but have simply happened together, come together συμβεβηκός, incidentally. Therefore, in determining the essence of the φύσει ὄντα, it is not enough merely to say they have the ἀρχή of their movedness in themselves. Rather, we are required to add this special determination: in themselves, specifically inasmuch as they are themselves and are in and with [*bei*] themselves.

[This word "specifically" does not restrict matters but requires us to look into the vast expanse of the unfathomable essence of a mode of being that is denied to all τέχνη because τέχνη renounces any claim to knowing and grounding *truth* as such.]

Aristotle concludes the first stage of his characterization of the essence of φύσις by what seems to be merely a superficial [329] clarification of the meaning of the concepts and expressions that gather around the essence and the concept and the word φύσις:

VIII. "Φύσις, therefore, is what has been said. Everything that possesses this kind of origin and ordering 'has' φύσις. And all these things *are* (have being) of the type called beingness. Φύσις is, in each case, such as lies present of and by itself, and is always *in* a thing that lies present in this way (constituting its lying-present). In accordance with φύσις, however, are these things as well as everything that belongs to these things in themselves, of and by themselves, as, e.g., it belongs to fire to be borne upward. In point of fact this (being borne upward) is not φύσις, nor does it possess φύσις, but it certainly is from φύσις and in accordance with φύσις. So now it has been settled what φύσις is, as well as what is meant by 'from φύσις,' and 'in accordance with φύσις.'" (192 b32–193 a2)

It may strike the reader that even at this point we continue to leave the basic word φύσις untranslated. We do not call it *natura* or "nature" because these names are too ambiguous and overburdened and, in general, because they get their validity as names for φύσις only by means of a peculiarly oriented interpretation of φύσις. In fact, we do not even have a word that would be appropriate for naming and thinking the essence of φύσις as we have explained it thus far. (We are tempted to say "emergence" [*Aufgang*], but without intermediate steps we cannot give this word the fullness and definiteness it requires.) However, the chief reason for continuing to use the untranslated and perhaps untranslatable word φύσις lies in the fact that everything said up to this point toward the clarification of its essence is only prologue. In fact, up until now we do not even know what kind of reflection and inquiry is already at work when we ask about φύσις as we have been doing. And these things Aristotle tells us only now in the passage we have just read, a text that establishes with extreme succinctness the horizon within which the discussion moves, both the preceding part and especially what is to follow.

The decisive sentence reads: καὶ ἔστι πάντα ταῦτα οὐσία, "and all these – namely, φύσει-beings – have being of the type called *beingness*." This expression "beingness," [330] which hardly strikes the ear as elegant, is the only adequate translation for οὐσία. Granted, even "beingness" says *very little*, in fact, almost nothing, but this is precisely its advantage. We avoid the usual and familiar "translations" (i.e., interpretations) of οὐσία as "substance" and "essence." Φύσις is οὐσία, beingness – that which characterizes a being as such; in a word: being. The word οὐσία was not originally a philosophical "term" any more than was the word κατηγορία, which we have already explained. The word οὐσία was first coined as a technical "term" by Aristotle. This coining consists in the fact that Aristotle thoughtfully draws out of the content of the word a crucial element and then holds on to it firmly and clearly. Nonetheless, at the time of Aristotle and even later, the word still retained its ordinary meaning, whereby it signified house and home, holdings, financial means; we might also say "present assets," "property," *what lies present*. We must think in terms of this meaning if we want to get at the naming power of οὐσία as a basic philosophical word. And then right away we also see how simple and obvious is the explanation Aristotle provides for the word οὐσία in the text above: ὑποκείμενον γάρ τι καὶ ἐν ὑποκειμένῳ ἐστὶν ἡ φύσις ἀεί, "for in each case φύσις is like a lying-present and 'in' a lying-present." One might object that our translation here is "wrong." Aristotle's sentence does *not* say ὑποκεῖσθαι γάρ τι, a "lying-present" [*Vorliegen*] but rather "something that lies present" [*ein Vorliegendes*]. But here we must pay strict attention to what the sentence is supposed to explain: namely, to what extent φύσις is οὐσία and thus has the character of beingness (being). This requires of us (as is so often the case with the philosophical use of the Greek language, but too little noticed by later thinkers) that we understand the participle ὑποκείμενον in a way analogous to our understanding of τὸ ὄν. Τὸ ὄν can mean *a being*, i.e., this particular being itself; but it can also mean that which *is*, that which has being. Analogously ὑποχείμενον can mean "that which lies present," but it can also mean "something distinguished by lying-present," and so it can mean the very lying-present itself. [331] (The unusually rich and manifold forms of the participle in the Greek language – the truly philosophical language – are no mere accident, but their meaning has hardly yet been recognized.)

In accordance with the explanation of οὐσία by way of ὑποχείμενον, the beingness of beings means for the Greeks the same as to lie present "there," i.e., "in front of..." In this connection let us recall that toward the beginning of this chapter, at 192 b13 (and later at 193 a36), instead of τὰ ὄντα Aristotle says συνεστῶτα (the stable: that which has taken a stand). Accordingly, "being" means the same as "standing on its own." But "to stand" is quite the opposite of "to lie." Yes, that is true if we take each of them separately. But if we take "to stand" and "to lie" in terms of what they share in common, then each manifests itself precisely through its opposite. Only what stands can fall and thus lie; and only what lies can be put upright and thus stand. The Greeks understand "being" sometimes as "to stand on its own" (ὑπόστασις, *substantia*) and sometimes as "lying present" (ὑποχείμενον, *subjectum*), but both have equal weight, for in both cases the Greeks have one and the same thing in view: being-present of and by itself, presencing. The decisive principle that guides Aristotle's interpretation of φύσις declares that φύσις must be understood as οὐσία, as a kind and mode of presencing.

Now, it has already been established through ἐπαγωγή that φύσει ὄντα are χινούμενα, that is to say: φύσει-beings are beings in the state of movedness. Accordingly, it is now a question of understanding movedness as a manner and mode of being, i.e., of presencing. Only when this is accomplished can we understand φύσις in its essence as the *origin and ordering of the movedness of what moves from out of itself* and toward itself.[5] Thus it is clear in principle that the question about the φύσις of the φύσει ὄντα is not a search for ontic properties to be found *in* beings of this sort, but rather an inquiry into the being of those beings, from which being it gets determined antecedently in what way beings of this kind of being can have properties at all.

[332] The next section, which forms the transition to a new attempt at determining the essence of φύσις, shows how decisively Aristotle's explanation of φύσις heretofore has, in the meanwhile, broadened explicitly into a principled reflection, and it shows how necessary this reflection is for the task confronting us:

IX. "But it is ridiculous to want to prove *that* φύσις *is*, because this (being as φύσις) appears of and by itself, insofar as [not 'that'] beings of this type show up everywhere among beings. But to demonstrate something that appears of and by itself (and above all) to prove something that refuses to appear – these are the actions of someone who cannot distinguish (from one another) something that of and by itself is familiar to all knowledge from something that of and by itself is not. But that such a thing can happen (i.e., such an inability to make the distinction) is not outside the realm of possibility: Someone born blind might try, through a sequence of reflections, to acquire some knowledge about colors. Of necessity in this case, such people arrive at an assertion about the nominal meanings of the words for colors, but by these means they never perceive the least thing about colors themselves." (193 a3–9)

"But it is ridiculous to try to prove *that* φύσις *is*." But why? Should we not take seriously some such procedure? Without a prior proof *that* something like φύσις "is," all explanations about φύσις remain pointless. So let us attempt such a proof. But in *that* case we have to suppose that φύσις *is not*, or at least that it is not yet proven in its being and as being. Therefore, in the course of our demonstration we may not permit ourselves to appeal *to it*. But if we take this restriction seriously, how could we ever find or point to something like φύσει ὄντα, growing things – animals, for example – the very things by means of which the being of φύσις is supposed to be proven? Such a procedure is impossible because it must already appeal to the being of φύσις, [333] and precisely for that reason this kind of proof is always superfluous. Already by its first step it attests of and by itself that its project is unnecessary. In fact, the whole undertaking is ridiculous. The being of φύσις and φύσις as being remain unprovable because φύσις does not need a proof, for wherever a φύσει-being stands in the open, φύσις has already shown itself and stands in view.

Regarding those who demand and attempt such a proof, one can at best draw their attention to the fact that they do not see *the very thing* that they already see, that they have no eye for what already stands in view for them. To be sure, *this* eye – which is not just for what one sees but for what one already has in view when one sees what one sees – this eye does not belong to everyone. This eye has the ability to differentiate what appears of and by itself and comes into the open according to its own essence, from what does not appear of and by itself. What appears antecedently – as φύσις does in the φύσει ὄντα, as history does in all historical occurrences, as art does in all artworks, as "life" does in all living things – what already stands in view is seen with the greatest difficulty, is grasped very seldomly, is almost always falsified into a mere addendum, and for these reasons simply overlooked. Of course, not everyone needs to explicitly hold in view what is already seen in all experience, but only those who make a claim to deciding, or even to asking, about nature, history, art, human beings, or beings as a whole. Certainly not every one of us who through action or thinking dwells in these regions of beings needs to consider explicitly what is already seen. But of course neither may we overlook it or toss it off as insignificant, as something merely "abstract" – that is, if we really want to stand where we stand.

What appears in advance, the current *being* of a being, is not something abstracted from beings later on, something depleted and thinned out, finally no more than a vapor, [334] nor is it something that becomes accessible only when we who are thinking "reflect" on ourselves. On the contrary, the way to what is already seen but not yet understood, much less conceptualized, is the leading-toward that we already mentioned, namely, ἐπαγωγή. This is what lets us see ahead into the distance, into what we ourselves are not and least of all could ever be, into something far off that nevertheless is most near, nearer than everything that lies in our hand or resounds in our ear or lies before our eyes. In order *not* to overlook what is nearest yet likewise farthest, we must stand above the obvious and the "factual." Differentiating between what appears of and by itself from what does not appear of and by itself is a κρίνειν in the genuinely Greek sense: separating out what is *superior* from what is inferior. Through this "critical" ability for differentiating, which is always decision, the human being is lifted out of mere captivation by what presses upon and preoccupies him or her and is placed out beyond it, into the relation to being. In the real sense of the word, one becomes ek-sistent, one ek-sists instead of merely "living" and snatching at "reality" in the so-called "concern for real life," where "reality" is only a refuge in the long-standing flight from being. According to Aristotle, those who cannot make such a distinction live like people blind from birth who work at making colors accessible to themselves by reasoning about the names they have heard them called. They choose a way that can never bring them to their goal, because the only road leading there is "seeing," and that is precisely what is denied to the blind. Just as there are people blind to colors, so there are people *blind to* φύσις. And if we recall that φύσις has been defined as only one kind of οὐσία (beingness), then those blind to φύσις are merely one type of people blind to being. Presumably those blind to being far outnumber those blind to color, and what is more, the power of their blindness is even stronger and more obstinate, for they are less obvious and mostly go unrecognized. As a consequence they even pass for the only ones who really see. [335] But obviously our relation to that which, of and by itself, appears in advance and eludes all plans for proof must be hard to hold on to in its originality and truth. Otherwise Aristotle would not need to explicitly remind us of it nor attack this blindness to being. And our relation to being is hard to hold on to because it seems to be made easy for us by our common comportment toward beings – so easy, in fact, that our relation to being looks as if it could be supplanted *by* this comportment and be nothing else *but* this comportment.

Aristotle's remarks on the desire to prove *that* φύσις "shows up" play a special role within the whole of his exposition, and we immediately see this role from the following passage:

X. "But for some (thinkers) φύσις, and so too the beingness of beings from φύσις, appears to be whatever is already and primarily present in any given thing, but in itself lacking all form. In this view the φύσις of the bedstead is the wood, the φύσις of the statue is the bronze. According to Antiphon's explanation, this is shown in the following way: If one buries a bedstead in the earth and if the decay goes so far that a sprout comes up, then what is generated (from this sprout) is not a bedstead but wood. Consequently something that has been brought about in accordance with rules and know-how [e.g., the bedstead made out of wood] is certainly something there, but only insofar as it has appeared incidentally. But its beingness lies in that (the φύσις) which abides through it all, holding itself together throughout everything it 'undergoes.' Furthermore, if any one of these [wood, bronze] has already undergone the same process [of having been brought into a form] with respect to yet another – as have bronze and gold with respect to water, or bones and wood with respect to earth, or similarly anything else among all other beings – then it is precisely the latter (water, earth) that *are* φύσις and that therefore are the beingness of the former (as beings)." (193 a9–21)

[336] From a superficial point of view, it now seems Aristotle moves from clarifying the correct attitude for determining the essence of φύσις as a manner of being *over to* characterizing the opinion of other thinkers with regard to φύσις. But his purpose here is not *just* to mention other views for the sake of some sort of scholarly completeness. Nor does he intend simply to reject those other views in order to fashion a contrasting background for his own interpretation. Rather, Aristotle's intention is to explain Antiphon's interpretation of φύσις in the light of his own formulation of the question, and so to put Antiphon's interpretation, for the first time, on the *only* path that can lead to an adequate determination of the essence of φύσις as Aristotle envisions it. Up to now we know only this much: φύσις is οὐσία, the being of some beings, specifically of those beings that have been seen antecedently to have the character of κινούμενα, beings that are in movement. Even more clearly: φύσις is the origin and ordering (ἀρχή) of the movedness of something that moves of itself.

If φύσις is οὐσία, a manner of being, then the correct determination of the essence of φύσις depends, first, on an adequately original grasp of the essence of οὐσία and, second, on a corresponding interpretation of what it is that we encounter, in the light of a given conception of being, as a φύσει-being. Now, the Greeks understand οὐσία as stable presencing. They give no reasons for this interpretation of being any more than they question the ground of its truth. For in the first beginning of thought, the fact that the being of beings is grasped at all is more essential than the question of its ground.

But how does the Sophist Antiphon, who comes from the Eleatic school, interpret φύσις in the light of being, conceived as stable presencing? He says: *only* earth, water, air, and fire truly *are* in accordance with φύσις. With this, however, there occurs a decision of the greatest import: what always seems to be *more* than mere (pure) earth – e.g., the wood "formed" out of the earth and even more so [337] the bedstead fashioned from the wood – all this "more" is in fact *less* being, because this "more" has the character of articulating, impressing, fitting, and forming, in short, the character of ῥυθμός. Things of this sort change, are unstable, are without stability. From wood one can just as well make a table and a shield and a ship; what is more, the wood itself is only something formed out of the earth. The earth is what truly perdures throughout, whereas the changes of ῥυθμός happen to it only now and again. What properly is, is τὸ ἀρρύθμιστον πρῶτον, the primarily and intrinsically *un*formed, which remains stably present throughout the changes of shape and form that it undergoes. From Antiphon's theses it is clear that bedsteads, statues, robes, and gowns *are* only inasmuch as they are wood, iron, and the like, i.e., only inasmuch as they consist of something more stable. The most stable, however, are earth, water, fire, and air – the "elements." But if the "elemental" is what most is, then this interpretation of φύσις – as the primary formless that sustains everything that is formed – implies that a decision has likewise been made about the interpretation of every "being," and that φύσις, as conceived here, is equated with *being pure and simple.* But this means the essence of οὐσία as stable presencing is given a fixed and very specific direction. According to *this* definition of its essence, all things, whether growing things or artifacts, never truly are – and yet they are not nothing; hence they are non-being, not fully sufficing for beingness. In contrast with these non-beings, only the "elemental" qualifies as the essence of being.

The following section gives an insight into the importance of the interpretation of φύσις currently under discussion, i.e., as the πρῶτον ἀρρύθμιστον χαθ᾽ ἑαυτόν (the primarily and intrinsically unformed):

XI. "Therefore different people say that either fire, or earth, or air, or water, or some of these ('elements'), or all of them, are φύσις *proper* and thus are the being of beings as a whole. For whatever each of these people [338] has taken antecedently (ὑπό) to be such as lies present in this way, whether it be one or many, that he declares to be beingness as such, whereas all the rest are modifications or states of what properly is or that into which a being is divided (and thus dissolved into relations); and each of these (that in each case constitute φύσις) therefore remains the same, staying with itself (i.e., there does *not* accrue to them any change by which they might go out of themselves), whereas other beings come to be and pass away 'without limit.'" (193 a21–28)

Here Aristotle summarizes the distinction between φύσις as the "elemental," taken as the only proper beings (the πρῶτον ἀρρύθμιστον καθ᾽ αὑτό), and non-beings (πάθη, ἕξεις, διαθέσεις, ῥυθμός) by once again introducing the opinions of other teachers and by making clear reference to Democritus. [From the viewpoint of the history of being, the basis of "materialism" as a metaphysical stance becomes apparent here.]

But more important is the last sentence of the section, where Aristotle thinks out and defines this distinction even more precisely by formulating it in terms of the contrast between ἀίδιον and γινόμενον ἀπειράκις. We usually think of this contrast as one between the "eternal" and the "temporal." On those terms, the primarily-present unformed is the "eternal," whereas all ῥυθμός, as change, is the "temporal." Nothing could be clearer than this distinction; yet one does not consider that this understanding of the distinction between eternity and temporality erroneously reads back into the Greek interpretation of "beings" notions that are merely "Hellenistic" and "Christian" and, in general, "modern." The "eternal" is taken as what endures without limit, with neither beginning nor end, whereas the "temporal" is limited duration. The viewpoint guiding this distinction is based on duration. Certainly the Greeks are acquainted *also* with this distinction regarding beings, but they always think the difference on the basis of their understanding of being. And this is quite distorted by the "Christian" distinction. [339] Already just from the Greek words for these concepts it is clear that the opposition of ἀίδιον and γινόμενον ἀπειράκις cannot refer to what limitlessly endures as opposed to what is limited, for in the text the so-called temporal means *limitless* coming-to-be and passing away. What is opposed to the ἀίδιον, the "eternal" as supposedly "limitless," is *also* something *limitless*: ἄπειρον (cf. πέρας). Now, how is all this supposed to hit upon *the decisive* contrast in terms of which "being" proper is determined? The so-called eternal is in Greek ἀίδιον – ἀείδιον; and ἀεί means not just "all the time" and "incessant." Rather, first of all it means "at any given time." Ὁ ἀεὶ βασιλεύων = the one who is ruler *at the time* – *not* the "eternal" ruler. With the word ἀεί what one has in view is the notion of "staying for a while," specifically in the sense of presencing. The ἀίδιον is something present of and by itself without other assistance, and *for this reason* perhaps something constantly present. Here we are thinking not with regard to "duration" but with regard to presencing. This is the clue for correctly interpreting the opposing concept, γινόμενον ἀπειράχις. In Greek thought, what comes to be and passes away is what is sometimes present, sometimes absent – without limit. But πέρας in Greek philosophy is not "limit" in the sense of the outer boundary, the point where something ends. The limit is always what limits, defines, gives footing and stability, that by which and in which something begins and is. Whatever becomes present and absent without limit has *of and by itself* no presencing, and it devolves into instability. The distinction between beings proper and non-beings does not consist in the fact that beings proper perdure without restriction whereas non-beings always have their duration broken off. With regard to duration both could be either restricted or unrestricted. The decisive factor is rather that beings proper are present of and by themselves and for this reason are encountered as what is always already present – ὑποχείμενον πρῶτον. Non-beings, on the other hand, are sometimes present, sometimes absent, because they are present *only* on the basis of something already present; that is, *along with* it they make their appearance or [340] remain absent. Beings (in the sense of the "elemental") are "always 'there,'" non-beings are "always gone" – where "there" and "gone" are understood on the basis of presencing and not with regard to mere "duration." The later distinction between *aeternitas* and *sempiternitas* would come closest to the Greek distinction we have just clarified. *Aeternitas* is the *nunc stans*, *sempiternitas* is the *nunc fluens*. But even here the original essence of being, as the Greeks experienced it, has already vanished. The distinction refers not to the mode of mere duration but only to that of change. What "stays" is the *unchanging*, what flows is the "fleeting," the changing. But both are equally understood in terms of something continuing without interruption.

For the Greeks, however, "being" means: *presencing into the unhidden*. What is decisive is not the duration and extent of the presencing but rather whether the presencing is dispensed into the unhidden and simple, and thus withdrawn into the hidden and inexhausted, or whether presencing is distorted (ψεῦδος) into a mere "looks like," into *"mere appearance,"* instead of being maintained in *un*distortedness (ἀ-τρέχεια). Only by seeing the opposition of unhiddenness and seeming can we adequately know what the essence of οὐσία is for the *Greeks*. Such knowledge is the condition for understanding *at all* Aristotle's interpretation of φύσις; in particular it determines whether we can follow the progression of the new approach, which now follows, toward the conclusive determination of the essence of φύσις.

Before attempting this, we must recall, in its simple coherence, what we have seen up to this point.

According to ἐπαγωγή, φύσει-beings are in the state of movedness. But φύσις itself is the ἀρχή, the origin and ordering, of movedness. From this we may readily conclude that the character of φύσις as origin and ordering will be adequately determined only when we achieve an essential insight into that *for which* φύσις is the origin and *over which* it is the ordering power: κίνησις.

[341] Aristotle lets us see this connection with perfect clarity at the beginning of Book III of the *Physics*, in the first three chapters of which he gives the crucial interpretation of the essence of κίνησις:

Ἐπεὶ δ᾽ ἡ φύσις μέν ἐστιν ἀρχὴ κινήσεως καὶ μεταβολῆς, ἡ δὲ μέθοδος ἡμῖν περὶ φύσεώς ἐστι, δεῖ μὴ λανθάνειν τί ἐστι κίνησις· ἀναγκαῖον γὰρ ἀγνοουμένης αὐτῆς ἀγνοεῖσθαι καὶ τὴν φύσιν. (200 b12–15)

"But now because φύσις is the origin and ordering of movedness, and thus of the change that breaks forth, and because our procedure inquires into φύσις (μέθοδος: the step-by-step inquiry that pursues the subject matter, not our later 'method' in the sense of a certain kind and manner of μέθοδος), in no way must we allow what κίνησις is (in its essence) to remain in hiddenness; for if it (κίνησις) were to remain unfamiliar, φύσις too would necessarily remain in unfamiliarity." [Compare the expression γνώριμον at B, 1, 193 a6, *supra*, where it was a question of blindness with regard to being and essence.]

But in the present context the point is merely to sketch out the basic outline of the essence of φύσις. Then, in section XV to follow (193 b7), the essence of the κίνησις proper to φύσις is finally grasped, but it is not properly developed. Rather, there it is only differentiated from the other realm of beings, the movedness and the rest of "artifacts."

Φύσις is the origin and ordering of the movedness (κίνησις) of a moving being (κινούμενον), and more precisely it is so καθ᾽ αὐτὸ καὶ μὴ κατὰ συμβεβηκός. A φύσει-being, in itself, from itself, and unto itself, *is* such an origin and ordering of the movedness of the moving being it is: moved of and by itself and never incidentally. Thus the characteristic of standing of and by itself must be accorded in a special way to φύσει-beings. A φύσει-being is οὐσία, beingness, in the sense of the German *Liegenschaften*, something lying present of and by itself. And for this reason, some thinkers are overwhelmed and deceived by what merely seems to be the case (δοκεῖ),[6] namely, that in general the essence of φύσις consists simply in being the unformed that is primally present, [342] the πρῶτον ἀρρύθμιστον, and, as such, in ruling (ὑπάρχον) normatively over the being of everything that in some other way still "is." Aristotle does not formally reject this way of conceiving φύσις. But the word δοχεῖ hints at such a rejection. We would do well to consider right now why the interpretation of φύσις as put forth by Antiphon must necessarily remain inadequate:

(1) Antiphon's doctrine does not consider the fact that φύσει-beings are *in* movedness, that is to say, that movedness co-constitutes the being of these beings. On the contrary, according to his understanding of φύσις, all character of movement, all alteration and changing circumstantiality (ῥυθμός) devolves into something only incidentally attaching to beings. Movement is unstable and therefore a non-being.

(2) Beingness is indeed conceived as stability, but one-sidedly in favor of the always-already-underlying. Thus,

(3) The other moment of the essence of οὐσία is omitted: *presencing*, which is the decisive factor in the Greek concept of being. We try to bring out in a word what is most proper to it by saying "presencing" [*Anwesung*] instead of "presentness" [*Anwesenheit*]. What we mean here is not mere presence [*Vorhandenheit*], and certainly not something that is exhausted merely in stability; rather: *presencing*, in the sense of coming forth into the unhidden, placing itself into the open. One does not get at the meaning of presencing by referring to mere duration.

(4) But the interpretation of φύσις given by Antiphon and the others understands the being of the φύσει ὄντα via a reference to "beings" (the "elemental"). This procedure of explaining being through beings instead of "understanding" beings from being results in the aforementioned mis-understanding of the character of κίνησις and the one-sided interpretation of οὐσία. Accordingly, because Antiphon's doctrine in no way reaches the proper area for thinking about being, [343] Aristotle obviously must re-ject this conception of φύσις as he makes the transition to his own proper interpretation of φύσις. We read:

XII. "Consequently, in one way φύσις is spoken of *as follows:* it is what primarily and antecedently underlies each single thing as 'the order-able' for beings that have in themselves the origin and ordering of movedness and thus of change. But in the other way, [φύσις is addressed] as the placing into the form, i.e., as the appearance, (namely, that) which shows itself for our addressing it." (193 a28–31)

We read and are astonished, for the sentence begins with οὖν, "con-sequently." The transition expresses no rejection of the aforementioned doctrine. On the contrary, the doctrine is obviously taken over, albeit with the stricture that in it we find only εἱς τρόπος, *one* way of understanding the essence of φύσις, namely, as ὕλη ("matter"). ῞Ετερος τρόπος, the other way, which Aristotle develops in the following sections, conceives of φύσις as μορφή ("form"). In this distinction between ὕλη and μορφή (matter and form) we quite easily recognize the distinction that we previously discussed: πρῶτον ἀρρύθμιστον, that which is primarily unstructured, and ῥυθμός, structure. But Aristotle does not simply replace Antiphon's distinction with that of ὕλη and μορφή. Antiphon considered ῥυθμός (structure) only as something unstable that happens to attach itself incidentally to what alone is stable, to what is unstructured (matter); but for Aristotle, according to the thesis we have just read, μορφή too has the distinction of determining the essence of φύσις. Both interpretations of φύσις are given equal rank, and this offers the possibility of constructing a double concept of φύσις. But in line with this, the first task incumbent upon us is to show that μορφή is the proper characteristic of the essence of φύσις.

This is the way it seems at first glance, but in fact everything shapes up quite differently. The ὕλη–μορφή distinction is not simply another formula for ἀρρύθμιστον–ῥυθμός. Rather, it lifts the question of φύσις onto an entirely new level where precisely the unasked question about the κίνησις-character of [344] φύσις gets answered, and where φύσις for the first time is adequately conceived as οὐσία, a kind of presencing. This likewise implies that, despite appearances to the contrary, the aforementioned theory of Antiphon is rejected with the sharpest kind of refutation. We can see all this with sufficient clarity only if we understand the now emerging distinction between ὕλη–μορφή in an Aristotelian – i.e., Greek – sense and do not lose this understanding again right away. We are constantly on the verge of losing it because the distinction between "matter" and "form" is a common road that Western thinking has traveled for centuries now. The distinction between content and form passes for the most obvious of all things obvious. Therefore, why should not the Greeks, too, have already thought according to this "schema"? ῞Υλη–μορφή was translated by the Romans as *materia* and *forma*. With the interpretation implied in this translation the distinction was carried over into the Middle Ages and modern times. Kant understands it as the distinction between "matter" and "form," which he explains as the distinction between the "determinable" and its "determination." (Cf. *The Critique of Pure Reason*, "The Amphiboly of Concepts of Reflection," A266, B322.) With this we reach the point furthest removed from Aristotle's Greek distinction.

῞Υλη in the ordinary sense means "forest," "thicket," the "woods" in which the hunter hunts. But it likewise means the woods that yield wood as construction material. From this, ὕλη comes to mean material for any and every kind of building and "production." By having recourse to the "original" meaning of words (as one likes to do) we are supposed to have demonstrated that ὕλη means the same as "material." Yes, except that on closer inspection it is only that the crucial *question* now obtrudes for the first time. If ὕλη means "material" *for* "production," then the determination of the essence of this so-called material depends on the interpretation of "production." But surely μορφή does not mean "production." Rather, it means "shape," and the shape is precisely the "form" into which the "material" is brought by imprinting and molding, i.e., by the act of "forming."

[345] Yes, except that fortunately Aristotle himself tells us how he thinks μορφή, and he does so in the very sentence that introduces this concept that is so crucial for his φύσις-interpretation: ἡ μορφὴ καὶ τὸ εἶδος τὸ κατὰ τὸν λόγον: "μορφή, and this means τὸ εἶδος that is in accordance with the λόγος." Μορφή must be understood from εἶδος, and εἶδος must be understood in relation to λόγος. But εἶδος (which Plato also expressed as ἰδέα) and λόγος name concepts that, under the titles "idea" and *"ratio"* (reason), indicate fundamental positions taken by Western humanity that are just as equivocal and just as removed from the Greek origin as are "matter" and "form." Nonetheless we must try to reach the original. Εἶδος means the appearance of a thing and of a being in general, but "appearance" in the sense of the aspect, the "looks," the view, ἰδέα, that it offers and can offer only because the being has been put forth into this appearance and, standing in it, is present of and by itself – in a word, *is*. Ἰδέα is "the seen," but not in the sense that it becomes such only through our seeing. Rather, ἰδέα is what something visible offers to our seeing; it is what offers a view; it is the *sightable*. But Plato, overwhelmed as it were by the essence of εἶδος, understood it in turn as something independently present and therefore as something common (κοινόν) to the individual "beings" that "stand in such an appearance." In this way individuals, as subordinate to the ἰδέα as that which properly is, were displaced into the role of non-beings.

As against this, Aristotle demands that we see that the individual beings in any given instance (this house here and that mountain there) are not at all non-beings, but indeed beings insofar as they put themselves forth into the appearance of house and mountain and so first place this appearance into presencing. In other words, εἶδος is genuinely understood as εἶδος only when it appears within the horizon of one's immediate addressing of a being, εἶδος τὸ κατὰ τὸν λόγον. In each case the statement immediately addresses a this and a that as this and that, i.e., as having such and such an appearance. The clue by which we can understand εἶδος and so also μορφή

[346] is λόγος. Therefore, in interpreting the ensuing determination of the essence of μορφή as εἶδος, we must watch whether and to what extent Aristotle himself follows this clue. In anticipation we can say: μορφή is "appearance," more precisely, the act of standing in and placing itself into the appearance; in general, μορφή means: placing into the appearance. Therefore, in what follows when we speak simply of "appearance," we always have in mind the appearance as (and insofar as) it puts *itself* forth into a given thing that is "there for a while" (for example, the "appearance" "table" that puts *itself* forth into this table here). We call an individual thing *das Jeweilige*, "that which is there for a while," because as an individual thing it "stays for a while" in its appearance and preserves the "while" (the presencing) of this appearance, and, by preserving the appearance, stands forth in it and out of it – which means that it *"is"* in the Greek sense of the word.

By translating μορφή as placing into the appearance, we mean to express initially two things that are of equal importance to the sense of the Greek term but that are thoroughly lacking in our word "form." First, placing into the appearance is a mode of presencing, οὐσία. Μορφή is not an *ontic* property present in matter, but a way of *being*. Second, "placing into the appearance" is movedness, κίνησις, which "moment" is radically lacking in the concept of form.

But this reference to the Greek way of understanding the meaning of μορφή in no way constitutes a demonstration of what Aristotle has undertaken to show, namely, that φύσις itself, according to a second way of addressing it, is μορφή. This demonstration, which takes up the rest of the chapter, goes through various stages in such a way that each stage lifts the task of the demonstration one level higher. The demonstration begins in this way:

XIII. "Just as we (loosely) call by the name τέχνη those things produced according to such a know-how, as well as whatever belongs to those kinds of beings, so too we (loosely) designate as φύσις whatever is according to φύσις and hence belongs to beings of this kind. But on the other hand, just as we would [347] never say that something behaves (and is present) in accordance with τέχνη, or that τέχνη is there, when something is a bedstead merely in terms of appropriateness (δυνάμει) but in fact does not at all have the appearance of the bedstead, so neither would we proceed that way in addressing something that has composed itself into a stand by way of φύσις. For whatever is flesh and bone only in terms of appropriateness does not have the φύσις that appertains to it until it achieves the appearance that we refer to in addressing the thing and that we delineate when we say *what* flesh or bone is; nor is (something that is merely appropriate) already a being from φύσις." (193 a31–b3)

How are these sentences supposed to prove that μορφή goes to make up the essence of φύσις? Nothing is said about μορφή at all. On the contrary, Aristotle begins the demonstration in a wholly extrinsic way with a reference to a way of speaking, one that in fact we still use. For example, we may say of a painting by van Gogh, "This is art," or, when we see a bird of prey circling above the forest, "That is nature." In such "language use" we take a being that, properly considered, is something by virtue of and on the basis of art, and we call this very thing itself "art." For after all, the painting is not art but a work of art, and the bird of prey is not nature but a natural being. Yet this manner of speaking manifests something essential. *When* do we say so emphatically, "This is art"? Not just when some piece of canvas hangs there smeared with dabs of color, not even when we have just any old "painting" there in front of us, but only when a being that we encounter steps forth preeminently into the appearance of a work of art, only when a being *is* insofar as it places itself into such an appearance. And the same holds when we say, "That is nature" – φύσις. Therefore, this way of speaking attests to the fact that we find what is φύσις-like only where we come upon a *placing into the appearance*; i.e., only where there is μορφή. Thus μορφή constitutes the essence of φύσις, or at least *co*-constitutes it.

[348] Yet the demonstration that such is the case is supported only by our way of speaking. And Aristotle gives here a splendid, if questionable, example befitting a philosophy based simply on "linguistic usage." This is what someone today might say if he or she were ignorant of what λόγος and λέγειν mean in Greek. However, to find the direction our thinking must take in order to grasp the essence of λόγος, we need only recall the Greek definition of the essence of the human being as ζῷον λόγον ἔχον. We can – in fact, we must – translate ἄνθρωπος – ζῷον λόγον ἔχον as: "the human being is the living entity to whom *the word* belongs." Instead of "word" we can even say "language," provided we think the nature of language adequately and originally, namely, from the essence of λόγος correctly understood. The determination of the essence of the human being that became common through the "definitions" *homo: animal rationale* and "the human being: the rational animal," does not mean that the human being "has" the "faculty of speech" as one property among others, but rather that the distinguishing characteristic of the essence of the human being consists in the fact that one has, and holds oneself in, λόγος.

What does λόγος mean? In the language of Greek mathematics the word "λόγος" means the same as "relation" and "proportion." Or we say "analogy," taken as "correspondence," and by this we mean a definite kind of relation, a relation of relations; but with the word "correspondence" we do not think of language and speech. Linguistic usage in mathematics, and partially in philosophy, holds on to something of the original meaning of λόγος. Λόγος belongs to λέγειν, which means and is the same as the German word *lesen*, "to collect" or "to gather" (as in "to gather grapes or grain at the harvest"). But still, nothing is yet gained by establishing that λέγειν means "to collect." Despite correct reference to root meanings, one can still misconstrue the *genuine* content of the *Greek* word and understand the concept of λόγος incorrectly by adhering to the meaning that has been prevalent up until now.

[349] "To collect," to gather, means: to bring various dispersed things together into a unity, and at the same time to bring this unity *forth* and hand it *over* (παρά). Into what? Into the unhidden of presencing [παρουσία = οὐσία (ἀπουσία)]. Λέγειν means to bring together into a unity and to bring forth this unity as gathered, i.e., above all as present; thus it means the same as to reveal what was formerly hidden, to let it be manifest in its presencing. Thus according to Aristotle the essence of an assertion is ἀπόφανσις: letting be seen, from the being itself, what and how the being is. He also calls this τὸ δηλοῦν, the act of revealing. In so doing, Aristotle is not giving a special "theory" of λόγος, but only preserves what the Greeks always recognized as the essence of λέγειν. Fragment 93 of Heraclitus shows this magnificently: ὁ ἄναξ, οὗ τὸ μαντεῖόν ἐστι τὸ ἐν Δελφοῖς, οὔτε λέγει οὔτε κρύπτει ἀλλὰ σημαίνει. The philologists (e.g., Diels, Snell) translate: "The lord whose oracle is at Delphi says nothing, does not speak and does not conceal, but gives a sign." This translation deprives Heraclitus's saying of its basic content and its authentic Heraclitean tension and resistance. Οὔτε λέγει οὔτε κρύπτει: here the word λέγειν is opposed to κρύπτειν, "to conceal," and for this reason we must translate it as "to unconceal," i.e., to reveal. The oracle does not directly *un*conceal nor does it simply conceal, but it points out. This means: it unconceals while it conceals, and it conceals while it unconceals. [For how this λέγειν is related to λόγος and for what λόγος means to Heraclitus, cf. fragments 1 and 2 and others.]

In the Greek definition of the essence of the human being, λέγειν and λόγος mean the relation on the basis of which what is present gathers itself for the first time as such around and for human beings. And only because human beings *are* insofar as they relate to beings as beings, unconcealing and concealing them, can they and must they have the "word," i.e., speak of the being of beings. But the words that language uses are only fragments that have precipitated out of the word, [350] and from them humans can never find their way to beings or find the path back to them, unless it be on the basis of λέγειν. Of itself λέγειν has nothing to do with saying and with language. Nonetheless, *if* the Greeks conceive of saying as λέγειν, then this implies an interpretation of the essence of word and of saying so unique that no later "philosophy of language" can ever begin to imagine its as yet unplumbed depths. Only when language has been debased to a means of commerce and organization, as is the case with us, does thought rooted in language appear to be a mere "philosophy of words," no longer adequate to the "pressing realities of life." This judgment is simply an admission that we ourselves no longer have the power to trust that the word is the essential foundation of all relations to beings as such.

But why do we lose ourselves in this wide-ranging digression into an explanation of the essence of λόγος when our question is about the essence of φύσις? Answer: in order to make clear that when Aristotle appeals to λέγεσθαι he is not relying extraneously on some "linguistic usage" but is thinking out of the original and fundamental relation to beings. Thus this seemingly superficial beginning to the demonstration regains its proper import: if beings having in themselves the origin and ordering of their movedness are experienced by means of λέγειν, then as a result μορφή itself and not just ὕλη (not to mention ἀρρύθμιστον) unveils itself as the φύσις-character of these beings. To be sure, Aristotle does not show this directly but rather in a way that clarifies the concept opposed to μορφή, a concept that has gone unexplained until now: ὕλη. We do not say, "That is φύσις" when there are only flesh and bones lying around. They are to a living entity what wood is to a bedstead: mere "matter." Then does ὕλη mean "matter"? But let us ask again: What does "matter" mean? Does it mean just "raw material"? No, Aristotle characterizes ὕλη as τὸ δυνάμει. Δύναμις means the capacity, or better, the appropriateness for ... The wood present in the workshop [351] is in a state of appropriateness for a "table." But it is not just any wood that has the character of appropriateness for a table; rather, only this wood, selected and cut to order. But the selection and the cut, i.e., the very character of appropriateness, is decided in terms of the "production" of "what is to be produced." But "to produce" means, both in Greek and in the original sense of the German *Herstellen*, to *place* something, as finished and as looking thus and so, *forth*, into presencing. Ὕλη is the appropriate orderable, that which, like flesh and bones, belongs to a being that has in itself the origin and ordering of its movedness. But only in being placed into the appearance is a being *what* and *how* it is in any given case. Thus Aristotle can conclude:

XIV. "For this reason (then), φύσις would be, in another way, the placing into the appearance in the case of *those* beings that have in themselves the origin and ordering of their movedness. Of course, the placing and the appearance do not stand off by themselves; rather, it is only in a given being that they can be pointed out by addressing them. However, *that which* takes its stand from these (i.e., from the order-able and from the placing) is certainly not φύσις itself, although it is a φύσει-being – such as, for example, a human being." (193 b3–6)

These sentences do not simply recapitulate the already proven thesis, namely, that φύσις can be spoken of in *two* ways. Much more important is the emphasis given to the crucial thought that φύσις, spoken of in two ways, is not a being but a manner of *being*. Therefore, Aristotle again presses home the point: the appearance and the placing into the appearance must not be taken Platonically as standing apart unto themselves, but as the being [*Sein*] in which an individual being stands at any given moment – for example, this person here. To be sure, this individual being is *from* ὕλη and μορφή, but precisely for this reason it is a being and *not a way of being* – not φύσις, as are μορφή and ὕλη in their inherent togetherness. In other words, it now becomes clear to what extent Aristotle's [352] distinction between ὕλη and μορφή is not simply another formula for Antiphon's distinction between ἀρρύθμιστον and ῥυθμός. These latter terms are intended to define φύσις, but they only designate beings – the stable as distinct from the unstable. They do not grasp, much less conceptualize, φύσις as being, i.e., as what makes up the stability or standing-on-its-own of φύσει ὄντα. Such being can be understood only if we use λόγος as our clue. But addressing things shows that the appearance and the placedness into the appearance are primary, and from them what we call ὕλη is then determined as the orderable. But with that, yet another issue already gets decided, but one that prompts the next step in the demonstration that φύσις is μορφή. Although ὕλη and μορφή both constitute the essence of φύσις, they do not carry equal weight. Μορφή has *priority*. With that we are saying that the *course* of the demonstration as carried out so far now lifts the *task* of the demonstration one level higher. And Aristotle loses no time in saying so:

XV. "What is more, this (namely, μορφή as the placing into the appearance) is φύσις *to a greater degree* than the orderable is. For each individual thing is addressed [as properly being] when it 'is' in the mode of having-itself-in-its-end rather than when it is (only) in the state of appropriateness for . . ." (193 b6–8)

Why is it that μορφή is φύσις not only on a par with ὕλη but "*to a greater degree*"? Because we speak of something as properly in being only *when* it is in the mode of ἐντελέχεια. Accordingly, μορφή must somehow have the intrinsic character of ἐντελέχεια. To what degree this is true, Aristotle does not explain here. Neither does he explain what ἐντελέχεια means. This term, coined by Aristotle himself, is the fundamental word of his thinking, and it embodies that knowledge of being that brings Greek philosophy to its fulfillment. "Ἐντελέχεια" comprises the basic concept of Western metaphysics in whose changes of meaning we can best estimate, and indeed must see, the distance between Greek thought in the beginning [353] and the metaphysics that followed. But at first it is not clear why Aristotle introduces ἐντελέχεια here in order to ground the fact that and the degree to which μορφή is μᾶλλον φύσις. Only one thing do we see clearly: Aristotle again appeals to λέγειν, to the addressing of things, in order to show where the proper being of a being can be glimpsed. But we can clear up the initially obscure *grounding* of the proof by clearing up beforehand *what is to be grounded*. What is the meaning of the new claim that overrides the previously equal status of ὕλη and μορφή by maintaining that μορφή is φύσις *to a greater degree?* Earlier we came upon the crucial guiding principle: φύσις is οὐσία, a kind of beingness or presencing. Therefore, the proposition to be grounded maintains that μορφή fulfills what beingness is more than ὕλη does. Earlier still it was established that φύσει ὄντα are κινούμενα: their being is movedness.

We now have to grasp movedness as οὐσία; i.e., we must say what movedness *is*. Only in this way do we clarify what φύσις is as ἀρχὴ κινήσεως, and only from the *thus* clarified essence of φύσις will we see why μορφή more fulfills what οὐσία is and therefore why it is φύσις to a greater degree.

What is movedness, taken as the being – i.e., the presencing – of a moving being? Aristotle gives the answer in *Physics* Γ 1–3. It would be presumptuous to try to capture in a few sentences an essential insight into Aristotle's interpretation of movedness, the most difficult thing Western metaphysics has had to ponder in the course of its history. Still we must try to do so, at least to a degree that will allow us to follow the demonstration of the μορφή-character of φύσις. The reason for the difficulty in Aristotle's definition of the essence [of movedness] lies in the strange simplicity of the essential insight. It is a simplicity we seldom achieve because even now we hardly have an inkling of the *Greek* concept of being, and likewise, in reflecting on the Greek experience of movedness, we forget what is decisive, namely, that the Greeks conceive of movedness in terms of rest. [354] At this point we must distinguish between movedness and movement, as well as between rest and repose. Movedness means the essence from which both movement and rest are determined. Rest is then the "cessation" (παύεσθαι, *Metaphysics* Θ 6, 1048 b26) of movement. The lack of movement can be calculated as its limit-case (= 0). But in fact even rest, which we thus take to be a derivative of movement, also has movedness as its essence. The purest manifestation of the essence of movedness is to be found where rest does not mean the breaking off and cessation of movement, but rather where movedness is gathered up into *standing still*, and where this ingathering, far from excluding movedness, includes and for the first time discloses it. For example: ὁρᾷ ἄμα καὶ ἑώραχε (*Metaphysics* Θ 6, 1048 b23): "Someone sees, and in seeing he or she has also at the same time (precisely) already seen." The movement of seeing and inspecting what is around one *is* properly the *highest* state of movedness only in the *repose* of (simple) seeing, gathered into itself. Such seeing is the τέλος, the end where the movement of seeing first *gathers itself up* and essentially is movedness. ("End" is not the result of stopping the movement, but is the beginning of movedness as the ingathering and storing up of movement.) Thus the movedness of a movement consists above all in the fact that the movement of a moving being gathers itself into its end, τέλος, and as so gathered within its end, "has" itself: ἐν τέλει ἔχει, ἐντελέχεια, having-itself-in-its-end. Instead of the word ἐντελέχεια, which he himself coined, Aristotle also uses the word ἐνέργεια. Here, in place of τέλος, there stands ἔργον, the "work" in the sense of what is to be produced and what has been pro-duced. In Greek thought ἐνέργεια means "standing in the work," where "work" means that which stands fully in its "end." But in turn the "fully ended or fulfilled" [*das "Vollendete"*] does not mean "the concluded," any more than τέλος means "conclusion." Rather, in Greek thought τέλος and ἔργον are defined by εἶδος; they name the manner and mode in which something stands "finally and finitely" [*"endlich"*] in its appearance.

From *movedness*, understood as ἐντελέχεια, we must now try to understand the movement of what moves as one manner [355] of being, namely, that of a κινούμενον. Relying on an example can make the direction of our essential insight more secure. And following Aristotle's approach we choose our example from the field of "production," the "making" of an artifact. Take a case of generation: a table coming into existence. Here we obviously find movements. But Aristotle does not mean the "movements" performed by the carpenter in handling the tools and the wood. Rather, in the generation of the table, Aristotle is thinking precisely *of the movement of what is being generated itself and as such*. Κίνησις is μεταβολή, the change of something into something, such that in the change the very act of change itself breaks out into the open, i.e., comes into appearance along with the changing thing. The orderable wood in the workshop changes into a table. What sort of being does this change have? The thing that changes is the wood lying present here, not just any wood but *this* wood that is appropriate.

But "appropriate for" means: tailored to the appearance of a table, hence for that wherein the generating of the table – the movement – comes to its *end*. The change of the appropriate wood into a table consists in the fact that the very appropriateness of what is appropriated emerges more fully into view and reaches its fulfillment in the appearance of a table and thus comes to stand in the table that has been pro-duced, placed *forth*, i.e., into the unhidden. In the rest that goes with this standing (of what has attained its stand), the emerging appropriateness (δύναμις) of the appropriate (δυνάμει) gathers itself up and "has" itself (ἔχει) as in its end (τέλος). Therefore Aristotle says (*Physics* Γ 1, 201 b4f.): ἡ τοῦ δυνατοῦ ᾗ δυνατὸν ἐντελέχεια φανερὸν ὅτι κίνησίς ἐστιν: "The having-itself-in-its-end of what is appropriate as something appropriate (i.e., in its appropriateness) is clearly (the essence of) movedness."

But generation is *this* kind of generation – i.e., κίνησις in the narrower sense of movement as opposed to rest – *only* insofar as that which is appropriate has *not yet* brought its appropriateness to its end, and so is ἀ-τελές – that is, only insofar as the standing-in-the-work is not yet within its end. Accordingly Aristotle says (*Physics*, Γ 2, 201 b31f.), ἥ τε κίνησις ἐνέργεια μέν τις εἶναι δοκεῖ, ἀτελὴς δέ: "Movement does appear as [356] something like standing-in-the-work, but as not yet having come into its end."

But therefore having-itself-within-its-end (ἐντελέχεια) is the essence of movedness (that is, it is *the being* of a moving being), because this repose most perfectly fulfills what οὐσία is: the intrinsically stable presencing in the appearance. Aristotle says this in his own way in a sentence we take from the treatise that deals explicitly with ἐντελέχεια (*Metaphysics* Θ 8, 1049 b5): φανερὸν ὅτι πρότερον ἐνέργεια δυνάμεώς ἐστιν: "Manifestly standing-in-the-work is prior to appropriateness for..." In this sentence Aristotle's thinking and *pari passu* Greek thinking, reaches its peak. But if we translate it in the usual way, it reads: "Clearly actuality is prior to potentiality." Ἐνέργεια, standing-in-the-work in the sense of presencing into the appearance, was translated by the Romans as *actus*, and so with one blow the Greek world was toppled. From *actus*, *agere* (to effect) came *actualitas*, "actuality." Δύναμις became *potentia*, the ability and potential that something has. Thus the assertion, "Clearly actuality is prior to potentiality" seems to be evidently in error, for the contrary is more plausible. Surely in order for something to be "actual" and to be able to be "actual," it must first be possible. Thus, potentiality is prior to actuality. But if we reason this way, we are not thinking either with Aristotle or with the Greeks in general. Certainly δύναμις also means "ability" and it can be used as the word for "power," but when Aristotle employs δύναμις as the opposite concept to ἐντελέχεια and ἐνέργεια, he uses the word (as he did analogously with κατηγορία and οὐσία) as a thoughtful name for an essential basic concept in which being-ness, οὐσία, is thought. We already translated δύναμις as appropriateness and being appropriate for . . . , *but even here* the danger persists that we will not think consistently enough in the Greek manner and will shrink from the hard work of getting clear about the meaning of appropriateness for . . . as that manner of emergence which, while still holding itself back and within itself, comes forth into the appearance [357] wherein such appropriateness is fulfilled. Δύναμις is a mode of presencing. But Aristotle says, ἐνέργεια (ἐντελέχεια) is πρότερον, "prior" to δύναμις, "prior," namely, with regard to οὐσία (cf. *Metaphysics* Θ 8, 1049 b10, 11). Ἐνέργεια more originally fulfills what pure presencing is insofar as it means a having-itself-in-the-work-and-within-the-end that has left behind the entire "not yet" of appropriateness for . . . , or better, has precisely brought it *forth along with it* into the realization of the finite, fulfilled [*voll-"endeten"*] appearance. The basic thesis Aristotle has put forth concerning the hierarchy of ἐντελέχεια and δύναμις can be expressed briefly as follows: ἐντελέχεια is οὐσία "to a greater degree" than δύναμις is. Ἐνέργεια fulfills the essence of intrinsically stable presencing more essentially than δύναμις does.

In *Physics* B, 1, 193 b6–8 Aristotle says, "What is more, this (namely, μορφή) is φύσις *to a greater degree* than ὕλη is. For each individual is addressed [as properly being] when it 'is' in the manner of having-itself-within-its-end rather than when it is (only) in appropriateness for . . ." It is still unclear to what degree the second sentence can serve to ground the claim that μορφή is not just another τρόπος set on a par with ὕλη, but rather is *φύσις to a greater degree* than ὕλη is. Μορφή is the placing into the appearance; i.e., it is κίνησις itself, the changing of the appropriate as a breaking out of its appropriateness. But the essence of κίνησις is ἐντελέχεια, which for its part fulfills what οὐσία is to a greater degree and more originally than δύναμις does. The determination of the essence of φύσις is ruled by the guiding principle that φύσις is a kind of οὐσία. Therefore, because μορφή is, in essence, ἐντελέχεια, and thus is οὐσία to a greater degree, then likewise μορφή intrinsically is μᾶλλον φύσις. The placing into the appearance more fulfills what φύσις is: the being of the κινούμενον καθ᾽ αὐτό.

Therefore, now more than ever we need a correct insight into the kind of priority that μορφή has over ὕλη, because along with the priority of μορφή, the essence proper to μορφή is still more clearly revealed. And this means the task of grasping φύσις as μορφή has inevitably moved up to a new level. Therefore, as we take the step into that next level, we must have clearly [358] in view what we saw at the previous level. Μορφή is φύσις "to a greater degree," but not because it supposedly is "form" that has subordinate to it a "matter" that it molds. Rather, as the placing into the appearance, μορφή surpasses the orderable (ὕλη) insofar as μορφή is the presencing of the appropriateness of that which is appropriate, and consequently, in terms of presencing, is more original. But that granted, what now is the perspective within which the essence of μορφή is still more clearly revealed? The following sentence establishes that perspective:

XVI. "Moreover, a human being is generated from a human being, but not a bedstead from a bedstead." (193 b8–9)

Is this sentence anything more than an empty truism? Yes, it certainly is. Even the transitional word ἔτι, "moreover," indicates the relation to what went before and at the same time points to an "advance." Ἔτι γίνεται: we should translate it more strongly: "Moreover, in the area we are talking about, what is at stake is generation (γένεσις), and generation is different in the cases of human beings and of bedsteads, i.e., of φύσει ὄντα (growing things) and of ποιούμενα (artifacts)." (Here where we are dealing with γένεσις, the human being is taken as only a ζῷον, a "living being.") In other words, μορφή as placing into the appearance is *only now explicitly* grasped as γένεσις. But γένεσις is *that kind* of movedness Aristotle omitted when he listed the types of movement in his introductory characterization of κίνησις as μεταβολή, because to *it* he reserved the task of distinguishing the essence of φύσις as μορφή.

Two kinds of generation are contrasted with each other. And from the way the two are sharply distinguished we have a good opportunity to discern the essence of generation. For the crucial characteristic of μορφή as movedness – namely, ἐντελέχεια – was certainly brought to our attention with regard to the generation of a table. But at the same time we have unwittingly carried over what was said about the generation of an artifact into the question of the μορφή that pertains to φύσις. But is not φύσις then *misunderstood* as some sort of self-making artifact? Or is this [359] not a misunderstanding at all but the only possible interpretation of φύσις, namely, as a kind of τέχνη? That almost seems to be the case, because modern metaphysics, in the impressive terms of, for example, Kant, conceives of "nature" as a "technique" such that this "technique" that constitutes the essence of nature provides the metaphysical *ground* for the possibility, or even the necessity, of subjecting and mastering nature through machine technology. Be that as it may, Aristotle's seemingly all-too-obvious statement about the difference between the generation of a human being and the generation of a table forces us into some crucial reflections in which we will have to clarify what role is assigned to the contrast of growing things with artifacts that has been operative from the very beginning of the chapter and has run through the whole explanation.

When Aristotle time and again characterizes growing things by way of analogy with artifacts, does this mean he already understands the φύσει ὄντα as self-making artifacts? No, quite the contrary, he conceives of φύσις as self-production. But is not "production" the same as "making"? It is for us so long as we wander thoughtlessly among worn-out ideas instead of holding on to what was already pointed out. But what if we should find our way back to the realm of being as understood by the Greeks? Then we see that making, ποίησις, is *one* kind of production, whereas "growing" (the going back into itself and emerging out of itself), φύσις, is *another*. Here "to pro-duce" cannot mean "to make" but rather: to place something into the unhiddenness of its appearance; to let something become present; presencing. From this notion of pro-duction the essence of generation [*Ent-stehen*] and of its various kinds may be determined. Instead of "generation" we should have to say "derivation" [*Ent-stellung*], which is not to be taken in its usual sense but rather as meaning: to derive from one appearance that appearance into which something pro-duced (in any given instance) is placed and thus *is*. Now there are different kinds of such "derivation." Something generated (say, a table) can be derived from one appearance (the appearance of "table") and placed forth into the same kind of appearance without the first appearance, from which [360] the table is derived, itself performing the placing into the appearance. The first appearance (εἶδος), "table," remains only a παράδειγμα, something that certainly shows up in the production but does *nothing more* than that and therefore requires something else that can first place the orderable wood, as something appropriate for appearing as a table, *into* that appearance. In those cases where the appearance merely shows up, and in showing up only guides a know-how in the producing of it and plays an accompanying role rather than actually *performing* the production – there production is a *making*.

This way of showing up is certainly one kind of presencing, but it is not the only kind. It is also possible that an appearance – without showing up *specifically* as a παράδειγμα, namely, in and for a τέχνη – can directly present *itself* as what takes over the placing into itself. The appearance places itself forth. Here we have the placing of an appearance. And in thus placing itself forth it places itself into itself; i.e., it itself produces something with its kind of appearance. This is μορφή as φύσις. And we can easily see that a ζῷον (an animal) does not "make" itself and its kind, because its appearance is not and never can be merely a measure or paradigm *according to which* something is produced from something orderable. Rather, such appearance is that which comes to presence [*das An-wesende*] itself, the self-placing appearance that alone in each case orders up the orderable and places it as appropriate into appropriateness. In γένεσις as self-placing, production is entirely the presencing of the appearance itself without the importation of outside help – whereas such outside help is what characterizes all "making." Whatever produces itself, i.e., places itself into its appearance, needs no fabrication. If it did, this would mean an animal could not reproduce itself without mastering the science of its own zoology. All this indicates that μορφή – not just more than ὕλη, but in fact alone and completely – is φύσις. And this is exactly what the supposed truism above would have us understand. But as soon as it becomes clear that φύσις is γένεσις in this sense, its state of movedness requires a definition, one that in every respect identifies its uniqueness. Therefore a further step is necessary [361]:

XVII. "Furthermore, φύσις, which is addressed as γένεσις – i.e., as deriving-and-placing-something so that it stands *forth* – is (nothing less than) being-on-the-way toward φύσις. (And this), of course, not as the practice of medicine is said to be the way not toward the art of medicine but toward health. For whereas the practice of medicine necessarily comes from the art of medicine, it is not directed toward this art (as its end). But φύσις is not related to φύσις in this way (namely, as medicine is to health). Rather, whatever is a being from and in the manner of φύσις goes from something toward something insofar as this being is determined by φύσις (in the movedness of this going). But 'toward what' does it go forth in the manner of φύσις? Not toward that 'from which' (it is derived in any given instance) but rather toward that as which it is generated in each instance." (193 b12–18)

Characterized as γένεσις in the previous section, φύσις is now understood as determined by ὁδός. We immediately translate ὁδός with "way," and we think of this as a stretch lying between the starting point and the goal. But the "way-ness" of a way must be looked for in another perspective. A way *leads* through an area; it opens itself up and opens up the area. A way is therefore the same as the process of passage from something to something else. It is way as *being-on-the-way*.

If we are to determine the γένεσις-character of φύσις more exactly, we have to clarify the movedness of this kind of movement. The movedness of movement is ἐνέργεια ἀτελής, the standing-in-the-work that has not yet come into its end. But according to what we said earlier, ἔργον, work, means neither making nor the artifact made, but that which is to be pro-duced, brought into presencing. In itself, ἐνέργεια ἀτελής is already a being-on-the-way that, as such and as a process, places forth what is to be pro-duced. The being-on-the-way in φύσις is μορφή (self-placing). Now, the previous section pointed out that *from* which μορφή as self-placing is on the way: the appearance of the φύσει ὄν is what *places itself* in the self-placing. But what is yet to be determined is the "whereunto" of the process, or better, the meaning of ὁδός that results from the determination of the "whereunto."

[362] Φύσις is ὁδὸς ἐκ φύσεως εἰς φύσιν, the being-on-the-way of a self-placing thing toward itself as what is to be pro-duced, and this in such a way that the self-placing is itself wholly of a kind with the self-placing thing to be pro-duced. What could be more obvious than the opinion that φύσις is therefore a kind of self-making, hence a τέχνη, the only difference being that the end of this making has the character of φύσις? And we do know of such a τέχνη. Ἰατρική, the art of medicine, has its τέλος as ὑγίεια, a φύσις-like condition. Ἰατρική is ὁδὸς εἰς φύσιν. But just when the road seems open to an analogy between φύσις and ἰατρική, the basic difference between the two ways of generating a φύσει ὄν comes to light. Ἰατρική, as ὁδὸς εἰς φύσιν, is a being-on-the-way *toward* something that precisely is *not* ἰατρική, not the art of medicine itself, i.e., not a τέχνη. Ἰατρική would have to be ὁδὸς εἰς ἰατρικήν in order to be at all analogous to φύσις. But if it were, it would no longer be ἰατρική, because practicing medicine has as its end the state of health and this alone. Even if a doctor practices medicine in order to attain a higher degree of the τέχνη, he or she does so only in order all the more to reach the τέλος of restoring health – provided, of course, that we are talking about a real doctor and not a medical "entrepreneur" or "time-server."

The renewed attempt to clarify the essence of φύσις by way of an analogy with τέχνη fails precisely here *from every conceivable point of view*. This means: we must understand the essence of φύσις entirely from out of itself, and we should not detract from the astonishing fact of φύσις as ὁδὸς φύσεως εἰς φύσιν by overhasty analogies and explanations.

But even when we give up pressing the analogy to τέχνη, one last tempting "explanation" now urges itself upon us. As φύσεως ὁδὸς εἰς φύσιν, is not φύσις a constant circling back upon itself? However, this is precisely what is not the case. As *on the way* to φύσις, φύσις does not fall back on whatever it comes forth from. What is generated *never* places itself back into what it comes from, [363] precisely because the essence of generation is the self-placing into the appearance. If such placing lets the self-placing appearance be present, and if the appearance is, in each case, present only in an individual "this" which has such an appearance, then to this extent, that *into which* the generation places the appearance surely must in each instance be something other than that "from which" it is generated.

Certainly φύσεως ὁδὸς εἰς φύσιν is a mode of coming forth into presencing, in which the "from which," the "to which," and the "how" of the presencing remain the same. Φύσις is a "going" in the sense of a going-forth toward a going-forth, and in this sense it is indeed a going *back* into itself; i.e., the *self* to which it returns remains a going-forth. The merely spatial image of a circle is essentially inadequate because this going-forth that goes back into itself precisely lets something go forth from which and to which the going-forth is in each instance on the way.

This essence of φύσις as κίνησις is fulfilled only by the kind of movedness that μορφή is. Therefore the decisive sentence, the one toward which this whole treatment of the essence of φύσις has been moving, says succinctly:

XVIII. "And so this, the self-placing into the appearance, is φύσις." (193 b18)

In the self-placing, as the ἐνέργεια ἀτελής characteristic of γένεσις, only the εἶδος, the appearance, is present as the "whence," the "whereunto," and the "how" of this being-on-the-way. So μορφή is not only φύσις "to a greater degree" than ὕλη is, and still less can it be put *merely on a par* with ὕλη such that the definition of the essence of φύσις would leave us with two τρόποι of equal weight, and Antiphon's doctrine would be entitled to equal authority next to Aristotle's. Antiphon's doctrine now gets its stiffest rejection with the sentence, "Μορφή, and it alone, fulfills the essence of φύσις." But in the transition to his own interpretation (193 a28: ἕνα μὲν οὖν τρόπον οὕτως ἡ φύσις λέγεται),[7] Aristotle did, after all, take over the doctrine of Antiphon. How can this fact be reconciled with the sentence we have just reached, which allows *one and only one* τρόπος? To understand this, we must know the extent to which [364] Aristotle's acceptance of Antiphon's doctrine nevertheless constitutes the sharpest rejection of it. The most drastic way to reject a proposition is not to dismiss it brusquely as disproven and merely brush it *aside*, but on the contrary to take it over and work it *into* an essential and grounded connection with one's own argument – i.e., to take it over and work it in as the non-essence that necessarily belongs to the essence. For if it is possible at all to have two τρόποι in the interpretation of φύσις with regard to μορφή and ὕλη, with the result that ὕλη can be mistakenly interpreted as something formless that is stably at hand, then the reason must lie in the essence of φύσις, and that now means: in μορφή itself. Aristotle refers to this reason in the following passage, where his interpretation of φύσις reaches its conclusion:

XIX. "However, the self-placing into the appearance – and therefore φύσις as well – is spoken of *in two ways*, for 'privation' too is something like appearance." (193 b18–20)

The reason why φύσις can be looked at from two viewpoints and spoken of in two ways consists in the fact that μορφή in itself – and consequently the essence of φύσις as well – is *twofold*. The sentence asserting the twofold essence of φύσις is grounded in the remark following it: "for 'privation' too is something like appearance."

As a word, a concept, and an "issue," στέρησις is introduced in this chapter just as brusquely as was ἐντελέχεια before it, probably because it has as decisive a significance in Aristotle's thought as does ἐντελέχεια. (On στέρησις, cf. *Physics* A, 7 and 8, although there, too, it is not explained.)

To interpret this last section of Aristotle's reading of φύσις, we must answer four questions:

(1) What does στέρησις mean?
(2) How is στέρησις related to μορφή, such that στέρησις can help clarify the twofoldness of μορφή? [365]
(3) In what sense, then, is the essence of φύσις twofold?
(4) What consequence does the twofoldness of φύσις have for the final determination of its essence?

Re (1) What does στέρησις mean? Literally translated, στέρησις means "privation," but this does not get us very far. On the contrary, this meaning of the word can even bar the way to understanding the issue if, as always in such cases, we lack a prior familiarity with, and a knowledge of, the realm in which the word arises as a name for the issue at stake. The realm is shown us by the claim that στέρησις, too, is something like εἶδος. But we know that the εἶδος, specifically the εἶδος κατὰ τὸν λόγον, characterizes μορφή, which in turn fulfills the essence of φύσις as οὐσία τοῦ κινουμένον καθ᾽ αὐτό, i.e., of φύσις as κίνησις. The essence of κίνησις is ἐντελέχεια. This is enough to let us know that we can adequately understand the essence of στέρησις only within the area of, and on the basis of, the *Greek* interpretation of *being*.

The Romans translated στέρησις as *privatio*. This word is taken as a kind of *negatio*. But negation can be understood as a form of denial, of "*saying no.*" Thus στέρησις belongs within the realm of "saying" and "addressing" – κατηγορία in the *pre*terminological sense we noted earlier.

Even Aristotle seems to understand στέρησις as a kind of saying. As evidence of this we offer a text from the treatise Περὶ γενέσεως καὶ φθορᾶς (A 3, 318 b16f.), a text that is, at one and the same time, appropriate for clarifying the sentence we are discussing from the *Physics* while, in addition, offering us a concrete example of a στέρησις: τὸ μὲν θερμὸν κατηγορία τις καὶ εἶδος. ἡ δὲ ψυχρότης στέρησις. "'Warm' is in a sense a way we can address things and therefore, properly speaking, an appearance; but 'cold,' on the other hand, is a στέρησις." Here "warm" and "cold" are opposed to each other as κατηγορία τις versus στέρησις. But observe carefully that Aristotle says κατηγορία τις. "Warm" is a way of addressing things only in a certain sense – in fact, the word is written in quotation marks. Hence, saying something is "warm" is [366] an attribution, saying something *to* something; correspondingly, στέρησις is, in a certain sense, a denial, saying something *away from* something. But to what extent is "cold" a denial?

When we say, "The water is cold," we attribute something *to* that being, yes, but in such a way that, in the very attribution, "warm" is *denied* of the water. But what is at stake in this distinction between warm and cold is not the distinction between attribution and denial; what is at stake, rather, is *that which is attributable or deniable* in accordance with its εἶδος. And therefore the chapter's concluding sentence, which is supposed to ground the twofold essence of μορφή, and therefore of φύσις, by means of a reference to στέρησις, says: καὶ γὰρ ἡ στέρησις εἶδός πώς ἐστιν. "For privation, too, – i.e., what is denied or 'said-away' – is a kind of appearance." In the coldness something appears and is present, something, therefore, that we "sense." In this "sensed something" that is present, something else is likewise absent, indeed in such a way that we sense what is present in a special way precisely because of this absencing. In στέρησις, "privation," it is a matter of "taking something *away*" by a kind of saying-it-away. Στέρησις certainly refers to an "away," but always and above all it means something falls away, has gone away, remains away, becomes absent. If we bear in mind that οὐσία, being-ness, means presencing, then we need no further long-winded explanations to establish where στέρησις as absencing belongs.

And yet right here we reach a danger point in our comprehension. We could make matters easy for ourselves by taking στέρησις (absencing) merely as the opposite of presencing. But στέρησις is *not* simply absentness [*Abwesenheit*]. Rather, as absencing, στέρησις is precisely στέρησις for presencing. What then is στέρησις? (Cf. Aristotle, *Metaphysics* Δ 22, 1022 b22ff.) When today, for example, *we* say, "My bicycle is gone!" we do not mean simply that it is somewhere else; we mean it is missing. When something is missing, the missing *thing* is gone, to be sure, but the *goneness* itself, the lack itself, is what irritates and upsets us, and the "lack" can do this only if the lack itself is "there," i.e., only if the lack *is*, i.e., constitutes a manner of being. Στέρησις as absencing is not simply absentness; rather, [367] it is a *presencing*, namely, that kind in which the *absencing* (but not the absent thing) is present. Στέρησις is εἶδος, but εἶδός πως, an appearance and presencing *of sorts*. Today we are all too inclined to reduce something like this presencing-by-absencing to a facile dialectical play of concepts rather than hold on to what is astonishing about it. For in στέρησις is hidden the essence of φύσις. To see this we must first answer the next question.

Re (2) How is στέρησις related to μορφή? The self-placing into the appearance is κίνησις, a change from something to something, a change that in itself is the "breaking out" of something. When wine becomes sour and turns to vinegar, it does not become nothing. When we say, "It has turned to vinegar," we mean to indicate that it came to "nothing," i.e., to what we had not expected. In the "vinegar" lies the nonappearance, the absencing, of the wine. Μορφή as γένεσις is ὁδός, the being-on-the-way of a "not yet" to a "no more." The self-placing into the appearance always lets something be present in such a way that *in* the presencing an absencing simultaneously becomes present. While the blossom "buds forth" (φύει), the leaves that prepared for the blossom now fall off. The fruit comes to light, while the blossom disappears. The self-placing into the appearance, the μορφή, has a στέρησις-character, and this now means: μορφή is διχῶς, *intrinsically twofold*, the presencing of an absencing. Consequently the third question already has its answer.

Re (3) In what sense is the essence of φύσις twofold? As φύσεως ὁδός εἰς φύσιν, φύσις is a kind of ἐνέργεια, a kind of οὐσία. Specifically it is production of itself, from out of itself, unto itself. Nonetheless, in essentially "being-on-the-way," each being that is *pro*-duced or put *forth* (excluding artifacts) is also put *away*, as the blossom is put away by the fruit. But in this putting *away*, the self-placing into the appearance – φύσις – does not cease to be. On the contrary, the plant in the form of fruit goes back into its seed, which, according to its essence, is nothing else but a going-forth into the appearance, ὁδὸς φύσεως εἰς φύσιν. With its very coming-to-life every living thing already begins to die, and conversely, dying is but a [368] kind of living, because only a living being has the ability to die. Indeed, dying *can* be the highest "act" of living. Φύσις is the self-productive putting-away of itself, and therefore it possesses the unique quality of delivering over to itself that which *through it* is first transformed from something orderable (e.g., water, light, air) into something appropriate for it alone (for example, into nutriment and so into sap or bones). One can take this "appropriate" for itself as the orderable and consider this orderable as material, and therefore take φύσις as mere "change of material." One can further reduce the material to what is most constantly present in it, and take this as the stable, indeed as the most stable, and thus in a certain sense as that which most is – and then declare this to be φύσις. Looked at in this way, φύσις offers the dual possibility of being addressed in terms of matter and form. *This* dual way of addressing φύσις has its basis in the original twofold essence of φύσις. More precisely it is grounded in a misinterpretation of the δυνάμει ὄν, one that changes the δυνάμει ὄν from "the appropriate" to something merely orderable and on hand. The doctrine of Antiphon and of his successors, who have continued in an unbroken line down to today, seizes upon the most extreme non-essence of φύσις and inflates it into the real and only essence. In fact, such inflation remains the essence of all nonessence.

Re (4) What is the consequence of the twofoldness of φύσις for the final determination of its essence? Answer: the simplicity of this essence. If we keep the whole in mind, then we now have *two* conceptual determinations of the essence of φύσις. The one takes φύσις as ἀρχὴ κινήσεως τοῦ κινουμένον καθ᾽ αὐτό, the origin and ordering of the movedness of what moves of and by itself. The other takes φύσις as μορφή, which means as γένεσις, which means κίνησις. If we think both determinations in their unity, then from the viewpoint of the first one, φύσις is nothing other than ἀρχὴ φύσεως, which is precisely what the second definition says: φύσις is φύσεως ὁδὸς εἰς φύσιν – φύσις is itself the origin and ordering of itself. From the viewpoint of the second definition, φύσις is the μορφὴ ἀρχῆς, the self-placing in which the origin places itself *into* the ordering process and [369] *as* that which orders the self-placing into the appearance. Μορφή is the essence of φύσις as ἀρχή, and ἀρχή is the essence of φύσις as μορφή, insofar as the uniqueness of μορφή consists in the fact that, in φύσις, the εἶδος, of and by itself and as such, brings itself into presencing. Unlike τέχνη, φύσις does not first require a supervening ποίησις that takes just something lying around (e.g., wood) and brings it into the appearance of "table." Such a product is never, of and by itself, on-the-way and never can be on-the-way to a table.

Φύσις, on the other hand, is the presencing of the absencing of itself, one that is on-the-way from itself and unto itself. As such an absencing, φύσις remains a going-back-into-itself, but this going-back is only the going of a going-forth.

But here in the *Physics* Aristotle conceives of φύσις as the beingness (οὐσία) of a particular (and in itself limited) region of beings, things that grow as distinguished from things that are made. With regard to their kind of *being*, these beings stem precisely from φύσις, of which Aristotle therefore says: ἕν γάρ τι γένος τοῦ ὄντος ἡ φύσις, "Φύσις is *one* branch of being [among others] for (the many-branched tree of) beings." Aristotle says this in a treatise that later, in the definitive ordering of his writings by the

Peripatetic school, was catalogued with those treatises that ever since have borne the name μετὰ τὰ φυσικά – which are writings that both do and do not belong to the φυσικά. The sentence we just read comes from chapter three of the treatise now called Book Γ (IV) of the *Metaphysics*, and the information it provides about φύσις is identical with the guiding principle put forth in *Physics*, Book B, chapter one, which we have just interpreted: φύσις *is one kind of* οὐσία. But this *same* treatise of the *Metaphysics*, in its first chapter, says exactly the opposite: οὐσία (the being of beings as such in totality) is φύσις τις, something like φύσις. But Aristotle is far from intending to say that the essence of being in general is, properly speaking, of the same kind as the φύσις which, a little later, he explicitly characterizes as only *one* branch of being [370] among others. Rather, this barely adequately expressed assertion that οὐσία is φύσις τις is an *echo* of the great beginning of Greek philosophy, the first beginning of Western philosophy. In this beginning being was thought as φύσις, such that the φύσις that Aristotle conceptualized can be only a late derivative of originary φύσις. And a much weaker, much harder-to-hear echo of the original φύσις that was projected as the being of beings, is still left for *us* when we speak of the "nature" of things, the nature of the "state," and the "nature" of the human being, by which we do not mean the natural "foundations" (thought of as physical, chemical, or biological) but rather the pure and simple *being and essence* of those beings.

But how should we think φύσις in the way it was originally thought? Are there still traces of its projection in the fragments of the original thinkers? In fact there are, and not just traces, for everything they said that we can still understand speaks *only* of φύσις, provided we have the right ear for it. The *indirect* witness thereof is the *nonessence* that is the historiographical interpretation of original Greek thinking as a "philosophy of *nature*" in the sense of a "primitive" "chemistry," an interpretation that has been prevalent for some time now. But let us leave this nonessence to its own ruin.

In conclusion let us give thought to the saying of a thinker from those beginnings, one who speaks directly of φύσις and who means by it (cf. Fragment 1) the being of beings as such as a whole. Fragment 123 of Heraclitus (taken from Porphyry) says: φύσις χρύπτεσθαι φιλεῖ, "Being loves to hide itself." What does this mean? It has been suggested, and still is suggested, that this fragment means being is difficult to get at and requires great efforts to be brought out of its hiding place and, as it were, purged of its self-hiding. But what is needed is precisely the opposite. Self-hiding belongs to the predilection [*Vor-liebe*] of being; i.e., it belongs to that wherein being has secured its essence. And the essence of being is to unconceal itself, to emerge, to come out into the unhidden [371] – φύσις. Only what in its very essence *un*conceals and must unconceal itself, can love to conceal itself. Only what is unconcealing can be concealing. And therefore the κρύπτεσθαι of φύσις is not to be overcome, not to be stripped from φύσις. Rather, the task is the much more difficult one of allowing to φύσις, in all the purity of its essence, the κρύπτεσθαι that belongs to it.

Being is the self-concealing revealing, φύσις in the original sense. Self-revealing is a coming-forth into unhiddenness, and this means: first preserving unhiddenness as such by taking it back into its essence. Unhiddenness is called ἀ-λήθεια. Truth, as we translate this word, is of the origin, i.e., it is essentially not a characteristic of human knowing and asserting, and still less is it a mere value or an "idea" that human beings (although they really do not know why) are supposed to strive to realize. Rather, truth as self-revealing belongs to being itself. Φύσις is ἀλήθεια, unconcealing, and therefore κρύπτεσθαι φιλεῖ.

[Because φύσις in the sense of the *Physics* is one kind of οὐσία, and because οὐσία itself stems in its essence from φύσις as projected in the beginning, therefore ἀλήθεια belongs to being and *therefore presencing* into the open of the ἰδέα (Plato) and into the open of the εἶδος κατὰ τὸν λόγον (Aristotle) is revealed as *one* characteristic of οὐσία; *therefore* for Aristotle the essence of κίνησις becomes *visible* as ἐντελέχεια and ἐνέργεια.]

Postscript to "What Is Metaphysics?" [1]

Translated by William McNeill[2]

[99] The question "What is metaphysics?" remains a question. For those who stay with the question, the following postscript is a more originary foreword. The question "What is metaphysics?" questions beyond metaphysics. It springs from a thinking that has already entered into the overcoming of metaphysics. It belongs to the essence of such transitions that, within certain limits, they must continue to speak the language of that which they help overcome. The special occasion on which the question concerning the essence of metaphysics is discussed should not mislead us into the opinion that such questioning must necessarily take its point of departure from the sciences. Modern research, with its different ways of representing beings and its different means of producing them, has assumed the fundamental trait of that truth which characterizes all beings by the will to will, itself prefigured by the appearance of the "will to power." Understood as a fundamental trait of the beingness of beings, "will" is the equating of beings with the actual, in such a way that the actuality of the actual comes to power in the unconditional attainability of pervasive objectification. Modern science neither serves a purpose first assigned to it, nor does it seek a "truth in itself." As a way of objectifying beings in a calculative manner, modern science is a condition posited by the will to will itself, through which the will to will secures the dominance of its essence. However, because all objectification of beings is preoccupied with procuring and securing beings and obtains from beings the possibilities of its own continuation, this objectification keeps to beings and even considers beings to be being. All comportment toward beings thus attests to a knowledge of being, yet at the same time to [100] an inability to stand of its own accord within the law [*Gesetz*][a] of truth of this knowledge. This truth is a truth about beings.

---

[a] Fifth edition, 1949: Gathered setting [*Ge-setz*]; event [*Ereignis*].

Metaphysics is the history of this truth. It says what beings are in bringing to a concept the beingness of beings. In the beingness of beings, metaphysics thinks being, yet without being able to ponder the truth of being in the manner of its own thinking. Metaphysics everywhere moves in the realm of the truth of being, which truth, metaphysically speaking,[3] remains its unknown and ungrounded ground. Granted, however, that not only do beings stem from being, but that being too, in a still more originary manner, itself rests within its own truth and that the truth of being unfolds in its essence as the being of truth, then it is necessary to ask what metaphysics is in its ground. This questioning must think metaphysically and at the same time think out of the ground of metaphysics, i.e., in a manner that is no longer metaphysical. Such questioning remains ambivalent in an essential sense.

Every attempt to follow the train of thought of the lecture will therefore meet with obstacles. That is good. Questioning thereby becomes more genuine. Every question that does justice to its issue is already a bridge to the answer. Essential answers are always only the last step in questioning. This last step, however, cannot be taken without the long series of initial and subsequent steps. The essential response draws its sustaining power from the inherent stance [Inständigkeit] assumed by questioning. The essential response is only the beginning of a responsibility. In such responsibility, questioning awakens in a more originary manner. For this reason too the genuine question is not superseded by the answer that is found.

The obstacles to following the train of thought of the lecture are of two kinds. The first arise from the enigmas that conceal themselves in the realm of what is thought here. The second spring from the inability, indeed often from the unwillingness, to think. In the realm of thoughtful questioning, even fleeting reservations – but especially those that are carefully weighed – may help. Gross errors of opinion may also bear fruit, even when they are voiced in the heat [101] of blind polemic. Careful thought need only restore everything to the releasement [Gelassenheit] of patient reflection.

The chief reservations and errors of opinion arising from this lecture may be gathered into three main objections. It is said that:

(1) The lecture makes "the nothing" into the sole object of metaphysics. Yet because the nothing is that which is altogether null, such thinking leads to the view that all is nothing, so that it is worth neither living nor dying. A "philosophy of nothing" is complete "nihilism."

(2) The lecture elevates an isolated and indeed depressed mood, namely, that of anxiety, to the status of the only fundamental attunement. Yet since anxiety is the psychic state of the "anxious" and cowardly, such thinking

denies the high-spirited composure of courage. A "philosophy of anxiety" paralyzes the will to act.

(3) The lecture decides against "logic." Yet since the intellect contains the criteria for all calculation and classification, such thinking leaves any judgment concerning truth to our arbitrary moods. A "philosophy of mere feelings" endangers "exact" thinking and security of action.

The correct response to these propositions will emerge from a renewed attempt to think through the lecture. Such an attempt may query whether the nothing, which attunes anxiety in its essence, exhausts itself in an empty negation of all beings, or whether that which is never and nowhere a being unveils itself as that which distinguishes itself from all beings, as that which we call being. No matter where or to what extent all research investigates beings, it nowhere finds being. It only ever encounters beings, because from the outset it remains intent on explaining beings. Being, however, is not an existing quality found in beings. Unlike beings, being cannot be represented or brought forth in the manner of an object. As that which is altogether other[a] than all beings, being is that which is not. But this nothing[b] essentially prevails [102] as being. We too quickly abdicate thinking when, in a facile explanation, we pass off the nothing as a mere nullity and equate it with the unreal. Instead of giving way to the haste of such empty acumen and relinquishing the enigmatic ambiguities of the nothing, we must prepare ourselves solely in readiness to experience in the nothing the pervasive expanse of that which gives every being the warrant[c] to be. That is being itself. Without being, whose abyssal but yet to be unfolded essence dispenses the nothing to us in essential anxiety, all beings would remain in an absence of being. Yet such absence too, as being's abandonment, is again not a null nothing if indeed the truth of being entails that being[d] never[4] prevails in its essence[e] without beings, that a being never[5] is without being.

An experience of being as that which is other than all beings is bestowed in anxiety, provided that, out of "anxiety" in the face of anxiety, i.e., in the mere anxiousness that pertains to fear, we do not evade the silent[f] voice that attunes us toward the horror of the abyss. Certainly if, with this hint

---

[a] Fourth edition, 1943: This too still said metaphysically, starting from beings.
[b] Fourth edition, 1943: Of beings.
[c] Fifth edition, 1949: That which grants.
[d] Fourth edition, 1943: In the sense of beyng.
[e] Fifth edition, 1949: Essential prevailing of being: beyng, difference; "essential prevailing" [*"Wesen"*] of being ambiguous: (1) Event [*Ereignis*], not effected by beings, event – the granting; (2) Beingness – whatness: enduring, duration, ἀεί.
[f] Fifth edition, 1949: "Being" (carrying out [*Austrag*]) as the silent voice, the voice of stillness.

concerning such essential anxiety, we willfully abandon the train of thought of the lecture; if we dissociate anxiety, as the mood attuned by that voice,[6] from its relation to the nothing; then we are left with anxiety as an isolated "feeling" that can be distinguished from other feelings and dissected amid a familiar assortment of psychic states observed by psychology. Along the guidelines of a facile distinction between "higher" and "lower" these "moods" can then be classified as either uplifting or depressing. The zealous pursuit of "types" and "countertypes" of "feelings" and of varieties and subspecies of these "types" will never run out of prey. Yet such anthropological investigation of human beings always remains outside of the possibility of following the train of thought of the lecture; for this lecture thinks out of an attentiveness to the voice of being and into the attunement coming from this voice, attuning the human being in [103] his essence to its claim, so that in the nothing he may learn to experience being.

Readiness for anxiety is a Yes to assuming a stance that fulfills the highest claim, a claim that is made upon the human essence alone. Of all beings, only the human being, called upon by the voice of being, experiences the wonder of all wonders: *that* beings *are*. The being that is thus called in its essence into the truth of being is for this reason always attuned in an essential manner. The lucid courage for essential anxiety assures us the enigmatic possibility of experiencing being. For close by essential anxiety as the horror of the abyss dwells awe. Awe clears and cherishes that locality of the human essence within which humans remain at home in that which endures.

By contrast, "anxiety" in the face of anxiety can stray to such an extent that it fails to recognize the simple relations that obtain in the essence of anxiety. What would all courage be if it did not find its permanent counterpart in the experience of essential anxiety? To the degree that we degrade such essential anxiety, together with the relationship of being to humans that is cleared within it, we denigrate the essence of courage. Yet courage is able to withstand the nothing. In the abyss of horror, courage recognizes the scarcely broached realm of being from whose clearing every being first returns to what it is and can be. This lecture neither propounds a "philosophy of anxiety," nor does it seek to impress upon us by devious means a "heroic philosophy." It thinks only that which dawned on Western thinking from its beginning as that which has to be thought, and yet has remained forgotten: being. Yet being is not a product of thinking. By contrast, essential thinking is presumably an event proper to being [*ein Ereignis des Seins*].

For this reason, it now also becomes necessary to ask the question, which is barely posed, of whether this thinking already stands within the law of its truth when it merely follows the thinking whose forms and rules are conceived by "logic." Why does the lecture place this term [104] in quotation marks? So as to indicate that "logic" is only *one* interpretation of the essence of thinking, indeed the one that, as its very name shows, rests upon the experience of being attained in Greek thought. The suspicion regarding "logic," whose consequential development degenerates into logistics, springs from a knowledge belonging to that thinking which finds its source in the experience of the truth of being, but not in contemplating the objectivity of beings. Exact thinking is never the most rigorous thinking, if rigor indeed receives its essence from the kind of rigorous effort whereby knowledge in each case maintains itself within a relation to what is essential in beings. Exact thinking merely binds itself to the calculation of beings and serves this end exclusively.

All calculation lets what is countable be resolved into something counted that can then be used for subsequent counting. Calculation refuses to let anything appear except what is countable. Everything is only whatever it counts. What has been counted in each instance secures the continuation of counting. Such counting progressively consumes numbers, and is itself a continual self-consumption. The calculative process of resolving beings into what has been counted counts as the explanation of their being. Calculation uses all beings in advance as that which is countable, and uses up what is counted for the purpose of counting. This use of beings that consumes them betrays the consuming character of calculation. Only because number can be infinitely multiplied, irrespective of whether this occurs in the direction of the large or the small, can the consuming essence of calculation hide behind its products and lend to calculative thinking the semblance of productivity – whereas already in its anticipatory grasping, and not primarily in its subsequent results, such thinking lets all beings count only in the form of what can be set at our disposal and consumed. Calculative thinking compels itself into a compulsion to master everything on the basis of the consequential correctness of its procedure. It is unable to foresee that everything calculable by calculation – prior to the sum-totals and products that it produces by calculation in each case – is already a whole, a whole whose unity indeed [105] belongs to the incalculable that withdraws itself and its uncanniness from the claws of calculation. Yet that which everywhere and always from the outset has closed itself off from the intent behind calculation, and yet, in its enigmatic unfamiliarity, is at all times nearer to the human being than all those beings in which he establishes himself and his intentions, can at times attune the essence of the human being to a thinking whose truth no "logic" is capable of grasping. That thinking whose thoughts not only cannot be calculated, but are in general determined by that which is other than beings, may be called essential thinking.[a] Instead of calculatively counting on beings by means of beings, it expends itself in being for the truth of being. Such thinking responds to the claim of being, through the human being letting his historical essence be responsible to the simplicity of a singular necessity, one that does not necessitate by way of compulsion, but creates the need that fulfills itself in the freedom of sacrifice. The need is for the truth of being to be preserved, whatever may happen to human beings and to all beings. The sacrifice is that of the human essence expending itself – in a manner removed from all compulsion, because it arises from the abyss of freedom – for the preservation of the truth of being for beings. In sacrifice there occurs [ereignet sich] the concealed thanks that alone pays homage to the grace that being has bestowed upon the human essence in thinking, so that human beings may, in their relation to being, assume the guardianship of being. Originary thinking [Das anfängliche Denken][7] is the echo of being's favor, of a favor in which a singular event is cleared and lets come to pass [sich ereignen]:[8][b] that beings are. This echo is the human response to the word of the silent voice of being. The response of thinking[9] is the origin of the human word, which word first lets language arise as the sounding of the word into words. Were there not at times a concealed thinking[10] in the ground of the essence of historical human beings, then human beings would never be capable of thanking[11] – granted that in all thinking of something and in every thanking[12] there must indeed be a thinking that thinks the truth of being in an originary manner. [106] Yet how else would a particular humankind ever find its way into an originary thanking unless the favor of being, through an open relation to such favor, granted human beings the nobility of a poverty in which the freedom of sacrifice conceals the treasure of its essence? Sacrifice is the departure from beings on the path to preserving the favor of being. Sacrifice can indeed be prepared and served by working and achievement with respect to beings, yet never fulfilled by such activities. Its accomplishment stems from that inherent stance [Inständigkeit] out of which every historical human being through action – and essential thinking is an action – preserves the Dasein he has attained

[a] Fifth edition, 1949: Calculating: domination – ordering into place; Thinking: releasement for the propriation of usage – telling renunciation [Ent-sagen].
[b] Fifth edition, 1949: Event [Ereignis].

for the preservation of the dignity of being. Such a stance is the equanimity that allows nothing to assail its concealed readiness for the essential departure that belongs to every sacrifice. Sacrifice is at home in the essence of the event [*Ereignis*] whereby being lays claim upon[a] the human being for the truth of being. For this reason, sacrifice tolerates no calculation, which can only ever miscalculate it in terms of utility or uselessness, whether the ends are placed low or set high. Such miscalculation distorts the essence of sacrifice. The obsession with ends confuses the clarity of the awe, ready for anxiety, that belongs to the courage of sacrifice which has taken upon itself the neighborhood of the indestructible.

The thinking of being seeks no hold in beings. Essential thinking heeds the measured signs of the incalculable and recognizes in the latter the unforeseeable arrival of the unavoidable. Such thinking is attentive to the truth of being and thus helps the being of truth to find its site within historical humankind. This help does not effect any results, because it has no need of effect. Essential thinking helps in its simple stance within Dasein insofar as such a stance, without being able to dispose over or even know of this, kindles its own kind.

Thinking, obedient to the voice of being, seeks from being the word through which the truth of being comes to language. Only when the language of historical human beings springs from the word [107] does it ring true. Yet if it does ring true, then it is beckoned by the testimony granted it from the silent voice of hidden sources. The thinking of being protects the word, and in such protectiveness fulfills its vocation. It is a care for our use of language. The saying of the thinker comes from a long-protected speechlessness and from the careful clarifying of the realm thus cleared. Of like provenance is the naming of the poet. Yet because that which is like is so only as difference allows, and because poetizing and thinking are most purely alike in their care of the word, they are at the same time farthest separated in their essence. The thinker says being. The poet names the holy. And yet the manner in which – thought from out of the essence of being – poetizing, thanking, and thinking are directed toward one another and are at the same time different, must be left open here. Presumably thanking and poetizing each in their own way spring from originary thinking, which they need, yet without themselves being able to be a thinking.

We may know much about the relation between philosophy and poetry. Yet we know nothing of the dialogue between poets and thinkers, who "dwell near one another on mountains most separate."

---

[a] Fifth edition, 1949: Appropriates in its event [*er-eignet*], needs and uses.

One of the essential sites of speechlessness is anxiety in the sense of the horror to which the abyss of the nothing attunes human beings. The nothing, as other than beings, is the veil of being.[a] Every destiny of beings has already in its origins come to its completion in being.

The last poetizing of the last poet in the dawn of the Greek world, namely, Sophocles' *Oedipus at Colonus*, closes with words that, in a manner impossible for us to follow, hark back to the concealed history of that people and preserve their entry into the unknown truth of being:

ἀλλ᾽ ἀποπαύετε μηδ᾽ ἐπὶ πλείω
θρῆνον ἐγείρετε·
πάντως γὰρ ἔχει τάδε κῦρος.

[108] But cease now, and nevermore hereafter
Awaken such lament;
For what has happened keeps with it everywhere preserved a decision
of completion.

---

[a] Fifth edition, 1949: The nothing: That which annuls, i.e., as difference, is as the veil of being, i.e., of beyng in the sense of the appropriative event of usage.

Letter on "Humanism" [a]

Translated by Frank A. Capuzzi[1]

[145] We are still far from pondering the essence of action decisively enough. We view action only as causing an effect. The actuality of the effect is valued according to its utility. But the essence of action is accomplishment. To accomplish means to unfold something into the fullness of its essence, to lead it forth into this fullness – *producere*. Therefore only what already is can really be accomplished. But what "is" above all is being. Thinking accomplishes the relation of being to the essence of the human being. It does not make or cause the relation. Thinking brings this relation to being solely as something handed over to thought itself from being. Such offering consists in the fact that in thinking being comes to language. Language is the house of being. In its home human beings dwell. Those who think and those who create with words are the guardians of this home. Their guardianship accomplishes the manifestation of being insofar as they bring this manifestation to language and preserve it in language through their saying. Thinking does not become action only because some effect issues from it or because it is applied. Thinking acts insofar as it thinks. Such action is presumably the simplest and at the same time the highest because it concerns the relation of being to humans. But all working or effecting lies in being and is directed toward beings. Thinking, in contrast, lets itself be claimed by being so that it can say the truth of being. Thinking accomplishes this letting. Thinking is *l'engagement par l'Être pour l'Être* [engagement by being for being]. I do not know whether it is linguistically possible to say both of these ("*par*" and "*pour*") at once in this way: penser,

[a] First edition, 1949: What is said here was not first thought up when this letter was written, but is based on the course taken by a path that was begun in 1936, in the "moment" of an attempt to say the truth of being in a simple manner. The letter continues to speak in the language of metaphysics, and does so knowingly. The other language remains in the background.

239

c'est l'engagement de l'Être [thinking is the engagement of being]. Here the possessive form "de l' ..." is supposed to express both subjective and objective genitive. In this regard "subject" and "object" are inappropriate terms of metaphysics, which very early on in [146] the form of Occidental "logic" and "grammar" seized control of the interpretation of language. We today can only begin to descry what is concealed in that occurrence. The liberation of language from grammar into a more original essential framework is reserved for thought and poetic creation. Thinking is not merely *l'engagement dans l'action* for and by beings, in the sense of whatever is actually present in our current situation. Thinking is *l'engagement* by and for the truth of being. The history of being is never past but stands ever before us; it sustains and defines every *condition et situation humaine*. In order to learn how to experience the aforementioned essence of thinking purely, and that means at the same time to carry it through, we must free ourselves from the technical interpretation of thinking. The beginnings of that interpretation reach back to Plato and Aristotle. They take thinking itself to be a τέχνη, a process of deliberation in service to doing and making. But here deliberation is already seen from the perspective of πρᾶξις and ποίησις. For this reason thinking, when taken for itself, is not "practical." The characterization of thinking as θεωρία and the determination of knowing as "theoretical" comportment occur already within the "technical" interpretation of thinking. Such characterization is a reactive attempt to rescue thinking and preserve its autonomy over against acting and doing. Since then "philosophy" has been in the constant predicament of having to justify its existence before the "sciences." It believes it can do that most effectively by elevating itself to the rank of a science. But such an effort is the abandonment of the essence of thinking. Philosophy is hounded by the fear that it loses prestige and validity if it is not a science. Not to be a science is taken as a failing that is equivalent to being unscientific. Being,[a] as the element of thinking, is abandoned by the technical interpretation of thinking. "Logic," beginning with the Sophists and Plato, sanctions this explanation. [147] Thinking is judged by a standard that does not measure up to it. Such judgment may be compared to the procedure of trying to evaluate the essence and powers of a fish by seeing how long it can live on dry land. For a long time now, all too long, thinking has been stranded on dry land. Can then the effort to return thinking to its element be called "irrationalism"?

---

[a] First edition, 1949: Being as event of appropriation [*Ereignis*], event of appropriation: the saying [*Sage*]; thinking: renunciative saying in response [*Entsagen*] to the saying of the event of appropriation.

Surely the questions raised in your letter would have been better answered in direct conversation. In written form thinking easily loses its flexibility. But in writing it is difficult above all to retain the multidimensionality of the realm peculiar to thinking. The rigor of thinking,[a] in contrast to that of the sciences, does not consist merely in an artificial, that is, technical-theoretical exactness of concepts. It lies in the fact that saying remains purely in the element of the truth of[2] being and lets the simplicity of its manifold dimensions rule. On the other hand, written composition exerts a wholesome pressure toward deliberate linguistic formulation. Today I would like to grapple with only one of your questions. Perhaps its discussion will also shed some light on the others.

You ask: "Comment redonner un sens au mot 'Humanisme'?" [How can we restore meaning to the word "humanism"?] This question proceeds from your intention to retain the word "humanism." I wonder whether that is necessary. Or is the damage caused by all such terms still not sufficiently obvious? True, "-isms" have for a long time now been suspect. But the market of public opinion continually demands new ones. We are always prepared to supply the demand. Even such names as "logic," "ethics," and "physics" begin to flourish only when originary thinking comes to an end. During the time of their greatness the Greeks thought without such headings. They did not even call thinking "philosophy." Thinking comes to an end when it slips out of its element. The element is what enables thinking to be a thinking. The element is what properly enables: it is the enabling [das Vermögen]. It embraces thinking and so brings it into its essence. [148] Said plainly, thinking is the thinking of being. The genitive says something twofold. Thinking is of being inasmuch as thinking, propriated[b] by being, belongs to being. At the same time thinking is of being insofar as thinking, belonging to being, listens to being. As the belonging to being that listens, thinking is what it is according to its essential origin. Thinking is – this says: Being has embraced its essence in a destinal manner in each case. To embrace a "thing" or a "person" in their essence means to love them, to favor them. Thought in a more original way such favoring means the bestowal of their essence as a gift. Such favoring [Mögen] is the proper essence of enabling [Vermögen], which not only can achieve this or that but also can let something essentially unfold in its provenance, that is, let it be. It is on the "strength" of such enabling by favoring that something is properly able

[a] First edition, 1949: "Thinking" already conceived here as thinking of the truth of being.
[b] First edition, 1949: Only a pointer in the language of metaphysics. For "Ereignis," "event of appropriation," has been the guiding word of my thinking since 1936.

to be. This enabling is what is properly "possible" [das "Mögliche"], whose essence resides in favoring. From this favoring being enables thinking. The former makes the latter possible. Being is the enabling-favoring, the "may be" [das "Mög-liche"]. As the element, being is the "quiet power" of the favoring-enabling, that is, of the possible. Of course, our words möglich [possible] and Möglichkeit [possibility], under the dominance of "logic" and "metaphysics," are thought solely in contrast to "actuality"; that is, they are thought on the basis of a definite – the metaphysical – interpretation of being as actus and potentia, a distinction identified with that between existentia and essentia.³ When I speak of the "quiet power of the possible" I do not mean the possibile of a merely represented possibilitas, nor potentia as the essentia of an actus of existentia; rather, I mean being itself, which in its favoring presides over thinking and hence over the essence of humanity, and that means over its relation to being. To enable something here means to preserve it in its essence, to maintain it in its element.

When thinking comes to an end by slipping out of its element it replaces this loss by procuring a validity for itself as τέχνη, as an instrument of education and therefore as a classroom matter [149] and later a cultural concern. By and by philosophy becomes a technique for explaining from highest causes. One no longer thinks; one occupies oneself with "philosophy." In competition with one another, such occupations publicly offer themselves as "-isms" and try to outdo one another. The dominance of such terms is not accidental. It rests above all in the modern age upon the peculiar dictatorship of the public realm. However, so-called "private existence" is not really essential, that is to say free, human being. It simply ossifies in a denial of the public realm. It remains an offshoot that depends upon the public and nourishes itself by a mere withdrawal from it. Hence it testifies, against its own will, to its subservience to the public realm. But because it stems from the dominance of subjectivity the public realm itself is the metaphysically conditioned establishment and authorization of the openness of beings in the unconditional objectification of everything. Language thereby falls into the service of expediting communication along routes where objectification – the uniform accessibility of everything to everyone – branches out and disregards all limits. In this way language comes under the dictatorship of the public realm, which decides in advance what is intelligible and what must be rejected as unintelligible. What is said in Being and Time (1927), sections 27 and 35, about the "they" in no way means to furnish an incidental contribution to sociology. Just as little does the "they" mean merely the opposite, understood in an ethical-existentiell way, of the selfhood of persons. Rather, what is said there contains a reference, thought in terms of the question of the truth of being, to the primordial belonging of the word to being. This relation remains concealed amid the dominance of subjectivity that presents itself as the public realm. But if the truth of being has become thought-provoking for thinking, then reflection on the essence of language must also attain a different rank. It can no longer be a mere philosophy of language. [150] That is the only reason *Being and Time* (section 34) contains a reference to the essential dimension of language and touches upon the simple question as to what mode of being language as language in any given case has. The widely and rapidly spreading devastation of language not only undermines aesthetic and moral responsibility in every use of language; it arises from a threat to the essence of humanity. A merely cultivated use of language is still no proof that we have as yet escaped this danger to our essence. These days, in fact, such usage might sooner testify that we have not yet seen and cannot see the danger because we have never yet placed ourselves in view of it. Much bemoaned of late, and much too lately, the decline of language is, however, not the grounds for, but already a consequence of, the state of affairs in which language under the dominance of the modern metaphysics of subjectivity almost irremediably falls out of its element. Language still denies us its essence: that it is the house of the truth of being. Instead, language surrenders itself to our mere willing and trafficking as an instrument of domination over beings. Beings themselves appear as actualities in the interaction of cause and effect. We encounter beings as actualities in a calculative businesslike way, but also scientifically and by way of philosophy, with explanations and proofs. Even the assurance that something is inexplicable belongs to these explanations and proofs. With such statements we believe that we confront the mystery. As if it were already decided that the truth of being lets itself at all be established in causes and explanatory grounds or, what comes to the same, in their incomprehensibility.

But if the human being is to find his way once again into the nearness of being he must first learn to exist in the nameless. In the same way he must recognize the seductions of the public realm as well as the impotence of the private. Before he speaks the human being must first let himself be claimed again by being, taking the risk that under this claim he will seldom have much to say. Only thus will [151] the pricelessness of its essence be once more bestowed upon the word, and upon humans a home for dwelling in the truth of being.

But in the claim upon human beings, in the attempt to make humans ready for this claim, is there not implied a concern about human beings? Where else does "care" tend but in the direction of bringing the human being back to his essence? What else does that in turn betoken but that man (*homo*) become human (*humanus*)? Thus *humanitas* really does remain the concern of such thinking. For this is humanism: meditating and caring, that human beings be human and not inhumane, "inhuman," that is, outside their essence. But in what does the humanity of the human being consist? It lies in his essence.

But whence and how is the essence of the human being determined? Marx demands that "the human being's humanity" be recognized and acknowledged. He finds it in "society." The "social" human is for him the "natural" human. In "society" human "nature," that is, the totality of "natural needs" (food, clothing, reproduction, economic sufficiency), is equably secured. The Christian sees the humanity of man, the *humanitas* of *homo*, in contradistinction to *Deitas*. He is the human being of the history of redemption who as a "child of God" hears and accepts the call of the Father in Christ. The human being is not of this world, since the "world," thought in terms of Platonic theory, is only a temporary passage to the beyond.

Humanitas, explicitly so called, was first considered and striven for in the age of the Roman Republic. *Homo humanus* was opposed to *homo barbarus*. *Homo humanus* here means the Romans, who exalted and honored Roman *virtus* through the "embodiment" of the παιδεία [education] taken over from the Greeks. These were the Greeks of the Hellenistic age, whose culture was acquired in the [152] schools of philosophy. It was concerned with *eruditio et institutio in bonas artes* [scholarship and training in good conduct]. Παιδεία thus understood was translated as *humanitas*. The genuine *romanitas* of *homo romanus* consisted in such *humanitas*. We encounter the first humanism in Rome: it therefore remains in essence a specifically Roman phenomenon, which emerges from the encounter of Roman civilization with the culture of late Greek civilization. The so-called Renaissance of the fourteenth and fifteenth centuries in Italy is a *renascentia romanitatis*. Because *romanitas* is what matters, it is concerned with *humanitas* and therefore with Greek παιδεία. But Greek civilization is always seen in its later form and this itself is seen from a Roman point of view. The *homo romanus* of the Renaissance also stands in opposition to *homo barbarus*. But now the in-humane is the supposed barbarism of Gothic Scholasticism in the Middle Ages. Therefore a *studium humanitatis*, which in a certain way reaches back to the ancients and thus also becomes a revival of Greek civilization, always adheres to historically understood humanism. For Germans this is apparent in the humanism of the eighteenth century supported by Winckelmann, Goethe, and Schiller. On the other hand, Hölderlin does not belong to "humanism," precisely because he thought the destiny of the essence of the human being in a more original way than "humanism" could.

But if one understands humanism in general as a concern that the human being become free for his humanity and find his worth in it, then humanism differs according to one's conception of the "freedom" and "nature" of the human being. So too are there various paths toward the realization of such conceptions. The humanism of Marx does not need to return to antiquity any more than the humanism that Sartre conceives existentialism to be. In this broad sense Christianity too is a humanism, in that according to its teaching everything depends on human salvation (*salus aeterna*); the history of the [153] human being appears in the context of the history of redemption. However different these forms of humanism may be in purpose and in principle, in the mode and means of their respective realizations, and in the form of their teaching, they nonetheless all agree in this, that the *humanitas* of *homo humanus* is determined with regard to an already established interpretation of nature, history, world, and the ground of the world, that is, of beings as a whole.

Every humanism is either grounded in a metaphysics or is itself made to be the ground of one. Every determination of the essence of the human being that already presupposes an interpretation of beings without asking about the truth of being, whether knowingly or not, is metaphysical. The result is that what is peculiar to all metaphysics, specifically with respect to the way the essence of the human being is determined, is that it is "humanistic." Accordingly, every humanism remains metaphysical. In defining the humanity of the human being, humanism not only does not ask about the relation of being[a] to the essence of the human being; because of its metaphysical origin humanism even impedes the question by neither recognizing nor understanding it. On the contrary, the necessity and proper form of the question concerning the truth of being, forgotten[b] in and through metaphysics, can come to light only if the question "What is metaphysics?" is posed in the midst of metaphysics' domination. Indeed, every inquiry into "being," even the one into the truth of being, must at first introduce its inquiry as a "metaphysical" one.

The first humanism, Roman humanism, and every kind that has emerged from that time to the present, has presupposed the most universal "essence" of the human being to be obvious. The human being is considered to be an *animal rationale*. This definition is not simply the Latin translation of

[a] First edition, 1949: "Being" and "being itself" at once enter the *isolation of the Absolute* through this way of saying things. Yet so long as the event of appropriation is held back, this way of saying things is unavoidable.

[b] *Plato's Doctrine of Truth*, first edition, 1947: But this "forgetting" is to be thought starting from ᾿Αλήθεια in terms of the event of appropriation.

the Greek ζῷον λόγον ἔχον, but rather a metaphysical interpretation of it. This essential definition of the human being is [154] not false. But it is conditioned by metaphysics. The essential provenance of metaphysics, and not just its limits, became questionable in *Being and Time*. What is questionable is above all commended to thinking as what is to be thought, but not at all left to the gnawing doubts of an empty skepticism.

Metaphysics does indeed represent beings in their being, and so it also[4] thinks the being of beings. But it does not think being as such,[5] does not think the difference between being and beings. (Cf. "On the Essence of Ground" [1929], p. 8; also *Kant and the Problem of Metaphysics* [1929], p. 225; and *Being and Time*, p. 230.) Metaphysics does not ask about the truth of being itself. Nor does it therefore ask in what way the essence of the human being belongs to the truth of being. Metaphysics has not only failed up to now to ask this question, the question is inaccessible to metaphysics as such. Being is still waiting for the time when It itself will become thought-provoking to the human being. With regard to the definition of the essence of the human being, however one may determine the *ratio* of the *animal* and the reason of the living being, whether as a "faculty of principles" or a "faculty of categories" or in some other way, the essence of reason is always and in each case grounded in this: for every apprehending of beings in their being, being in each case[6] is already cleared, it is[7] propriated in its truth. So too with *animal*, ζῷον, an interpretation of "life" is already posited that necessarily lies in an interpretation of beings as ζωή and φύσις, within which what is living appears. Above and beyond everything else, however, it finally remains to ask[8] whether the essence of the human being primordially and most decisively lies in the dimension of *animalitas* at all. Are we really on the right track toward the essence of the human being as long as we set him off as one living creature among others in contrast to plants, beasts, and God? We can proceed in that way; we can in such fashion locate the human being among beings as one being among others. We will thereby always be able to state something correct about the human being. [155] But we must be clear on this point, that when we do this we abandon the human being to the essential realm of *animalitas* even if we do not equate him with beasts but attribute a specific difference to him. In principle we are still thinking of *homo animalis* – even when *anima* [soul] is posited as *animus sive mens* [spirit or mind], and this in turn is later posited as subject, person, or spirit. Such positing is the manner of metaphysics. But then the essence of the human being is too little heeded and not thought in its origin, the essential provenance that is always the essential future for historical mankind. Metaphysics thinks of the human being on the basis of *animalitas* and does not think in the direction of his *humanitas*.

Metaphysics closes itself to the simple essential fact that the human being essentially occurs in his essence only where he is claimed by being. Only from that claim "has" he found that wherein his essence dwells. Only from this dwelling does he "have" "language" as the home that preserves the ecstatic for his essence. Such standing in the clearing of being I call the ek-sistence of human beings. This way of being is proper only to the human being. Ek-sistence so understood is not only the ground of the possibility of reason, *ratio*, but is also that in which the essence of the human being preserves the source that determines him.

Ek-sistence can be said only of the essence of the human being, that is, only of the human way "to be." For as far as our experience shows, only the human being is admitted to the destiny of ek-sistence. Therefore ek-sistence can also never be thought of as a specific kind of living creature among others – granted that the human being is destined to think the essence of his being and not merely to give accounts of the nature and history of his constitution and activities. Thus even what we attribute to the human being as *animalitas* on the basis of the comparison with "beasts" is itself grounded in the essence of ek-sistence. The human body is something essentially [156] other than an animal organism. Nor is the error of biologism overcome by adjoining a soul to the human body, a mind to the soul, and the existentiell to the mind, and then louder than before singing the praises of the mind – only to let everything relapse into "life-experience," with a warning that thinking by its inflexible concepts disrupts the flow of life and that thought of being distorts existence. The fact that physiology and physiological chemistry can scientifically investigate the human being as an organism is no proof that in this "organic" thing, that is, in the body scientifically explained, the essence of the human being consists. That has as little validity as the notion that the essence of nature has been discovered in atomic energy. It could even be that nature, in the face it turns toward the human being's technical mastery, is simply concealing its essence. Just as little as the essence of the human being consists in being an animal organism can this insufficient definition of the essence of the human being be overcome or offset by outfitting the human being with an immortal soul, the power of reason, or the character of a person. In each instance its essence is passed over, and passed over on the basis of the same metaphysical projection.

What the human being is – or, as it is called in the traditional language of metaphysics, the "essence" of the human being – lies in his ek-sistence.

But ek-sistence thought in this way is not identical with the traditional concept of *existentia*, which means actuality in contrast to the meaning of *essentia* as possibility. In *Being and Time* (p. 42) this sentence is italicized: "The 'essence' of Dasein lies in its existence." However, here the opposition between *existentia* and *essentia* is not what is at issue, because neither of these metaphysical determinations of being, let alone their relationship, is yet in question. Still less does the sentence contain a universal statement [157] about *Dasein*, in the sense in which this word came into fashion in the eighteenth century, as a name for "object," intending to express the metaphysical concept of the actuality of the actual. On the contrary, the sentence says: the human being occurs essentially in such a way that he is the "there" [*das "Da"*], that is, the clearing of being. The "being" of the *Da*, and only it, has the fundamental character of ek-sistence, that is, of an ecstatic inherence in the truth of being. The ecstatic essence of the human being consists in ek-sistence, which is different from the metaphysically conceived *existentia*. Medieval philosophy conceives the latter as *actualitas*. Kant represents *existentia* as actuality in the sense of the objectivity of experience. Hegel defines *existentia* as the self-knowing Idea of absolute subjectivity. Nietzsche grasps *existentia* as the eternal recurrence of the same. Here it remains an open question whether through *existentia* – in these explanations of it as actuality that at first seem quite different – the being of a stone or even life as the being of plants and animals is adequately thought. In any case living creatures are as they are without standing outside their being as such and within the truth of being, preserving in such standing the essential nature of their being. Of all the beings that are, presumably the most difficult to think about are living creatures, because on the one hand they are in a certain way most closely akin to us, and on the other they are at the same time separated from our ek-sistent essence by an abyss. However, it might also seem as though the essence of divinity is closer to us than what is so alien in other living creatures, closer, namely, in an essential distance that, however distant, is nonetheless more familiar to our ek-sistent essence than is our scarcely conceivable, abysmal bodily kinship with the beast. Such reflections cast a strange light upon the current and therefore always still premature designation of the human being as *animal rationale*. Because plants and animals are lodged in their respective environments but are never placed freely into the clearing of being which alone is "world," they lack language. [158] But in being denied language they are not thereby suspended worldlessly in their environment. Still, in this word "environment" converges all that is puzzling about living creatures. In its essence, language is not the utterance of an organism; nor is it the expression of a living thing. Nor can it ever be thought in an essentially correct way in terms of its symbolic character, perhaps not even in terms of the character of signification. Language is the clearing-concealing advent of being itself.

Ek-sistence, thought in terms of ecstasis, does not coincide with *existentia* in either form or content. In terms of content ek-sistence means standing out[a] into the truth of being. *Existentia* (*existence*) means in contrast *actualitas*, actuality as opposed to mere possibility as Idea. Ek-sistence identifies the determination of what the human being is in the destiny of truth. *Existentia* is the name for the realization of something that is as it appears in its Idea. The sentence "The human being ek-sists" is not an answer to the question of whether the human being actually is or not; rather, it responds to the question concerning the "essence" of the human being. We are accustomed to posing this question with equal impropriety whether we ask what the human being is or who he is. For in the *Who?* or the *What?* we are already on the lookout for something like a person or an object. But the personal no less than the objective misses and misconstrues the essential unfolding of ek-sistence in the history of being. That is why the sentence cited from *Being and Time* (p. 42) is careful to enclose the word "essence" in quotation marks. This indicates that "essence" is now being defined neither from *esse essentiae* nor from *esse existentiae* but rather from the ek-static character of Dasein. As ek-sisting, the human being sustains Da-sein in that he takes the *Da*, the clearing of being, into "care." But Da-sein itself occurs essentially as "thrown." It unfolds essentially in the throw of being as a destinal sending.

But it would be the ultimate error if one wished to explain the sentence about the human being's eksistent essence as if it were the [159] secularized transference to human beings of a thought that Christian theology expresses about God (*Deus est ipsum esse*[9] [God is his being]); for ek-sistence is not the realization of an essence, nor does ek-sistence itself even effect and posit what is essential. If we understand what *Being and Time* calls "projection" as a representational positing, we take it to be an achievement of subjectivity and do not think it in the only way the "understanding of being" in the context of the "existential analysis" of "being-in-the-world" can be thought – namely, as the ecstatic relation[b] to the clearing of being. The adequate execution and completion of this other thinking that abandons subjectivity is surely made more difficult by the fact that in the publication of *Being and Time* the third division of the first part, "Time and Being," was

---

[a] *Plato's Doctrine of Truth*, first edition, 1947: "Out": into the "out" of the "out of one another" of the difference (the "there"), not "out" out of an interior.

[b] First edition, 1949: Imprecise, better: ekstatic in-standing within the clearing.

held back (cf. *Being and Time*, p. 39). Here everything[a] is reversed. The division in question was held back because thinking failed in the adequate saying[b] of this turning [*Kehre*] and did not succeed with the help of the language of metaphysics. The lecture "On the Essence of Truth," thought out and delivered in 1930 but not printed until 1943, provides a certain insight into the thinking of the turning from "Being and Time" to "Time and Being." This turning is not a change of standpoint[c] from *Being and Time*, but in it the thinking that was sought first arrives at the locality of that dimension out of which *Being and Time* is experienced, that is to say, experienced in[10] the fundamental experience of the oblivion of being.[d]

By way of contrast, Sartre expresses the basic tenet of existentialism in this way: Existence precedes essence. In this statement he is taking *existentia* and *essentia* according to their metaphysical meaning, which from Plato's time on has said that *essentia* precedes *existentia*. Sartre reverses this statement. But the reversal of a metaphysical statement remains a metaphysical statement. With it he stays with metaphysics in oblivion of the truth of being. For even if philosophy wishes to determine the relation of *essentia* and *existentia* in the sense it had in medieval controversies, in Leibniz's sense, or in some other way, it still [160] remains to ask first of all from what destiny of being this differentiation[e] in being as *esse essentiae* and *esse existentiae* comes to appear to thinking. We have yet to consider why the question about the destiny of being was never asked and why it could never be thought. Or is the fact that this is how it is with the differentiation of *essentia* and *existentia* not a sign of forgetfulness of being? We must presume that this destiny does not rest upon a mere failure of human thinking, let alone upon a lesser capacity of early Western thinking. Concealed in its essential provenance, the differentiation of *essentia* (essentiality) and *existentia* (actuality) completely dominates the destiny of Western history and of all history determined by Europe.

Sartre's key proposition about the priority of *existentia* over *essentia* does, however, justify using the name "existentialism" as an appropriate title for a philosophy of this sort. But the basic tenet of "existentialism" has nothing at all in common with the statement from *Being and Time* – apart from the

---

[a] First edition, 1949: In terms of the "what" and "how" of that which is thought-worthy and of thinking.

[b] First edition, 1949: Letting itself show.

[c] First edition, 1949: I.e., of the question of being.

[d] First edition, 1949: Forgottenness – Λήθη – concealing – withdrawal – expropriation: event of appropriation.

[e] First edition, 1949: This distinction, however, is not identical with the ontological difference. Within the latter, the said distinction belongs on the "side" of being.

fact that in *Being and Time* no statement about the relation of *essentia* and *existentia* can yet be expressed, since there it is still a question of preparing something precursory. As is obvious from what we have just said, that happens clumsily enough. What still today remains to be said could perhaps become an impetus for guiding the essence of the human being to the point where it thoughtfully attends to that dimension of the truth of being that thoroughly governs it. But even this could take place only to the honor of being and for the benefit of Da-sein, which the human being ek-sistingly sustains; not, however, for the sake of the human being, so that civilization and culture through human doings might be vindicated.

But in order that we today may attain to the dimension of the truth of being in order to ponder it, we should first of all make clear how being concerns the human being and how it claims him. Such an essential experience happens to us when it dawns on us that [161] the human being is in that he ek-sists. Were we now to say this in the language of the tradition, it would run: the ek-sistence of the human being is his substance. That is why in *Being and Time* the sentence often recurs, "The 'substance' of the human being is existence" (pp. 117, 212, 314). But "substance," thought in terms of the history of being, is already a blanket translation of οὐσία, a word that designates the presence of what is present and at the same time, with puzzling ambiguity, usually means what is present itself. If we think the metaphysical term "substance" in the sense already suggested in accordance with the "phenomenological destruction" carried out in *Being and Time* (cf. p. 25), then the statement "The 'substance' of the human being is ek-sistence" says nothing else but that the way that the human being in his proper essence becomes present to being is ecstatic inherence in the truth of being. Through this determination of the essence of the human being the humanistic interpretations of the human being as *animal rationale*, as "person," as spiritual-ensouled-bodily being, are not declared false and thrust aside. Rather, the sole implication is that the highest determinations of the essence of the human being in humanism still do not realize the proper dignity[a] of the human being. To that extent the thinking in *Being and Time* is against humanism. But this opposition does not mean that such thinking aligns itself against the humane and advocates the inhuman, that it promotes the inhumane and deprecates the dignity of the human being. Humanism is opposed because it does not set the *humanitas* of the human being high enough. Of course the essential worth of the human being does

---

[a] First edition, 1949: The dignity proper to him, i.e., that has come to be appropriate, appropriated in the event: propriation and event of appropriation.

not consist in his being the substance of beings, as the "Subject" among them, so that as the tyrant of being he may deign to release the beingness of beings into an all too loudly glorified "objectivity."

The human being is rather "thrown" by being itself into the truth of being, so that ek-sisting in this fashion he might guard the truth of being, in order that beings might appear in the light of being [162] as the beings they are. Human beings do not decide whether and how beings appear, whether and how God and the gods or history and nature come forward into the clearing of being, come to presence and depart. The advent of beings lies in the destiny[a] of being. But for humans it is ever a question of finding what is fitting in their essence that corresponds to such destiny; for in accord with this destiny the human being as ek-sisting has to guard the truth of being. The human being is the shepherd of being. It is in this direction alone that *Being and Time* is thinking when ecstatic existence is experienced as "care" (cf. section 44c, pp. 226ff.).

Yet being – what is being? It "is"[11] It itself. The thinking that is to come must learn to experience that and to say it. "Being" – that is not God and not a cosmic ground. Being is essentially[12] farther[b] than all beings and is yet nearer to the human being than every being, be it a rock, a beast, a work of art, a machine, be it an angel or God. Being is the nearest. Yet the near remains farthest[13] from the human being. Human beings at first cling always and only to beings. But when thinking represents beings as beings it no doubt relates itself to being. In truth, however, it always thinks only of beings as such; precisely not, and never, being as such. The "question of being" always remains a question about beings. It is still not at all what its elusive name indicates: the question in the direction of being. Philosophy, even when it becomes "critical" through Descartes and Kant, always follows the course of metaphysical representation. It thinks from beings back to beings with a glance in passing toward being. For every departure from beings and every return to them stands already in the light of being.

But metaphysics recognizes the clearing of being either solely as the view of what is present in "outward appearance" (ἰδέα) or critically as what is seen in the perspect of categorial representation on the part of subjectivity. This means that the truth of being as the clearing itself remains concealed for metaphysics. [163] However, this concealment is not a defect of metaphysics but a treasure withheld from it yet held before it, the treasure of

---

[a] First edition, 1949: Gathered sending [*Ge-schick*]: gathering of the epochs of being used by the need of letting-presence.

[b] First edition, 1949: Expanse: not that of an embracing, but rather of the locality of appropriation; as the expanse of the clearing.

its own proper wealth. But the clearing itself is being. Within the destiny of being in metaphysics the clearing first affords a view by which what is present comes into touch with the human being, who is present to it, so that the human being himself can in apprehending (νοεῖν) first touch upon being (θιγεῖν, Aristotle, *Metaphysics* Θ, 10). This view first draws the perspect toward it. It abandons itself to such a perspect when apprehending has become a setting-forth-before-itself in the *perceptio* of the *res cogitans* taken as the *subiectum* of *certitudo*.

But how – provided we really ought to ask such a question at all – how does being relate to ek-sistence? Being itself is the relation[a] to the extent that It, as the locality of the truth of being amid beings, gathers to itself and embraces ek-sistence in its existential, that is, ecstatic, essence. Because the human being as the one who ek-sists comes to stand in this relation that being destines for itself, in that he ecstatically sustains it, that is, in care takes it upon himself, he at first fails to recognize the nearest and attaches himself to the next nearest. He even thinks that this is the nearest. But nearer than the nearest, than beings,[14] and at the same time for ordinary thinking farther than the farthest is nearness itself: the truth of being.

Forgetting the truth of being in favor of the pressing throng of beings unthought in their essence is what "falling" [*Verfallen*] means in *Being and Time*. This word does not signify the Fall of Man understood in a "moral-philosophical" and at the same time secularized way; rather, it designates an essential relationship of humans to being within being's relation to the essence of the human being. Accordingly, the terms "authenticity"[b] and "inauthenticity," which are used in a provisional fashion, do not imply a moral-existentiell or an "anthropological" distinction but rather a relation that, because it has been hitherto concealed from philosophy, has yet to be thought for the first time, an "ecstatic" relation of the essence of the human being to the truth of being. But this [164] relation is as it is not by reason of ek-sistence; on the contrary, the essence of ek-sistence is destined[15] existentially-ecstatically from the essence of the truth of being.

The one thing thinking would like to attain and for the first time tries to articulate in *Being and Time* is something simple. As such, being remains mysterious, the simple nearness of an unobtrusive prevailing. The nearness[c] occurs essentially as language itself. But language is not mere

---

[a] *Plato's Doctrine of Truth*, first edition, 1947: Relation from out of restraint (withholding) of refusal (of withdrawal).

[b] First edition, 1949: To be thought from out of what is proper to ap-propriating.

[c] First edition, 1949: In the sense of nearing: holding ready in clearing, holding as safeguarding.

speech, insofar as we represent the latter at best as the unity of phoneme (or written character), melody, rhythm, and meaning (or sense). We think of the phoneme and written character as a verbal body for language, of melody and rhythm as its soul, and whatever has to do with meaning as its spirit. We usually think of language as corresponding to the essence of the human being represented as *animal rationale*, that is, as the unity of body-soul-spirit. But just as ek-sistence – and through it the relation of the truth of being to the human being – remains veiled in the *humanitas* of *homo animalis*, so does the metaphysical-animal explanation of language cover up the essence of language in the history of being. According to this essence, language is the house of being, which is propriated by being and pervaded by being. And so it is proper to think the essence of language from its correspondence to being and indeed as this correspondence, that is, as the home of the human being's essence.

But the human being is not only a living creature who possesses language along with other capacities. Rather, language is the house of being in which the human being ek-sists by dwelling, in that he belongs to the truth of being, guarding it.

So the point is that in the determination of the humanity of the human being as ek-sistence what is essential is not the human being but being – as the dimension of the ecstasis of ek-sistence. However, the dimension is not something spatial in the familiar sense. Rather, everything spatial[a] and all time-space occur essentially in the dimensionality that being itself is.

[165] Thinking attends to these simple relationships. It tries to find the right word for them within the long-traditional language and grammar of metaphysics. But does such thinking – granted that there is something in a name – still allow itself to be described as humanism? Certainly not so far as humanism thinks metaphysically. Certainly not if humanism is existentialism and is represented by what Sartre expresses: précisément nous sommes sur un plan où il y a seulement des hommes [We are precisely in a situation where there are only human beings] (*Existentialism Is a Humanism*, p. 36). Thought from *Being and Time*, this should say instead: précisément nous sommes sur un plan où il y a principalement l'Être [We are precisely in a situation where principally there is being]. But where does *le plan* come from and what is it? *L'Être et le plan* are the same. In *Being and Time* (p. 212) we purposely and cautiously say, il y a l'Être: "there is / it gives" ["*es gibt*"] being. *Il y a* translates "it gives" imprecisely. For the "it" that here "gives" is

---

[a] *Plato's Doctrine of Truth*, first edition, 1947: Space neither alongside time, nor dissolved into time, nor deduced from time.

being itself. The "gives" names the essence of being that is giving, granting its truth. The self-giving into the open, along with the open region itself, is being itself.

At the same time "it gives" is used preliminarily to avoid the locution "being is"; for "is" is commonly said of some thing that is. We call such a thing a being. But being "is" precisely not "a being." If "is" is spoken without a closer interpretation of being, then being is all too easily represented as a "being" after the fashion of the familiar sorts of beings that act as causes and are actualized as effects. And yet Parmenides, in the early age of thinking, says, ἔστι γὰρ εἶναι, "for there is being." The primal mystery for all thinking is concealed in this phrase. Perhaps "is" can be said only of being in an appropriate way, so that no individual being ever properly "is." But because thinking should be directed only toward saying being in its truth, instead of explaining it as a particular being in terms of beings, whether and how being is must remain an open question for the careful attention of thinking.

The ἔστι γὰρ εἶναι of Parmenides is still unthought today. That allows us to gauge how things stand with the progress of philosophy. [166] When philosophy attends to its essence it does not make forward strides at all. It remains where it is in order constantly to think the Same. Progression, that is, progression forward from this place, is a mistake that follows thinking as the shadow that thinking itself casts. Because being is still unthought, *Being and Time* too says of it, "there is / it gives." Yet one cannot speculate about this *il y a* precipitately and without a foothold. This "there is / it gives" rules as the destiny of being. Its history comes to language in the words of essential thinkers. Therefore the thinking that thinks into the truth of being is, as thinking, historical. There is not a "systematic" thinking and next to it an illustrative history of past opinions. Nor is there, as Hegel thought, only a systematics that can fashion the law of its thinking into the law of history and simultaneously subsume history into the system. Thought in a more primordial way, there is the history of being to which thinking belongs as recollection of this history, propriated by it. Such recollective thought differs essentially from the subsequent presentation of history in the sense of an evanescent past. History does not take place primarily as a happening. And its happening is not evanescence. The happening of history occurs essentially as the destiny of the truth of being and from it (cf. the lecture on Hölderlin's hymn "As when on feast day..." [1941], p. 31). Being comes to its destiny in that It, being, gives itself. But thought in terms of such destiny this says: It gives itself and refuses itself simultaneously. Nonetheless, Hegel's definition of history as the development of "Spirit" is not untrue. Neither is it partly correct and partly false. It is as true as metaphysics, which through Hegel first brings to language its essence – thought in terms of the absolute – in the system. Absolute metaphysics, with its Marxian and Nietzschean inversions, belongs to the history of the truth of being. Whatever stems from it cannot be countered or even cast aside by refutations. It can only be taken up in such a way that its truth is more primordially sheltered in being itself [167] and removed from the domain of mere human opinion. All refutation in the field of essential thinking is foolish. Strife among thinkers is the "lovers' quarrel" concerning the matter itself. It assists them mutually toward a simple belonging to the Same, from which they find what is fitting for them in the destiny of being.

Assuming that in the future the human being will be able to think the truth of being, he will think from ek-sistence. The human being stands ek-sistingly in the destiny of being. The ek-sistence of the human being is historical as such, but not only or primarily because so much happens to the human being and to things human in the course of time. Because it must think the ek-sistence of Da-sein, the thinking of *Being and Time* is essentially concerned that the historicity of Dasein be experienced.

But does not *Being and Time* say on p. 212, where the "there is / it gives" comes to language, "Only so long as Dasein is, is there [*gibt es*] being"? To be sure. It means that only so long as the clearing of being propriates does being convey itself to human beings. But the fact that the *Da*, the clearing as the truth of being itself, propriates is the dispensation of being itself. This is the destiny of the clearing. But the sentence does not mean that the Dasein of the human being in the traditional sense of *existentia*, and thought in modern philosophy as the actuality of the *ego cogito*, is that entity through which being is first fashioned. The sentence does not say that being is the product of the human being. The Introduction to *Being and Time* (p. 38) says simply and clearly, even in italics, "Being is the *transcendens* pure and simple." Just as the openness of spatial nearness seen from the perspective of a particular thing exceeds all things near and far, so is being essentially broader than all beings, because it is the clearing itself. For all that, being is thought on the basis of beings, a consequence of the approach – at first unavoidable – within a metaphysics that is still dominant. Only from such a perspective does being show itself in and as a transcending.

[168] The introductory definition, "Being is the *transcendens* pure and simple," articulates in one simple sentence the way the essence of being hitherto has been cleared for the human being. This retrospective definition of the essence of the being of beings[16] from the clearing of beings

as such[17] remains indispensable for the prospective approach of thinking toward the question concerning the truth of being. In this way thinking attests to its essential unfolding as destiny. It is far from the arrogant presumption that wishes to begin anew and declares all past philosophy false. But whether the definition of being as the *transcendens* pure and simple really does name the simple essence of the truth of being – this and this alone is the primary question for a thinking that attempts to think the truth of being. That is why we also say (p. 230) that how being *is*, is to be understood chiefly from its "meaning" [*Sinn*], that is, from the truth of being. Being is cleared for the human being in ecstatic projection [*Entwurf*]. But this projection does not create being.

Moreover, the projection is essentially a thrown projection. What throws in such projection is not the human being but being itself, which sends the human being into the ek-sistence of Da-sein that is his essence. This destiny propriates as the clearing of being – which it is. The clearing grants nearness to being. In this nearness, in the clearing of the *Da*, the human being dwells as the ek-sisting one without yet being able properly to experience and take over this dwelling today. In the lecture on Hölderlin's elegy "Homecoming" (1943) this nearness "of" being, which the *Da* of Dasein is, is thought on the basis of *Being and Time*; it is perceived as spoken from the minstrel's poem; from the experience of the oblivion of being it is called the "homeland." The word is thought here in an essential sense, not patriotically or nationalistically, but in terms of the history of being. The essence of the homeland, however, is also mentioned with the intention of thinking the homelessness of contemporary human beings from the essence of being's history. Nietzsche was the last to experience this homelessness. [169] From within metaphysics he was unable to find any other way out than a reversal of metaphysics. But that is the height of futility. On the other hand, when Hölderlin composes "Homecoming" he is concerned that his "countrymen" find their essence. He does not at all seek that essence in an egoism of his people. He sees it rather in the context of a belongingness to the destiny of the West. But even the West is not thought regionally as the Occident in contrast to the Orient, nor merely as Europe, but rather world-historically out of nearness to the source. We have still scarcely begun to think the mysterious relations to the East that have come to word in Hölderlin's poetry (cf. "The Ister"; also "The Journey," third strophe ff.). "German" is not spoken to the world so that the world might be reformed through the German essence; rather, it is spoken to the Germans so that from a destinal belongingness to other peoples they might become world-historical along with them (see remarks on Hölderlin's poem

"Remembrance" ["*Andenken*"]. *Tübinger Gedenkschrift* [1943], p. 322). The homeland of this historical dwelling is nearness to being.[a]

In such nearness, if at all, a decision may be made as to whether and how God and the gods withhold their presence and the night remains, whether and how the day of the holy dawns, whether and how in the upsurgence of the holy an epiphany of God and the gods can begin anew. But the holy, which alone is the essential sphere of divinity, which in turn alone affords a dimension for the gods and for God, comes to radiate only when being itself beforehand and after extensive preparation has been cleared and is experienced in its truth. Only thus does the overcoming of homelessness begin from being, a homelessness in which not only human beings but the essence of the human being stumbles aimlessly about.

Homelessness so understood consists in the abandonment of beings by being. Homelessness is the symptom of oblivion of being. Because of it the truth of being remains unthought. The oblivion of being makes itself known indirectly through the fact that the [170] human being always observes and handles only beings. Even so, because humans cannot avoid having some notion of being, it is explained merely as what is "most general" and therefore as something that encompasses beings, or as a creation of the infinite being, or as the product of a finite subject. At the same time "being" has long stood for "beings" and, inversely, the latter for the former, the two of them caught in a curious and still unraveled confusion.

As the destiny that sends truth, being remains concealed. But the destiny of world is heralded in poetry, without yet becoming manifest as the history of being. The world-historical thinking of Hölderlin that speaks out in the poem "Remembrance" is therefore essentially more primordial and thus more significant for the future than the mere cosmopolitanism of Goethe. For the same reason Hölderlin's relation to Greek civilization is something essentially other than humanism. When confronted with death, therefore, those young Germans who knew about Hölderlin lived and thought something other than what the public held to be the typical German attitude.

Homelessness is coming to be the destiny of the world. Hence it is necessary to think that destiny in terms of the history of being. What Marx recognized in an essential and significant sense, though derived from Hegel, as the estrangement of the human being has its roots in the homelessness of modern human beings. This homelessness is specifically evoked from the destiny of being in the form of metaphysics, and through metaphysics

---

[a] *Plato's Doctrine of Truth*, first edition, 1947: Being itself preserves and shelters itself as this nearness.

is simultaneously entrenched and covered up as such. Because Marx by experiencing estrangement attains an essential dimension of history, the Marxist view of history is superior to that of other historical accounts. But since neither Husserl nor – so far as I have seen till now – Sartre recognizes the essential importance of the historical in being, neither phenomenology nor existentialism enters that dimension within which a productive dialogue with Marxism first becomes possible.

[171] For such dialogue it is certainly also necessary to free oneself from naive notions about materialism, as well as from the cheap refutations that are supposed to counter it. The essence of materialism does not consist in the assertion that everything is simply matter but rather in a metaphysical determination according to which every being appears as the material of labor. The modern metaphysical essence of labor is anticipated in Hegel's *Phenomenology of Spirit* as the self-establishing process of unconditioned production, which is the objectification of the actual through the human being, experienced as subjectivity. The essence of materialism is concealed in the essence of technology, about which much has been written but little has been thought. Technology is in its essence a destiny within the history of being and of the truth of being, a truth that lies in oblivion. For technology does not go back to the τέχνη of the Greeks in name only but derives historically and essentially from τέχνη as a mode of ἀληθεύειν, a mode, that is, of rendering beings manifest. As a form of truth technology is grounded in the history of metaphysics, which is itself a distinctive and up to now the only surveyable phase of the history of being. No matter which of the various positions one chooses to adopt toward the doctrines of communism and to their foundation, from the point of view of the history of being it is certain that an elemental experience of what is world-historical speaks out in it. Whoever takes "communism" only as a "party" or a "Weltanschauung" is thinking too shallowly, just as those who by the term "Americanism" mean, and mean derogatorily, nothing more than a particular lifestyle. The danger[a] into which Europe as it has hitherto existed is ever more clearly forced consists presumably in the fact above all that its thinking – once its glory – is falling behind[b] the essential course[18] of

---

[a] First edition, 1949: The danger has in the meantime come more clearly to light. The collapse of thinking back into metaphysics is taking on a new form: it is the end of philosophy in the sense of its complete dissolution into the sciences, whose unity is likewise unfolding in a new way in cybernetics. The power of science cannot be stopped by an intervention or offensive of whatever kind, because "science" belongs in the gathered setting-in-place [*Ge-stell*] that continues to obscure the place [*verstellt*] of the event of appropriation.

[b] First edition, 1949: Falling back into metaphysics.

a dawning world destiny that nevertheless in the basic traits of its essential provenance remains European by definition. No metaphysics, whether idealistic, materialistic, or Christian, can in accord with its essence, and surely not in [172] its own attempts to explicate itself, "get a hold on" this destiny, and that means thoughtfully to reach and gather together what in the fullest sense of being now is.[a]

In the face of the essential homelessness of human beings, the approaching destiny of the human being reveals itself to thought on the history of being in this, that the human being find his way into the truth of being and set out on this find. Every nationalism is metaphysically an anthropologism, and as such subjectivism. Nationalism is not overcome through mere internationalism; it is rather expanded and elevated thereby into a system. Nationalism is as little brought and raised to *humanitas* by internationalism as individualism is by an ahistorical collectivism. The latter is the subjectivity[b] of human beings in totality. It completes subjectivity's unconditioned self-assertion, which refuses to yield. Nor can it be even adequately experienced by a thinking that mediates in a one-sided fashion. Expelled from the truth of being, the human being everywhere circles around himself as the *animal rationale*.

But the essence of the human being consists in his being more than merely human, if this is represented as "being a rational creature." "More" must not be understood here additively, as if the traditional definition of the human being were indeed to remain basic, only elaborated by means of an existentiell postscript. The "more" means: more originally and therefore more essentially in terms of his essence. But here something enigmatic manifests itself: the human being is in thrownness. This means that the human being, as the ek-sisting counterthrow [*Gegenwurf*] of being,[c] is more than *animal rationale* precisely to the extent that he is less bound up with the human being conceived from subjectivity. The human being is not the lord of beings. The human being is the shepherd of being. Human beings lose nothing in this "less"; rather, they gain in that they attain the truth of being. They gain the essential poverty of the shepherd, whose dignity consists in [173] being called by being itself into the preservation of being's truth. The call comes as the throw from which the thrownness of Da-sein

---

[a] *Plato's Doctrine of Truth*, first edition, 1947: What is it that now is – now in the era of the will to will? What now is, is unconditional neglect of preservation [*Verwahrlosung*], this word taken in a strict sense in terms of the history of being: *wahr-los* [without preservation]; conversely: in terms of destining.

[b] First edition, 1949: Industrial society as the subject that provides the measure – and thinking as "politics."

[c] First edition, 1949: Better: within being qua event of appropriation.

derives. In his essential unfolding within the history of being, the human being is the being whose being as ek-sistence consists in his dwelling in the nearness of being. The human being is the neighbor of being.

But – as you no doubt have been wanting to rejoin for quite a while now – does not such thinking think precisely the *humanitas* of *homo humanus*? Does it not think *humanitas* in a decisive sense, as no metaphysics has thought it or can think it? Is this not "humanism" in the extreme sense? Certainly. It is a humanism that thinks the humanity of the human being from nearness to being. But at the same time it is a humanism in which not the human being but the human being's historical essence is at stake in its provenance from the truth of being. But then does not the ek-sistence of the human being also stand or fall in this game of stakes? Indeed it does.

In *Being and Time* (p. 38) it is said that every question of philosophy "returns to existence." But existence here is not the actuality of the *ego cogito*. Neither is it the actuality of subjects who act with and for each other and so become who they are. "Ek-sistence," in fundamental contrast to every *existentia* and "*existence,*" is ek-static dwelling in the nearness of being. It is the guardianship, that is, the care for being. Because there is something simple to be thought in this thinking it seems quite difficult to the representational thought that has been transmitted as philosophy. But the difficulty is not a matter of indulging in a special sort of profundity and of building complicated concepts; rather, it is concealed in the step back that lets thinking enter into a questioning that experiences – and lets the habitual opining of philosophy fall away.

It is everywhere supposed that the attempt in *Being and Time* ended in a blind alley. Let us not comment any further upon that opinion. The thinking that hazards a few steps in *Being and Time* [174] has even today not advanced beyond that publication. But perhaps in the meantime it has in one respect come further into its own matter. However, as long as philosophy merely busies itself with continually obstructing the possibility of admittance into the matter for thinking, i.e., into the truth of being, it stands safely beyond any danger of shattering against the hardness of that matter. Thus to "philosophize" about being shattered is separated by a chasm from a thinking that is shattered. If such thinking were to go fortunately for someone, no misfortune would befall him. He would receive the only gift that can come to thinking from being.

But it is also the case that the matter of thinking is not achieved in the fact that idle talk about the "truth of being" and the "history of being" is set in motion. Everything depends upon this alone, that the truth of being come to language and that thinking attain to this language. Perhaps, then, language requires much less precipitate expression than proper silence. But who of us today would want to imagine that his attempts to think are at home on the path of silence? At best, thinking could perhaps point toward the truth of being, and indeed toward it as what is to be thought. It would thus be more easily weaned from mere supposing and opining and directed to the now rare handicraft of writing. Things that really matter, although they are not defined for all eternity, even when they come very late still come at the right time.

Whether the realm of the truth of being is a blind alley or whether it is the free space in which freedom conserves its essence is something each one may judge after he himself has tried to go the designated way, or even better, after he has gone a better way, that is, a way befitting the question. On the penultimate page of *Being and Time* (p. 437) stand the sentences: "The *conflict* with respect to the interpretation of being (that is, therefore, not the interpretation of beings or of the being of the human being) cannot be settled, [175] *because it has not yet been kindled.* And in the end it is not a question of 'picking a quarrel,' since the kindling of the conflict does demand some preparation. To this end alone the foregoing investigation is under way." Today after two decades these sentences still hold. Let us also in the days ahead remain as wanderers on the way into the neighborhood of being. The question you pose helps to clarify the way.

You ask, "Comment redonner un sens au mot 'Humanisme'?" "How can some sense be restored to the word 'humanism'?" Your question not only presupposes a desire to retain the word "humanism" but also contains an admission that this word has lost its meaning.

It has lost it through the insight that the essence of humanism is metaphysical, which now means that metaphysics not only does not pose the question concerning the truth of being but also obstructs the question, insofar as metaphysics persists in the oblivion of being. But the same thinking that has led us to this insight into the questionable essence of humanism has likewise compelled us to think the essence of the human being more primordially. With regard to this more essential *humanitas* of *homo humanus* there arises the possibility of restoring to the word "humanism" a historical sense that is older than its oldest meaning chronologically reckoned. The restoration is not to be understood as though the word "humanism" were wholly without meaning and a mere *flatus vocis* [empty sound]. The *"humanum"* in the word points to *humanitas*, the essence of the human being; the "-ism" indicates that the essence of the human being is meant to be taken essentially. This is the sense that the word "humanism" has as such. To restore a sense to it can only mean to redefine the meaning of the word.

That requires that we first experience the essence of the human being more primordially; but it also demands that we show to what extent this essence in its own way becomes destinal. The essence of [176] the human being lies in ek-sistence. That is what is essentially – that is, from being itself – at issue here, insofar as being appropriates the human being as ek-sisting for guardianship over the truth of being into this truth itself. "Humanism" now means, in case we decide to retain the word, that the essence of the human being is essential for the truth of being, specifically in such a way that what matters is not the human being simply as such. So we are thinking a curious kind of "humanism." The word results in a name that is a *lucus a non lucendo* [literally, a grove where no light penetrates].

Should we still keep the name "humanism" for a "humanism" that contradicts all previous humanism – although it in no way advocates the inhuman? And keep it just so that by sharing in the use of the name we might perhaps swim in the predominant currents, stifled in metaphysical subjectivism and submerged in oblivion of being? Or should thinking, by means of open resistance to "humanism," risk a shock that could for the first time cause perplexity concerning the *humanitas* of *homo humanus* and its basis? In this way it could awaken a reflection – if the world-historical moment did not itself already compel such a reflection – that thinks not only about the human being but also about the "nature" of the human being, not only about his nature but even more primordially about the dimension in which the essence of the human being, determined by being itself, is at home. Should we not rather suffer a little while longer those inevitable misinterpretations to which the path of thinking in the element of being and time has hitherto been exposed and let them slowly dissipate? These misinterpretations are natural reinterpretations of what was read, or simply mirrorings of what one believes he knows already before he reads. They all betray the same structure and the same foundation.

Because we are speaking against "humanism" people fear a defense of the inhuman and a glorification [177] of barbaric brutality. For what is more "logical" than that for somebody who negates humanism nothing remains but the affirmation of inhumanity?

Because we are speaking against "logic" people believe we are demanding that the rigor of thinking be renounced and in its place the arbitrariness of drives and feelings be installed and thus that "irrationalism" be proclaimed as true. For what is more "logical" than that whoever speaks against the logical is defending the alogical?

Because we are speaking against "values" people are horrified at a philosophy that ostensibly dares to despise humanity's best qualities. For what is more "logical" than that a thinking that denies values must necessarily pronounce everything valueless?

Because we say that the being of the human being consists in "being-in-the-world" people find that the human being is downgraded to a merely terrestrial being, whereupon philosophy sinks into positivism. For what is more "logical" than that whoever asserts the worldliness of human being holds only this life as valid, denies the beyond, and renounces all "Transcendence"?

Because we refer to the word of Nietzsche on the "death of God" people regard such a gesture as atheism. For what is more "logical" than that whoever has experienced the death of God is godless?

Because in all the respects mentioned we everywhere speak against all that humanity deems high and holy our philosophy teaches an irresponsible and destructive "nihilism." For what is more "logical" than that whoever roundly denies what is truly in being puts himself on the side of nonbeing and thus professes the pure nothing as the meaning of reality?

What is going on here? People hear talk about "humanism," "logic," "values," "world," and "God." They hear something about opposition to these. They recognize and accept these things [178] as positive. But with hearsay – in a way that is not strictly deliberate – they immediately assume that what speaks against something is automatically its negation and that this is "negative" in the sense of destructive. And somewhere in *Being and Time* there is explicit talk of "the phenomenological destruction." With the assistance of logic and *ratio* often invoked, people come to believe that whatever is not positive is negative and thus that it seeks to degrade reason and therefore deserves to be branded as depravity. We are so filled with "logic" that anything that disturbs the habitual somnolence of prevailing opinion is automatically registered as a despicable contradiction. We pitch everything that does not stay close to the familiar and beloved positive into the previously excavated pit of pure negation, which negates everything, ends in nothing, and so consummates nihilism. Following this logical course we let everything expire in a nihilism we invented for ourselves with the aid of logic.

But does the "against" which a thinking advances against ordinary opinion necessarily point toward pure negation and the negative? This happens – and then, to be sure, happens inevitably and conclusively, that is, without a clear prospect of anything else – only when one posits in advance what is meant as the "positive" and on this basis makes an absolute and simultaneously negative decision about the range of possible opposition to it. Concealed in such a procedure is the refusal to subject to reflection this presupposed "positive" together with its position and opposition in which it is thought to be secure. By continually appealing to the logical one conjures up the illusion that one is entering straightforwardly into thinking when in fact one has disavowed it.

It ought to be somewhat clearer now that opposition to "humanism" in no way implies a defense of the inhuman but rather opens other vistas.

"Logic" understands thinking to be the representation of beings in their being, which representation proposes to itself in the generality of the concept. [179] But how is it with meditation on being itself, that is, with the thinking that thinks the truth of being? This thinking alone reaches the primordial essence of λόγος, which was already obfuscated and lost in Plato and in Aristotle, the founder of "logic." To think against "logic" does not mean to break a lance for the illogical but simply to trace in thought the λόγος and its essence, which appeared in the dawn of thinking, that is, to exert ourselves for the first time in preparing for such reflection. Of what value are even far-reaching systems of logic to us if, without really knowing what they are doing, they recoil before the task of simply inquiring into the essence of λόγος? If we wished to bandy about objections, which is of course fruitless, we could say with more right: irrationalism, as a denial of *ratio*, rules unnoticed and uncontested in the defense of "logic," which believes it can eschew meditation on λόγος and on the essence of *ratio*, which has its ground in λόγος.

To think against "values" is not to maintain that everything interpreted as "a value" – "culture," "art," "science," "human dignity," "world," and "God" – is valueless. Rather, it is important finally to realize that precisely through the characterization of something as "a value" what is so valued is robbed of its worth. That is to say, by the assessment of something as a value what is valued is admitted only as an object for human estimation. But what a thing is in its being is not exhausted by its being an object, particularly when objectivity takes the form of value. Every valuing, even where it values positively, is a subjectivizing. It does not let beings: be. Rather, valuing lets beings: be valid – solely as the objects of its doing. The bizarre effort to prove the objectivity of values does not know what it is doing. When one proclaims "God" the altogether "highest value," this is a degradation of God's essence. Here as elsewhere thinking in values is [180] the greatest blasphemy imaginable against being. To think against values therefore does not mean to beat the drum for the valuelessness and nullity of beings. It means rather to bring the clearing of the truth of being before thinking, as against subjectivizing beings into mere objects.

The reference to "being-in-the-world" as the basic trait of the *humanitas* of *homo humanus* does not assert that the human being is merely a "worldly" creature understood in a Christian sense, thus a creature turned away from God and so cut loose from "Transcendence." What is really meant by this word would be more clearly called "the transcendent." The transcendent is a supersensible being. This is considered the highest being in the sense of the first cause of all beings. God is thought as this first cause. However, in the name "being-in-the-world," "world" does not in any way imply earthly as opposed to heavenly being, nor the "worldly" as opposed to the "spiritual." For us "world" does not at all signify beings or any realm of beings but the openness of being. The human being is, and is human, insofar as he is the ek-sisting one. He stands out into the openness of being. Being itself, which as the throw has projected the essence of the human being into "care," is as this openness. Thrown in such fashion, the human being stands "in" the openness of being. "World" is the clearing of being into which the human being stands out on the basis of his thrown essence. "Being-in-the-world" designates the essence of ek-sistence with regard to the cleared dimension out of which the "ek-" of ek-sistence essentially unfolds. Thought in terms of ek-sistence, "world" is in a certain sense precisely "the beyond" within eksistence and for it. The human being is never first and foremost the human being on the hither side of the world, as a "subject," whether this is taken as "I" or "We." Nor is he ever simply a mere subject that always simultaneously is related to objects, so that his essence lies in the subject-object relation. Rather, before all this, the human being in his essence is ek-sistent [181] into the openness of being, into the open region that first clears the "between" within which a "relation" of subject to object can "be."

The statement that the essence of the human being consists in being-in-the-world likewise contains no decision about whether the human being in a theologico-metaphysical sense is merely a this-worldly or an other-worldly creature.

With the existential determination of the essence of the human being, therefore, nothing is decided about the "existence of God" or his "nonbeing," no more than about the possibility or impossibility of gods. Thus it is not only rash but also an error in procedure to maintain that the interpretation of the essence of the human being from the relation of his essence to the truth of being is atheism. And what is more, this arbitrary classification betrays a lack of careful reading. No one bothers to notice that in my essay "On the Essence of Ground" (1929) the following appears

(p. 28, note 1): "Through the ontological interpretation of Dasein as being-in-the-world no decision, whether positive or negative, is made concerning a possible being toward God. It is, however, the case that through an illumination of transcendence we first achieve *an adequate concept of Dasein*, with respect to which it can now be asked how the relationship of Dasein to God is ontologically ordered." If we think about this remark too quickly, as is usually the case, we will declare that such a philosophy does not decide either for or against the existence of God. It remains stalled in indifference. Thus it is unconcerned with the religious question. Such indifferentism ultimately falls prey to nihilism.

But does the foregoing observation teach indifferentism? Why then are particular words in the note italicized – and not just random ones? For no other reason than to indicate that the thinking that thinks from the question concerning the truth of being questions more primordially than metaphysics can. Only from the truth of being can the essence of the holy be thought. [182] Only from the essence of the holy is the essence of divinity to be thought. Only in the light of the essence of divinity can it be thought or said what the word "God" is to signify. Or should we not first be able to hear and understand all these words carefully if we are to be permitted as human beings, that is, as eksistent creatures, to experience a relation of God to human beings? How can the human being at the present stage of world history ask at all seriously and rigorously whether the god nears or withdraws, when he has above all neglected to think into the dimension in which alone that question can be asked? But this is the dimension of the holy, which indeed remains closed as a dimension if the open region of being is not cleared and in its clearing[a] is near to humans. Perhaps what is distinctive about this world-epoch consists in the closure of the dimension of the hale [*des Heilen*]. Perhaps that is the sole malignancy [*Unheil*].

But with this reference the thinking that points toward the truth of being as what is to be thought has in no way decided in favor of theism. It can be theistic as little as atheistic. Not, however, because of an indifferent attitude, but out of respect for the boundaries that have been set for thinking as such, indeed set by what gives itself to thinking as what is to be thought, by the truth of being. Insofar as thinking limits itself to its task it directs the human being at the present moment of the world's destiny into the primordial dimension of his historical abode. When thinking of this kind speaks the truth of being it has entrusted itself to what is more essential than

---

[a] First edition, 1949: Clearing as clearing of self-concealing sheltering.

all values and all types of beings. Thinking does not overcome metaphysics by climbing still higher, surmounting it, transcending it somehow or other; thinking overcomes metaphysics by climbing back down into the nearness of the nearest. The descent, particularly where human beings have strayed into subjectivity, is more arduous and more dangerous than the ascent. The descent leads to the poverty of the ek-sistence of *homo humanus*. In ek-sistence [183] the region of *homo animalis*, of metaphysics, is abandoned. The dominance of that region is the mediate and deeply rooted basis for the blindness and arbitrariness of what is called "biologism," but also of what is known under the heading "pragmatism." To think the truth of being at the same time means to think the humanity of *homo humanus*. What counts is *humanitas* in the service of the truth of being, but without humanism in the metaphysical sense.

But if *humanitas* must be viewed as so essential to the thinking of being, must not "ontology" therefore be supplemented by "ethics"? Is not that effort entirely essential which you express in the sentence, "Ce que je cherche à faire, depuis longtemps déjà, c'est péciser le rapport de l'ontologie avec une éthique possible" ["What I have been trying to do for a long time now is to determine precisely the relation of ontology to a possible ethics"]?

Soon after *Being and Time* appeared a young friend asked me, "When are you going to write an ethics?" Where the essence of the human being is thought so essentially, i.e., solely from the question concerning the truth of being, and yet without elevating the human being to the center of beings, a longing necessarily awakens for a peremptory directive and for rules that say how the human being, experienced from ek-sistence toward being, ought to live in a fitting manner. The desire for an ethics presses ever more ardently for fulfillment as the obvious no less than the hidden perplexity of human beings soars to immeasurable heights. The greatest care must be fostered upon the ethical bond at a time when technological human beings, delivered over to mass society, can attain reliable constancy only by gathering and ordering all their plans and activities in a way that corresponds to technology.

Who can disregard our predicament? Should we not safeguard and secure the existing bonds even if they hold human beings together ever so tenuously and merely for the present? Certainly. But does this need ever release thought from the task of thinking what still remains principally [184] to be thought and, as being, prior to all beings, is their guarantor and their truth? Even further, can thinking refuse to think being after the latter has lain hidden so long in oblivion but at the same time has made itself known in the present moment of world history by the uprooting of all beings?

Before we attempt to determine more precisely the relationship between "ontology" and "ethics" we must ask what "ontology" and "ethics" themselves are. It becomes necessary to ponder whether what can be designated by both terms still remains near and proper to what is assigned to thinking, which as such has to think above all the truth of being.

Of course if both "ontology" and "ethics," along with all thinking in terms of disciplines, become untenable, and if our thinking therewith becomes more disciplined, how then do matters stand with the question about the relation between these two philosophical disciplines?

Along with "logic" and "physics," "ethics" appeared for the first time in the school of Plato. These disciplines arose at a time when thinking was becoming "philosophy," philosophy ἐπιστήμη (science), and science itself a matter for schools and academic pursuits. In the course of a philosophy so understood, science waxed and thinking waned. Thinkers prior to this period knew neither a "logic" nor an "ethics" nor "physics." Yet their thinking was neither illogical nor immoral. But they did think φύσις in a depth and breadth that no subsequent "physics" was ever again able to attain. The tragedies of Sophocles – provided such a comparison is at all permissible – preserve the ἦθος in their sayings more primordially than Aristotle's lectures on "ethics." A saying of Heraclitus that consists of only three words says something so simply that from it the essence of *ethos* immediately comes to light.

[185] The saying of Heraclitus (Fragment 119) goes: ἦθος ἀνθρώπῳ δαίμων. This is usually translated, "A man's character is his daimon." This translation thinks in a modern way, not a Greek one. ἦθος means abode, dwelling place. The word names the open region in which the human being dwells. The open region of his abode allows what pertains to the essence of the human being, and what in thus arriving resides in nearness to him, to appear. The abode of the human being contains and preserves the advent of what belongs to the human being in his essence. According to Heraclitus's phrase this is δαίμων, the god. The fragment says: The human being dwells, insofar as he is a human being, in the nearness of god. A story that Aristotle reports (*De partibus animalium*, A, 5, 645 a17ff.) agrees with this fragment of Heraclitus. It runs:

Ἡράκλειτος λέγεται πρὸς τοὺς ξένους εἰπεῖν τοὺς βουλομένους ἐντυχεῖν αὐτῷ, οἳ ἐπειδὴ προσιόντες εἶδον αὐτὸν θερόμενον πρὸς τῷ ἰπνῷ ἔστησαν, ἐκέλευε γὰρ αὐτοὺς εἰσιέναι θαρροῦντας· εἶναι γὰρ καὶ ἐνταῦθα θεοὺς...

The story is told of something Heraclitus said to some strangers who wanted to come visit him. Having arrived, they saw him warming himself at a stove. Surprised, they stood there in consternation – above all because he encouraged them, the astounded ones, and called to them to come in, with the words, "For here too the gods are present."

The story certainly speaks for itself, but we may stress a few aspects.

The group of foreign visitors, in their importunate curiosity about the thinker, are disappointed and perplexed by their first glimpse of his abode. They believe they should meet the thinker in circumstances that, contrary to the ordinary round of human life, everywhere bear traces of the exceptional and rare and so of the exciting. The group hopes that in their visit to the thinker they will find things that will provide material for entertaining conversation – at least for a while. The foreigners who wish to visit the thinker [186] expect to catch sight of him perchance at that very moment when, sunk in profound meditation, he is thinking. The visitors want this "experience" not in order to be overwhelmed by thinking but simply so they can say they saw and heard someone everybody says is a thinker.

Instead of this the sightseers find Heraclitus by a stove. That is surely a common and insignificant place. True enough, bread is baked here. But Heraclitus is not even busy baking at the stove. He stands there merely to warm himself. In this altogether everyday place he betrays the entire poverty of his life. The vision of a shivering thinker offers little of interest. At this disappointing spectacle even the curious lose their desire to come any closer. What are they supposed to do here? Such an everyday and unexciting occurrence – somebody who is chilled warming himself at a stove – anyone can find any time at home. So why look up a thinker? The visitors are on the verge of going away again. Heraclitus reads the frustrated curiosity in their faces. He knows that for the crowd the failure of an expected sensation to materialize is enough to make those who have just arrived leave. He therefore encourages them. He invites them explicitly to come in with the words εἶναι γὰρ καὶ ἐνταῦθα θεούς, "Here too the gods come to presence."

This phrase places the abode (ἦθος) of the thinker and his deed in another light. Whether the visitors understood this phrase at once – or at all – and then saw everything differently in this other light the story does not say. But the story was told and has come down to us today because what it reports derives from and characterizes the atmosphere surrounding this thinker. καὶ ἐνταῦθα, "even here," at the stove, in that ordinary place where every thing and every circumstance, each deed and [187] thought is intimate and commonplace, that is, familiar [geheuer], "even there" in the sphere of the familiar, εἶναι θεούς, it is the case that "the gods come to presence."

Heraclitus himself says, ἦθος ἀνθρώπῳ δαίμων, "The (familiar) abode for humans is the open region for the presencing of god (the unfamiliar one)."

If the name "ethics," in keeping with the basic meaning of the word ἦθος, should now say that ethics ponders the abode of the human being, then that thinking which thinks the truth of being as the primordial element of the human being, as one who eksists, is in itself originary ethics. However, this thinking is not ethics in the first instance because it is ontology. For ontology always thinks solely the being (ὄν) in its being. But as long as the truth of being is not thought all ontology remains without its foundation. Therefore the thinking that in *Being and Time* tries to advance thought in a preliminary way into the truth of being characterizes itself as "fundamental ontology." It strives to reach back into the essential ground from which thought concerning the truth of being emerges. By initiating another inquiry this thinking is already removed from the "ontology" of metaphysics (even that of Kant). "Ontology" itself, however, whether transcendental or precritical, is subject to critique, not because it thinks the being of beings and in so doing reduces being to a concept, but because it does not think the truth of being and so fails to recognize that there is a thinking more rigorous than conceptual thinking. In the poverty of its first breakthrough, the thinking that tries to advance thought into the truth of being brings only a small part of that wholly other dimension to language. This language even falsifies itself, for it does not yet succeed in retaining the essential help of phenomenological seeing while dispensing with the inappropriate concern with "science" and "research." But in order to make the attempt at thinking recognizable and at the same time understandable for existing philosophy, it could at first be expressed only within the horizon of [188] that existing philosophy and the use of its current terms.

In the meantime I have learned to see that these very terms were bound to lead immediately and inevitably into error. For the terms and the conceptual language corresponding to them were not rethought by readers from the matter particularly to be thought; rather, the matter was conceived according to the established terminology in its customary meaning. The thinking that inquires into the truth of being and so defines the human being's essential abode from being and toward being is neither ethics nor ontology. Thus the question about the relation of each to the other no longer has any basis in this sphere. Nonetheless, your question, thought in a more original way, retains a meaning and an essential importance.

For it must be asked: If the thinking that ponders the truth of being defines the essence of *humanitas* as ek-sistence from the latter's belongingness to being, then does thinking remain only a theoretical representation of being and of the human being; or can we obtain from such knowledge directives that can be readily applied to our active lives?

The answer is that such thinking is neither theoretical nor practical. It comes to pass [*ereignet sich*] before this distinction. Such thinking is, insofar as it is, recollection of being and nothing else. Belonging to being, because thrown by being into the preservation of its truth and claimed for such preservation, it thinks being. Such thinking has no result. It has no effect. It satisfies its essence in that it is. But it is by saying its matter. Historically, only one saying [*Sage*] belongs to the matter of thinking, the one that is in each case appropriate to its matter. Its material relevance is essentially higher than the validity of the sciences, because it is freer. For it lets being – be.

Thinking builds upon the house of being, the house in which the jointure of being, in its destinal unfolding, enjoins the essence of the human being in each case to dwell in the truth of being. [189] This dwelling is the essence of "being-in-the-world." The reference in *Being and Time* (p. 54) to "being-in" as "dwelling" is not some etymological play. The same reference in the 1936 essay on Hölderlin's word, "Full of merit, yet poetically, man dwells upon this earth," is not the adornment of a thinking that rescues itself from science by means of poetry. The talk about the house of being is not the transfer of the image "house" onto being. But one day we will, by thinking the essence of being in a way appropriate to its matter, more readily be able to think what "house" and "dwelling" are.

And yet thinking never creates the house of being. Thinking conducts historical eksistence, that is, the *humanitas* of *homo humanus*, into the realm of the upsurgence of healing [*des Heilen*].

With healing, evil appears all the more in the clearing of being. The essence of evil does not consist in the mere baseness of human action, but rather in the malice of rage. Both of these, however, healing and the raging, can essentially occur in being only insofar as being itself is in strife. In it is concealed the essential provenance of nihilation. What nihilates comes to the clearing as the negative. This can be addressed in the "no." The "not" in no way arises from the no-saying of negation. Every "no" that does not mistake itself as willful assertion of the positing power of subjectivity, but rather remains a letting-be of ek-sistence, answers to the claim of the nihilation that has come to the clearing. Every "no" is simply the affirmation of the "not." Every affirmation consists in acknowledgment. Acknowledgment lets that toward which it goes come toward it. It is believed that nihilation is nowhere to be found in beings themselves. This is correct as long as one seeks nihilation as some kind of being, as an existing quality in beings. But in so seeking, one is not seeking nihilation. Neither is being any existing quality that allows itself to be ascertained among beings. [190] And yet being is more in being[a] than any beings. Because nihilation occurs essentially in being itself we can never discern it as something in beings. Reference to this impossibility never in any way proves that the origin of the not is no-saying. This proof appears to carry weight only if one posits beings as what is objective for subjectivity. From this alternative it follows that every "not," because it never appears as something objective, must inevitably be the product of a subjective act. But whether no-saying first posits the "not" as something merely thought, or whether nihilation first requires the "no" as what is to be said in the letting-be of beings – this can never be decided at all by a subjective reflection of a thinking already posited as subjectivity. In such a reflection we have not yet reached the dimension where the question can be appropriately formulated. It remains to ask, granting that thinking belongs to ek-sistence, whether every "yes" and "no" are not themselves already eksistent in the truth of being. If they are, then the "yes" and the "no"[b] are already intrinsically in thrall to being. As enthralled, they can never first posit the very thing to which they themselves belong.

Nihilation unfolds essentially in being itself, and not at all in the existence of the human being – so far as this existence is thought as the subjectivity of the *ego cogito*. Existence [*Dasein*] in no way nihilates as a human subject who carries out nihilation in the sense of denial; rather, Da-sein nihilates inasmuch as it belongs to the essence of being as that essence in which the human being ek-sists. Being nihilates – as being. Therefore the "not" appears in the absolute Idealism of Hegel and Schelling as the negativity of negation in the essence of being. But there being is thought in the sense of absolute actuality as the unconditioned will that wills itself and does so as the will of knowledge and of love. In this willing being as will to power is still concealed. But just why the negativity of absolute subjectivity is "dialectical," and why nihilation comes to the fore through this dialectic but at the same time is veiled in its essence, cannot be discussed here.

[191] The nihilating in being is the essence of what I call the nothing. Hence, because it thinks being, thinking thinks the nothing.

To healing being first grants ascent into grace; to raging its compulsion to malignancy.

[a] First edition, 1949: Insofar as being lets beings "be."
[b] First edition, 1949: Affirmation and denial, acknowledgment and rejection already used in the gathered call [*Geheiß*] of the event of appropriation – called into renunciative saying in response [*Entsagen*] to the gathered call of the distinction.

Only so far as the human being, ek-sisting into the truth of being, belongs to being can there come from being itself the assignment of those directives that must become law and rule for human beings. In Greek, to assign is νέμειν. Νόμος is not only law but more originally the assignment contained in the dispensation of being. Only this assignment is capable of enjoining humans into being. Only such enjoining is capable of supporting and obligating. Otherwise all law remains merely something fabricated by human reason. More essential than instituting rules is that human beings find the way to their abode in the truth of being. This abode first yields the experience of something we can hold on to. The truth of being offers a hold for all conduct. "Hold" in our language means protective heed. Being is the protective heed that holds the human being in his ek-sistent essence to the truth of such protective heed – in such a way that it houses ek-sistence in language. Thus language is at once the house of being and the home of the human essence. Only because language is the home of the essence of the human being can historical humankind and human beings not be at home in their language, so that for them language becomes a mere container for their sundry preoccupations.

But now in what relation does the thinking of being stand to theoretical and practical comportment? It exceeds all contemplation because it cares for the light in which a seeing, as *theoria*, can first live and move. Thinking attends to the clearing of being in that it puts its saying of being into language as the home of eksistence. Thus thinking is a deed. But a deed that also surpasses all *praxis*. Thinking permeates action and production, not through the grandeur of its achievement and not as a consequence of [192] its effect, but through the humbleness of its inconsequential accomplishment.

For thinking in its saying merely brings the unspoken word of being to language.

The usage "bring to language" employed here is now to be taken quite literally. Being comes, clearing itself, to language. It is perpetually under way to language. Such arriving in its turn brings ek-sisting thought to language in its saying. Thus language itself is raised into the clearing of being. Language thus *is* only in this mysterious and yet for us always pervasive way. To the extent that language that has thus been brought fully into its essence is historical, being is entrusted to recollection. Ek-sistence thoughtfully dwells in the house of being. In all this it is as if nothing at all happens through thoughtful saying.

But just now an example of the inconspicuous deed of thinking manifested itself. For to the extent that we expressly think the usage "bring to language," a usage destined to language, thinking only that and nothing further, to the extent that we retain this thought in the heedfulness of saying as what in the future continually has to be thought, we have brought something of the essential unfolding of being itself to language.

What is strange in this thinking of being is its simplicity. Precisely this keeps us from it. For we look for thinking – which has its world-historical prestige under the name "philosophy" – in the form of the unusual, which is accessible only to initiates. At the same time we conceive of thinking on the model of scientific knowledge and its research projects. We measure deeds by the impressive and successful achievements of *praxis*. But the deed of thinking is neither theoretical nor practical, nor is it the conjunction of these two forms of comportment.

Through its simple essence, the thinking of being makes itself unrecognizable to us. But if we become acquainted with the unusual character of the simple, then another plight immediately befalls us. The suspicion arises that such thinking of [193] being falls prey to arbitrariness; for it cannot cling to beings. Whence does thinking take its measure? What law governs its deed?

Here the third question of your letter must be entertained: Comment sauver l'élément d'aventure que comporte toute recherche sans faire de la philosophie une simple aventurière? [How can we preserve the element of adventure that all research contains without simply turning philosophy into an adventuress?] I shall mention poetry now only in passing. It is confronted by the same question, and in the same manner, as thinking. But Aristotle's words in the *Poetics*, although they have scarcely been pondered, are still valid – that poetizing is truer than the exploration of beings.

But thinking is an *aventure* not only as a search and an inquiry into the unthought. Thinking, in its essence as thinking of being, is claimed by being. Thinking is related to being as what arrives (*l'avenant*). Thinking as such is bound to the advent of being, to being as advent. Being has already been destined to thinking. Being *is* as the destiny of thinking. But destiny is in itself historical. Its history has already come to language in the saying of thinkers.

To bring to language ever and again this advent of being that remains, and in its remaining waits for human beings, is the sole matter of thinking. For this reason essential thinkers always say the Same. But that does not mean the identical. Of course they say it only to one who undertakes to meditate on them. Whenever thinking, in historical recollection, attends to the destiny of being, it has already bound itself to what is fitting for it, in accord with its destiny. To flee into the identical is not dangerous. To venture into discordance in order to say the Same is the danger. Ambiguity threatens, and mere quarreling.

The fittingness of the saying of being, as of the destiny of truth, is the first law of thinking – not the rules of logic, which can become rules only on the basis of the law of being. [194] To attend to the fittingness of thoughtful saying does not only imply, however, that we contemplate at every turn *what* is to be said of being and *how* it is to be said. It is equally essential to ponder *whether* what is to be thought is to be said – to what extent, at what moment of the history of being, in what sort of dialogue with this history, and on the basis of what claim, it ought to be said. The threefold issue mentioned in an earlier letter is determined in its cohesion by the law of the fittingness of thought on the history of being: rigor of meditation, carefulness in saying, frugality with words.

It is time to break the habit of overestimating philosophy and of thereby asking too much of it. What is needed in the present world crisis is less philosophy, but more attentiveness in thinking; less literature, but more cultivation of the letter.

The thinking that is to come is no longer philosophy, because it thinks more originally than metaphysics – a name identical to philosophy. However, the thinking that is to come can no longer, as Hegel demanded, set aside the name "love of wisdom" and become wisdom itself in the form of absolute knowledge. Thinking is on the descent to the poverty of its provisional essence. Thinking gathers language into simple saying. In this way language is the language of being, as clouds are the clouds of the sky. With its saying, thinking lays inconspicuous furrows in language. They are still more inconspicuous than the furrows that the farmer, slow of step, draws through the field.

Introduction to "What Is Metaphysics?"

Translated by Walter Kaufmann[1]

THE WAY BACK INTO THE GROUND
OF METAPHYSICS

[195] Descartes, writing to Picot, who translated the *Principia Philosophiae* into French, observed: "Ainsi toute la Philosophie est comme un arbre, dont les racines sont la Métaphysique, le tronc est la Physique, et les branches qui sortent de ce tronc sont toutes les autres sciences..." [Thus the whole of philosophy is like a tree: the roots are metaphysics, the trunk is physics, and the branches that issue from the trunk are all the other sciences...] (Opp. ed. Ad. et Ta. IX, 14).

Staying with this image, we ask: In what soil do the roots of the tree of philosophy take hold? Out of what ground do the roots, and thereby the whole tree, receive their nourishing juices and strength? What element, concealed in the ground and soil, enters and lives in the roots that support and nourish the tree? What is the basis and element of the essence[2] of metaphysics? What is metaphysics, viewed from its ground? What is metaphysics itself, at bottom?

Metaphysics thinks beings as beings. Wherever the question is asked what beings are, beings as such are in sight. Metaphysical representation owes this sight to the light[a] of Being. The light itself, i.e., that which such thinking experiences as light, no longer comes within the range of metaphysical thinking; for metaphysics always represents beings only as beings. Within this perspective, metaphysical thinking does, of course, inquire about the being that is the source and originator of this light. But the light itself is considered sufficiently illuminated through its granting the transparency for every perspective upon beings.

[a] Fifth edition, 1949: Clearing.

277

In whatever manner beings are interpreted – whether as spirit, after the fashion of spiritualism; or as matter and force, after the fashion of materialism; or as becoming and life; or as representation, will, substance, subject, or energeia; or as the eternal recurrence of the same – every time, [196] beings as beings appear in the light of Being. Wherever metaphysics represents beings, Being has been cleared. Being has arrived in a state of unconcealedness (Ἀλήθεια). But whether and how Being brings such unconcealedness with it, whether and how It brings itself within, and as, metaphysics,[a] remains veiled. Being in its essence as revealing, i.e., in its truth, is not thought. Nevertheless, when metaphysics gives answers to its question concerning beings as such, metaphysics speaks from out of the unnoticed manifestness of Being. The truth of Being may thus be called the ground in which metaphysics, as the root of the tree of philosophy, is kept and from which it is nourished.

Because metaphysics interrogates beings as beings, it remains concerned with beings and does not turn itself to Being as Being. As the root of the tree, it sends all nourishment and all strength into the trunk and its branches. The root branches out into the soil and ground to enable the tree to grow out of the ground and thus to leave it. The tree of philosophy grows out of the soil in which metaphysics is rooted. The ground and soil is the element in which the root of the tree lives, but the growth of the tree is never able to absorb this soil in such a way that it disappears in the tree as part of the tree. Instead, the roots, down to the subtlest tendrils, lose themselves in the soil. The ground is ground for the roots, and in the ground the roots forget themselves for the sake of the tree. The roots still belong to the tree even when they abandon themselves, after a fashion, to the element of the soil. They squander themselves and their element on the tree. As roots, they do not turn toward the soil – at least not as if it were their essence to grow only into this element and to spread out in it. Presumably, the element would not be the element either if the roots did not live in it.

Metaphysics, insofar as it always represents only beings as beings, does not recall Being itself. Philosophy [197] does not gather itself upon its ground.[b] It always leaves its ground – leaves it by means of metaphysics. And yet it never escapes its ground. Insofar as a thinking sets out to experience the ground of metaphysics, insofar as such thinking attempts to

---

[a] Fifth edition, 1949: Bringing within: Granting unconcealment, and therein what is unconcealed, present. In presencing there lies concealed: The bringing of unconcealment that lets presence that which is present. "Being itself" is Being in its truth, which truth belongs to Being, i.e., into which truth "Being" disappears.

[b] Fifth edition, 1949: Being and ground: the Same.

recall the truth of Being itself instead of merely representing beings as beings, thinking has in a sense left metaphysics. From the point of view of metaphysics, such thinking goes back into the ground of metaphysics. But what still appears as ground[a] from this point of view is presumably something else, once it is experienced in its own terms – something as yet unsaid, and accordingly the essence of metaphysics, too, is something other than metaphysics.

Such thinking, which recalls the truth of Being, is no longer satisfied with metaphysics, to be sure; but it does not oppose and think against metaphysics either. To return to our image, it does not tear up the root of philosophy. It tills the ground and plows the soil for this root. Metaphysics remains what comes first in philosophy. What comes first in thinking, however, it does not reach. When we think the truth of Being, metaphysics is overcome. We can no longer accept the claim of metaphysics to preside over our fundamental relation to "Being" or to decisively determine every relation to beings as such. But this "overcoming of metaphysics" does not abolish metaphysics. As long as man remains the *animal rationale*, he is the *animal metaphysicum*. As long as man understands himself as the rational animal, metaphysics belongs, as Kant said, to the nature of man. But if our thinking should succeed in its efforts to go back into the ground of metaphysics, it might well help to bring about a change in the human essence, a change accompanied by a transformation of metaphysics.

If, as we unfold the question concerning the truth of Being, we speak of overcoming metaphysics, this means: recalling Being itself. Such recalling goes beyond the traditional failure to think the [198] ground of the root of philosophy. The thinking attempted in *Being and Time* (1927) sets out on the way to prepare an overcoming of metaphysics, so understood. That, however, which sets such thinking on its way can only be that which is to be thought.[b] That Being itself and how Being itself concerns our thinking does not depend upon our thinking alone. That Being itself, and the manner in which Being itself, strikes a particular thinking, lets such thinking spring forth in springing from Being itself in such a way as to respond to Being as such.[c]

Why, however, should such an overcoming of metaphysics be necessary? Is the point merely to underpin that discipline of philosophy which was the root hitherto and to supplant it with a yet more original discipline? Is it a question of changing the philosophic system of instruction? No. Or are

[a] Fifth edition, 1949: Being as nonground, ground.
[b] Fifth edition, 1949: What *calls for* thinking?
[c] Fifth edition, 1949: Event of appropriation [*Ereignis*].

we trying to go back into the ground of metaphysics in order to uncover a hitherto overlooked presupposition of philosophy, and thereby to show that philosophy does not yet stand on an unshakable foundation and therefore cannot yet be the absolute science? No.

It is something else that is at stake with the arrival of the truth of Being or its failure to arrive: it is neither the state of philosophy nor philosophy itself alone, but rather the proximity or remoteness of that from which philosophy, insofar as it means the representation of beings as such, receives its essence and its necessity. What is to be decided is whether Being itself, out of its own proper truth, can come to pass[a] in a relation appropriate to the essence of human beings; or whether metaphysics, in turning away from its own ground, continues to prevent the relation of Being to man from lighting up, out of the essence of this very relation, in such a way as to bring human beings into a belonging to Being.

In its answers to the question concerning beings as such, metaphysics operates with a prior representation of Being. It speaks of Being necessarily and hence continually. But [199] metaphysics does not induce Being itself to speak, for metaphysics does not give thought to Being in its truth, nor does it think such truth as unconcealedness, nor does it think this unconcealedness in its essence.[b] To metaphysics the essence of truth always appears only in the already derivative form of the truth of cognitive knowledge and the truth of propositions that formulate such knowledge. Unconcealedness, however, could be something more primordial than all truth in the sense of *veritas*.[c] Ἀλήθεια could be the word that offers a hitherto unnoticed hint concerning the unthought essence of *esse*. If this should be so, then the representational thinking of metaphysics could certainly never attain this essence of truth, however zealously it might devote itself to historical studies of pre-Socratic philosophy; for what is at stake here is not some renaissance of pre-Socratic thinking: any such attempt would be vain and absurd. What is at stake is rather an attentiveness to the arrival of the hitherto unspoken essence of unconcealedness that Being has announced itself to be.[d] Meanwhile the truth of Being has remained concealed from metaphysics during its long history from Anaximander to Nietzsche. Why does metaphysics not recall it? Is the failure to recall it due simply to the nature of metaphysical thinking? Or does it belong to the essential destiny of metaphysics that its own ground withdraws from it because in the rise of

---

[a] Fifth edition, 1949: Usage [*Brauch*].

[b] Fifth edition, 1949: Gathered, revealing-sheltering granting as *Ereignis*.

[c] Fifth edition, 1949: *Veritas* in Thomas Aquinas always *in intellectu*, be it the *intellectus divinus*.

[d] Fifth edition, 1949: Being, truth, world, ~~Being~~, *Ereignis*.

unconcealedness its essential core, namely, concealedness,[a] remains absent in favor of that which is unconcealed, which can thereby first appear as beings?[3]

Metaphysics, however, speaks continually, and in the most various ways, of Being. Metaphysics gives, and seems to confirm, the appearance that it asks and answers the question concerning Being. In fact, metaphysics never answers the question concerning the truth of Being, for it never asks this question. Metaphysics does not ask this question because it thinks Being only by representing beings as beings. It means beings as a whole, although it speaks of Being. It names Being and means beings as beings. From its beginning to its completion, the propositions of metaphysics have been [200] strangely involved in a persistent confusion[b] of beings and Being. This confusion, to be sure, must be considered an event and not a mere mistake. It cannot by any means have its ground in a mere negligence of thought or a carelessness of expression. Owing to this persistent confusion, the claim that metaphysics poses the question of Being lands us in utter error.

Due to the manner in which it thinks of beings, metaphysics almost seems to be, without knowing it, the barrier that refuses human beings the primordial[c] relation of Being[d] to the human essence.

What if the absence of this relation and the oblivion of this absence determined the entire modern age from afar? What if the absence of Being abandoned man more and more exclusively to beings, leaving him forsaken and far from any relation of Being to his (human) essence, while this forsakenness itself remained veiled? What if this were the case – and had been the case for a long time now? What if there were signs that this oblivion will enter into oblivion still more decisively in the future?

Would there still be occasion for a thinker to give himself arrogant airs in view of this destiny of Being? Would there still be occasion, if this forsakenness of Being should be our situation, to indulge in some other pretense, and to do so in some artificially induced elation? If the oblivion of Being that has been described here should be our situation, would there not be occasion enough for a thinking that recalls Being to experience a genuine horror? What can such thinking do other than to endure anxiously

[a] Fifth edition, 1949: Λήθη as concealing.
[b] Fifth edition, 1949: Confusion: remaining tied to passing over to Being and back to beings. One always stands *in* the other and *for* the other, "interchange," "exchange," first this way, then the other.
[c] Fifth edition, 1949: The initiatory event [*an-fangende Ereignis*] that prevails in initiation – in usage – disappropriation [*Enteignis*].
[d] Fifth edition, 1949: Being itself = B̶e̶i̶n̶g̶.

this destiny of Being, so as first of all to bring the oblivion of Being to bear upon us? But how could thought achieve this if the anxiety destined to it were merely a mood of depression? What does such anxiety, as a destiny of Being, have to do with psychology or psychoanalysis?

[201] Granted that the overcoming of metaphysics corresponded to the endeavor to first learn to attend to the oblivion of Being, in order to experience this oblivion and to absorb this experience into the relation of Being to man, and to preserve it there, then in the need belonging to the oblivion of Being, the question "What is metaphysics?" might well remain what is most needed of all that is necessary for thought.

Thus everything depends on this: that our thinking should become more thoughtful in its season. This is achieved when our thinking, instead of implementing a higher degree of exertion, is directed toward another provenance. The thinking that is set in place by beings as such, and is therefore representational and illuminating in that way, must then be relinquished to a thinking that is brought to pass by Being itself and is therefore in thrall to Being.

All attempts are futile that seek to make representational thinking, which remains metaphysical, and only metaphysical, effective, and useful for immediate action in everyday public life. For the more thoughtful our thinking becomes and the more responsive it is in accomplishing its relation to Being, the more purely our thinking will stand of its own accord in the sole action appropriate to it: namely, in the thinking of that which is thought for it[a] and has thus already been thought.

But who still recalls what has been thought? One makes inventions. The thinking attempted in *Being and Time* is "under way" toward bringing our thinking onto a way through which it may enter the relation of the truth of Being to the essence of man, toward opening up a path for thinking on which it may explicitly ponder Being itself in its truth.[b] On this way – that is, in the service of the question concerning the truth of Being – it becomes necessary to meditate upon the essence of human beings; for the experience of the oblivion of Being, which is not specifically mentioned because it still had to be demonstrated, involves the crucial conjecture that in accordance with the unconcealedness of Being the relation of Being to the human essence belongs to Being itself. But how could this [202] conjecture, which is experienced here, become an explicit question before every attempt had been made to liberate the determination of the human essence from subjectivity,

---

[a] Fifth edition, 1949: Addressed to it, gathered and granted it, appropriated for it.
[b] Fifth edition, 1949: Preservation [*Wahrnis*] as *Ereignis*.

but also from the definition of *animal rationale?* To characterize with a *single* term both the relation of Being to the essence of man and the essential relation of man to the openness ("there" ["*Da*"]) of Being [*Sein*] as such, the name of "Dasein" [there-being] was chosen for the essential realm in which man stands as man. This term was employed even though in metaphysics it is used interchangeably with *existentia*, actuality, reality, and objectivity, and although this metaphysical usage is further supported by the common [German] expression "*menschliches Dasein*" [human existence]. Any attempt at thoughtfulness is therefore thwarted as long as one is satisfied with the observation that in *Being and Time* the term "Dasein" is used in place of "consciousness." As if this were simply a matter of using different words! As if it were not the one and only thing at stake here: namely, to bring us to think the relation of Being to the essence of man and thus, from our point of view,[a] to present initially an experience of the human essence that may prove sufficient to direct our inquiry. The term "Dasein" neither takes the place of the term "consciousness," nor does the "matter" designated as "Dasein" take the place of what we represent to ourselves when we speak of "consciousness." Rather, "Dasein" names that which is first of all to be experienced, and subsequently thought accordingly, as a place[b] – namely, as the locality of the truth of Being.

What the term "Dasein" means throughout the treatise *Being and Time* is indicated already by the guiding thesis: "*The 'essence' of Dasein lies in its existence*" (*Being and Time*, p. 42).

To be sure, in the language of metaphysics the word "existence" is a synonym of "Dasein": both refer to the actuality of anything at all that is actual, from God to a grain of sand. As long, therefore, as the quoted sentence is understood only superficially, [203] the difficulty of what is to be thought is merely transferred from the word "Dasein" to the word "existence." In *Being and Time*, the term "existence" is used exclusively for the Being of the human being. Once "existence" is understood correctly, the "essence" of Dasein can be thought, in whose openness Being itself announces and conceals itself, grants itself and withdraws; at the same time, this truth of Being does not exhaust itself in Dasein, nor can it by any means simply be identified with it after the fashion of the metaphysical proposition that all objectivity is as such also subjectivity.

What does "existence" mean in *Being and Time?* The word names a way of Being; specifically, the Being of that being which stands open for the

---

[a] Fifth edition, 1949: But no longer starting from "us" as subjects.

[b] Fifth edition, 1949: Inadequately said: the locality dwelt in by mortals, the mortal region of the locality.

openness of Being in which it stands in withstanding it. This withstanding is experienced under the name of "care." The ecstatic essence of Dasein is thought in terms of care, and, conversely, care is experienced adequately only in its ecstatic essence. Withstanding, experienced in this manner, is the essence of the ecstasis that is to be thought here. The ecstatic essence of existence is therefore still understood inadequately as long as one thinks of it as merely a "standing out," while interpreting the "out" as meaning "away from" the interior of an immanence of consciousness or spirit. For in this manner, existence would still be represented in terms of "subjectivity" and "substance"; while, in fact, the "out" ought to be understood in terms of the "outside itself" of the openness of Being itself. The stasis of the ecstatic consists – strange as it may sound – in standing in the "out" and "there" of unconcealedness, which prevails as the essence of Being itself. What is meant by "existence" in the context of a thinking that is prompted by, and directed toward, the truth of Being, could be most felicitously designated by the word "in-standing" [*Inständigkeit*]. We must think at the same time, however, of standing in the openness of Being, of sustaining this standing-in (care), and of enduring in what is most extreme (being toward death);[a] for together they constitute the full essence of existence.[b]

[204] The being that exists is the human being. The human being alone exists. Rocks are, but they do not exist. Trees are, but they do not exist. Horses are, but they do not exist. Angels are, but they do not exist. God is, but he does not exist. The proposition "the human being alone exists" does not at all mean that the human being alone is a real being while all other beings are unreal and mere appearances or human representations. The proposition "the human being exists" means: the human being is that being whose Being is distinguished by an open standing that stands in the unconcealedness of Being, proceeding from Being, in Being. The[c] existential essence of the human being is the reason why human beings can represent beings as such, and why they can be conscious of such representations. All consciousness presupposes existence, thought as ecstatic, as the *essentia* of the human being – *essentia* meaning that as which the human being essentially prevails insofar as he is human. But consciousness does not itself create the openness of beings, nor is it consciousness that makes it possible for the human being to stand open for beings. Whither and whence

---

[a] Fifth edition, 1949: Letting death come toward and upon oneself, holding oneself in the arrival of death as the gathered shelter [*Ge-Birg*] of Being.

[b] Fifth edition, 1949: Dwelling, as "building."

[c] Fifth edition, 1949: Used and appropriated.

and in what free dimension could the intentionality of consciousness move, if in-standing were not the essence of the human being in the first instance? What else could be the meaning – if anybody has ever seriously thought about this – of the word *sein* [being] in the [German] words *Bewußtsein* ["consciousness"; literally: "being conscious"] and *Selbstbewußtsein* ["self-consciousness"] if it did not name the existential essence of that which is insofar as it exists? To be a self is admittedly one feature of the essence of that being which exists; but existence does not consist in being a self, nor can it be defined in such terms. Yet because metaphysical thinking understands the human being's selfhood in terms of substance or – and at bottom this amounts to the same – in terms of the subject, the first path that leads from metaphysics to the ecstatic existential essence of the human being must lead through the metaphysical determination of human selfhood (*Being and Time*, §§63 and 64).

The question concerning existence, however, is always subservient to the singular question of thought. This question, yet [205] to be unfolded, concerns the truth of Being as the concealed ground of all metaphysics. For this reason the treatise that seeks to point the way back into the ground of metaphysics does not bear the title "Existence and Time," nor "Consciousness and Time," but *Being and Time*. Nor can this title be understood as if it were parallel to the customary juxtapositions of Being and Becoming, Being and Seeming, Being and Thinking, or Being and Ought. For in all these cases Being is conceived as limited, as if Becoming, Seeming, Thinking, and Ought did not belong to Being, although it is obvious that they are not nothing and thus do belong to Being. In *Being and Time*, Being is not something other than time: "Time" is a preliminary name for the truth of Being, and this truth is what prevails as essential in Being and thus is Being itself. But why "time" and "being"?

By recalling the beginnings of that history in which Being unveiled itself in the thinking of the Greeks, it can be shown that the Greeks from early on experienced the Being of beings as the presence of what is present. When we translate εἶναι as "being," our translation is linguistically correct. Yet we merely substitute one set of sounds for another. As soon as we examine ourselves it becomes obvious that we neither think εἶναι in a Greek manner, nor do we think a correspondingly clear and univocal determination when we speak of "being." What, then, are we saying when instead of εἶναι we say "being," and instead of "being," εἶναι and *esse*? We are saying nothing. The Greek, Latin, and German words all remain equally obtuse. As long as we adhere to customary usage we merely betray ourselves as the pacemakers of the greatest thoughtlessness that has ever gained currency in human thought and that has remained dominant until this moment. This εἶναι, however, means: to presence. The essence of this presencing lies deeply concealed in the early names for Being. But for us εἶναι and οὐσία as παρ- and ἀπουσία mean this in the first instance: in presencing there prevails, in an unthought and concealed manner, presence and duration – there prevails time. Being as such is thus unconcealed [206] in terms of time. Thus time points to unconcealedness, i.e., to the truth of Being. But the time that is to be thought here is not experienced through the changing course that beings take. Time is evidently of an altogether different essence,[a] which not only has not yet been thought by way of the concept of time belonging to metaphysics, but never can be thought in this way. Thus time becomes the preliminary name – a name that has first to be pondered – for the truth of Being that is yet to be experienced.

Just as a concealed essence of time speaks not only in the first metaphysical names for Being, so too it speaks in its last name, in "the eternal recurrence of the same." In the epoch of metaphysics,[b] the history of Being is pervaded by an unthought essence of time. Space is neither simply co-ordinated nor merely subordinated to such time.[c]

An attempt to make a transition from the representation of beings as such to recalling the truth of Being must, in starting from such representation, still represent, in a certain sense, the truth of Being, too; with the result that this latter representation must necessarily be of another kind and ultimately, insofar as it is representation, inappropriate to that which is to be thought. This relation, which comes out of metaphysics and tries to enter into the relation of the truth of Being to the human essence, is conceived as "understanding." But here understanding is thought at the same time from out of the unconcealedness of Being. Understanding is ecstatic, thrown projection,[d] ecstatic here meaning: standing in the realm of the open. The realm that opens up for us[e] in projection, in order that something (Being in this case) may prove itself as something (in this case, Being as itself in its unconcealedness), is called meaning[f] (cf. *Being and Time*, p. 151). "Meaning of Being" and "truth of Being" say the same.

[a] Fifth edition, 1949: Time is four-dimensional: The *first* dimension, which gathers everything, is *nearness*.

[b] Fifth edition, 1949: This epoch is the whole history of Being.

[c] Fifth edition, 1949: Time-space.

[d] Fifth edition, 1949: Thrownness and *Ereignis*. Throwing, throwing toward, sending; projection: responding to the throw.

[e] Fifth edition, 1949: Brings itself to us.

[f] Fifth edition, 1949: Meaning – pointing the path toward the matter [*Sach-verhalt*].

Granted that time belongs to the truth of Being in a way that is still concealed: then every projective holding open of the truth of Being, as an understanding of Being, must look toward time as the possible[a] horizon of an understanding of Being (cf. *Being and Time*, §§31–34 and 68).

The preface to *Being and Time*, on the first page of the treatise, ends with these sentences: "The concrete working out of [207] the question concerning the meaning of '*Being*' is the intention of the following treatise. The interpretation of *time* as the possible horizon of every understanding of Being whatsoever is its provisional goal."

All philosophy has fallen into the oblivion of Being that has, at the same time, become and remained the destinal claim upon thinking in *Being and Time*; and philosophy could hardly have given a clearer demonstration of the power of this oblivion of Being than it has furnished us by the somnambulistic assurance with which it has passed by the proper and singular question of *Being and Time*. What is at stake here is, therefore, not a series of misunderstandings of a book but our abandonment by Being.

Metaphysics states what beings are as beings. It offers a λόγος (statement) about the ὄν (beings). The later title "ontology" characterizes its essence, provided, of course, that we understand it in accordance with its proper significance and not through its narrow Scholastic meaning. Metaphysics moves in the sphere of the ὄν ἧ ὄν. Its representing concerns beings as beings. In this manner, metaphysics always represents beings as such in their totality; it represents the beingness of beings (the οὐσία of the ὄν). But metaphysics represents the beingness of beings in a twofold manner: in the first place, the totality of beings as such with an eye to their most universal traits (ὄν καθόλου, κοινόν); but at the same time also the totality of beings as such in the sense of the highest and therefore divine being (ὄν καθόλου, ἀκρότατον, θεῖον). In the metaphysics of Aristotle, the unconcealedness of beings as such has specifically developed in this twofold manner (cf. *Metaphysics*, Γ, Ε, Κ).

Because it represents beings as beings, metaphysics is, in a twofold and yet unitary manner, the truth of beings in their universality and in the highest being. According to its essence, metaphysics is at the same time both ontology in the narrower sense, and theology. This ontotheological essence of philosophy proper (πρώτη φιλοσοφία) must indeed be grounded [208] in the way in which the ὄν opens up in it, namely, as ὄν. Thus the theological character of ontology is not merely due to the fact that Greek metaphysics was later taken up and transformed by the ecclesiastic

---

[a] Fifth edition, 1949: Enabling.

theology of Christianity. Rather it is due to the manner in which beings as beings have revealed themselves from early on. It was this unconcealedness of beings that first provided the possibility for Christian theology to take possession of Greek philosophy – whether for better or for worse may be decided by the theologians on the basis of their experience of what is Christian, in pondering what is written in the First Epistle of Paul the Apostle to the Corinthians: οὐχὶ ἐμώρανεν ὁ θεὸς τὴν σοφίαν τοῦ κόσμου: "Has not God let the wisdom of this world become foolishness?"(I Corinthians 1:20). The σοφία τοῦ κόσμου [wisdom of this world], however, is that which, according to 1:22, the Ἕλληνες ζητοῦσιν, the Greeks seek. Aristotle even calls πρώτη φιλοσοφία (philosophy proper) quite explicitly ζητουμένη, that which is sought after. Will Christian theology one day resolve to take seriously the word of the apostle and thus also the conception of philosophy as foolishness?

As the truth of beings as such, metaphysics has a twofold character. The reason for this twofoldness, however, let alone its origin, remains closed to metaphysics; and this is no accident, nor due to mere neglect. Metaphysics has this twofold character because it is what it is: the representation of beings as beings. Metaphysics has no choice. As metaphysics, it is by its very essence excluded from the experience of Being; for it always represents beings (ὄν) only with an eye to that aspect of them that has already manifested itself as being (ᾗ ὄν). But metaphysics never pays attention to what has concealed itself in this very ὄν insofar as it became unconcealed.

Thus the time came when it became necessary to make a fresh attempt to attend thoughtfully to what precisely is said when we speak of ὄν or use the word "being" [seiend]. Accordingly, the question concerning the ὄν was [209] retrieved for thinking (cf. Being and Time, Preface). But this retrieval is no mere repetition of the Platonic-Aristotelian question; instead it asks about that which conceals itself in the ὄν.[a]

Metaphysics is founded upon that which remains concealed in the ὄν as long as its representing devotes itself to the ὄν ᾗ ὄν. The attempt to inquire back into what is thus concealed therefore seeks, from the point of view of metaphysics, the fundament of ontology. For this reason, that attempt is called, in Being and Time (p. 13), "fundamental ontology." Yet this title, like any title, is soon seen to be inappropriate. From the point of view of metaphysics, to be sure, it says something that is correct; but precisely for that reason it is misleading, for what matters is undertaking the transition from metaphysics to recalling the truth of Being. As long as this thinking

---

[a] Fifth edition, 1949: The distinction.

calls itself "fundamental ontology" it blocks and obscures its own path by this very designation. For what the title "fundamental ontology" suggests is that the thinking that attempts to think the truth of Being – and not, like all ontology, the truth of beings – is, as fundamental ontology, still a kind of ontology. In fact, the attempt to recall the truth of Being, as a going back into the ground of metaphysics, has already left the realm of all ontology with its very first step. On the other hand, every philosophy that revolves around an indirect or direct representation of "transcendence" remains of necessity essentially an ontology, whether it achieves a new foundation of ontology or whether it assures us that it repudiates ontology as a conceptual freezing of experience.

If, coming from the old custom of representing beings as such, the very thinking that attempts to think the truth of Being itself becomes entangled in such representation, then it would seem that both for a preliminary orientation and in order to prepare the transition from representational thinking to a thinking that recalls [das andenkende Denken], nothing becomes more necessary than the question: What is metaphysics?

[210] The unfolding of this question in the following lecture culminates, for its part, in another question. This is called the grounding question of metaphysics: Why are there beings at all, and not rather Nothing? In the interim, people have talked back and forth a great deal about anxiety and the Nothing, both of which are spoken of in this lecture. But one has never yet deigned to ask oneself why a lecture that attempts to recall the Nothing from out of a thinking of the truth of Being, and from there tries to think into the essence of metaphysics, should claim that this question is the grounding question of metaphysics. How can an attentive reader help feeling on the tip of his tongue an objection that is far more weighty than all protests against anxiety and the Nothing? The final question provokes the objection that a meditation that attempts to recall Being by way of the Nothing returns in the end to a question concerning beings. On top of that, the question even proceeds in the customary manner of metaphysics by beginning with a causal "Why?" To this extent, then, the attempt to recall Being is fully repudiated in favor of a representational knowledge of beings in terms of beings. And to make matters still worse, the final question is obviously the question that the metaphysician Leibniz posed in his *Principes de la nature et de la grâce:* "Pourquoi il y a plutôt quelque chose que rien?" (Opp. ed. Gerh. tom. VI, 602 n. 7).

Does the lecture, then, fall short of its intention? After all, this would be quite possible in view of the difficulty of effecting a transition from metaphysics to another kind of thinking. Does the lecture end up by asking with

Leibniz[a] the metaphysical question about the supreme cause of all that is? Why, then, is Leibniz's name not mentioned, as would seem appropriate?

Or is the question asked in an altogether different sense? If it does not concern itself with beings and inquire about their first cause among all beings, then the question must begin from that which is not a being. And this is precisely what the question names, and it capitalizes the word: the Nothing. This is the sole [211] topic of the lecture. The demand seems obvious that the end of the lecture should be thought through, for once, in its own perspective that guides the whole lecture. What is called the grounding question of metaphysics would then have to be understood and asked in terms of fundamental ontology as the question that comes out of the ground of metaphysics and as the question about this ground.

But if we grant this lecture that in the end it thinks in the direction of its own distinctive concern, how then are we to understand this question?

The question is: Why are there beings at all, and not rather Nothing? Granted that we do not remain within metaphysics to ask metaphysically in the customary manner, but that we recall the truth of Being out of the essence and truth of metaphysics, then this might be asked as well: How does it come about that beings take precedence everywhere and lay claim to every "is," while that which is not a being – namely, the Nothing thus understood as Being itself – remains forgotten? How does it come about that with Being[b] It[c] is really nothing and that the Nothing does not properly prevail? Is it perhaps from this that the as yet unshaken presumption has entered all metaphysics that an understanding of "Being" may simply be taken for granted and that the Nothing can therefore be dealt with more easily than beings? That is indeed the situation regarding Being and Nothing. If it were different, then Leibniz could not have said in the same place by way of an explanation: "Car le rien est plus simple et plus facile que quelque chose [For the nothing is simpler and easier than any thing]."

What is more enigmatic: that beings are, or that Being "is"? Or does even this reflection fail to bring us close to that enigma which has occurred [sich ereignet][d] with the Being of[e] beings?

Whatever the answer may be, the time should have ripened meanwhile for thinking through the lecture "What Is Metaphysics?," which has been subjected to so many attacks, from its end, for once – from *its* end and not from some imaginary end.

[a] Fifth edition, 1949: And Schelling.
[b] Fifth edition, 1949: As such.
[c] Fifth edition, 1949: For metaphysics.
[d] Fifth edition, 1949: The event [*Ereignis*] of the forgottenness of the distinction.
[e] Fifth edition, 1949: The distinction.

On the Question of Being

Translated by William McNeill[1]

FOREWORD

[213] This essay presents the unaltered, slightly expanded (pp. 24ff.) text of a contribution to a publication in honor of Ernst Jünger (1955). The title has been altered. It formerly read: *Concerning "The Line"* [*Über "Die Linie"*]. The new title is meant to indicate that the meditation on the essence of nihilism stems from a discussion [*Erörterung*][2] locating being as ~~being~~. In accordance with the tradition, philosophy understands the question of being as the question concerning beings as beings. This is *the* question of metaphysics. The answers to this question in each case appeal to an interpretation of being that remains unquestioned and that prepares the ground and soil for metaphysics. Metaphysics does not go back into its ground. Such a return is addressed in the "Introduction to 'What Is Metaphysics?'," which since the fifth edition (1949) has been placed before the text of the lecture (seventh edition [1955], pp. 7–23).

CONCERNING "THE LINE"

Dear Herr Jünger!

My greeting on your sixtieth birthday adopts, with a slight change, the title of the treatise that you dedicated to me on the same occasion. Your contribution *Across the Line* [*Über die Linie*] has meanwhile appeared as a separate publication, expanded in a few places. It is an "assessment of our situation," concerned with "crossing" the line, yet does not confine itself merely to describing the situation. The line is also called the "zero meridian" (p. 29). You speak (on pp. 22 and 31) of the "zero point." [214] The zero indicates the nothing, indeed an empty nothing. Where everything presses toward nothing, nihilism reigns. At the zero meridian it approaches

its consummation. Taking up an interpretation of Nietzsche's, you understand nihilism as the process whereby *"the highest values become devalued"*
(*The Will to Power*, aphorism no. 2, from the year 1887).

As meridian, the zero-line has its zone. The realm of consummate
nihilism constitutes the border between two world eras. The line that designates this realm is the critical line. By this line will be decided whether the
movement of nihilism comes to an end in a nihilistic nothing, or whether it
is the transition to the realm of a "new turning of being" (p. 32). The movement of nihilism must thus of its own accord be disposed toward different
possibilities and in keeping with its essence be ambiguous.

Your assessment of the situation follows the signs whereby we may recognize whether and to what extent we are crossing the line and thereby
exiting from the zone of consummate nihilism. In the title of your essay
Über die Linie the *über* means as much as: across, *trans*, μετά. By contrast, the
following remarks understand the *über* only in the sense of *de*, περί. They
deal "with" the line itself, with the zone of self-consummating nihilism.
Keeping to the image of the line, we find that it traverses a space that
is itself determined by a locale. The locale gathers. Gathering shelters
that which is gathered in the direction of its essence. From the locale of
the line, the provenance of the essence of nihilism and its consummation
emerge.

My letter seeks to think ahead to this locale of the line and thus locate the
line. Your assessment of the situation under the title *trans lineam* and my
discussion locating the line under the title *de linea* belong together. Yours
entails mine. Mine remains directed toward yours. With this, I am telling
you nothing special. You know that an assessment of the human situation
in relation to the movement of nihilism and within this movement demands
an [215] adequate determination of the essential. Such knowledge is extensively lacking. This lack dims our view in assessing our situation. It makes a
judgment concerning nihilism ready and easy and blinds us to the presence
of "this most uncanny of all guests" (Nietzsche, *The Will to Power*, Outline. *Werke*, vol. XV, p. 141). It is called the "most uncanny" [*unheimlichste*]
because, as the unconditional will to will, it wills homelessness [*Heimat-
losigkeit*] as such. This is why it is of no avail to show it the door, because
it has long since been roaming around invisibly inside the house. The task
is to catch sight of and see through this guest. You yourself write (p. 11):
"A good definition of nihilism would be comparable to making visible the
cancer-causing agent. It would not mean the healing, but presumably its
precondition, insofar as human beings in general play a role here. We are,
after all, concerned with a process that far exceeds history."

"A good definition of nihilism" could thus be expected from a discussion *de linea*, provided that a humanly possible concern for healing can indeed be compared to being escorted *trans lineam*. You indeed emphasize that nihilism is not to be equated with illness, nor for that matter with chaos or evil. As with the cancer-causing agent, nihilism itself is not something diseased. With regard to the *essence* of nihilism there is no prospect and can be no meaningful claim of healing. And yet your text maintains the stance of a doctor, as indicated by its division into prognosis, diagnosis, and therapy. The young Nietzsche once named the philosopher the "doctor of culture" (*Werke*, vol. X, p. 225). Yet now it is no longer merely a matter of culture. You rightly say: "The whole is at stake." "It is a matter of the planet in general" (p. 28). Healing can concern itself only with the malevolent consequences and threatening phenomena that accompany this planetary process. An awareness and knowledge of the cause, i.e., of the essence, of nihilism are all the more urgently needed. Thinking is needed all the more urgently, granted that an adequate experience of this essence can be prepared only in a responsive [216] thinking. Yet in the same measure that the possibilities of any immediately effective healing disappear, the capability for thought has also already diminished. The essence of nihilism is neither healable nor unhealable. It is the heal-less, and yet, as such, a unique pointer toward the salutary. If thinking is to approach the realm of the essence of nihilism, it must necessarily become more precursory, and thereby become other.

Whether a discussion of the line can furnish "a good definition of nihilism," and whether it may even strive for such a thing, becomes questionable for a thinking that is precursory. A discussion of the line must attempt something else. This explicit renunciation of a definition appears to relinquish the rigor of thought. Yet it could also happen that this renunciation could first bring thinking onto the path of a rigorous effort that might let us experience the kind of rigor of thought appropriate to this issue. This can never be decided by the judiciary of *ratio*. The latter is not at all a legitimate judge. It unthinkingly thrusts everything that is inappropriate *to it* into the alleged mire of the irrational, a mire that, moreover, it itself first delimits. Reason and its representational activity are only *one* kind of thinking and are by no means self-determined. They are determined, rather, by that which has called upon thinking to think in the manner of *ratio*. That the domination of *ratio* is erecting itself as the rationalization of all order, as standardization, and as leveling out in the course of the unfolding of European nihilism, should give us just as much to think about as the accompanying attempts to flee into the irrational.

What is most thought-provoking, however, is the way in which rationalism and irrationalism become equally entwined in a reciprocal exchange from which they not only are unable to extricate themselves, but from which they no longer wish to escape. Thus, one denies any possibility that thinking might be brought before a call that maintains itself outside of the alternative of rational or irrational. Such a thinking could [217] nonetheless be prepared by the tentative steps attempted in the manner of historical elucidation, reflection, and discussion.

My discussion seeks an encounter with the medical assessment of the situation that you have provided. You look across and go across the line; I simply take a look at the line that you have represented. These two perspectives provide mutual assistance in extending and clarifying our experience. Perhaps they could both help to awaken the "sufficient power of mind" (p. 28) that you claim is necessary for crossing the line.

In order to catch sight of nihilism in the phase of its consummation, we must accompany its movement in action. The description of this action will impress itself upon us particularly if, as description, it itself partakes of this action. Thereby, however, the description runs into an extraordinary danger and faces a far-reaching responsibility. The responsibility of whoever participates in this manner must gather itself in a responsive word that springs from a persistent questioning within the greatest possible worthiness of question that nihilism displays, and which is assumed and sustained as responsive to such worthiness.

Your essay *The Worker* [*Der Arbeiter*][3] (1932) has provided a description of European nihilism in its phase following the first world war. This essay develops from your treatise *Total Mobilization* [*Die Totale Mobilmachung*] (1930). The figure of "the worker" belongs to the phase of "active nihilism" (Nietzsche). The action of work consisted – and with a transformed function continues to consist – in making visible, through the figure of the worker, the "total work-like character" of all that is actual. Nihilism, at first merely European, thereby appears in its planetary tendency. Of course there is no description in itself that would be capable of showing what is actual in itself. Every description, the more incisively it proceeds, moves all the more decisively in its own manner within a particular perspective. The manner of seeing and the perspective – the "optics," as you put it – of [218] human representation result from fundamental experiences with beings as a whole. Yet they are already preceded by a clearing [*Lichtung*] of the way in which beings "are," a clearing that can never first be made by human beings. The fundamental experience that sustains and traverses your representation and depiction arose from the matériel battles of the first world war. Beings as a whole, however, show themselves to you in the light and shadow of the metaphysics of the will to power, which Nietzsche interprets in the form of a doctrine of values.

In the winter of 1939–40 I discussed *The Worker* among a small circle of university teachers. People were astonished that such a clear-sighted book had been available for years, and that they themselves had not yet learned even to venture the attempt to let their view of the present move within the optics of *The Worker* and to think in planetary terms. One could sense that even a universal, historiographical consideration of world history was inadequate for such a task. At that time, people read enthusiastically *The Marble Cliffs* [*Die Marmorklippen*], but, as it seemed to me, without a sufficiently broad, i.e., planetary, horizon. And we were not surprised, either, that an attempt to elucidate *The Worker* was kept under surveillance and eventually prohibited. For it belongs to the essence of the will to power not to let the actual that it gains power over appear in *that* actuality which prevails as the will to power itself.

You will permit me to reproduce a note that I made during this attempt to elucidate your book. I do so in the hope that I can say some things more clearly and freely in the present letter. The note reads:

Ernst Jünger's text *The Worker* is important because, in a different way from Spengler, it achieves what all Nietzsche literature thus far has been unable to achieve, namely, to impart an experience of beings and the way in which they are, in the light of Nietzsche's projection of beings as will to power. Nietzsche's metaphysics, however, is by no means comprehended thoughtfully; not even the ways to do so are indicated; on the contrary: instead of being worthy of question in a genuine sense, this metaphysics becomes self-evident and seemingly superfluous.

[219] As you can see, the critical question thinks in a direction that admittedly does not belong to the sphere of tasks to be pursued by the descriptions undertaken in *The Worker*. Much of what your descriptions brought into view and brought to language for the first time is now seen and stated by everyone. Moreover, "The Question concerning Technology" owes a lasting debt to the descriptions in *The Worker*. It is appropriate to note that your "descriptions" do not merely depict something actual that is already familiar, but make accessible a "new actuality," in which it is "not so much a matter of new thoughts or a new system . . ." (Preface to *The Worker*).

Even today the fruitful aspect of what you say is gathered within "description" properly understood – and how should it not be? Yet the optics and perspective that guide such description are no longer or not yet determined in the way they were before. For you no longer partake in that action of active nihilism that, already in *The Worker*, is conceived in a Nietzschean sense as oriented toward an overcoming. Yet no longer partaking in no way already means: standing outside of nihilism, especially not if the essence of nihilism is nothing nihilistic and if the history of that essence is older and remains younger than the phases of the various forms of nihilism, phases that can be ascertained historiographically. For this reason, both your book *The Worker* and the treatise *On Pain* [*Über den Schmerz*] (1934) that followed it in leaping even further ahead are not discarded records of the nihilistic movement. On the contrary: It seems to me that these works *remain* with us because, to the extent that they speak the language of our century, they can ignite anew the critical encounter with the *essence* of nihilism, an encounter that has by no means as yet been achieved.

As I write this, I recall our dialogue that took place toward the end of the last decade. As we walked along a forest path we came to a halt at a place where a trail branched off. At that point I encouraged you to have *The Worker* [220] reissued, indeed in its original form. You followed this suggestion only with some hesitation, for reasons that concerned not so much the content of the book as the right moment to reissue it. Our dialogue about *The Worker* broke off. I myself was not focused enough to articulate with sufficient clarity the reasons for my suggestion. Since then, the time may have become more ready to say something about this.

On the one hand, the movement of nihilism in the many forms of its inexorable and planetary character that eats away at and consumes everything has become more evident. No one of any insight would today wish to deny that nihilism in its most diverse and hidden forms is the "normal condition" of humankind (cf. Nietzsche, *The Will to Power*, no. 23). The best evidence of this is provided by the exclusively re-active attempts to oppose nihilism that, instead of entering into a critical encounter with its essence, undertake a restoration of the past. They seek salvation in taking flight, namely, in taking flight from any insight into the metaphysical position of the human being as worthy of question. The same flight presses upon us too where one appears to give up all metaphysics and replace it with logistics, sociology, and psychology. The will to knowledge that breaks forth here and the way in which its entire organization can be directed points to an intensification of the will to power that is of another kind than that which Nietzsche designated as active nihilism.

On the other hand, your own endeavors and writings are now intent on helping us to extricate ourselves from the zone of consummate nihilism, without your giving up the fundamental outline of the perspective opened up by *The Worker* and emerging from Nietzsche's metaphysics.

You write (*Über die Linie*, p. 36): "Total mobilization has entered a stage whose threat exceeds that of the previous stage. For the German is no longer the subject of such mobilization, and the danger thereby grows that he will be conceived as its object." Even now you rightly regard total mobilization as a distinctive [221] characteristic of what is actual. Yet its actuality is for you now no longer determined by the "*will to* (my emphasis) total mobilization" (*Der Arbeiter*, p. 148), and is no longer determined in such a way that this will can have validity as the sole source that "gives meaning" and justifies everything. Hence you write (*Über die Linie*, p. 30): "There is no doubt that our subsistence (i.e., according to p. 31, 'persons, works, and institutions') as a whole is moving across the critical line. The dangers and our security are thereby altered." In the zone belonging to the line, nihilism approaches its consummation. The whole of "human subsistence" can cross the line only if this subsistence steps out of the zone of consummate nihilism.

Accordingly, a discussion of the line must ask: Wherein consists the consummation of nihilism? The answer seems to be at hand. Nihilism is consummated when it has seized all subsisting resources and appears wherever nothing can assert itself as an exception anymore, insofar as such nihilism has become our normal condition. Yet in this condition of normality the consummation only *becomes actualized*. The condition of normality is a consequence of the consummation. Consummation [*Vollendung*] means the gathering of all essential possibilities of nihilism, possibilities that remain difficult to see through as a whole and individually. The essential possibilities of nihilism can be pondered only if we think back toward its essence. I say "back" because the essence of nihilism prevails ahead and thus in advance of individual nihilistic phenomena, gathering them into its consummation. Yet the consummation of nihilism is not already its end. With the consummation of nihilism there first *begins* the final phase of nihilism. The zone of this end-phase, because it is pervaded by a condition of normality that sets in, is presumably unusually broad. For this reason the zero-line, where the consummation becomes an end, is not yet visible at all in the end.

Yet how do matters stand, then, concerning the prospect of crossing over the line? Is human subsistence already in a transition [222] *trans lineam*, or is it now first entering the broad field that stands before the line? But perhaps our eyes deceive us here in an unavoidable way. Perhaps the zero-line will emerge suddenly before us in the form of a planetary catastrophe.

Who will cross over it then? And what can catastrophes accomplish? The two world wars have neither halted the movement of nihilism, nor steered it from its course. What you say about total mobilization (p. 36) confirms this. How do matters stand now regarding the critical line? In such a way, in any case, that a discussion locating its locale might awaken a reflection on whether and to what extent we may think of crossing over the line.

Yet the attempt to say something *de linea* in a dialogue with you by letter confronts a peculiar difficulty. The reason for this difficulty lies in the fact that in your "crossing" over the line, i.e., in the space on this and on the other side of the line, you speak the same language. The position of nihilism is, it seems, already relinquished in a certain way by crossing over the line, but *its language has remained*. I here mean language not as a mere means of expression that can be taken off and exchanged like a garment, without that which has come to language being touched by it. In language there appears and prevails for the first time that which, in using words that are decisive, we apparently express only after the event, using expressions that we believe could be arbitrarily discarded and replaced by others. The language of *The Worker* manifests its chief traits, it seems to me, most evidently in the subtitle of the work. It reads: "Domination and *Gestalt*." The subtitle characterizes the fundamental outline of the work. You understand the word *Gestalt* [figure] initially in the sense of the *Gestalt* psychology of the time, as "a whole that contains more than the sum of its parts." One could ponder to what extent this characterization of *Gestalt*, by speaking of "more" and of "the sum," still depends on a way of representing that sums things up, and leaves indeterminate whatever has the character of *Gestalt* as such. [223] But you give *Gestalt* a cultist status and thereby rightly set it off from a "mere idea."

In this context, "idea" is understood in the modern sense of *perceptio*, of representation by a subject. On the other hand, for you too *Gestalt* is accessible only in a seeing. The seeing in question is that which the Greeks call ἰδεῖν, a word that Plato uses to refer to a looking that catches sight not of that which is changeable and can be perceived by the senses, but of the unchangeable, being, the ἰδέα. You too characterize *Gestalt* as "being that is at rest." The *Gestalt* is not an "idea" in the modern sense, and thus not a regulative representation of reason in Kant's sense either. For Greek thinking, being that is at rest remains purely distinguished (different) from changeable beings. This difference between being and beings then appears, when seen starting from beings and moving toward being, as transcendence, i.e., as the meta-physical. Yet the distinction is not an absolute separation. It is so far from being the latter that in presencing (being) that which comes to presence (beings) is brought to the fore [*her-vor-gebracht*], but not caused in the sense of an efficient causality. That which brings to the fore is on occasion thought by Plato as that which gives shape (τύπος) (cf. *Theaetetus*, 192a, 194b). You too think the relation of *Gestalt* to that which it "forms" as a relation of stamping and shaping. However, you understand shaping in a modern sense as a conferring of "meaning" or "sense" upon that which is meaning- or sense-less. The *Gestalt* is the "source that gives meaning" (*Der Arbeiter*, p. 148).

This historical pointer to the way in which *Gestalt*, ἰδέα, and being belong together is not meant to discount your work by historiographical means, but to indicate *that it remains housed within metaphysics*. In accordance with metaphysics, all beings, changeable and moved, mobile and mobilized, are represented from the perspective of a "being that is at rest," and this even where, as in Hegel and Nietzsche, "being" (the actuality of the actual) is thought as pure becoming and absolute movement. The *Gestalt* is "metaphysical power" (*Der Arbeiter*, pp. 113, 124, 146).

[224] In another respect, however, the metaphysical representation that occurs in *The Worker* is distinct from Platonic and even from modern representation, that of Nietzsche excepted. The source that gives meaning, the power that is present in advance and thus shapes everything, is *Gestalt* as the *Gestalt* of a particular *kind of human*: "The *Gestalt* of the worker." The *Gestalt* resides in the essential configuration of a kind of human that, as *subiectum*, underlies all beings. It is not the individual human being as an "I," the subjective aspect of being an *ego*, but the preformed and *Gestalt*-like presence of a particular cast (type) of human that constitutes the most extreme subjectity, which comes to the fore in the consummation of modern metaphysics and is presented through its thinking.

In the *Gestalt* of the worker and its domination it is no longer the subjective, let alone the subjectivistic, subjectity of the human essence that is seen. The metaphysical seeing of the *Gestalt* of the worker corresponds to the projection of the essential *Gestalt* of Zarathustra within the metaphysics of the will to power. What is concealed in this appearing of the objective subjectity of the *subiectum* (of the being of beings), which is meant as a *Gestalt* of human being and not as an individual human being?

Talk of the subjectity (not subjectivity) of the human essence as the foundation for the objectivity of every *subiectum* (everything present) appears in every respect to be paradoxical and contrived. This appearance has its grounds in the fact that we have scarcely begun to question why, and in what way, within modern metaphysics a thinking becomes necessary that represents Zarathustra as *Gestalt*. The statement often made that

Nietzsche's thinking became fatefully embroiled in poetizing is itself only
the relinquishing of any thoughtful questioning. Yet we do not even need
to think back to Kant's transcendental deduction of the categories to see
that catching sight of the *Gestalt* as the source that gives meaning is a matter
of the *legitimation* of the being of beings. It would be an all too crude explanation were one to say that [225] here in a secularized world the human
being takes the place of God as originator of the being of beings. Certainly,
there can be no doubt that the human essence plays a role. But the essence
(*Wesen* in the verbal sense)[4] of the human being, "the Dasein in the human
being" (cf. *Kant and the Problem of Metaphysics*, first edition [1929], §43), is
nothing human. For the *idea* of the human essence to be able to attain the
status of that which, as ground, already underlies everything present as that
presence that first permits a "representation" among beings and thus "legit-
imizes" the latter *as* beings, the human being must first of all be represented
in the sense of an authoritative, underlying ground. Yet authoritative for
what? For securing beings in their being. What meaning does "being"
assume when the securing of beings is at stake? It appears as that which can
be ascertained, i.e., represented, anywhere and at any time. Understanding
being in this way, Descartes found the subjecty of the *subiectum* in the
ego cogito of the finite human being. The appearance of the metaphysical
Gestalt of the human being as the source that gives meaning is the ultimate
consequence of positing the human essence as the authoritative *subiectum*.
As a consequence, the inner form of metaphysics, which resides in what
one can call transcendence, becomes transformed. Within metaphysics,
transcendence is for essential reasons ambiguous. Where such ambiguity is
not heeded, a hopeless confusion spreads, a confusion that may serve as the
characteristic sign of the metaphysical representation that is still customary
today.

On the one hand, transcendence refers to the relation proceeding from
beings and passing over to *being*, and which transpires between the two.
At the same time, however, transcendence refers to the relation leading
from changeable beings to an *entity that is at rest*. Finally, corresponding
to the use of the title "Excellence," transcendence can refer to that *supreme
entity itself*, which is then also called "being," resulting in it being strangely
confused with the first meaning.

Why bore you with this hint concerning these distinctions, which are
bandied about all too readily today, i.e., are scarcely [226] thought through
in their diversity or in their belonging together? In order to clarify from
this how the meta-physical in metaphysics, namely, transcendence, comes
to be transformed whenever, within the realm of these distinctions, *the*

Gestalt of the human essence appears as the source that gives meaning. Transcendence, understood in its multiple meanings, turns around into a corresponding rescendence and disappears therein. This kind of descent via the *Gestalt* occurs in such a way that the presence of the latter represents itself, becomes present again in what is shaped by its shaping. The presence that belongs to the *Gestalt* of the worker is power. The representation of presence is his domination as a "new and special kind of will to power" (*Der Arbeiter*, p. 70).

What is new and special has been experienced and recognized by you in "work" as the totalitarian character of the actuality of the actual. Thereby, metaphysical representation in the light of the will to power comes to be twisted more decisively out of the biological and anthropological domain that led Nietzsche's path all too greatly astray. Evidence may be provided by a note such as the following: "Who will prove to be the *strongest* in this? (in the ascendancy of the doctrine of the eternal recurrence of the same) . . . – human beings who *are sure of their power* and who represent the strength *achieved* by man with conscious pride" (*The Will to Power*, no. 55, end). According to *The Worker*, "Domination is today possible only as representation of the *Gestalt* of the worker, which lays claim to planetary validity" (p. 192). "Work" in the highest sense, which pervades all mobilization, is "representation of the *Gestalt* of the worker" (ibid., p. 202). "But the way in which the *Gestalt* of the worker is beginning to penetrate the world is the totalitarian character of work" (ibid., p. 99). Later we read the almost synonymous sentence: "Technology is the way in which the *Gestalt* of the worker mobilizes the world" (ibid., p. 150).

This is preceded by the following decisive remark: "In order to possess a real relationship to technology, one must [227] be something more than a technologist" (ibid., p. 149). I can understand this statement only in the following way: by a "real" [*wirklichen*] relationship you mean a true relationship. What is true is that which corresponds to the essence of technology. This relationship to its essence can never be achieved by way of a directly technical undertaking, i.e., by way of the specialized character of work in each case. The relationship resides in a relation to the totalitarian character of work. But "work," thus understood, is identical to being, in the sense of the will to power (ibid., p. 86).

What determination of the essence of technology results from this? It is "the symbol of the *Gestalt* of the worker" (ibid., p. 72). Technology, "as mobilization of the world through the *Gestalt* of the worker" (ibid., p. 154), is manifestly grounded in that reversal of transcendence into the rescendence of the *Gestalt* of the worker, whereby the presence of this

Gestalt unfolds into the representation of its power. Thus you can write: "Technology is... like the destroyer of every belief whatsoever, and thus the most decisive anti-Christian power that has yet appeared" (ibid.).

Already by its subtitle "Domination and *Gestalt*," your book *The Worker* maps out the fundamental traits of this emergent new metaphysics of the will to power as a whole, insofar as the will to power now presents itself everywhere entirely as work. Even as I first read this book, the questions that I must continue to pose today arose for me: In terms of what is the essence of work to be determined? Does it follow from the *Gestalt* of the worker? Through what is this *Gestalt* that of the worker, unless the essence of work pervades it? Does not this *Gestalt* thus acquire its presence with respect to a particular humankind from out of the essence of work? From where does the meaning of working and worker arise with the high status that you ascribe to *Gestalt* and to its domination? Does this meaning spring from the fact that work is here thought as a shaping that belongs to the will to power? Does this specification even stem from the essence of technology "as the mobilization of the world through the *Gestalt* [228] of the worker"? And does the essence of technology, thus determined, point into still more originary realms?

It would be all too easy to point out that in your analyses of the relationship between the totalitarian character of work and the *Gestalt* of the worker a circle encloses the reciprocal relationship between that which is determinative (work) and what is determined (the worker). Instead of regarding this as indicative of an illogical thinking, I take the circle to be a sign of the fact that here we must think the circularity of a whole, but in a thinking that can never have as its standard a "logic" measured in accordance with freedom from contradiction.

The questions posed above become worthy of a more incisive questioning if I formulate them as I recently sought to do for you in connection with my lecture in Munich ("The Question concerning Technology"). If technology is the mobilization of the world through the *Gestalt* of the worker, it occurs through the presence that shapes the will to power belonging to this particular kind of human being. In presence and in representation there is announced the fundamental trait of what was unveiled to Western thinking as being. From the early period of Greek civilization to the recent period of our century, "being" has meant: presencing. Every kind of presence and of presentation stems from the event [*Ereignis*] of presence. The "will to power" as the actuality of the actual is one way in which the "being" of beings appears. "Work," from which the *Gestalt* of the worker for its part receives its meaning, is identical with "being." Here it remains to be pondered whether and to what extent the essence of "being" is intrinsically a relation to the human essence (cf. *What Calls for Thinking?*, pp. 73ff.). The relation between "work," understood metaphysically, and the "worker" would then necessarily be grounded in this relation. It seems to me that the following questions can hardly be circumvented:

May we think the *Gestalt* of the worker as *Gestalt*, and Plato's ἰδέα as εἶδος, more originarily with respect to their essential provenance? If not, what reasons prevent [229] this and demand instead that we simply accept *Gestalt* and ἰδέα as something ultimate for us and as something primordial in themselves? If we may do so, what paths can this question concerning the essential provenance of ἰδέα and *Gestalt* take? To put it in a formulaic manner, does the essence of *Gestalt* spring in its provenance from the realm of what I call *Ge-Stell?*[5] Does the essential provenance of the ἰδέα accordingly belong to the same realm from which the related essence of *Gestalt* stems? Or is *Ge-Stell* only a function of the *Gestalt* of a particular humankind? If this latter were the case, then the *essential unfolding* [*Wesen*] of being and above all the being of beings would be a product of human representation. The era in which European thinking came to this opinion continues to cast its last shadow over us.

Initially these questions concerning *Gestalt* and *Ge-Stell* remain peculiar considerations. They should not be imposed upon anyone, especially since their very concern is of a precursory nature. Nor are the questions in this letter raised as questions that ought necessarily to have been posed in *The Worker*. To demand such a thing would be to misjudge the style of the work. Its task is to provide an interpretation of actuality with respect to the totalitarian character of work that belongs to it, and indeed in such a way that the interpretation itself participates in this character and announces the special working character of an author in this era. Thus, in the "Overview" at the end of the book (the note on p. 296), you write the following: "*Nota bene:* all these concepts (*Gestalt*, type, organic construction, totalitarian) are there for the purpose of comprehending. Our concern is not with them. They may be forgotten or set aside without further ado, after being used as working factors for grasping a particular actuality that subsists despite and beyond any concept; the reader must see *through* the description as through an optical system."

I have meanwhile followed this *nota bene* each time I read your writings, and asked myself whether concepts, the meanings of words, and before that, language, can be only an "optical system" [230] for you, whether these systems subsist over and against an independent actuality from which the systems, like screwed-on pieces of apparatus, can be unscrewed and replaced again by others. Does it not lie already in the meaning of "working factors" that they in each case co-determine actuality, the totalitarian character of work pertaining to everything actual, only inasmuch as they themselves are already determined by it? Certainly, concepts are "there for the purpose of comprehending." Yet the modern representing of the actual, an objectifying within which our grasping comprehending moves in advance, everywhere remains an attack that seizes upon the actual insofar as the latter is challenged to show itself within the perspective of our representing grasp. Within the sphere of this modern, grasping comprehending, the consequence of such challenging is that actuality as it is grasped passes over – quite unexpectedly, and in a way that initially goes unheeded for a long time – into a counterattack. This counterattack suddenly, and despite Kant, catches modern natural science by surprise, and such science must first approach and secure its knowledge of this surprising event by way of specific discoveries within the scientific manner of proceeding.

Heisenberg's relation of indeterminacy can certainly never be directly derived from Kant's transcendental interpretation of our cognitive knowledge of physical nature. Yet nor can that relation ever be represented, i.e., thought, without this representing initially reverting to the transcendental realm of the subject-object relation. Only when this has occurred can the question begin concerning the essential provenance of our objectifying of beings, i.e., concerning the essence of our "grasping."

In your case and in mine, however, our concern is not only with concepts of a science, but with fundamental words like *Gestalt*, domination, representation, power, will, value, security; with presence (presencing) and with the nothing, which as absence interrupts ("nullifies") presence, without ever annihilating it. Rather, insofar as the nothing "nullifies," it confirms itself as a distinctive presence, veiling [231] itself as such presence. In the fundamental words listed, there prevails a saying that is other than that of scientific assertions. To be sure, metaphysical representation too is familiar with concepts. Yet these are distinct from scientific concepts not only with regard to their degree of universality. Kant was the first to see this with full clarity (*Critique of Pure Reason*, A 843, B 871). Metaphysical concepts are in essence other in kind insofar as that which they grasp and comprehend is in an originary sense the same as this very grasping. For this reason, it is much less a matter of indifference within the realm of fundamental words of thinking whether one forgets them or whether one persistently continues to use them unexamined, and above all to use them where we are supposed to step out of the zone in which the "concepts" to which you refer say what is authoritative, namely, in the zone of consummate nihilism.

Your book *Across the Line* speaks of nihilism as a "fundamental power" (p. 60); it poses the question of what will be the "fundamental value" in the future (p. 31); once again, it names *"Gestalt,"* "including the *Gestalt* of the worker" (p. 41). The latter, if I perceive things correctly, is no longer the sole *Gestalt* "in which rest is found to dwell" (ibid.). Rather, you say that the realm of power pertaining to nihilism is of such a kind that there "the princely appearance of the human being is missing" (p. 10). Or is the *Gestalt* of the worker in fact that "new" *Gestalt* in which such princely appearing is yet concealed? Even in the realm of the line that has been crossed, "security" is the issue. Even now pain remains the touchstone. The "metaphysical" prevails even in the new realm. Does the fundamental word "pain" here still speak from out of the same meaning as that delimited in your treatise *On Pain*, in which the position of "the worker" is pushed farthest? Does the metaphysical even on the other side of the line retain the same meaning as in *The Worker*, where it means that which is *"Gestalt*-like"? Or does the "transcending" in the direction of a [232] "transcendence" and excellence that is *non*human, and, rather, divine in kind, now take the place of the representation of the *Gestalt* of an essential kind of human being as the sole previous form of the legitimation of the actual? Does the theological that prevails in all metaphysics come to the fore? (*Über die Linie*, pp. 32, 39, 41). When in your work *The Book of the Sandclock* [*Das Sanduhrbuch*] (1954) you say, *"Gestalt* is confirmed in pain" (p. 106), then, so far as I can see, you retain the fundamental configuration of your thinking, but let the fundamental words "pain" and *"Gestalt"* speak in a transformed sense, although one that is not yet explicitly clarified. Or am I mistaken?

This would be the place to go into your treatise *On Pain* and to bring to light the intrinsic connection between "work" and "pain." This connection points to metaphysical relations that manifest themselves to you in terms of the metaphysical position of your book *The Worker*. To be able to trace more clearly the relations that sustain the connection between "work" and "pain," nothing less would be necessary than to think through the fundamental trait of Hegel's metaphysics, the unifying unity of the *Phenomenology of Spirit* and the *Science of Logic*. This fundamental trait is "absolute negativity" as the "infinite force" of actuality, i.e., of the "existing concept." In the same (not the identical) belonging to the negation of negation, work and pain manifest their innermost metaphysical relatedness. This pointer is already sufficient to indicate the extensive discussions that would be required here in order to respond to this issue. And if one ventured to think through the relations between "work," as the fundamental trait of beings, and "pain" by moving back via Hegel's *Logic*, then the Greek word for pain, namely, ἄλγος, would first come to speak for us. Presumably, ἄλγος is related to ἀλέγω, which as the *intensivum* of λέγω means intimate gathering. In that case, pain would be that which gathers most intimately. Hegel's concept of the "concept" and, when correctly understood, the "strenuous effort" it entails say the Same on the transformed soil of the absolute metaphysics of subjectivity.

[233] That you have been led on other paths to the metaphysical relations between work and pain is a fine testimony to the fact that, in the manner of your metaphysical representing, you are attempting to hear the voice that becomes audible from out of those relations.

In what language does the fundamental outline of that thinking speak that prefigures a crossing of the line? Is the language of the metaphysics of the will to power, of *Gestalt*, and of values to be saved over beyond the critical line? What if the language of metaphysics and metaphysics itself, whether it is that of the living god or of the dead god, in fact constituted, *as* metaphysics, that limit which prevents a transition over the line, i.e., the overcoming of nihilism? If this were the case, would not crossing the line then necessarily have to become a transformation of our saying and demand a transformed relation to the essence of language? And is not your own relation to language of such a kind as to demand of you a different characterization of the conceptual language of the sciences? In frequently representing such language as nominalism, one continues to remain entangled in the logical-grammatical conception of the essence of language.

I write all this in the form of questions; for, as far as I can see, thinking can today do no more than to continually ponder what is evoked in the said questions. Perhaps the moment will come when the essence of nihilism will show itself more clearly in other ways and in a brighter light. Until that point, I remain content to presume that the only way in which we might reflect upon the essence of nihilism is by first setting out on a path that leads to a discussion of the essence [*Wesen*] of being. On this path alone can the question concerning the nothing be discussed. *But the question concerning the essence of being dies off if it does not relinquish the language of metaphysics, because metaphysical representation prevents us from thinking the question concerning the essence of being.*

[234] It ought to be evident that the transformation of that saying which gives thought to the essence of being is subject to other demands than exchanging an old terminology for a new one. The fact that an endeavor to undertake such transformation will presumably remain tentative for a long time to come is not an adequate reason for failing to do so. Today we are especially tempted to evaluate the thoughtfulness of thinking according to

the tempo of reckoning and planning, which justifies its technical inventions directly for everyone by its economic successes. This evaluation of thinking puts excessive demands on it through standards that are alien to such thinking. At the same time, one subjects thinking to the presumptuous demand of knowing the solution to riddles and bringing the salutary. In the face of such demands, your pointing to the necessity of allowing all as yet intact sources of strength to flow and of bringing all assistance to bear so as to enable us to survive "in the wake of nihilism" merits full approval.

In addition, however, we must not have scant regard for a discussion of the *essence* of nihilism, and may not do so for the very reason that nihilism has the tendency to dissemble its own essence and thereby to withdraw from the all-decisive encounter and confrontation with it. The latter alone could help to open and to prepare a free realm within which we may experience what you call "a new turning of being" (*Über die Linie*, p. 32).

You write: "The moment at which the line is crossed brings a new turning of being, and with it that which is actual begins to shimmer."

This sentence is easy to read and yet difficult to think. Above all, I would wish to ask whether, conversely, it is not a new turning of being that would first bring the moment for crossing the line. This question seems merely to reverse your statement. Yet a mere reversal is always a fraught undertaking. The solution it might offer remains entangled in the question that has been reversed. Your statement says that "that which is actual," the actual, i.e., beings, begins to shimmer [235] because being takes a new turn. Thus we may now ask more appropriately whether "being" is something independent, something that in addition and on occasion also turns toward human beings. Presumably the turning itself, albeit in a way that is as yet veiled, is That which, in a quite perplexed and indeterminate manner, we name "being." Yet does not such turning also, and in a strange way, occur under the domination of nihilism, namely, in such a way that "being" turns away and withdraws into absence? Turning away and withdrawal, however, are not nothing. They prevail in a manner that is almost more oppressive for human beings, so that they draw the human being away, suck into his endeavors and activities, and thus ultimately suck these activities up into their withdrawing wake in such a way that the human being can come to the opinion that he now everywhere encounters only himself. In truth, however, his self is nothing more than his ek-sistence being used up in service of the domination of what you characterize as the totalitarian character of work.

Certainly, the turning and turning away of being, if we pay sufficient heed to them, can never be represented as though they affected human beings only on particular occasions and at particular moments. Rather, the human essence resides in the fact that at all times it endures and dwells in one way or another within such turning or turning away. We always say *too little* of "being itself" when, in saying "being," we omit its essential presencing *in the direction of* the human *essence* and thereby fail to see that this essence itself is part of "being." We also always say *too little* of the human being when, in saying "being" (not being human) we posit the human being as independent and then first bring what we have thus posited into a relation to "being." Yet we also always say *too much* when we mean being as the all-encompassing, and in so doing represent the human being only as one particular entity among others (such as plant and animal), and place them in relation to one another. For there already lies within the human essence the relation to that which – through a relation, a relating in the sense of needful usage [*Brauchen*] – is determined as "being" and so through this relation is removed from its supposed "self-independence." The talk of "being" drives [236] representation from one perplexity to another, without the source of such being at a loss becoming manifest.

Yet everything comes to be in the best of order, or so it appears, if we do not purposely fail to attend to something long since thought of: the subject-object relation. This relation says that to every subject (human being) there belongs an object (being), and vice versa. Certainly; were it not for the fact that all of this – the relation, the subject, and the object – already resides within the essence of what we are representing, quite inadequately as has been shown, as the relation between being and human being. Subjectivity and objectivity are for their part already grounded in a peculiar manifestness of "being" and of the "human essence." Such manifestness establishes representation in terms of the distinction between the two as subject and object. This distinction henceforth becomes absolute and banishes thinking into a dead end. Any positing of "being" that would seek to name "being" from the perspective of the subject-object relation fails to ponder something worthy of question that it has left unthought. Thus the talk of a "turning of being" remains a makeshift measure that is thoroughly worthy of question, because being resides within the turning, so that the latter can never first come to "being" from the outside.

Presencing ("being") is, as presencing, on each and every occasion a presencing directed toward the human essence, insofar as presencing is a call [*Geheiß*] that on each occasion calls upon the human essence. The human essence as such is a hearing, because the essence of human beings belongs to the calling of this call, to the approach of presencing [*ins Anwesen*]. That which is the Same each time, the belonging together of call and hearing, would then be "being"? What am I saying? It is no longer "being" at all – if we attempt fully to think through "being" in its destinal prevailing, namely, as presencing, in which manner alone we respond to its destinal essence. We would then have to relinquish the isolating and separating word "being" just as decisively as the name "human being." The question concerning the relation between the two revealed itself to be inadequate, because it never attains to the realm of what it seeks to ask after. In truth we cannot then even [237] continue to say that "being" and "the human being" "are" the Same in the sense that *they* belong together; for when we say it in *this* way, we continue to let both subsist independently.

Yet why, in a letter about the essence of consummate nihilism, am I mentioning these laborious and abstract things? On the one hand, in order to indicate that it is by no means easier to say "being" than to speak of the nothing; yet also in order to show once more how inevitably everything here depends on the correct saying, on that Λόγος whose essence the logic and dialectic that come from metaphysics are never able to experience.

Is it due to "being" – if for a moment we let this word name that Same that is worthy of question, and in which the essence of being and the essence of the human being belong together – is it due to "being" that our saying fails in a telling manner in its response, remaining only what is all too readily suspected as so-called "mysticism"? Or does it have to do with our saying that such saying does not yet speak, because it is not yet able to respond in a fitting manner to the essence of "being"? Is the question of which language of fundamental words is spoken at the moment of crossing the line, i.e., in traversing the critical zone of consummate nihilism, left to the whim of those who are speaking? Is it enough for this language to be universally comprehensible, or do other laws and measures prevail here that are just as unique as the world-historical moment of the planetary consummation of nihilism and the critical confrontation of its essence?

These are questions that are scarcely beginning to become worthy of question in such a way that we could find ourselves at home in them and never again let them go, even at the peril of having to relinquish old and established habits of thinking in the sense of metaphysical representation and of being accused of disdain for all sound reasoning.

These are questions that, in our passing "over the line," still display a particularly acute character; for such passage moves within the [238] realm of the nothing. Does the nothing vanish with the consummation or at least with the overcoming of nihilism? Presumably this overcoming can be attained only when, instead of the appearance of the nihilative nothing, the essence of the nothing in its former kinship with "being" can arrive and be accommodated among us mortals.

From where does this essence come? Where must we seek it? What is the locale of the nothing? We shall not be asking too much in an unthinking manner if we search for the locale and in our discussion locate the essence of the line. Yet is this something other than the attempt to provide what you demand: "a good definition of nihilism"? It looks as though thinking is continually led around or even chased around the Same as though in a magical circle, yet without ever being able to approach this Same. But perhaps the circle is a concealed spiral. Perhaps this spiral has in the meantime become more constricted. This means: the manner and way in which we are approaching the essence of nihilism are being transformed. Whatever is good in the "good definition" that you rightfully demand will prove its worth in our giving up the desire to define, to the extent that this desire must become fixed in propositional statements in which thinking dies out. Yet it remains a slight, because merely negative, gain if we learn to heed the fact that no information can be provided concerning the nothing or being or nihilism, concerning their essence or concerning the essential (verbal) unfolding of such essence (nominal), that might lie ready before us in the form of propositional statements waiting to be seized.

This remains a gain to the extent that we come to experience the fact that what the "good definition" is supposed to be valid for, namely, the essence of nihilism, points us toward a realm that demands a different saying. If a turning belongs to "being," and indeed in such a way that the latter resides in the former, then "being" dissolves into the turning. The latter now becomes that which is worthy of question, that in terms of which we henceforth think being, which has returned and been taken up into its essence. Accordingly, a thoughtful look ahead into this realm can write "being" only in the following [239] way: b̶e̶i̶n̶g̶. The crossing out of this word initially has only a preventive role, namely, that of preventing the almost ineradicable habit of representing "being" as something standing somewhere on its own that then on occasion first comes face-to-face with human beings. In accordance with this way of representing matters, it appears as though the human being is excepted from "being." However, he is not only not excepted, i.e., not only included in "being," but "being," in needing the human being, is obliged to relinquish this appearance of independence. And this is why it is also other in essence than the representation of an inclusive concept might have it, one that embraces the subject-object relation.

From what has been said, the sign of this crossing through cannot, however, be the merely negative sign of a crossing out. It points, rather, toward the four regions of the fourfold and their being gathered in the locale of this crossing through (cf. *Vorträge und Aufsätze* [1954], pp. 145–204).

Coming to presence is turned as such toward the human essence, wherein such turning first finds its consummation insofar as the human essence thoughtfully commemorates [*gedenkt*] this turning. In his essence the human being is the thoughtful memory [*Gedächtnis*] of being, but of ~~being~~. This means: the human essence also belongs to that which, in the crossing out of being, takes thinking into the claim of a more originary call.[a] Coming to presence is grounded in the turning that, as such, turns the human essence in toward it, so that this essence may expend itself for such turning.

Like ~~being~~, the nothing would also have to be written – and that means, thought – in the same way. This implies that the human essence, in its thoughtful commemoration, belongs to the nothing, and not merely as some addition. If, therefore, in nihilism the nothing attains domination in a particular way, then the human being is not only affected by nihilism, but essentially participates in it. In that case, however, the entire "subsistence" of human beings does not stand somewhere on this side of the line, in order then to cross over it and take up residence on the other side with being. The human essence itself belongs to the essence of nihilism and thereby to the phase of its consummation. As [240] that being which is in essence brought into the need of ~~being~~, the human being is part of the zone of ~~being~~, i.e., at the same time of the nothing. The human being not only stands *within* the critical zone of the line. He himself – but not taken independently, and especially not through himself alone – is this zone and thus the line. In no case does the line, thought as a sign of the zone of consummate nihilism, lie before the human being in the manner of something that could be crossed. In that case, however, the possibility of a *trans lineam* and of such a crossing collapses.

The more we think carefully about "the line," the more this immediately persuasive image disappears, without the thoughts that have thereby been ignited having to lose their significance. In the essay *Across the Line*, you provide a description of the locale of nihilism and an assessment of the situation and possible mobility of the human being with respect to the locale described and designated by the image of the line. Certainly a topography of nihilism is required, of its process and its overcoming. Yet the topography must be preceded by a topology: a discussion locating that locale which gathers being and nothing into their essence, determines the essence of

---

[a] First edition, 1956: Ereignis.

nihilism, and thus lets us recognize those paths on which the ways toward a possible overcoming of nihilism emerge.

To where do being and nothing belong, between which the play of nihilism unfolds its essence? In *Across the Line* (pp. 22ff.) you name "reduction" as a chief characteristic of nihilistic trends: "The superabundance dries up: the human being feels himself exploited in manifold, not merely economic relations." You rightly add, however: "this does not exclude that it (the reduction) is extensively connected with a growing unfolding of power and effective force," just as decline "is of course not merely decline" (p. 23).

What else does this say but the fact that the movement toward less and less fullness and originariness within beings [241] as a whole is not merely accompanied but determined by a growth in the will to power? The will to power is that will which wills *itself*. As this will and within the orders established by it there appears, prefigured early on and prevailing in many different ways, that which, represented from the perspective of beings, surpasses such beings and within such surpassing in turn has an effect on beings, whether as the ground of beings, or as their causation. The reduction that can be ascertained within beings rests on a production of being, namely, on the unfolding of the will to power into the unconditional will to will. The disappearance, the absence, is determined from out of a presence and through such presence. Such presence precedes all that disappears, surpasses it. Thus, wherever beings disappear, there prevails not only such beings taken on their own, but, in an authoritative manner, something else. Everywhere the surpassing that returns to beings, the "*transcendens* pure and simple" (*Being and Time*, §7), is "the being" of beings. Surpassing is metaphysics itself, where this name now refers not to a doctrine and discipline of philosophy, but rather to the fact that such surpassing is "given" [*daß "es" jenen Überstieg "gibt"*] (*Being and Time*, §43c). It is given to the extent that it is brought onto the path of its prevailing, i.e., destined. The incalculable fullness and suddenness of what unfolds as surpassing is called the destiny of (objective genitive) metaphysics.

In accordance with this destiny, human representation itself becomes metaphysical. The metaphysical representations of beings can indeed be historiographically presented in their happening as a sequence. But such happening is not the history of being which, rather, prevails as the destiny of the surpassing. The fact that, and the way that, the being of beings is "given" is meta-physics in the sense designated.

Even if we mean it only in the sense of the complete negation of anything present, the nothing belongs, in its being absent, to presencing as one possibility of the latter. Accordingly, if the nothing prevails within nihilism and the essence of the nothing belongs to being, [242] yet being is the destiny of the surpassing, then the essential locale of nihilism shows itself to be the essence of metaphysics. This can be said only if, and so long as, we experience the essence of metaphysics as the destiny of the surpassing.

Wherein does the overcoming of nihilism then consist? In the recovery [Verwindung] of metaphysics.[6] This is a disagreeable thought. People try to avoid it. This is all the more reason not to make it any easier. Yet taking up this thought will encounter less resistance if we heed the fact that the thought entails that the essence of nihilism is nothing nihilistic, and that nothing is detracted from the ancient worthiness of metaphysics by the fact that its own essence shelters nihilism within it.

The zone of the critical line, i.e., the locality of the essence of consummate nihilism, would thus have to be sought where the essence of metaphysics unfolds its most extreme possibilities and gathers itself in them. This occurs where the will to will wills, i.e., challenges, *sets in place* everything that presences, and does so solely in the thoroughgoing and uniform orderability of its standing reserve. As the unconditional gathering of such setting in place, being does not disappear. It irrupts in a singular uncanniness. Only what was previously present, that which the will to will had not yet seized, but continued to leave in the will of spirit and its totalizing self-movement in which Hegel's thinking moves, shows itself as having disappeared and been reduced.

The disappearance of what was previously present is not a vanishing of presencing. Rather, presencing presumably withdraws. Yet such withdrawal remains concealed from representation as nihilistically determined. It appears as though that which presences in the manner of standing reserve were self-sufficient. The subsistence of such standing reserve and that which sets it into such constancy, namely, the coming to presence of that which presences, appear – whenever they are talked about – as an invention of a thinking that roams about and is no longer able to see the supposedly sole "reality" on account of its seeing only the "being" of beings.

[243] In the phase of consummate nihilism, it looks as though there were no such thing as the *being of* beings, as though there were nothing (in the sense of a negative nothing) to being. Being remains absent in a strange way. It conceals itself. It maintains itself in a concealment that conceals itself. In such concealing, however, there lies the essence of oblivion as experienced by the Greeks. In the end, i.e., from the beginning of its essence, such oblivion is nothing negative. As a sheltering in concealment, rather, it is presumably a sheltering that preserves what is as yet

unrevealed. For ordinary representation, being oblivious readily takes on the appearance of merely missing something, of a lack, of something unfortunate. We habitually take oblivion and forgetfulness exclusively as an omission that can be found frequently enough as a condition belonging to human beings represented in their independence. We still remain far removed from a determination of the essence of oblivion. Yet even where we have caught sight of the essence of oblivion in its full extent, we all too readily run the danger of understanding oblivion merely as a human act or activity.

People have indeed tended to represent the "oblivion of being" as though, to say it by way of an image, being were the umbrella that has been left sitting somewhere through the forgetfulness of some philosophy professor.

Yet oblivion does not simply *befall* the essence of being, as something apparently separate from the latter. It belongs to the issue of being itself, prevails as a destiny of its essence. Correctly thought, oblivion, the concealing of the as yet unrevealed essence (in the verbal sense of essential unfolding) of being, shelters untapped treasures and is the promise of a find that awaits only the appropriate seeking. To have some premonition of this requires no prophetic gift, nor the affectation of preachers, but only an attentiveness, practiced for decades, to that which has been and which announces itself in the metaphysical thinking of the Western world. That which has been stands here within the sign of the unconcealment of that which is present. Unconcealment resides in the concealment [244] of presencing. Recollective thinking [*Andenken*] has the task of attending to *this* concealment, in which unconcealment (Ἀλήθεια) is grounded. It recollects thoughtfully what presences as that which has been, and which is not past, since it remains that which does not become past in all enduring granted by the event [*Ereignis*] of being in each case.

The recovery of metaphysics is recovery of the oblivion of being. Such recovery turns toward the essence of metaphysics. It entwines itself around it by way of what this essence itself demands, insofar as it calls for that realm that can raise it into the free dimension of its truth. In order to respond to a recovery of metaphysics, thinking must for this reason first clarify the essence of metaphysics. To such an attempt, the recovery of metaphysics initially appears to be an overcoming that merely brings exclusively metaphysical representation behind it, so as to lead thinking into the free realm attained by a recovery from the essence of metaphysics. But in this recovery, the enduring truth of the metaphysics that has seemingly been rejected first returns explicitly as the now appropriated *essence* of metaphysics.

Here there occurs something other than a mere restoration of metaphysics. Moreover, there is no restoration that could simply take up what has been handed down in the way that one picks up the apples that have fallen from a tree. Every restoration is an interpretation of metaphysics. Whoever today is of the opinion that he is able to see through and follow more clearly metaphysical inquiry as a whole in its specificity and history should, in his predilection for moving in these illuminated realms in such a superior manner, one day think carefully about where he has acquired the light to see more clearly. One can scarcely exaggerate the grotesque way in which people proclaim my attempts at thinking to be a demolishing of metaphysics and at the same time, with the aid of those attempts, keep to paths of thought and ideas that have been taken from – I do not say, are thanks to – that alleged demolition. It is not thanks that is needed here, but reflection. Yet the failure to reflect began already with the superficial [245] misconstrual of the "destruction" ["*Destruktion*"] discussed in *Being and Time* (1927), a "destruction" that has no other intent than to reattain the originary experiences of being belonging to metaphysics by deconstructing [*Abbau*] representations that have become commonplace and empty.

In order to rescue metaphysics in its essence, however, the role of mortals in such rescuing must content itself with first asking: "What is metaphysics?" At the peril of becoming long-winded and of repeating things that have been said on other occasions, I would like to take the opportunity of this letter to elucidate once more the meaning and import of that question. Why? Because *your* intention too is concerned with assisting in the overcoming of nihilism in your own way. Such overcoming, however, occurs in the realm of a recovery of metaphysics. We enter this realm with the question: "What is metaphysics?" This question, if we ask it in a thoughtful way, already contains an intimation that the question itself unsettles its own manner of questioning. "What is . . . ?" indicates the way in which one is accustomed to inquire concerning the "essence" of something. Yet when the question is concerned with a discussion locating metaphysics as the surpassing of beings by being, then this surpassing on the part of "being" immediately calls into question the elements that have been distinguished from one another in that distinction within which the doctrines of metaphysics have moved from time immemorial, the distinction from which they receive the basic outline of their language. This is the distinction between essence and existence, what-being and that-being.

The question "What is metaphysics?" at first makes indiscriminate use of this distinction. Yet reflection on being's surpassing of beings soon proves to be one of those questions that must stab itself in the heart, not so that thinking may thereby die, but so that it may live in a transformed manner. When I attempted to discuss the question "What is metaphysics?" – one year before the appearance of your treatise *Total Mobilization* – I was from the outset not looking for a definition belonging to some discipline of scholastic philosophy. Rather, with regard to the determination [246] of metaphysics according to which there occurs in metaphysics a surpassing of beings toward beings as such,[7] I discussed a question that ponders what is other than beings. Yet this question too was not just vaguely taken up or asked in an indeterminate manner.

After a quarter of a century it might be time to point for once to a fact that people still brush aside today, as though it were an external circumstance. The question "What is metaphysics?" was discussed in an inaugural philosophical lecture before all the assembled faculties. For this reason, it places itself into the sphere of all sciences and speaks to them. Yet in what way? Not with the presumptuous intention of improving their work, let alone disparaging it.

The representational activity of the sciences everywhere concerns beings, and indeed special regions of beings. The task was to proceed from such representation of beings and, in following it, to comply with a view that is dear to the sciences. They are of the opinion that the representation of beings exhausts the entire realm of what can be researched and questioned, and that apart from beings there is "nothing else." In the question concerning the essence of metaphysics, the attempt is made to assume this view belonging to the sciences and apparently to share it with them. Yet anyone who thinks carefully must also already know that an inquiry into the essence of metaphysics can only have in view that which distinguishes metaphysics: that is, the surpassing: *the being of* beings. By contrast, within the perspective of scientific representation, which is acquainted only with beings, that which is not in any way a being (namely, being) can present itself only as nothing. This is why the lecture asks concerning "*this* nothing." It does not ask in an arbitrary or indeterminate manner about "the" nothing. It asks: how do things stand with what is thus quite other than anything that is, with that which is not a being? Here it becomes manifest that the Dasein of the human being is "held into" "*this*" nothing, into that which is quite other than beings. To put it another way, this means, and could only [247] mean: "The human being holds the place of the nothing." This sentence says that the human being holds free the locale for that which is quite other than beings, so that within this openness something like coming to presence (being) can be given. This nothing, which is not beings and which is nevertheless *given [und das* es *gleichwohl gibt]*,[8] is nothing negative. It belongs to presencing. Being and nothing are not given alongside one another. The one employs itself for the other in a kinship whose essential fullness we have as yet scarcely pondered. Nor can we ponder it so long as we fail to ask: What is "it" that does the "giving" here? In what kind of giving does it give? To what extent does there belong to this "giving of being and nothing" something that gives and entrusts itself to this gift in preserving it? We can easily say: There is a giving *[es gibt]*. Being no more "is" than nothing. But *there is a giving* of both.

Leonardo da Vinci writes: "The nothing has no middle, and its limits are the nothing." "Among the great things that are to be found among us, the being of nothing is the greatest" (*Tagebücher und Aufzeichnungen*, translated from the Italian manuscripts and edited by Theodor Lücke [1940], pp. 4f.). This word from one of the greats cannot, and is not meant to, prove anything; but it points to the questions: In what way is being, is nothing, given? From whence does such giving come to us? To what extent are we already given over to it, insofar as we are human beings?

Because the lecture "What Is Metaphysics?", in keeping with the occasion at hand, inquires in a deliberately restricted manner from the perspective of the surpassing, i.e., of the *being of* beings, and does so with regard to *that* nothing which initially presents itself to the scientific representation of beings, people have seized upon and extracted "the" nothing and made the lecture into a testament to nihilism. Now that a considerable time has passed, it might be permitted to ask the question: Where, in which sentence and in which turn of phrase, is it ever said that the nothing named in the lecture is a nothing in the sense of a negative nothing and as such the first and last goal of all representation and existing?

[248] The lecture closes with the question: "Why are there beings at all, and why not far rather Nothing [*Nichts*]?" Here, contrary to custom, the word *Nichts*, "Nothing," is deliberately capitalized. In terms of the wording, the question brought up here is indeed that posed by Leibniz and taken up by Schelling. Both thinkers understand it as the question concerning the supreme ground and primary existing cause of all beings. The contemporary attempts to restore metaphysics are fond of addressing the said question.

Yet the lecture "What Is Metaphysics?", in accordance with its differently construed path through another realm, also thinks this question in a transformed manner. The question now asked is: Why is it that everywhere only beings have priority, without our giving thought to the "not" of beings, to "this nothing," i.e., to being with regard to its essence? Whoever thinks through this lecture as a stretch on the path from *Being and Time* can understand the question only in the sense indicated. To attempt this was initially a strange and excessive demand. This is why the transformed question was explicitly clarified in the "Introduction" that was placed at the beginning of the fifth edition of "What Is Metaphysics?" (1949, pp. 20ff.).

What is the point of this hint? It is meant to indicate with what difficulty and hesitancy thinking lets itself enter a reflection that reflects upon what is also the concern of your text *Across the Line:* the essence of nihilism.

The question "What is metaphysics?" attempts only one thing: to bring the sciences to think about the fact that they necessarily and thus at all times and everywhere encounter that which is quite other than beings, the nothing of beings. They already stand, without *their* knowing it, in a relation to being. Only from the truth of being that prevails on each occasion do they receive a light that first enables them to see and observe *as such* the beings represented by them. Asking "What is metaphysics?", i.e., the thinking that emerges from metaphysics, is no longer science. But the surpassing as such, [249] i.e., *the being of* beings with regard to its essence, becomes worthy of question for thinking, and thus never worthy of nothing or nihilistic. Here, the apparently empty word "being" is always thought in the essential fullness of those determinations that, from Φύσις and Λόγος to the "will to power," refer to one another and everywhere show a fundamental trait that we attempt to name in the word "presencing" [*An-wesen*] (*Being and Time*, §6). Only *because* the question "What is metaphysics?" from the start recalls the surpassing, the *transcendens*, the *being of* beings, can it think the "not" of beings, *that* nothing which is equioriginarily the Same as being.

Of course, those who have never seriously pondered the context and fundamental orientation of the question concerning metaphysics, the point of departure of its path, the occasion of its unfolding, and the sphere of the sciences it addresses itself to, must come to the conclusion that here a philosophy of nothing (in the sense of a negative nihilism) is being proclaimed.

The misinterpretations of the question "What is metaphysics?" – misinterpretations that apparently cannot yet be eradicated – and the failure to recognize its vantage point, are least of all mere consequences of an aversion to thinking. Their origin lies more deeply concealed. They nevertheless belong to those phenomena that shed light upon the course of our history: We and our entire subsistence are still moving within the zone of nihilism, granted that the essence of nihilism indeed resides in the oblivion of being.

How do things then stand concerning the crossing of the line? Does it lead us out of the zone of consummate nihilism? The attempt to cross the line remains captivated in a form of representation that belongs to the dominion of the oblivion of being. This is why it continues to speak in terms of fundamental metaphysical concepts (*Gestalt*, value, transcendence).

Can the image of the line adequately depict the zone of consummate nihilism? Is the image of the zone better?

[250] Doubts arise as to whether such images are suited to depict the overcoming of nihilism, i.e., the recovery of the oblivion of being. Yet presumably every image is subject to such doubts. These doubts, however, are unable to touch the illuminative force of images, their originary and uncircumventable presence. Such considerations testify only to how little experience we have in the saying of thinking, how little we know the essence of such saying.

The essence of nihilism, which finds its ultimate consummation in the domination of the will to will, resides in the oblivion of being. We seem to respond best to such oblivion by forgetting it, which here means: casting it to the winds. Yet in so doing we fail to heed what is meant by oblivion as concealment of b̶e̶i̶n̶g̶. If we pay heed to this, we experience an unsettling necessity: Instead of wanting to overcome nihilism, we must attempt to first turn in toward its *essence*. Turning in into its essence is the first step through which we may leave nihilism behind us. The path of this turning takes the form and direction of a turning back. This does not, however, mean going back to times past in the attempt to freshen these up in some contrived form. "Back" here means the direction pointing to that locality (the oblivion of being) from which metaphysics already received and retains its provenance.

In accordance with this provenance, metaphysics as metaphysics remains prevented from ever experiencing its essence; for it is within a surpassing and for it that the *being* of beings *shows* itself to metaphysical representation. Appearing in this way, it expressly makes its claim upon metaphysical representation. No wonder metaphysical representation rebels against the thought that it moves within the *oblivion* of being.

And yet an adequate and sustained meditation can attain the insight that, in keeping with its essence, metaphysics can never grant human dwelling the possibility of settling expressly within the locality, i.e., within the essence of the oblivion of being. For this reason, [251] thinking and poetizing must return to where, in a certain way, they have always already been but have never yet built. Only through building, however, can we prepare a dwelling in that locality. Such building can scarcely think of establishing a house for the god and dwelling sites for mortals. It must content itself with building the *path* that leads back into the locality of a recovery of metaphysics and thereby lets us journey through what is destined in an overcoming of nihilism.

Whoever ventures such a word, particularly in a text for publication, knows all too well how overhastily and readily this saying, which is meant to provoke reflection, comes to be discarded as an obscure mumbling or dismissed as pompous proclamation. Despite this, he who continues to learn must direct his thought toward examining more originarily and with greater care the saying of recollective thinking. One day he may come to leave such saying in the realm of the mystery, as a supreme gift and greatest danger, as something seldom successful and frequently unsuccessful.

Here we may recognize why all saying of this kind proceeds awkwardly and with difficulty. It must always pass through the essential ambiguity of the word and its turns of phrase. The ambiguity of saying by no means consists in a mere accumulation of significations that arise arbitrarily. It resides in a play that, the richer it unfolds, remains all the more rigorously maintained in a concealed rule. Via the latter, the ambiguity plays in the balance of scales whose oscillation we rarely experience. This is why the saying remains bound to a supreme law. This law is the freedom that frees us for the ever playful jointure of never resting transformation. The ambiguity of those words that "arise like flowers" (Hölderlin, "Bread and Wine") is the garden of the wilderness in which growth and nurturance are attuned to one another out of an incomprehensible intimacy. It should not surprise you that the discussion of the essence of nihilism at every point of our path unavoidably comes upon that which provokes and is worthy of thought, and which we awkwardly enough [252] name the saying of thinking. This saying is not the expression of thinking, but thinking itself, its course and its song.

What is the purpose of this letter? It attempts to raise into a higher ambiguity the title "*Über die Linie,*" i.e., everything that it describes in your sense and in mine and tries to demonstrate by saying it in writing. This higher ambiguity lets us experience to what extent the overcoming of nihilism demands a turning in into its essence, a turning in whereby the desire to overcome becomes untenable. The recovery of metaphysics calls thinking into a more originary calling.

Your assessment of the situation *trans lineam* and my discussion *de linea* are referred to one another. Together they are directed not to cease the endeavor to practice planetary thinking for part of its path, however short in measurement. And here no prophetic gifts or gestures are needed in order to realize that planetary building will encounter issues to which those involved are today nowhere equal. This is equally true for both the language of Europe and that of East Asia, and is true above all for the realm of possible dialogue between them. Neither is able on its own to open or to found this realm.

Nietzsche, in whose light or shadow every contemporary thinks and poetizes in being "for him" or "against him," heard a calling that demands that human beings prepare for assuming domination over the earth. He saw and understood the erupting struggle for domination (XIV, p. 320; XVI, p. 337; XII, p. 208). This is no war, but the Πόλεμος that first lets gods and humans, freemen and slaves, appear in their respective essence and leads to a critical encounter of being. Compared to this encounter, world wars remain superficial. They are less and less capable of deciding anything the more technological their armaments.

Nietzsche heard that call to reflect on the essence of a planetary domination. He followed the call on the [253] path of the metaphysical thinking granted him and collapsed on the way. So it seems, at least, to a historiographical account. Perhaps, however, he did not collapse, but went as far as his thinking was able to go.

That his thinking has left us with much that is grave and difficult should remind us more rigorously and otherwise than hitherto that the question awakened in this thinking concerning the essence of nihilism stems from an ancient provenance indeed. The question has not become any easier for us. For this reason it must restrict itself to something more precursory, namely, giving careful thought to ancient, venerable words whose saying addresses to us the essential realm of nihilism and of its recovery. Is there any more worthy endeavor to save what has been destined for us and handed down to us in its destiny than such recollective thinking? I know of none. Yet it appears subversive to those for whom the conventions that have come down to us remain without provenance. They regard that which appears in its innocence as something absolutely valid. They demand that the latter appear in grandiose systems. By contrast, where careful thought is concerned always and only with drawing our attention to the use of language in thinking, it has no use. Yet at times it serves what is needed by that which is to be thought.

What this letter attempts to clarify may all too soon prove to be inadequate.

The *way* in which it seeks to tend to reflection and discussion, however, is said by Goethe in a statement with which I should like to close:

If someone regards words and expressions as sacred testimonials, rather than merely bringing them into quick and fleeting circulation like tokens or paper money, seeking instead to employ them as true equivalents in intellectual exchange, then one cannot chide him for drawing attention to the way in which conventional expressions that no one takes exception to any longer indeed have a damaging influence, obfuscating opinions, distorting concepts, and leading entire disciplines in a wrong direction.

With hearty greetings.

Hegel and the Greeks

Translated by Robert Metcalf[1]

[255] The title of the lecture can be reformulated as a question. It reads: How does Hegel present the philosophy of the Greeks within the horizon of his own philosophy? We can answer this question by taking a historiographical look at Hegel's philosophy from a present-day standpoint, and in so doing investigate the relation in which Hegel for his part represents Greek philosophy historiographically. This way of proceeding yields a historiographical investigation into historiographical connections. Such a project has its own justification and usefulness.

However, something else is at stake, in play [auf dem Spiel]. With the name "the Greeks" we are thinking of the commencement of philosophy; with the name "Hegel," of its completion. Hegel himself understands his philosophy according to this determination.

In the title "Hegel and the Greeks," the whole of philosophy in its history addresses itself to us, and does so now, at a time when the disintegration of philosophy is becoming manifest; for philosophy is migrating into logistics, psychology, and sociology. These independent areas of research secure for themselves their increasing validity and influence at many levels as devices and instruments for the success of the political-economic world, that is to say, of what is, in an essential sense, the technological world.

But the incessant disintegration of philosophy, determined from afar, is not after all the end of thinking, but rather something else, yet something that has withdrawn from public ascertainability. The following discourse seeks to meditate on this for a while, as an attempt to awaken attention to the matter of thinking. The matter of thinking is at stake. "Matter" means here: that which of its own accord demands discussion. In order to be able to respond to such a demand, it is necessary that we allow ourselves to be looked upon by the matter of thinking and prepare ourselves [256] to allow thinking, as determined by its matter, to transform itself.

323

The following limits itself to pointing out one possibility through which the matter of thinking becomes visible. But why, then, this roundabout approach through Hegel and the Greeks in order to arrive at the matter of thinking? Because we need to take this path, which indeed, in its essence, is not a roundabout one; for the tradition, experienced in the right way, provides us the present that stands over against us as the matter of thinking and, for that reason, is at issue. Genuine tradition is so far from being the dragging weight of what is past that it much rather frees us for what approaches us as present, and thus becomes the enduring directive toward the matter of thinking.

Hegel and the Greeks – this sounds like: Kant and the Greeks, Leibniz and the Greeks, medieval Scholasticism and the Greeks. It sounds like this, and yet is nonetheless different. For it is Hegel who, for the first time, thinks the philosophy of the Greeks as a whole and thinks this whole philosophically. In what way is this possible? By virtue of the fact that Hegel determines history as such in such a way that it must be philosophical in its fundamental trait. The history of philosophy is for Hegel the intrinsically unitary and hence necessary process of the advance of spirit toward itself. The history of philosophy is no mere sequence of diverse opinions and teachings that supersede each other without any connection.

Hegel says in an introduction to his Berlin lectures on the history of philosophy: "The history which we have before us is the history of thought finding itself" (*Vorlesungen über die Geschichte der Philosophie*, ed. Hoffmeister 1940, vol. I, p. 81, note). "For only philosophy itself unfolds the history of philosophy" (ibid., pp. 235f.). Accordingly, for Hegel, philosophy as the self-unfolding of spirit toward absolute knowing and the history of philosophy are identical. No philosopher *before* Hegel gained such a fundamental philosophical position [257] as to make possible and require that philosophizing itself move at the same time within its history and that this movement be philosophy itself. But according to a statement of Hegel's from the introduction to his first lecture here in Heidelberg, philosophy has for its "goal": "truth" (ibid., p. 14).

As Hegel says in a marginal note to the manuscript of this lecture, philosophy is as its history the "*realm of pure truth*, – not the deeds *of external reality*, but rather the inner remaining-with-itself of spirit" (ibid., p. 6, note). "Truth" means here: what is true in its pure realization, which at the same time brings to presentation the truth of what is true, truth in its essence.

May we now take Hegel's determination of the goal of philosophy, which is truth, as hinting at a meditation upon the matter of thinking? Presumably so, as soon as we have sufficiently clarified the theme, "Hegel and the

Greeks," that is to say, philosophy taken in all of its destiny with regard to its goal, truth.

We therefore ask initially: In what way must the history of philosophy, as history, be philosophical in its fundamental trait? What is meant here by "philosophical"? What is meant here by "history"?

The answers cannot but immediately incur the risk of saying what seemingly is already familiar. However, for thinking there is never anything familiar. Hegel explains: "With him (namely, with Descartes), we properly enter upon a self-supporting philosophy. Here, we can say that we are home and, like the sailor who has journeyed on the stormy sea for a long time, cry: 'Land-ho!'" (*Werke*, vol. XV, p. 328). With this image Hegel means to suggest the following: The *"ego cogito sum,"* the "I think, I am," is the solid ground upon which philosophy can settle truly and completely. In the philosophy of Descartes, the ego becomes the authoritative *subiectum*, i.e., that which already lies before. However, this subject [258] is first taken hold of in the right way – namely, in the Kantian sense, transcendentally and completely, i.e., in the sense of speculative idealism – when the whole structure and movement of the subjectivity of the subject unfolds and is taken up into absolute self-knowing. In *knowing* itself as this knowing that conditions all objectivity, the subject *is*, as this knowing, the absolute itself. True being is the thinking that thinks itself absolutely. For Hegel, being and thinking are the same, specifically in the sense that everything is taken back into thinking and is determined according to what Hegel simply calls "thought."

Subjectivity, as the *ego cogito*, is consciousness that represents something, draws what is represented back to itself and in this way gathers it to itself. In Greek, gathering is called λέγειν. To gather what is manifold for the I into the I is called, expressed in the middle voice, λέγεσθαι. The thinking I gathers what is represented in going through that which is represented, in going through it in its representability. "Going through something" in Greek is called διά. Διαλέγεσθαι, dialectic, signifies here that the subject brings its subjectivity before it, produces it in and as the said process.

Dialectic is the process of the production of the subjectivity of the absolute subject and, as such, its "necessary activity." In accordance with the structure of subjectivity, the production process involves three stages. First of all, the subject as consciousness relates itself immediately to its object. This immediately and yet indeterminately represented object Hegel also calls "being," the universal, the abstract. For in this connection abstraction is still made from the relation of the object to the subject. Only through this relating back, or reflection, does the object come to be represented *as* object for the subject, and the subject come to be represented for itself, i.e., as itself relating to the object. However, so long as we merely differentiate object and subject, being and reflection, over against each other, and persist with this differentiation, the movement from the object to the subject does not yet set forth the whole of [259] subjectivity *for* subjectivity. The object, being, is indeed mediated with the subject through reflection, but the mediation itself, *as* the innermost movement of the subject, is not yet represented *for* the subject. Only when the thesis of the object and the antithesis of the subject are detected in their necessary synthesis is the movement of the subjectivity of the subject-object relation complete in its course. This course is a proceeding from the thesis, advancing to the antithesis, going over into the synthesis, and, from out of this synthesis as the whole, the return to itself of the positing posited. This course gathers the whole of subjectivity into the unfolded unity of subjectivity. In this way, subjectivity grows together, *con-crescit*, becomes concrete. Dialectic is speculative in this manner. For *speculari* means detecting, catching sight of, apprehending, com-prehending. Hegel says in the Introduction to the *Science of Logic* (ed. Lasson, vol. I, p. 38) that speculation consists "in the apprehending of opposites in their unity." Hegel's way of characterizing speculation becomes clearer if we notice that, in speculation, what is at stake is not only the apprehending of unity, the phase of synthesis, but in the first instance and always the apprehending "of opposites" as opposites. This requires apprehending the shining of opposites against one another and in one another, which is the manner in which antithesis reigns as it is presented in the "Logic of Essence" (i.e., the logic of reflection). From this self-re-flecting shining, or mirroring, *speculari* (*speculum:* mirror) receives its conclusive determination. Considered in this way, speculation is the positive whole of that which "dialectic" is meant to signify here: not a transcendental, critically restrictive, or even polemical way of thinking, but rather the mirroring and uniting of opposites as the process of the production of spirit itself.

Hegel also calls "speculative dialectic" simply "method." By this title he means neither an instrument of representing nor merely a special way of proceeding in [260] philosophy. "Method" is the innermost movement of subjectivity, "the soul of being," the production process through which the web of the whole actuality of the absolute is woven. "Method," "the soul of being" – that sounds like fantasy. It is commonly thought that our age has left behind such errors of speculation. Yet we are living right in the midst of this supposed fantasy.

When modern physics aims at a formula for the world, then it becomes apparent that the being of beings has dissolved itself in the method of total calculability. The first writing of Descartes, through whom, according to

Hegel, philosophy and with it modern science set foot upon solid ground, bears the title: *Discours de la méthode* (1637). Method, i.e., speculative dialectic, is for Hegel the fundamental trait of all actuality. For this reason, method determines all happening, i.e., history, as such movement.

Now it becomes clear to what extent the history of philosophy is the innermost movement of spirit, i.e., of absolute subjectivity, on its course toward itself. The departure, advance, transition, and return on this course are determined in a speculative and dialectical manner.

Hegel says: "In philosophy as such, in its present and final stage, is contained everything that the work of millennia has brought forth; it is the result of everything that has gone before" (Hoffmeister, vol. I, p. 118). In the system of speculative idealism philosophy comes to completion; i.e., it has arrived at its highest stage and received its completion from here. People take offense at Hegel's statement concerning the completion of philosophy. People regard it as arrogant and characterize it as an error that has long since been refuted by history. For after Hegel's time there continued to be philosophy and there still is philosophy. But the statement concerning the completion of philosophy does not mean that philosophy is at an end in the sense of a cessation and breaking off. Rather the completion first provides the possibility of diverse transformations down to the simplest forms: brutal inversion and vehement opposition. Marx and Kierkegaard [261] are the greatest of Hegelians. They are this against their will. The completion of philosophy is neither its end, nor does it consist in the isolated system of speculative idealism. The completion *is* only as the whole course of the history of philosophy, in whose course the beginning remains as essential as the completion: Hegel and the Greeks.

How then is the philosophy of the Greeks determined in terms of the fundamental speculative-dialectical trait of history? In the course of this history, Hegel's metaphysical system is the highest stage, that of synthesis. Preceding it, there is the stage of antithesis, which begins with Descartes inasmuch as his philosophy for the first time posits the subject *as* subject. Thereby, objects too first become representable *as* objects. The subject-object relation now comes to light as op-position, as antithesis. By comparison, all philosophy before Descartes exhausts itself in the mere representing of what is objective. Even soul and spirit are represented in the manner of objects, though, to be sure, not *as* objects. Accordingly, for Hegel the thinking subject is also already everywhere at work in pre-Cartesian philosophy, but it is not yet conceived *as* subject, as that in which all objectivity is grounded. Hegel says in his lectures on the history of philosophy: "The human being (of the Greek world) was not yet turned inward upon himself as he is in our times. He was indeed subject, but he had not yet posited himself as such" (Hoffmeister, vol. I, p. 144). The antithesis of the subject to the object is not yet solid ground in philosophy prior to Descartes. That stage which precedes the antithesis is the stage of thesis. With it, philosophy "proper" *begins*. The philosophy of the Greeks is the complete unfolding of this beginning. That which concerns the Greeks and which allows philosophy to begin is, according to Hegel, the purely objective. It is the first "manifestation," the first "emergence" of spirit, that in which all objects are united. Hegel calls it "the universal in general." Because the universal does not yet relate to the subject as such, is not yet conceived as mediated and disclosed through mediation by the subject, [262] and that is to say, has not yet "grown together" or become concrete, it remains "abstract." "The first emergence is necessarily the most abstract; it is the simplest, the poorest, to which the concrete is opposed." Hegel adds here: "and thus the most ancient philosophers are the poorest of all." The stage of Greek "consciousness," the stage of thesis is "the stage of abstraction." But, at the same time, Hegel characterizes "the stage of Greek consciousness" as "the stage of beauty" (*Werke*, vol. XIII, p. 175).

How do these two go together? The beautiful and the abstract are surely not identical. Yet they are if we understand the one and the other in Hegel's sense. The abstract is the first manifestation that remains purely with itself, the most universal of all beings, being as unmediated, simple shining. But such shining constitutes the fundamental trait of the beautiful. That which shines purely in itself indeed arose from spirit as the ideal, i.e., from the subject, but spirit "does not yet have itself as medium (in order therein) to represent itself and upon which to ground the world" (ibid.).

Here we are unable to trace out how Hegel articulates and presents the history of Greek philosophy within the horizon of the stage of beauty as the stage of abstraction. In lieu of this there follows but a mere indication of Hegel's interpretation of four basic words of Greek philosophy. They speak the language of the guiding word, "being," εἶναι (ἐόν, οὐσία). In the subsequent philosophy of the West, they speak time and again up to the present day.

According to Hegel's translation, the four basic words read: (1) ῞Εν, the all; (2) Λόγος, reason; (3) ᾽Ιδέα, concept; (4) ᾽Ενέργεια, actuality.

῞Εν is the word of Parmenides.
Λόγος is the word of Heraclitus.
᾽Ιδέα is the word of Plato.
᾽Ενέργεια is the word of Aristotle.

[263] In order to understand how Hegel interprets these basic words, there are two things to which we must pay attention: first, that which is decisive for Hegel in the interpretation of the philosophers referred to, as opposed to what he mentions only incidentally; second, the manner in which Hegel determines his interpretation of the four basic words within the horizon of the guiding word, "being."

In the introduction to his lectures on the history of philosophy (Hoffmeister, vol. I, p. 240), Hegel explains: "The first universal is the immediate universal, i.e., being. The content, the object, is thus the objective thought, the thought that is." Hegel means to say: being is the pure being-thought of what is immediately thought, without regard as yet to the thinking that thinks this thought apart from mediated disclosure. The determination of what is purely thought is "indeterminacy," its mediated disclosure, immediacy. Being, so understood, is that which simply is represented immediately and indeterminately, indeed in such a way that what is thus initially thought even keeps from itself the absence of determining and mediating, inveighs against it, as it were. From this it becomes clear that being, as the first, simple objectivity of the object, is thought by way of pure abstraction from its relation to the subject that remains to be thought. This is worth heeding, first, in order to understand the direction Hegel follows in explicating the philosophy of the four philosophers mentioned, but also so that we may weigh the importance that Hegel attributes to the basic words in each case.

The basic word of Parmenides reads: ῝Εν, the One, that which unites everything and hence is universal. Parmenides discusses the σήματα, the signs through which the ῝Εν shows itself, in the long fragment VIII, which was known to Hegel. Still, Hegel finds the "main thought" of Parmenides *not* in the ῝Εν, being as the universal. Rather, the "main thought" is, according to Hegel, expressed in the sentence that says: "Being and thinking are the same." Hegel explicates this sentence to mean that being, as "the thought that is," is a [264] production of thinking. Hegel sees in the sentence of Parmenides a first step toward Descartes, with whose philosophy there first begins the determination of being on the basis of the explicitly posited subject. For this reason, Hegel can explain: "With Parmenides, philosophizing proper began.... This beginning is admittedly still confused and indeterminate" (*Werke*, vol. XIII, pp. 296f.).

The basic word of Heraclitus reads: Λόγος, the gathering which lets everything that is as a whole lie before and appear as beings. Λόγος is the name that Heraclitus gives to the being of beings. But Hegel's explication of the philosophy of Heraclitus takes its direction precisely *not* from the

Λόγος. That is strange, but all the stranger since Hegel closes the Foreword to his interpretation of Heraclitus with the words: "there is no sentence of Heraclitus that is not taken up in my logic" (ibid., p. 328). But for this "logic" of Hegel, Λόγος is reason in the sense of absolute subjectivity, the "logic" itself is speculative dialectic, through whose movement what is immediately universal and abstract, being, is reflected as what is objective in opposition to the subject, and this reflection is determined as mediation in the sense of becoming. In becoming, what is opposed comes together, becomes concrete and in this way comes to unity. To apprehend this unity is the essence of that speculation which unfolds itself as dialectic.

In Hegel's judgment, Heraclitus is the first to recognize dialectic as a principle, and thereby to advance further beyond Parmenides. Hegel explains: "Being (as Parmenides thinks it) is the One, the first; the second is becoming – he (Heraclitus) has advanced to this determination. That is what is first of all concrete, the absolute, as in it the unity of opposites. Thus, with him (Heraclitus), the philosophical idea in its speculative form is first to be found" (ibid.). In this way, then, Hegel places the main emphasis of his interpretation of Heraclitus on the sentences in which the dialectical, the unity and uniting of contradictions, comes to language.

[265] The basic word of Plato reads: Ἰδέα. For Hegel's explication of Platonic philosophy, it remains to be considered that he apprehends the Ideas as "the intrinsically determinate universal." "Intrinsically determinate" means: the Ideas are thought in their state of belonging together; they are not mere prototypes existing in themselves, but are rather "what is in and for itself" as distinct from "the sensibly existing" (*Werke*, vol. XIV, p. 199). "In and for itself" – therein lies a coming-to-be-itself, namely, con-ceiving oneself. Accordingly, Hegel can explain: the Ideas are "not immediately in consciousness (namely, as intuitions), rather they are (mediated in consciousness) in cognition." "For this reason, one does not *have* them, but rather they are brought forth within spirit through cognition" (ibid., p. 201). This bringing-forth, producing, is conceiving as the activity of absolute knowing, i.e., "science." Therefore Hegel says: "With Plato begins philosophical science as science" (ibid., p. 169). "What is distinctive of Platonic philosophy is its orientation toward the intellectual, supersensible world..." (ibid., p. 170).

The basic word of Aristotle reads: Ἐνέργεια, which Hegel translates as "actuality" (the Roman *actus*). Ἐνέργεια is "still more determinately" the "*entelechy* (ἐντελέχεια), which is in itself end and realization of the end." Ἐνέργεια is "pure efficacy from out of itself." "Only energy, form, is activity, that which effects, self-relating negativity" (ibid., p. 321).

330

Here ἐνέργεια is also thought on the basis of speculative dialectic as the pure activity of the absolute subject. When the thesis is negated by the antithesis, and the latter, for its part, is negated by the synthesis, there holds sway in such negating that which Hegel calls "the self-relating negativity." It is nothing negative. The negation of negation is rather that position in which spirit posits itself as the absolute through its activity. Hegel sees in the ἐνέργεια of Aristotle the first stage of the absolute self-movement [266] of spirit, i.e., of actuality in and for itself. Hegel makes clear his assessment of the whole of Aristotelian philosophy in the following sentence: "If one were to take philosophy seriously, then nothing would be worthier than to hold lectures on Aristotle" (ibid., p. 314).

According to Hegel, philosophy becomes "serious" when it no longer loses itself in objects and in subjective reflection upon objects, but rather becomes active as the activity of absolute knowing.

Clarifying the four basic words allows us to recognize that Hegel understands Ἕν, Λόγος, Ἰδέα, and Ἐνέργεια within the horizon of being, which he conceives as the abstract universal. Being, and accordingly that which is represented in the basic words, is *not yet* determined and *not yet* mediated in and through the dialectical movement of absolute subjectivity. The philosophy of the Greeks is the stage of this "not yet." It is not yet the completion, but for all that it is nonetheless understood from the perspective of this completion, which has determined itself as the system of speculative idealism.

According to Hegel, it is the innermost "drive," "the need" of spirit to detach itself from what is abstract by absolving itself into the concreteness of absolute subjectivity and so freeing itself for itself. Hence, Hegel can say: "philosophy is what is most opposed to the abstract; it is precisely the struggle against what is abstract, the constant war with the understanding's reflection" (Hoffmeister, vol. I, p. 113). In the Greek world, spirit indeed comes for the first time into free and open opposition to being. But spirit does not yet properly come to absolute certainty of itself as self-knowing subject. Only where this latter occurs, in the system of speculative-dialectical metaphysics, does philosophy come to be what it is: "what is holiest, what is innermost to spirit itself" (ibid., p. 125).

Hegel determines "truth" to be the "goal" of philosophy. This is achieved only at the stage of completion. The [267] stage of Greek philosophy remains in the "not yet." As the stage of beauty, it is not yet the stage of truth.

Here – when we look through the entire history of philosophy, "Hegel and the Greeks," its completion and its beginning – we begin to ponder and ask: With Parmenides, does not Ἀλήθεια, truth, stand over the beginning of the path of philosophy? Why does Hegel not bring *it* to language? Does he understand by "truth" something other than unconcealment? To be sure. Truth, for Hegel, is the absolute certainty of the self-knowing absolute subject. But for the Greeks, according to his interpretation, the subject does not yet come to appearance *as subject*. Thus, Ἀλήθεια cannot be what determines truth in the sense of certainty.

So the matter stands for Hegel. And yet if Ἀλήθεια, however veiled and unthought, holds sway over the beginning of Greek philosophy, we must surely ask: Is not precisely certainty in its essence referred to Ἀλήθεια, granted that we do not explicate the latter indeterminately and arbitrarily as truth in the sense of certainty, but rather carefully ponder it as disclosure? If we venture to think Ἀλήθεια in this way, then two issues remain to be considered from the outset: First, the experience of Ἀλήθεια as unconcealment and disclosure in no way bases itself upon the etymology of a selected word, but rather upon the matter to be thought here – a matter from which even Hegel's philosophy cannot entirely withdraw. If Hegel designates being as the first emergence and first manifestation of spirit, then it remains to be considered whether, in this emerging and self-revealing, disclosure must not already be in play, no less here than in the pure shining of beauty that, according to Hegel, determines the stage of Greek "consciousness." If Hegel allows the fundamental position of his system to culminate in the absolute idea, in the complete self-appearing of spirit, this provokes the question as to whether *disclosure* must not *also* be in play even in this shining, i.e., [268] in the phenomenology of spirit and therefore in absolute self-knowing and its certainty. And at once we are faced with the further question as to whether disclosure has its site in spirit as the absolute subject, or whether disclosure itself is the site and points to the site wherein something like a representing subject can first "be" what it is.

With this, we are already involved with another issue that is to be considered as soon as Ἀλήθεια comes to language as disclosure. What this name names is not the crude key that unlocks every enigma of thinking; rather, Ἀλήθεια is the enigma itself – the matter of thinking.

Yet it is not we who establish this issue as the matter of thinking. It has long since been addressed to us and passed down through the whole history of philosophy. It is simply a matter of listening to this tradition in return, and thereby examining the prejudices and pre-judgments in which every thinking, in its own way, must dwell. Of course, such an examination, too, can never conduct itself as the court of justice that ultimately decides upon the essence of history and our possible relation to it. For this examination has its limit, which can be circumscribed as follows: the more thoughtful a thinking is, that is, the more it is claimed by its language, the more authoritative what is unthought becomes for it, and even what is unthinkable for it.

When, from the perspective of absolute subjectivity, Hegel interprets being in a speculative and dialectical manner as the indeterminate immediate, the abstract universal, and explicates the basic words for being in Greek – "Εν, Λόγος, 'Ιδέα, 'Ενέργεια – within *this* horizon of modern philosophy, we are tempted to judge this explication to be historiographically incorrect.

Yet every historiographical statement and its grounds move already within a relation to history. For this reason, we must, before deciding upon the historiographical correctness of our representation, consider whether and how history is experienced, whence it is determined in its fundamental traits.

[269] With regard to Hegel and the Greeks, this means that, prior to all correct or incorrect historiographical assertions, Hegel experienced the essence of history in terms of the essence of being in the sense of absolute subjectivity. To this day there has been no experience of history that, seen philosophically, could respond to this experience of history. But the speculative-dialectical determination of history does entail that it remained denied to Hegel to see 'Αλήθεια and its holding sway expressly as *the matter of thinking*, and this occurs in precisely that philosophy which determined "the realm of pure truth" to be "the goal" of philosophy. For, when Hegel conceives being as the indeterminate immediate, he experiences it as what is posited by the determining and conceiving subject. Accordingly, he is *not* able to release εἶναι, being in the Greek sense, from the relation to the subject, and set it free into its own essence. This essence, however, is presencing, that is to say, an enduring coming *forth from* concealment into unconcealment. In coming to presence, disclosure is at play. It is at play in the "Εν and in Λόγος, i.e., in unifying, gathering, lying-before – i.e., in letting come to endure. 'Αλήθεια is at play in the 'Ιδέα and in the κοινωνία of the Ideas, insofar as these bring one another to shine and thus constitute being beings [*das Seiendsein*], the ὄντως ὄν. 'Αλήθεια is at play in 'Ενέργεια, which has nothing to do with *actus* and activity, but rather only with the ἔργον, experienced in a Greek manner, and with its state of being brought forth into presencing, through which the latter reaches completion.[2]

Yet 'Αλήθεια, disclosure, is at play not only in the basic words of Greek thinking, but in the Greek language as a whole, which speaks differently as soon as we put out of play Roman and medieval and modern ways of representing in our interpretations of it, and seek in the Greek world neither personalities nor consciousness.

But how then do matters stand with this enigmatic Ἀλήθεια itself, which has become something of an annoyance for interpreters of the Greek world, [270] because they focus only on this isolated word and its etymology instead of thinking in terms of the matter to which such issues as unconcealment and disclosure refer? Is Ἀλήθεια as unconcealment the same as being, i.e., coming to presence? This is testified by the fact that Aristotle still means the same thing by τὰ ὄντα, beings, that which presences, as by τὰ ἀληθέα, the unconcealed. But in what way do unconcealment and presence, ἀλήθεια and οὐσία, belong to one another? Are both of the same essential rank? Or is it that presence is referred to unconcealment, but not vice versa? In this case, being would indeed have to do with disclosure, but not disclosure with being. Moreover, if the essence of truth that straightaway comes to reign as correctness and certainty can subsist only within the realm of unconcealment, then truth indeed has to do with Ἀλήθεια, but not Ἀλήθεια with truth.

Wherein does Ἀλήθεια itself belong, if it must be released from its reference to truth and being, and set free into what is proper to it? Does thinking as yet have the scope of vision even to intimate what occurs in disclosure, and especially in *concealing*, which all disclosure needs?

The enigmatic character of Ἀλήθεια comes closer to us, and yet so does the danger that we may hypostatize it into a fantastical world-essence.

It has indeed often been remarked that there cannot be an unconcealment in itself, that unconcealment is after all always unconcealment "for someone." It is thereby unavoidably "subjectivized."

Nevertheless, must the human being – which is what is being thought here – necessarily be determined as subject? Does "for human beings" already unconditionally mean: posited *by* human beings? We may deny both options, and must recall the fact that ἀλήθεια, thought in a Greek manner, certainly holds sway for human beings, but that the human being remains determined by λόγος. The human being is the sayer. Saying, in Old High German *sagan*, means showing, letting appear [271] and letting be seen. The human being is the being that, in saying, lets what is presencing lie before us in its presence, apprehending what lies before. Human beings can speak only insofar as they are sayers.

The oldest evidence of ἀληθείη and ἀληθής, unconcealment and unconcealed, we find in Homer, and specifically in connection with verbs of saying. From this it has been somewhat precipitously concluded that unconcealment is therefore "dependent" upon the *verba dicendi*.[3] What does "dependent" mean here, if saying is letting-appear, as are accordingly

334

dissembling and hiding? It is not that unconcealment is "dependent" upon saying; rather, every saying already needs the realm of unconcealment. Only where unconcealment already holds sway can something become sayable, visible, showable, capable of being apprehended. When we keep in view the enigmatic sway of Ἀλήθεια, disclosure, we may come to intimate that even the whole essence of language resides in dis-closure, in the holding sway of Ἀλήθεια. However, the talk of holding-sway, too, remains still a makeshift expedient, if indeed the manner of its being in play receives its determination from disclosure itself, i.e., from the clearing of self-concealing.

"Hegel and the Greeks" – in the meantime, we seem to have arrived at a discussion of something strange, remote from our topic. Nonetheless we are closer to our topic than before. In the introduction to our lecture, it was said: The matter of thinking is at stake, in play. The attempt is to be made to bring this matter into view through our topic.

Hegel determines the philosophy of the Greeks as the beginning of "philosophy proper." However, this philosophy remains, as the stage of thesis and abstraction, in a "not yet."[4] The completion through antithesis and synthesis is as yet outstanding.[5]

[272] Our meditation on Hegel's interpretation of the Greek doctrine of being tried to show that "being," with which philosophy begins, unfolds essentially as presence only insofar as Ἀλήθεια already holds sway, and yet Ἀλήθεια itself remains unthought with respect to its essential provenance.

Thus in looking at Ἀλήθεια we come to experience the fact that, in regard to it, our thinking is addressed by something[a] that, already *before* the beginning of "philosophy," yet at the same time[6] throughout its entire history, has drawn thinking toward it. Ἀλήθεια comes before the history of philosophy, but in such a way that it withholds itself from philosophical determinability as something that demands to be discussed by a thinking that springs from it.[7] Ἀλήθεια is that which, unthought, is worthy of thought – *the* matter of thinking. Therefore, Ἀλήθεια remains for us what is first of all to be thought – to be thought freed from the perspective of the metaphysical representation of "truth" in the sense of correctness, freed also from the determination of "being" as actuality.[8]

Hegel says of the philosophy of the Greeks: "Satisfaction is to be found therein only to a certain degree," namely, the satisfaction of spirit's drive toward absolute certainty. This judgment of Hegel's as to the unsatisfying

---

[a] Separatum from *The Presence of the Greeks in Modern Thought* (1960): that which presses, the conflict.

character of Greek philosophy is spoken from the perspective of the completion of philosophy. Within the horizon of speculative idealism, the philosophy of the Greeks remains in the "not yet" of its completion.

Yet if we now attend to the enigma [9] [a] of Ἀλήθεια, which holds sway over the beginning of Greek philosophy and over the course of philosophy as a whole, then the philosophy of the Greeks shows itself to our thinking too in a "not yet." But this is the "not yet" of the unthought – not a "not yet" that does not satisfy us, but rather a "not yet" to which *we* are not sufficient, and which *we* fail to satisfy.

[a] Separatum from *The Presence of the Greeks in Modern Thought* (1960): the authority of the enigma.

Kant's Thesis about Being

Translated by Ted E. Klein Jr. and William E. Pohl[1]

[273] The title suggests that the following is to present a point from Kant's philosophy. It will give us instruction in a past philosophy. This may have its uses – but only, of course, if our sense of the tradition is still keen.

Such is hardly the case anymore, least of all where it is a question of the tradition of what has continually concerned us human beings always, and everywhere, but which we do not expressly consider.

We use "being" to name it. The name names that which we mean when we say "is" and "has been" and "is in the offing." Everything that reaches us and that we reach out for goes through the spoken or unspoken "it is." That this is the case – from that fact we can nowhere and never escape. The "is" remains known to us in all its obvious and concealed inflections. And yet, as soon as this word "being" strikes our ear, we assert that we cannot imagine what falls under the term, that we cannot be thinking of anything when using it.

Presumably this hasty conclusion is correct; it justifies our being annoyed at talk – not to say idle talk – about "being," so annoyed that "being" becomes a laughingstock. Without giving thought to being, without recollecting a path in thought to it, one has the presumption to make oneself the court that decides whether the word "being" speaks or not. Hardly anyone takes offense anymore at having thoughtlessness in this way elevated to a principle.

If things have reached such a state that what was once the source of our historical Dasein is bogged down in ridicule, it might be advisable to engage in some simple reflection.

[274] We can think nothing when the word "being" is used. How would the suggestion be that it is, therefore, the job of the thinker to furnish information about what is called "being"?

337

In case this should turn out to be too much even for thinkers, it could at least remain their task to show again and again that being is what is worthy of thought, and to show this in such a way, moreover, that this which is worthy of thought remains as such within the horizon of human beings.

We shall follow the suggestion mentioned and listen to a thinker and what he has to say to us concerning being. We shall listen to Kant.

Why do we listen to Kant to learn something about being? For two reasons. First, Kant took a far-reaching step in the discussion of being. Second, Kant took this step out of loyalty to the tradition, i.e., in a critical encounter with it, which threw new light on it. Both reasons for the reference to Kant's thesis about being impel us to reflect.

Kant's thesis about being goes as follows, according to the version in his main work, the *Critique of Pure Reason* (1781):

"*Being*" is obviously not a real predicate; that is, it is not a concept of something which could be added to the concept of a thing. It is merely the positing of a thing, or of certain determinations in and of themselves. (A 598, B 626)

In view of that which today *is*, which in being besets us and which as possible nonbeing threatens us, Kant's thesis about being strikes us as abstract, meager, and pale. For, meanwhile, it has also been demanded of philosophy that it no longer be satisfied with interpreting the world and roving about in abstract speculations, but rather that what really matters is changing the world practically. But changing the world in the manner intended requires beforehand that thinking be changed, just as a change of thinking already underlies the demand we have mentioned. (Cf. [275] Karl Marx, *The German Ideology:* "A. *Theses on Feuerbach* ad Feuerbach, 11": "The philosophers have only *interpreted* the world in various ways; the point is to *change* it.")

But in what way is thinking supposed to change if it does not take the path into that which is worthy of thought? Now, the fact that being presents itself as that which is worthy of thought is neither an optional presupposition nor an arbitrary invention. It is the verdict of a tradition that still governs us today, and this far more decisively than one might care to admit.

Kant's thesis offends us as abstract and inadequate only if we fail to consider what Kant said in elucidation of it and how he said it. We must follow the path of his elucidation of the thesis. We must bring before our eyes the region in which that path runs. We must bear in mind the site where what Kant discusses and situates under the name "being" belongs.[a]

---

[a] First edition, 1963: Topology of being.

When we attempt such a thing, something astounding becomes apparent. Kant elucidates his thesis in a merely "episodic way," i.e., in the form of insertions, notes, appendices to his main works. The thesis is not advanced as the first principle of a system commensurate with its content and its import. What appears to be a shortcoming has, however, the advantage that at each of the various episodic places Kant gives expression to an original reflection, which never pretends to be the conclusive one.

The following presentation will have to adapt itself to Kant's procedure. It will be guided by the intention of allowing one to see how, in all Kant's elucidations, i.e., in his fundamental philosophical position, his thesis everywhere shines through as the guiding idea, even when it does not form the scaffolding expressly constructed for the architectonic of his work. For that reason the procedure here followed aims at so balancing the suitable texts against each other that they will illuminate one another, and [276] what cannot be stated directly will nevertheless become evident.

Not until we retrace the thought in Kant's thesis in this kind of way shall we experience the full difficulty in the question about being, and also that which is decisive and that which is questionable in it. At this point we begin to wonder whether and to what extent present-day thinking is competent to attempt a critical encounter with Kant's thesis, i.e., to ask in what Kant's thesis about being is grounded, in what sense does it admit of proof, in what way can it be discussed. The tasks of thought herewith designated go beyond the possibilities of a first delineation, go beyond even the capacity of the thinking still customary today. All the more pressing is the need for reflectively listening to the tradition, a listening that does not devote itself to what is past but rather considers the present. Let us repeat Kant's thesis:

"Being" is obviously not a real predicate; that is, it is not a concept of something which could be added to the concept of a thing. It is merely the positing of a thing, or of certain determinations in and of themselves.

Kant's thesis contains two assertions. The first is a negative one, which denies to being the character of a real predicate, in no way, however, denying to it the character of a predicate in general. In accordance with this, the positive assertion of the thesis that follows it characterizes being as "merely the positing."

Even now, when the content of the thesis is distributed between both assertions, we resist with difficulty the opinion that the word "being" does not offer anything to thought. The prevailing perplexity, however, is lessened, and Kant's thesis becomes more familiar if, before a more precise classification, we note at what place within the structure and development of the *Critique of Pure Reason* Kant expresses his thesis.

Let us recall here in passing an undeniable development: Occidental-European thought is guided by the question "What are beings?" In this way it inquires about being. [277] In the history of this way of thinking, Kant effects a decisive turn, through the *Critique of Pure Reason*. With this in view, we expect Kant to bring the guiding thought of his main work into play by a discussion of being and by the assertion of his thesis. This is not the case. Instead, we do not encounter the thesis in question until the last third of the *Critique of Pure Reason*, in the section entitled "On the Impossibility of an Ontological Proof of the Existence of God" (A 592, B 620).

But if we recall once again the history of Occidental-European thought, then we see that the question about being, taken as a question about the being of beings, is double in form. It asks on the one hand: What are beings, in general, as beings? Considerations within the province of this question come, in the course of the history of philosophy, under the heading of ontology. The question "What are beings?" includes also the question, "Which being is the highest and in what way is it?" The question is about the divine and God. The province of this question is called theology. The duality of the question about the being of beings can be brought together in the title "onto-theo-logy." The twofold[a] question, What are beings? asks on the one hand, What are (in general) beings? The question asks on the other hand, What (which one) is the (ultimate) being?

Obviously, the twofold quality of the question about beings must result from the way the being of beings manifests itself.[b] Being manifests itself in the character of that which we call ground. Beings in general are the ground in the sense of the foundation upon which any further consideration of beings takes place. That which is the highest being is the ground in the sense of that which allows all beings to come into being.[c]

That being is defined as ground has until now been considered most self-evident; and yet it is most questionable. To what extent being is to be defined as ground, wherein [278] the essence of ground lies, cannot be discussed here. But already, in a seemingly external consideration, the suspicion forces itself upon us that in Kant's determination of being as

---

[a] First edition, 1963: The word "twofold" already says *more* than the mere "and" of ὂν ἢ ὄν "and" θεῖον.

[b] First edition, 1963: Being *and* beings, but not *as* difference or the latter as that which is worthy of question, indeed even the most worthy of question.

[c] First edition, 1963: χοινόν – χοινότατον; χοινόν – χαθόλου (θεῖον).

positing, there prevails a kinship with that which we call ground. *Positio, ponere*, means to set, place, lay, lie, to lie *before*, to lie at the ground.

In the course of the history of ontotheological inquiry the task has arisen not only of showing what the highest being is but of proving that this most supreme of beings *is*, that God exists. The words *Existenz, Dasein*, actuality, name a mode of being.

In the year 1763, almost two decades before the appearance of the *Critique of Pure Reason*, Kant published a work under the title *The Only Possible Ground of Proof for a Demonstration of the Existence of God*. The "First Consideration" in this work deals with the concepts of "Existence [*Dasein*] in general" and "being in general." Here we already find Kant's thesis about being, and even in the twofold form of the negative and the affirmative assertion. The wording of both assertions agrees in a certain manner with that in the *Critique of Pure Reason*. The negative assertion goes like this in the precritical work: "Existence is not a predicate or determination of anything whatever." The affirmative assertion goes: "The concept of positing or asserting [*Position oder Setzung*] is completely simple and identical with that of being in general."

At first it was necessary only to point out that Kant formulates the thesis within the province of the questions of philosophical theology. This dominates the entire question about the being of beings, i.e., metaphysics in its central content. From this it can be seen that the thesis about being is no out-of-the-way, abstract bit of doctrine, as its wording might at first easily persuade us.

In the *Critique of Pure Reason* the negative-defensive assertion is introduced with an "obviously." That means it is supposed to be immediately evident to everyone: being – [279] "obviously" not a real predicate. For us today the statement is by no means immediately clear. Being – this means, of course, reality. How, then, could being not count as a real predicate? But for Kant the word "real" still has its original meaning. It means that which belongs to a *res*, to a substance, to the substantive content of a thing. A real predicate, a determination belonging to a substance, is, for example, the predicate "heavy" with respect to the stone, regardless of whether the stone really exists or not. In Kant's thesis "real" means, then, not that which we mean today when we speak of *Realpolitik*, which deals with facts, with the actual. Reality is for Kant not actuality but rather substantiality. A real predicate is such as belongs to the substantive content of a thing and can be attributed to it. We represent and place before ourselves the substantive content of a thing in its concept. We can place before ourselves what the word "stone" names without it being necessary that the thing in question exists as a stone just now lying there before us. *Existenz, Dasein,* i.e., being, says Kant's thesis, is "obviously no real predicate." The obviousness of this negative assertion emerges as soon as we think of the word "real" in Kant's sense. Being is nothing real.

But how is that? After all, we do say of a stone lying before us that it, this stone here, exists. This stone *is.* Accordingly, the "is," i.e., being, shows itself just as obviously as predicate, namely, in the assertion about this stone as the subject of the assertion. Nor does Kant deny in the *Critique of Pure Reason* that the existence predicated of an existing stone is a predicate. But the "is" is no *real* predicate. Of what is the "is" predicated then? Obviously of the existing stone. And what does this "is" in the assertion "The stone is here" say? It says nothing about *what* the stone, as stone, is; it does say, however, *that* what belongs to the stone exists here, is. What is called being, then? Kant answers with the affirmative assertion in his thesis: Being "is merely the positing of a thing or of certain determinations in and of themselves."

[280] The wording of this statement easily misleads one into supposing that being as "merely the positing of a thing" concerns the thing in the sense of the thing in and for itself. This meaning the thesis cannot have, insofar as it is expressed within the *Critique of Pure Reason.* "Thing" here means something for which Kant also says "object" or "*Gegenstand.*" Nor does Kant say that the positing concerns the thing with all its real determinations; what he says is rather, "merely the positing of the thing, or of certain determinations in and of themselves." How the phrase "or of certain determinations" is to be interpreted we shall leave open for now.

The expression "in and of itself" does not mean: "something in itself," something that exists unrelated to a consciousness. The "in and of itself" we must understand as marking the distinction from what is represented as this or that with regard to something else. This sense of "in itself" is already expressed in Kant's statement, in his saying that being "is merely the positing." This "merely" sounds like a limitation, as if the positing were something inferior to the reality, i.e., to the substantiality of a thing. The "merely," however, indicates that being can never be explained by *what* any given being is, i.e., for Kant, by the concept. The "merely" does not limit, but rather assigns being to a domain where alone it can be characterized in its purity. "Merely" means here: purely. "Being" and "is" belong, with all their meanings and inflections, in a domain of their own. They are nothing thing-like, i.e., for Kant, nothing objective.

In order to think of "being" and "is," therefore, another view is required, one that is not guided exclusively by observing things and by reckoning with them. A stone lying before us obviously "is"; but one can explore and study it from every side without ever finding the "is" in it. And yet this stone *is*.

In what way does "being" receive the meaning of "merely the positing"? From what source and how is the meaning of the heading "pure positing" circumscribed? [281] Does not this interpretation of being as positing remain for us strange, even arbitrary, or in any case ambiguous and therefore inexact?

Kant himself, to be sure, translates "positing," "*Position,*" by *Setzung.* But this does not help much. For our German word *Setzung* is just as ambiguous as the Latin *positio.* The latter can mean: (1) Setting, placing, laying as action. (2) Something set, the theme. (3) Setness [*Gesetztheit*], site, constitution. But we can also understand *Position* and *Setzung* in such a way that they mean the unity of the positing of something posited as such in its positedness.

In every case the characterization of being as positing points to an ambiguity that is not accidental and also not unknown to us. For it plays about everywhere in the realm of that setting and placing that we know as representing. For this, the learned language of philosophy has two characteristic names: representing is *percipere, perceptio,* to take something to oneself, grasp; and: *repraesentare,* to hold opposite oneself, to hold present to oneself. In representing we place something before ourselves, so that it, as thus placed (posited), stands over against us as object. Being, as position, means the positedness of something in representational positing. According to what is posited and how it is posited, positing, position, being has a different meaning. Kant, therefore, after setting up his thesis about being in the text of the *Critique of Pure Reason,* continues:

In its logical use it [i.e., being as "merely the position"] is merely the copula of a judgment. The proposition "God is omnipotent" contains two concepts, each of which has its object – God and omnipotence. The small word "is" adds no new predicate, but only serves to posit the predicate *in its relation* to the subject.

In *The Only Possible Ground of Proof* the relationship between the subject and predicate of the sentence as posited by the "is" of the copula is called the *respectus logicus.* Kant's talk of the "logical use" of "being" causes one to suppose that there is yet another use [282] of "being." At the same time we are at this point already learning something essential about being. It is "used," in the sense of applied. This use is accomplished by the understanding, by thinking.

What other use of "being" and of the "is" is there, besides the "logical" one? In the sentence "God is," no substantive, real predicate is added on.

Rather, the subject, God, with all its predicates, is posited "in itself." The "is" now says: God exists, God is there. *"Dasein," "Existenz,"* mean being, to be sure, but "being" and "is" not in the sense of positing the relation between the subject and predicate of the sentence. The positing of the "is" in the sentence "God is" goes beyond the concept of God and brings to this concept the thing itself, the object God as existing. Being is used here, in contrast to the logical use, with reference to the existing object in and of itself. We could therefore speak of the ontic, or better, the objective, use of being. In the precritical work Kant writes:

> If not merely this relationship [namely, between subject and predicate of the sentence], but the thing posited in and of itself is considered, then such being is the same as existence.

And the heading of the section concerned begins: "Existence is the absolute position of a thing." In an undated note (*Werke*, Akademieausgabe vol. XVIII, n. 6276), Kant briefly summarizes what has been presented thus far:

> By the predicate "existence" I add nothing to the thing, but rather add the thing itself to the concept. In an existential sentence, therefore, I go beyond the concept, not to a predicate other than what was thought of in the concept, but rather to the thing itself with just the very same predicates, not more, not less, except that absolute position is now added over and beyond the relative.

[283] But now the question for Kant becomes, and remains, whether and how and within what limits the sentence "God is" is possible as absolute positing – the secret goad that prods all the thinking in the *Critique of Pure Reason* and is the moving force in his later major works. The talk about being as absolute positing, in contrast to relative positing, as the logical one, gives the impression that no relation is posited in absolute positing. If, in the case of absolute positing, however, it is a matter of the *objective* use of being in the sense of *Dasein* and *Existenz*, then for critical reflection it becomes not only clear but pressing that here also a relation is posited and consequently the "is" receives the character of a predicate, even if not of a real one.[a]

In the logical use of being (*a* is *b*) it is a matter of the positing of the relation between subject and predicate of a sentence. In the ontic use of being – this stone is ("exists") – it is a matter of the positing of the relation

---

[a] First edition, 1963: Presencing is attributed, but is not demonstrable in the manner of the empiricism of natural science.

between I-subject and object – this, however, in such a way that the subject-predicate relation cuts across, as it were, the subject-object relation. The significance of this is that the "is" as copula in the statement of an objective cognition has a different and richer sense than the merely logical sense. But it will be seen that Kant arrived at this insight only after long reflection and did not even express it until the second edition of the *Critique of Pure Reason*. Six years after the first edition he is able to say what is involved with the "is," i.e., with being. Not until the *Critique of Pure Reason* are fullness and certainty brought into the interpretation of being as positing.

Had someone at the time of the composition of his precritical essay asked Kant concerning *The Only Possible Ground of Proof for a Demonstration of the Existence of God* just how it might be determined more exactly what he understood "existence" in the sense of absolute positing to be, Kant would have referred to this work, wherein the following is found: "So simple is this concept [of *Dasein* and *Existenz*] that one can say nothing by way of unfolding it."

[284] Kant even adds a fundamental observation that gives us an insight into his philosophical position prior to the appearance of the *Critique of Pure Reason*:

If one sees that our entire knowledge ends ultimately in insoluble concepts,[a] then one also understands that there will be some that are almost insoluble, that is, where the characteristic features are barely clearer and simpler than the issue itself. This is the case with our explanation of existence. I gladly admit that by means of the latter the concept of that which is explained becomes clear to only a very small degree. But the nature of the object in relation to the capacities of our understanding permits no higher degree.

The "nature of the object," i.e., here the essence of being, permits no higher degree of clarification. Nevertheless, for Kant one thing stands firm from the beginning: he thinks of existence and being "in relation to the capacities of our understanding." Even in the *Critique of Pure Reason* being continues to be defined as positing. The critical reflection, to be sure, attains no "higher degree of clarification," that is, according to the precritical way of explaining and dissecting concepts. But the *Critique* achieves a different sort of explanation of being and of its different modes, which we are acquainted with as being possible, being actual, being necessary.

What has happened? What must have happened through the *Critique of Pure Reason*, if the reflection on being was begun as a reflection on the

[a] First edition, 1963: I.e., begins from there in terms of its subject-matter, proceeds from there as the all-governing ἀρχή (archetypes).

"relation" of being "to the capacities of our understanding"? Kant himself gives us the answer in the *Critique of Pure Reason* with the statement:

So long as the definition of possibility, existence,[a] and necessity is sought solely in pure understanding, they cannot be explained save through an obvious tautology.[b] (A 244, B 302)

[285] However, it is just such an explanation that Kant himself still attempts in his precritical period. Meanwhile the insight came to him that the relating of being and of the modes of being solely to "the capacities of our understanding" does not afford a sufficient horizon from which being and the modes of being can be explained, i.e., now – from which their meaning can be "verified."

What is lacking? In what regard must our thinking at once glimpse being together with all its modalities in order to arrive at a sufficient determination of essence? In a supplementary remark in the second edition of the *Critique of Pure Reason* (B 302) one finds:

[Possibility, existence, and necessity] cannot be *verified* by anything [i.e., authenticated or proved] . . . if all sensuous intuition (the only kind of intuition we have) is removed.[c]

Without this intuition the concepts of being lack the relation to an object, through which relation alone they acquire what Kant calls their "reference." To be sure, "being" means position, positedness in being posited by thinking as an act of understanding. But this positing can only posit something as object, i.e., as something brought over against us, and thus bring it to a stand as something standing over *against* us [*Gegen*stand], if something that can be posited is *given* to our positing through sensuous intuition, i.e., through the affection of the senses. Only positing as positing of an affection lets us understand what, for Kant, the being of beings means.

But in the affection through our senses, a manifold of representations is continually given to us. In order that the given "turmoil," the flux of this manifold, can come to a *stand* and thus show itself as something *standing* over against us [*Gegenstand*], the manifold must be ordered, i.e., connected.

[a] First edition, 1963: I.e., actuality.

[b] First edition, 1963: On the various possibilities of "tautology" of the καθ᾽ αὐτό, cf. Aristotle, *Metaphysics*, VII.

[c] First edition, 1963: Contrast with Husserl's "categorial intuition" (*Logical Investigations*, VI); but what does "category" mean for Husserl?

Such connection can, however, never come through the senses. All connecting comes, according to Kant, from that power of representation that is called understanding. Its basic feature is positing as synthesis. [286] Positing has the character of proposition, i.e., of judgment, whereby something is placed before us as something, a predicate is attributed to a subject by the "is." To the extent, however, that the positing is necessarily related as proposition to what is given in the affection, whenever an object is to be cognized by us, the "is" (as copula) receives from this a new sense. Kant does not define this until the second edition of the *Critique of Pure Reason* (§19, B 140ff.). He writes at the beginning of §19:

I have never been able to accept the interpretation which logicians give of judgment in general. It is, they declare, the representation of a relation between two concepts.

With respect to this explanation Kant finds "that it is not determined here wherein this *relationship* consists." In the logical explanation of judgment, Kant misses that wherein positing a predicate of a subject is grounded. Only as object for the cognizing I-subject can the sentence-subject of the statement be grounding. Kant continues, therefore, beginning a new section in the text:

But if I investigate more precisely the relation of the given modes of knowledge in any judgment, and distinguish it, as belonging to the understanding, from the relation according to laws of the reproductive imagination (which [relationship] has only subjective validity), I find that a judgment is nothing but the manner in which given modes of knowledge are brought to the *objective* unity of apperception. This is what is intended by the copula *is*. It is employed to distinguish the objective unity of given representations from a subjective unity.

In the attempt to give these sentences their due consideration, we must above all heed not only the fact that the "is" of the copula is now differently defined, but also the fact that along with it the relation of the "is" to the unity of connecting (gathering) comes to light.

[287] The belonging together of being and unity, of ἐόν and ἕν, already manifests itself to thought in the great beginning of Western philosophy. Today, if someone mentions to us simply the two titles, "being" and "unity," we are hardly in a position to give a satisfying answer concerning the belonging together of the two or even to discern the ground of this belonging together. For we do not think "unity" and unification in terms of the gathering-revealing character of λόγος and neither do we think of "being" as self-revealing presencing. We do not even

think of the belonging together of the two, which the Greeks also left unthought.[a]

Before we pursue the question of how, in Kant's thought, the belonging together of being and unity is presented and how Kant's thesis about being thereby manifests its richer content, only then grounded, we shall mention the example, cited by Kant, that clarifies for us the objective sense of the "is" as copula. It goes:

[If I consider the sequence of representations as only[b] a process in the subject, in accordance with laws of association, then] all that I could say would be: If I support a body, I feel an impression of weight; I could *not* say: It, the body, *is* heavy. Thus to say that the body is heavy is not merely to state that the two representations have been conjoined in my perception (however often that perception be repeated), but to say that these two representations are connected in the object, i.e., irrespective of the state of the subject.

According to Kant's interpretation of the "is," there speaks in it a connecting of subject and predicate of the sentence in the object. Every connecting brings with itself a unity with which and into which it connects the given manifold. If, however, the unity cannot first arise from the connecting, because the connecting remains dependent from the outset upon the unity, then where does the unity come from? According to Kant it is "to be sought higher up," above the positing that connects by way of the understanding. It is that ἕν (uniting unity) which lets all the σύν (together) of every θέσις (positing) arise in the first place. [288] Kant therefore calls it "the originally synthetic unity." From the outset it is already present (*adest*) in all representation, in perception. It is the unity of the original synthesis of apperception. Because it makes possible the being of beings, or in Kantian terms, the objectivity of the object, it lies higher, beyond the object. Because it makes possible the object [*Gegenstand*] as such, it is called "transcendental apperception." At the end of §15 (B 131) Kant says of it that it

itself contains the ground of the unity of diverse concepts in judgment, and therefore [the ground] of the possibility of the understanding, even as regards its logical employment.

While Kant in his precritical work is still content with the view that being and existence cannot be further explained in their relationship to the

[a] First edition, 1963: Unthought: propriating usage [*brauchendes Eignen*].
[b] First edition, 1963: "Only": the subjective as initially given.

capacities of understanding, he gets, through the *Critique of Pure Reason*, so far as not only to clarify expressly the capacities of understanding but even to explain fundamentally the possibility of understanding itself. With this regression to the locus of the possibility of the understanding, with this decisive step from his precritical considerations into the area of critical questioning, *one thing, however, remains untouched.* It is the guiding thread to which Kant holds in setting up and clarifying his thesis on being: namely, that it must be possible for being and its modes to be determined from their relation to the understanding.

Of course, the more original critical determination of the understanding now also gives the warrant for a changed and richer clarification of being. For now the modalities, the modes of "existence" and their determination, come expressly into the purview of Kantian thought. Kant himself lives in the certainty of having reached the place from which the determination of the being of beings can be set in motion. Once again, this is verified by a note that appears only in the text of the second edition of the *Critique of Pure Reason* (§16, B 134, note): [289]

The synthetic unity of apperception is therefore the highest point at which one must attach all employment of the understanding, even the whole of logic, and after it, transcendental philosophy. Indeed this faculty [of apperception] is the understanding itself.

Apperception purports: (1) In all representing, to be co-present before-hand as unifying; (2) in this pregiving of unity, to be dependent at the same time on affection. Apperception thus understood is "the highest point at which one must attach . . . the whole of logic." Kant does not say: to which one must attach it. In that case, all of logic would be only belatedly hung on to something that would subsist without this "logic." Transcendental apperception, rather, is the "highest point at which" logic as a whole, as such, is already attached and hanging, which point it fulfills in that its whole essence depends upon transcendental apperception, and this is why it must be thought of in terms of this origin and only so.

And what does this "after it" in the text mean? It does not mean that all logic, of itself, is of a higher order than transcendental philosophy, but rather: not until and only if all logic remains ordered into the place of transcendental apperception can it function within the critical ontology related to the given of sensuous intuition, that is to say, as the guiding thread of the determination of the concepts (categories) and the basic principles of the being of beings. It is this way because "the first pure cognition pertaining to the understanding [i.e., the decisive stamping of the being of beings] is the principle of the original *synthetic* unity of apperception" (§17, B 137). Accordingly, this principle is a unifying one, and the "unity" is no mere being together; rather, it is unifying-gathering, λόγος in the original sense, but transferred to and relocated in the I-subject. This λόγος holds "all logic" in its custody.

Kant gives the name transcendental philosophy to the ontology that, as a result of the transformation effected by the *Critique of Pure Reason*, considers the being of beings as the objectivity of the [290] object of experience. Transcendental philosophy has its ground in logic. The logic, however, is no longer formal logic, but the logic determined by the original synthetic unity of transcendental apperception. In such logic ontology is grounded. This confirms what we have already said: Being and existence are determined by their relationship to the use of the understanding.

Even now the main title for the interpretation of the being of beings is still: "Being and Thought." But the legitimate use of the understanding depends on the following: that thinking continues to be specified as representational thinking that posits and judges – i.e., as positing and proposition by virtue of transcendental apperception, and that thinking remains related to affection by the senses. Thinking is ensconced in human subjectivity, which is affected by sensibility, i.e., is finite. "I think" means: I connect a sensuously given manifold of representations by virtue of a prior glance toward the unity of apperception, which articulates itself into the limited multiplicity of pure concepts of the understanding, i.e., categories.

At one with the critical unfolding of the essence of the understanding is the limitation of its use, namely, its being limited to the determination of that which is given through sensuous intuition and its pure forms. Conversely, the restriction of the use of the understanding to experience opens the way at the same time to a more primordial determination of the essence of the understanding itself. What is posited in positing is what is posited of a given, which, for its part, becomes for the positing, by means of such positing and placing, something placed opposite and standing over against us, something thrown over against us [*Entgegengeworfenen*], i.e., an object [*Objekt*]. The positedness (positing), i.e., being, changes into objectness [*Gegenständigkeit*]. Even though Kant still speaks of "things" in the *Critique of Pure Reason*, as, for example, in the affirmative assertion of his thesis on being, "thing" always means: *Gegen-stand*, ob-ject in the broadest sense of something represented, of an "X." Accordingly, Kant says in the Preface to the second edition of the *Critique of Pure Reason* (B XXVII) that the critique [291] "teaches that the object is to be taken in *a twofold sense*, namely as appearance and as thing in itself."

The *Critique* divides (A 235, B 294) "all objects whatever into phenomena and noumena." These latter are divided into noumena in the negative and noumena in the positive sense. Whatever in general the pure understanding, i.e., without relation to sensibility, represents, but does not and cannot know, serves as the X that is only thought of as underlying the appearing object. The noumenon in the positive sense, i.e., the nonsensuous object intended as in itself, e.g., God, remains closed to our theoretical cognition since we have at our disposal no nonsensuous intuition for which the object in itself could be immediately present.

The *Critique* does not abandon the determination of being as positing nor even the concept of being in general. It is therefore an error of Neo-Kantianism, still being felt today, to say that through Kant's philosophy the concept of being is, as one says, "resolved." The age-old prevailing meaning of being (constant presence) not only is preserved in Kant's critical interpretation of being as the objectness of the object of experience, but even reappears in an exceptional form in the definition of "objectness," while the interpretation of being as the substantiality of substance, which otherwise prevails in the history of philosophy, virtually covers it up or even disguises it. Kant, however, defines "substantial" entirely in the sense of the critical interpretation of being as objectness: The substantial means nothing other

than the concept of object in general, which subsists in so far as we think in it merely the transcendental subject apart from all predicates. (A 414, B 441)

Let it be suggested at this point that we will do well to understand the words *"Gegen-stand"* and "ob-ject" in Kant's language literally as well, insofar as the relation to the [292] thinking I-subject resonates in them, from which relation being as positing receives its meaning.

Since from the side of transcendental apperception in its relation to sense impressions, the essence of positing is determined as objective proposition, as an objective statement of judgment, the "highest point" of thought, i.e., the possibility of the understanding itself, must also prove to be the ground [*Grund*] of all possible statements, and thus to be *the fundamental principle* [Grundsatz]. And so the title to §17 (B 136) reads: *The Fundamental Principle of the Synthetic Unity of Apperception Is the Supreme Principle of All Employment of the Understanding.*

Accordingly, the systematic interpretation of the being of beings, i.e., of the objectivity of the object of experience, can be stated only in fundamental principles. This situation affords the basis for the fact that through Hegel, and via Fichte and Schelling, "the science of logic" becomes dialectic, a movement of principles circling within themselves that is itself the absoluteness of being. Kant introduces the "Systematic Representation of All Synthetic Principles" of pure understanding with the following statement (A 158/59, B 197/98):

That there should be principles at all is entirely due to the pure understanding. Not only is it the faculty of rules in respect of that which happens, but it is itself the source of principles according to which everything (that can be presented to us only as an object) must conform to rules. For without such rules appearances would never yield knowledge of an object corresponding to them.

Those principles that expressly "explain" the modalities of being are called, according to Kant, "the postulates of empirical thought in general." Kant expressly remarks that the "designations" for the four groups in the "Table of Principles" (namely, "*Axioms* of Intuition," "*Anticipations* of Perception," "*Analogies* of Experience," "*Postulates* of Empirical Thought in General") were "chosen with care, [293] so as not to leave unnoticed the differences with regard to the evidence and the exercise of these principles" (A 161, B 200). We must limit ourselves now to characterizing only the fourth group, "the postulates," and, moreover, with the single intent of allowing us to see how in these principles the guiding concept of being as positing shows through.

We shall postpone clarification of the title "postulates" but shall remind ourselves that this title occurs again at the highest point of Kant's metaphysics proper, where it is a question of the postulates of practical reason.

Postulates are requirements. Who or what requires and for what? As "the postulates of empirical thought in general" they are required by this thought itself, from its source, from the essence of the understanding, and are, indeed, required for making possible the positing of that which sensuous perception provides, and thus for making possible the interconnecting of existence, i.e., of the actuality of the manifold of appearances. Anything actual is at any given time something actual that is possible; and that it is something actual ultimately points back to something necessary. "The postulates of empirical thought in general" are the principles by which being possible, being actual, or being necessary are explained, insofar as the existence of the object of experience is determined by them.

The first postulate reads: "That which agrees with the formal conditions of experience (in accordance with intuition and concepts) is *possible.*"

The second postulate reads: "That which is bound up with the material conditions of experience (with sensation) is *actual.*"

The third postulate reads: "That which in its connection with the actual is determined in accordance with universal conditions of experience, is (that is, exists as) *necessary.*"

[294] We shall not presume, at the first attempt, to understand the content of these principles with complete clarity. Nevertheless, we are already prepared for a first understanding, and this, indeed, by means of that which Kant explains about being in the negative assertion of his thesis: "*Being is obviously not a real predicate.*" This means: Being, and therefore also the modes of being – being possible, being actual, being necessary – do not say anything about *what* the *Gegenstand,* the object, is, but rather about *how* the object is related to the subject. With respect to this "how" the so-called concepts of being are called "modalities." Kant himself begins his clarification of the "postulates" with the following statement:

The categories of modality have the peculiarity that, in determining an object, they do not in the least enlarge the concept [namely, that of the subject of the sentence] to which they are attached as predicates. They only express the relation to our faculty of cognition. (A 219, B 266)

Once again let us note: Kant now no longer explains being and existence in terms of the relation to the faculty of *understanding* but rather in terms of the relationship to the faculty of *cognition,* i.e., of course, to the understanding, to the power of judgment, but in such a way that this latter gets its determination through its relation to experience (sensation). Being, to be sure, remains position, but drawn into the relationship to affection. In the predicates of being possible, being actual, and being necessary there lies a "determination of the object" – only, however, a "certain" determination, insofar as something is stated about the object in itself, about it as object – namely, with regard to its objectivity, i.e., its standing-over-against-ness [*Gegenständigkeit*], with regard to the existence peculiar to it, but not with regard to its reality, i.e., its substantiality [*Sachheit*]. For the critical-transcendental interpretation of the being of beings, the precritical thesis that being is "not a predicate at all" is no longer valid. Being, as being possible, being actual, being necessary, is not, to be sure, a real (ontic) predicate, but it is a transcendental (ontological) predicate.

[295] Now for the first time we understand the initially strange wording that Kant uses in the affirmative assertion of his thesis in the text of the *Critique of Pure Reason:* "Being ... is merely the positing of a thing or of certain determinations in and of themselves." "Thing" means now, according to the language of the *Critique,* object or *Gegenstand.* The "certain" determinations of the object as the object of the cognition are the

non-real ones, the modalities of being. As these, they are positings. To what extent this is accurate must become evident from the content of the three postulates of empirical thought in general.

We now attend only to this: that and how in Kant's interpretation of the modes of being, being is thought of as positing.

The being possible of an object consists in the positedness of something in such a way that this latter *"agrees with"* what is given in the pure forms of intuition, i.e., space and time, and is, as thus given, capable of being determined according to the pure forms of thought, i.e., the categories.

The being actual of an object is the positedness of something possible in such a way that what is posited *"coheres with"* sensuous perception.

The being necessary of an object is the positedness of what *"is connected with"* the actual according to general laws of experience.

Possibility is: agreement with . . . ; Actuality is: coherence with . . . ; Necessity is: connection with . . .

In each of the modalities there prevails the positing of a relationship – different in each instance – to that which is requisite for the existence of an object of experience. *The modalities are predicates of the relationship required in each instance.* The principles that these predicates explain require that which is requisite for the possible, actual, or necessary existence of an object. For that reason Kant calls these principles *postulates.* They are postulates of thought in the twofold sense that the requirements stem *from* the understanding [296] as the source of thought and also are at the same time valid *for* thought, insofar as it is supposed by means of its categories to determine what is given in experience as an existing object. "Postulates of empirical thought in general" – this "in general" means: though the postulates are not named in the Table of Principles of pure understanding until the fourth and last place, they are the first in rank, insofar as every judgment about an object of experience must from the outset satisfy them.

The postulates name that which is requisite in advance for the positing of an object of experience. The postulates name the being that belongs to the existence of that entity which, as appearance, is an object for the cognizing subject. Kant's thesis about being holds good; being is "merely the positing." But the thesis now shows a richer content. The "merely" means the pure relationship of the objectivity of objects to the subjectivity of human cognition. Possibility, actuality, necessity are positings of different modes of this relationship. The different ways of being posited are determined by the source of the original positing. This is the pure synthesis of transcendental apperception; and this synthesis is the primal act of cognitive thought.

Because being is no *real* predicate, but is nevertheless a predicate and therefore is attributed to the object, and yet cannot be elicited from the substantial content of the object, the ontological predicates of modality cannot stem from the object, but rather must, as modes of positing, have their origin in subjectivity. Positing and its modalities of existence are determined from the side of thought. Thus, there hovers unexpressed over Kant's thesis about being the heading: *Being and Thought*.

In the "Explanation" of the postulates and, before that already, in the presentation of the Table of Categories, Kant distinguishes possibility, actuality, and necessity without its being said, or even asked wherein the basis for the distinction between being possible and being actual might lie.

[297] Not until ten years after the *Critique of Pure Reason*, toward the end of his third main work, the *Critique of Judgment* (1790), does Kant touch upon this question, and then quite "episodically," in §76, which bears the heading, "Remark." Five years later, the twenty-year-old Schelling, in his first work, "On the Ego as the Principle of Philosophy; or, Concerning the Unconditional in Human Knowledge" (1795), ended the concluding remark of his work with the following statement:

But never, perhaps, have so many profound thoughts been compressed into so few pages as has happened in the *Critique of Teleological Judgment*, §76. (*Philosophische Schriften*, vol. I [1809], p. 114. *Werke* I, 242)

Because what Schelling says here hits the mark, we must not pretend to think through this §76 adequately. According to the intention of this presentation, the task is only to bring into view how Kant, even in the assertion about being now referred to, holds to the guiding determination of being as positing. Kant says,

The reason [for the distinction –] which is unavoidably necessary to the human understanding [– between the possibility and the actuality of things] lies in the subject and in the nature of its cognitive faculties.

For the exercise of these faculties there are for us human beings "two quite heterogenous factors ... required." To what extent? Understanding and sensuous intuition are quite different in kind; the former is requisite "for concepts," the latter "for objects that correspond to them." Our understanding is never capable of giving us an object. Our sensuous intuition, on the other hand, is not capable of positing as an object in its objectivity that which is given by it. Taken by itself, our understanding can, by means of its concepts, think of an object solely in its possibility. In order to recognize the object as actual, affection through the senses is required. [298] What was just remarked will help us to understand the following decisive statement of Kant's:

Now the whole distinction which we draw between the merely possible and the actual rests upon the fact that possibility signifies only the positing of the representation of a thing relative to our concept, and, in general, to our capacity of thinking, whereas actuality signifies the positing of a thing in itself (apart from this concept).

From Kant's own words we conclude: possibility and actuality are different modes of positing. The differentiation of them is unavoidable for us humans, because the substantiality of an object, its reality, is objective for us only if objectivity as sensuously given is determined by the understanding and if, conversely, that which is to be determined by the understanding is given to it.

Kant uses the title "objective reality," that is, the substantiality posited as an object, for the being of those beings that are accessible to us as objects of experience. Accordingly, Kant says in another decisive place in the *Critique of Pure Reason*:

If knowledge is to have objective reality, that is, if it is to relate to an object, and is to acquire meaning and significance in respect to it, the object must be capable of being in some manner given. (A 155, B 194)

Through the reference to the basis and the inevitability of the distinction between possibility and actuality, it becomes clear that in the essence of the being of beings, in positing, the articulation of the necessary difference between possibility and actuality prevails. With this glimpse of the basis of the articulation of being, the most Kant can say about being seems to be achieved. So it seems, indeed, when we are on the lookout for results instead of following Kant's path.

In the determination of being, however, Kant takes yet a further step, and this again only by way of an intimation, [299] so that he does not achieve a systematic presentation of being as positing. This does not mean a shortcoming from the viewpoint of Kant's work, because the episodic statements about being as positing belong to the style of his work.

We can make clear to ourselves what is unavoidable in Kant's ultimate step by the following reflection. Kant calls his statements about being "explanation" and "elucidation." Both are supposed to make it possible to see clearly and purely what he means by being. Insofar as he determines it as "merely the positing," he understands being as coming from a delimited site, namely, from positing as an act of human subjectivity, i.e., of the human understanding that is dependent on the sensuously given. Tracing something back to its site [*Ort*] we call situating by discussion [*Erörterung*]. Explanation and elucidation are based in situating by discussion. Thereby we first discern the site, but the situational context is not yet visible, i.e., that in terms of which being as positing, i.e., such positing itself, is in its turn expressly determined.

Now, Kant attached an appendix at the close of the positive part of his interpretation of human experience of beings and its object, i.e., at the close of his critical ontology, under the title: "On the Amphiboly of Concepts of Reflection." Presumably this "Appendix" was inserted very late, perhaps only after completion of the *Critique of Pure Reason*. Seen as part of the history of philosophy, it presents Kant's encounter with Leibniz. Seen with regard to Kant's own thought, this "Appendix" contains a reflection back over the completed steps of thought and the dimension through which they passed. This retrospective reflection is itself a new step, the most extreme one that Kant executed in the interpretation of being. So far as this interpretation consists in restricting the use of the understanding to experience, the question it deals with concerns the limits of the understanding. That is why Kant says, in the "Remark" on this "Appendix" (A 280, B 336), that the discussion situating the concepts of reflection is "of great utility as a reliable method of determining and securing the limits of the understanding."

[300] The "Appendix" secures the safeguard by means of which Kant's *Critique of Pure Reason* makes secure human theoretical cognition over its whole range. Here, too, we must be content with an indication that is supposed to show only to what extent Kant in this "Appendix" draws the lines in the situational context of the site in which being as positing belongs. The interpretation of being as positing includes the fact that positing and positedness of the object are elucidated in terms of various relations to the power of cognition, i.e., in reference back to it, in bending back, in reflection. If, now, these various reflexive relationships are taken expressly as such into view and thereby compared with one another, then it becomes obvious that the interpretation of these relationships of reflection must proceed according to definite perspectives.

This consideration then aims "at the condition of the mind," i.e., at the human subject. The consideration no longer goes directly to the object of experience; it bends itself back toward the experiencing subject, it is reflection [*Reflexion*]. Kant speaks of "deliberation" [*"Überlegung"*]. If now reflection attends to those conditions and relationships of representational thinking by which, in general, the delimitation of the being of beings becomes possible, then reflection on the situational context in the site of being is a transcendental reflection. In conformity with this, Kant writes:

The act by which I confront the comparison of representations in general with the cognitive faculty to which it belongs, and by means of which I distinguish whether it is as belonging to the pure understanding or to sensible intuition that they are to be compared with each other, I call *transcendental reflection* [Überlegung]. (A 261, B 317)

In the elucidation of *being possible* as positing, the relationship to the formal conditions of experience came into play and therewith the concept of *form*. With the elucidation of *being actual*, the material conditions of experience were expressed and thereby the concept of *matter*. The [301] elucidation of the modalities of being as positing is accordingly accomplished with a view to the difference of matter and form. This distinction belongs to the situational context belonging to the site of being as positing.

Because the relationship of reflection is determined with the help of these concepts, they are called concepts of reflection. The manner whereby the concepts of reflection are determined, however, is itself a reflection. The ultimate determination of being as positing is accomplished for Kant in a reflection on reflection – therefore, in a distinctive manner of thought. This fact increases the justification for bringing Kant's reflection on being under the title "Being and Thought." The title seems to speak unequivocally. Nevertheless, something unclarified is concealed in it.

In the course of the clarification and substantiation of the distinction between possibility and actuality, it turned out that the positing of the actual proceeds out of the bare concept of the possible, out into the outside, over against the inside of the subjective condition of the subject. Hereby the differentiation of "inside" and "outside" comes into play. The "inside" refers to the intrinsic determinations of a thing that are forthcoming out of the understanding (*qualitas–quantitas*) in distinction to the "outside," i.e., the determinations that show themselves in the intuition of space and time as the extrinsic relations of things as appearances among one another. The difference between these concepts (concepts of reflection), and they themselves, are forthcoming for transcendental reflection.

Even before the transcendental concepts of reflection named, "matter and form," "inner and outer," Kant names "identity and difference," "agreement and opposition." Of the concepts of reflection, "matter and form," which are named in fourth and last place, he says, however:

These two concepts underlie all other reflection, so inseparably are they bound up with all employment of the understanding. [302] The one [matter] signifies the determinable in general, the other its determination. (A 266, B 322)

Even the mere enumerating of the concepts of reflection gives us hints for a more thorough understanding of Kant's thesis about being as positing. Positing shows itself in the joining of form and matter. This is explained as the difference between determining and the determinable, i.e., with regard to the spontaneity of the act of understanding in its relation to the receptivity of sensuous perception. In this discussion, being as positing is situated, i.e., is located in relation to the structure of human subjectivity as the site of its essential provenance.

The access to subjectivity is reflection. To the extent that reflection as transcendental does not aim directly at objects but at the relationship of the objectivity of objects to the subjectivity of the subject, and therefore to the extent that the theme of reflection in its turn, as the named relation-ship, is already a relating back to the thinking ego, the reflection by which Kant elucidates being as positing and situates it, proves to be a reflection on reflection, as a thinking of the thinking related to perception. The al-ready frequently mentioned heading for Kant's interpretation of being, the title "Being and Thought," speaks more clearly now in its richer content. Nevertheless, the heading still remains obscure in its decisive sense. For in its formula-like version an ambiguity is concealed that must be thought about if the title "Being and Thought" is supposed not only to characterize Kant's interpretation of being but also to name the fundamental trait that forms the process of the entire history of philosophy.

Before, in conclusion, we bring to light the ambiguity mentioned, it might be helpful if we show – even though only roughly – how, in Kant's interpretation of being as positing, the tradition speaks. Already from Kant's early work, *The Only Possible Ground of Proof for a Demonstration of the Existence of God*, we gather that the explanation of being takes place with regard to existence, because the "demonstration of the existence of God" is the theme under consideration. Instead of *Dasein*, [303] the language of metaphysics says also *Existenz*. It suffices to remind oneself of this word in order to recognize in the *sistere*, the setting [*Setzen*], the connection with the *ponere* and with positing; the *exsistentia* is the *actus, quo res sistitur, ponitur extra statum possibilitatis* (cf. Heidegger, *Nietzsche* [1961], vol. II, pp. 417ff.).

Of course, with such allusions we must give up the predominating in-strumental and calculative relationship to language and keep ourselves open for the broad, sustained power of its utterance coming from afar.

359

In the Spanish language, the word for being is *ser.* It is derived from *sedere*, to sit. We speak of *"Wohnsitz"* (residence). That means where living settles down. This settling down is a presence-at... Hölderlin would like "to sing the palatial seats of princes and their ancestors." Now, it would be foolish to maintain that the question about being can be dealt with by dissecting the meaning of words. But listening to the utterance of language can, with the necessary precautions and with due regard for the context of the utterance, give us hints toward the proper subject matter of thought.

Thought must ask: What, then, is called being, such that it can be determined by way of representational thinking as positing and positedness? That is a question that Kant does not ask, just as he does not ask the following ones: What, then, is called being, such that positing can be determined by the structure of form and matter? What, then, is called being, such that in the determination of the positedness of that which is posited, these occur in the twofold form of the subject, on the one hand as sentence-subject in relation to the predicate and on the other hand as ego-subject in relation to the object? What, then, is called being, such that it becomes determinable in terms of the *subiectum*, i.e., in Greek, the ὑποχείμενον? This is, because it is constantly present, that which already lies before us from the outset. Because being is determined as presence, a being is that which is lying there before us, ὑποχείμενον. Our relation to beings is that of letting them lie there, as a mode of laying, of *ponere*. This includes the possibility of setting and placing them. Because being is cleared as presence, [304] our relation to beings as that which is lying there can become one of laying, placing, setting before us [*Vorstellen*], and positing. Being, in the sense of enduring presencing, is dominant in Kant's thesis about being as positing, and also in the entire realm of his interpretation of the being of beings as objectivity and objective reality.

Being as purely a positing unfolds itself into the modalities. Beings are posited in being posited by the proposition, which is related to sensuous affection; i.e., it is posited by empirical judgment in the empirical use of the understanding in thinking thus determined. Being is elucidated and situated by virtue of its relationship to thought. Elucidation and situational discussion have the character of reflection, which becomes explicit as thought about thought.

What still remains unclear in the title "Being and Thought"? If we insert into this title the results of our presentation of Kant's thesis then we shall say positing instead of being, reflection of reflection instead of thought. Then the title "Being and Thought" means positing and reflection of reflection.

What stands here on both sides of the conjunction "and" has been elucidated as Kant meant it.

But what does the "and" mean in "Being and Thought"? We are not embarrassed for the answer and can easily dispose of the matter. We can readily appeal in this case to one of the oldest maxims of philosophy, the saying of Parmenides that goes, τὸ γὰρ αὐτὸ νοεῖν ἐστίν τε καὶ εἶναι. "For thinking and being are the same."

The relationship between thinking and being is sameness, identity. The title "Being and Thought" says, being and thought are identical. As if it were decided what identical means, as if the sense of identity lay at hand, and in particular, lay at hand right here in this distinctive "case" in respect of the relation between being and thought. Both are obviously nothing like things or objects between which one might, unchallenged, calculate this way or that. In no case does "identical" mean the same as "equal." Being *and* thought: [305] in this "and" lies concealed that which is worthy of thought, both for philosophy up to now and for present-day thinking.

But the presentation of the Kantian thesis has shown that being as positing is determined in terms of its relationship to the empirical use of the understanding. The "and" in the title suggests this relationship, which, according to Kant, has its foothold in thinking, i.e., in an activity of the human subject.

Of what sort is this relationship? The characterization of thinking as reflection of reflection gives us a hint, even if only an approximate, not to say misleading, one. Thought plays a double role: in the first place as reflection and then as reflection of reflection. But what does all this mean?

Given the assumption that the characterization of thinking as reflection suffices to specify the relation to being, then this means that thinking as simple positing provides the horizon within which such qualities as positedness and objectivity can be seen. The function of thought is to provide a horizon for the elucidation of being and of its modalities as positing.

Thinking as reflection of reflection means, on the other hand, the process whereby, and also the instrument and organon wherewith, being as glimpsed in the horizon of positedness is interpreted. Thinking as reflection means the horizon, thinking as reflection of reflection means the organon for the interpretation of the being of beings. In the title "Being and Thought," thinking remains essentially ambiguous in the indicated sense, and this holds for the entire history of Western thought.

But how would it be, now, if we take being in the sense of originary Greek thought, as the self-clearing and enduring presence of that which is for a while, not only and not in the first instance as positedness in being posited by the understanding? Can representational thought form the horizon for being in this its originary character? Obviously not, if self-clearing and enduring [306] presence differs indeed from positedness, even though this positedness may remain akin to that presence, because positedness owes to presence its essential provenance.

If that is so, must not also, then, the *kind* of interpretation of being, the manner of thinking, have a correspondingly different character? From ancient times the theory of thought has been called "logic." But if, now, thinking is ambiguous in its relation to being – as offering both a horizon and an organon – does not what we call "logic" also remain ambiguous, according to the view under discussion? Does not "logic," then, as organon and as interpretive horizon of being, become completely questionable? A reflection that presses in this direction does not turn itself against logic but occupies itself with making a sufficient determination of the λόγος, i.e., of that saying in which being brings itself to language as what is *singularly* thoughtworthy for thinking.

In the unobtrusive "is" lies concealed everything of being that is worthy of thought. But what is most worthy of thought therein remains, nevertheless, that we consider whether "being," whether the "is," can itself be, or whether being never "is" and it yet remains true that being is given.

But whence comes, to whom goes, the gift in the "being is given," and what is the manner of giving?

Being cannot *be*. Were it to be, it would no longer remain being but would become a being, an entity.

But does not the thinker who first gave thought to being, does not Parmenides say (Fragment 6): ἔστι γὰρ εἶναι, "there is, namely, being" – "there is present, namely, presencing"? If we consider that in the εἶναι, presencing, it is really revealing, Ἀλήθεια, that speaks, then the presencing that in the ἔστι is said emphatically of the εἶναι means *letting be present*. Being – is properly that which grants presence.

Is being, being that is, here passed off as some entity, or is being, τὸ αὐτό (the Same), here said καθ᾽ αὐτό, with reference to itself? Does a tautology speak here? Indeed. However, it is tautology in that highest sense, which says not nothing but everything: that which [307] originarily was and throughout the future will be decisive for thought. That is why this tautology conceals within it something unsaid, unthought, unquestioned. "There is present, namely, presencing."

What does presence mean here? The present? Where does the determination of such things come from? Does an unthought character of a concealed essence of time here show itself, or more exactly, conceal itself?

If that is the situation, then the question about being must come under the heading: "Being and Time."

And Kant's thesis about being as pure positing?

If positedness, objectivity, proves to be a modification of presence, then Kant's thesis about being belongs to that which remains unthought in all metaphysics.

The guiding title for the metaphysical determination of the being of beings, "Being and Thought," does not so much as pose the question of being, let alone find an answer.

Nevertheless, Kant's thesis about being as pure positing remains a peak from which a perspective reaches back to the determination of being as ὑποχεῖσθαι, and points forward toward the speculative-dialectical interpretation of being as Absolute Concept.

Notes

1 The dedication appears only in the *Gesamtausgabe*, not in the first edition of *Wegmarken*. (Ed.)

Comments on Karl Jaspers's Psychology of Worldviews

1 Page references are to the first edition of Jaspers's *Psychologie der Weltanschauungen* (1919). (Ed.)

2 In using the two German words for history (*Historie* and *Geschichte*) interchangeably throughout this essay, Heidegger does not clearly distinguish them, as he does later in his 1925 Kassel lectures on Dilthey and in his *Being and Time*, where the former term is reserved for the discipline of "historiography," and the latter for the more original happening of "history." For the sake of economy, I have translated both terms and their variants without indicating which German term is being employed at the time. (Trans.)

3 In this early essay, Heidegger is already using *"Dasein"* as a central term. Thus, following John Macquarrie and Edward Robinson's translation of Heidegger's *Being and Time*, I have adopted the German term in my translation. However, since Heidegger plays on the literal meaning of the noun "Dasein" as "being there," and that of the verb "dasein" as "to be there," I have often also used the English translation, "existence or being there," or simply "being there." (Trans.)

Phenomenology and Theology

1 First published in *The Piety of Thinking*, translated with notes and commentary by James G. Hart and John C. Maraldo (Bloomington: Indiana University Press, 1976). Present version revised and edited by James G. Hart, John C. Maraldo, and William McNeill.

2 All theological concepts of existence that are centered on faith intend a specific *transition* of existence, in which pre-Christian and Christian existence are united in their own way. This transitional character is what motivates the multidimensionality of theological concepts – a feature we cannot examine more closely here.

3 Cf. *Being and Time*, Division Two, §58.

4   It should not require extensive discussion to show that it is a matter here of a basic
    (existential) confrontation of two possibilities of existence that does not exclude,
    but *includes*, an in each case factical, existentiell, and reciprocal acknowledgment
    and earnestness.

From the Last Marburg Lecture Course

1   Edited and revised by William McNeill. Translation adopted in part from *The
    Metaphysical Foundations of Logic*, translated by Michael Heim (Bloomington:
    Indiana University Press, 1984). Where translations of French or Latin are
    given in brackets they have been provided by the translator and do not appear
    in the German text.
2   Throughout the text, Heidegger's references are identified as follows:
    E.   Joh. Ed. Erdmann, *Leibnitii Opera Philosophica quae extant Latina, Gallica,
    Germanica Omnia*, 2 vols., Berlin, 1840.
    G.   C. I. Gerhardt, *Die philosophischen Schriften von Gottfried Wilhelm Leibniz*,
    7 vols., Berlin, 1875–90.
    B.   A. Buchenau, translator, *G. W. Leibniz, Hauptschriften zur Grundlegung der
    Philosophie*, edited by E. Cassirer, 2 vols. (Philosophische Bibliothek, vols.
    107 and 108), Leipzig, 1904–6.
    S.   H. Schmalenbach, *Leibniz* (Munich: Dreimasken Verlag, 1921).
3   *Leibnizens Mathematische Schriften*, ed. C. I. Gerhardt, 7 volumes (in 8) (Berlin
    and Halle, 1849–63) [reprint, Hildesheim, 1962].
4   In translations of German philosophy the customary rendering of *Vorstellung* is
    "(mental) representation," though sometimes "notion" or "idea" is also used. In
    discussing the monad's mode of apprehension, however, Heidegger plays on the
    temporal, out-stretching meaning of *vor-stellend* and thus suggests the necessity
    of a different English translation. To "pre-hend" does not share the same root
    meaning as *stellen* (to place) but derives from the Latin *prendere* (to grasp, reach).
    "Prehension" is nevertheless connected with "apprehension" and has enjoyed
    a felicitous usage in the English-language philosophy influenced by Leibniz,
    namely in the speculative thought of Alfred North Whitehead. (Trans.)

What Is Metaphysics?

1   Originally published in *Martin Heidegger: Basic Writings*, ed. David Farrell Krell
    (2nd, revised and expanded edition) (New York: HarperCollins, 1993), pp. 93–
    110. Present version edited and revised by David Farrell Krell and William
    McNeill.
2   The words "whether explicitly or not" (*ob ausdrücklich oder nicht*) are an addi-
    tion to the *Gesamtausgabe* edition. They do not appear in the first edition of
    Wegmarken. (Ed.)
3   The words "it seems" (*wie es scheint*) do not appear in the first edition of
    Wegmarken. (Ed.)
4   The first edition of *Wegmarken* reads: "In a familiar phrase . . .". (Ed.)

On the Essence of Ground

1 An existing translation by Terrence Malick, *The Essence of Reasons* (Evanston: Northwestern University Press, 1969), has been consulted throughout. In certain instances, I have gratefully adopted, or adapted, Malick's translation. Where translations of French, Latin, or Greek are given in brackets they have been provided by the translator and do not appear in the German text. Translations from the Latin that appear in brackets have been adopted, with minor alterations, from the Malick translation.

2 *Metaphysics* V, 1, 1013 a17ff.

3 Ibid., V, 2, 1013 b16ff.

4 Ibid., I, 7, 988 b16ff.

5 The German *Grund* means both "ground" and "reason"; thus, *der Satz vom Grund* (or the more archaic *Satz vom Grunde*) is usually translated as the "principle of reason" or "principle of sufficient reason." I have generally rendered it as "principle of reason." Part of Heidegger's argument will be that ground as *ratio* or λόγος is derivative upon the more primary sense of being (*Sein*) itself as ground. (Trans.)

6 *Dissertatio philosophica de usu et limitibus principii rationis determinantis vulgo sufficientis.* Cf. *Opuscula philosophico-theologica antea seorsum edita nunc secundis curis revisa et copiose aucta* (Lipsiae, 1750), pp. 152ff.

7 *Über die vierfache Wurzel des Satzes vom zureichenden Grunde.* Second edition (1847); third edition edited by Jul. Frauenstädt (1864).

8 *Principiorum primorum cognitionis metaphysicae nova dilucidatio* (1755).

9 *Über eine Entdeckung, nach der alle neue Kritik der reinen Vernunft durch eine ältere entbehrlich gemacht werden soll* (1790).

10 Cf. pp. 106f.

11 *Philosophische Untersuchungen über das Wesen der menschlichen Freiheit und die damit zusammenhängenden Gegenstände. Werke,* I. Abt., Bd. 7, pp. 333–416.

12 The first edition of *Wegmarken* has *vulgäre,* "ordinary," rather than *gewöhnliche,* "usual," "habitual," "customary." (Trans.)

13 Cf. *Opuscules et fragments inédits de Leibniz,* ed. L. Couturat (1903), pp. 518ff. Cf. also *Revue de Métaphysique et de Morale,* vol. X (1902), pp. 2ff. Couturat attributes a special significance to this treatise, since it supposedly provides him with definitive evidence for his own thesis "que la métaphysique de Leibniz repose toute entière sur la logique" ["that Leibniz's metaphysics is based entirely on logic"]. Although this treatise forms the basis for our following discussions, this does not indicate agreement with Couturat's interpretation of the treatise, nor with his view of Leibniz in general, nor indeed with his concept of logic. This treatise instead speaks most sharply *against* the *principium rationis* having its origin in logic; indeed, it speaks in general *against* the very question as to whether logic or metaphysics merits priority in Leibniz. The very possibility of such a question begins to vacillate precisely through Leibniz, and is first shattered in Kant, although here it does not issue in any further repercussions.

14 Cf. M. Heidegger, *Sein und Zeit* [*Being and Time*] I (*Jahrbuch für Philosophie und phänomenologische Forschung,* Bd. VIII, 1927), §44, pp. 212–230; on the assertion, cf. §33, pp. 154ff. (The pagination given agrees with the separate edition.)

15 Cf. ibid., §60, pp. 295ff.

16 On "finding oneself" [*Befindlichkeit*], cf. *Being and Time*, §29, pp. 134ff.

17 When "ontology" and "ontological" are today appealed to as catchwords and titles for various orientations, these expressions are employed in an utterly trivial manner that fails to appreciate any problematic whatsoever. One thrives on the erroneous opinion that ontology as the question concerning the being of beings means a "realistic" (naive or critical) "attitude" as opposed to an "idealistic" one. Ontological problematic has so little to do with "realism" that precisely Kant, in and through his *transcendental* way of questioning, was able to accomplish the first decisive step since Plato and Aristotle toward *explicitly* laying the ground for ontology. Defending the "reality of the outer world" is not yet an ontological orientation. "Ontological" – taken in its popular philosophical meaning – means, however (and this betrays the hopeless confusion), something that must instead be called ontic, i.e., a stance that lets *beings* in themselves be what and how they are. But this does not yet raise any *problem of being*, let alone attain the foundation for the possibility of an ontology.[a]

18 Cf. *Being and Time*, §69c, pp. 364ff.; also the note on p. 363.

19 Cf. Heidegger, *Kant und das Problem der Metaphysik* (1929). [Translated as *Kant and the Problem of Metaphysics* by Richard Taft (Bloomington: Indiana University Press, 1990).]

20 Cf. Kant, *Über eine Entdeckung, nach der alle neue Kritik der reinen Vernunft durch eine ältere entbehrlich gemacht werden soll* (1790), concluding appraisal of the three principal peculiarities of metaphysics in Leibniz. Cf. also the prize essay on the progress of metaphysics, Division I.

21 The words *der seiende Mensch*, "the human being that exists," do not appear in the first edition of *Wegmarken*. (Trans.)

22 Cf. K. Reinhardt, *Parmenides und die Geschichte der griechischen Philosophie* (1916), pp. 174ff. and p. 216 (note).

23 Cf. Diels, *Fragmente der Vorsokratiker:* Melissos, Fragment 7; and Parmenides, Fragment 2.

24 Ibid.: Anaxagoras, Fragment 8.

25 Ibid.: Heraclitus, Fragment 89.

26 Regarding the textual references in St. John's gospel, cf. the excursus on κόσμος in W. Bauer, *Das Johannesevangelium* (*Lietzmanns Handbuch zum Neuen Testament* 6), second, completely revised edition (1925), p. 18. On the theological interpretation, cf. the exceptional commentaries by A. Schlatter, *Die Theologie des Neuen Testaments*, Part II (1910), pp. 114ff.

27 Augustine, *Opera* (Migne), vol. IV, 1842.

28 Ibid., treatise II, chapter 1, no. 11 (vol. III, 1393).

29 Cf., e.g., *Summa theologica*, II/2, qu. CLXXXVIII, a 2, ad 3; *dupliciter aliquis potest esse in saeculo: uno modo per praesentiam corporalem, alio modo per mentis affectum.*

30 *Metaphysica* (ed. II, 1743), §354, p. 87.

[a] First edition, 1929: Furthermore, the task from the outset is not to produce or even to ground an "ontology," but to reach the truth of beyng, i.e., to be reached by it – history of beyng itself, not the demand for philosophical erudition, hence *being* and time.

31 *Entwurf der notwendigen Vernunft-Wahrheiten, wiefern sie den zufälligen entgegengesetzet werden* (Leipzig, 1745), §350, p. 657.

32 Ibid., §349, pp. 654ff.

33 Ibid., §348, p. 653.

34 Cf. on this *Kant und das Problem der Metaphysik* (1929).

35 *De mundi sensibilis atque intelligibilis forma et principiis, Sectio I. De notione mundi generatim.* §§1, 2.

36 Cf. *Critique of Pure Reason*, A 568, B 596.

37 Ibid., A 832, B 860.

38 Ibid., A 328, B 384.

39 Ibid., A 327, B 384.

40 Ibid., A 310, B 367; also A 333, B 390.

41 Ibid., A 322, B 379. On the classification of the "idea" as a particular "kind of representation" in the "serial arrangement" of representations, cf. A 320, B 376f.

42 Ibid., A 334, B 391.

43 *Was heißt: sich im Denken orientieren?* (1786). *Werke* (Cassirer) IV, p. 355.

44 *Critique of Pure Reason*, A 407f., B 434.

45 "In the application of pure concepts of understanding to possible experience, the employment of their synthesis is either *mathematical* or *dynamical*; for they are concerned partly with the mere *intuition* of an appearance in general, partly with its *existence*." (Ibid., A 160, B 199.) With regard to the corresponding division of the "principles," Kant states: "But it should be noted that we are as little concerned in the one case with the principles of mathematics as in the other with the principles of general (physical) dynamics. We treat only of the principles of pure understanding in their relation to inner sense (all differences among the given representations being ignored). It is through these principles of pure understanding that the special principles of mathematics and of dynamics become possible. I have named them, therefore, on account rather of their application than of their content..." (Ibid., A 162, B 302.) Cf. in relation precisely to a more radical problematic of the concept of world and of beings as a whole the distinction between the mathematical sublime and the dynamical sublime. (*Critique of Judgment*, especially §28.)

46 Ibid., A 419ff., B 446ff.

47 Ibid.

48 Ibid., A 572, B 600 (note).

49 *Anthropologie in pragmatischer Hinsicht abgefaßt* (1800), 2nd edition, Preface. *Werke* (Cassirer) VIII, p. 3.

50 Ibid., p. 4.

51 Ibid. "A man of the world is a participator in the great game of life." "*Man of the world* means knowing one's relations to other human beings and how things go in human life." "*To have class [world]* means to have maxims and to emulate great examples. It comes from the French. One attains one's end through *conduite*, morals, dealings etc." (Lecture on Anthropology.) Cf. *Die philosophischen Hauptvorlesungen I. Kants. Nach den neuaufgefundenen Kolleghesten des Grafen Heinrich zu Dohna-Wundlacken.* Edited by A. Kowalewski (1924), p. 71.

52 Cf. *Grundlegung zur Metaphysik der Sitten. Werke* (Cassirer) IV, p. 273 (note).

53 Ibid., p. 274 (note).

54 Cf. p. 72 of the Anthropology Lecture cited in note 51.

55 *Critique of Pure Reason*, A 839, B 867f. Cf. also *Logik* (ed. G. B. Jäsche), Introduction, Part III.

56 Ibid., A 569, B 597.

57 Ibid., A 840, B 868 (note).

58 In the present context we can neither develop nor indeed answer the following questions: (1) To what extent does something like "Weltanschauung" belong necessarily to the essence of Dasein as being-in-the-world? (2) In what manner must the essence of Weltanschauung be delimited in general and grounded in terms of its intrinsic possibility with respect to the transcendence of Dasein? (3) How, in accordance with its transcendental character, does Weltanschauung relate to philosophy?

59 If indeed one identifies the ontic contexture of items of utility, or equipment, with world and interprets being-in-the-world as dealing with items of utility, then there is certainly no prospect of any understanding of transcendence as being-in-the-world in the sense of a "fundamental constitution of Dasein."

The ontological structure of beings in our "environing world" – insofar as they are discovered as equipment – does, however, have the advantage, in terms of an *initial characterization* of the phenomenon of world, of leading over into an analysis of this phenomenon[a] and of preparing the transcendental problem of world. And this is also the *sole* intent – an intent indicated clearly enough in the structuring and layout of §§14–24 of *Being and Time* – of the analysis of the environing world, an analysis that as a whole, and considered with regard to the *leading goal*, remains of subordinate significance.

Yet if nature is apparently missing – not only nature as an object of natural science, but also nature in an originary sense (cf. *Being and Time*, p. 65 below) – in this orientation of the analytic of Dasein, then there are reasons for this. The decisive reason lies in the fact that nature does not let itself be encountered either within the sphere of the environing world, nor in general primarily as something *toward which* we *comport* ourselves. Nature is originally manifest in Dasein through Dasein's existing as finding itself attuned *in the midst of* beings. But insofar as finding oneself [*Befindlichkeit*] (thrownness) belongs to the essence of Dasein, and comes to be expressed in the unity of the full concept of *care*, it is only here that the *basis* for the *problem* of nature can first be attained.

60 The German *zeitigen* is used in *Being and Time* to designate the "temporalizing" of Dasein as ecstatic temporality. Its more conventional usage implies maturation, flourishing, arising. Thus, the present usage suggests that Dasein's selfhood first comes into being in and through a temporalizing. (Trans.)

61 The words "i.e., belongs to Dasein" (*d.h. daseinszugehörig*) do not appear in the first edition of *Wegmarken*. (Trans.)

---

[a] First edition, 1929: And indeed in such a way that the manner in which the concept of world is grasped avoids from the outset the path of *ens creatum* taken by the traditional, ontic metaphysics of nature.

62 The ontological interpretation of Dasein as being-in-the-world decides neither positively nor negatively concerning a possible being toward God. Presumably, however, the elucidation of transcendence first achieves an *adequate concept* of *Dasein*, and with respect to this being it can then be *asked* how things stand ontologically concerning the relation of Dasein to God.

63 *Republic* VI, 509 B.

64 This parenthetical addition is not found in the first edition of *Wegmarken*. (Trans.)

65 Ibid., 509 A.

66 Here we may be permitted to point out that what has been published so far of the investigations on "Being and Time" has no other task than that of a concrete projection unveiling *transcendence* (cf. §§12–83; especially §69). This in turn occurs for the purpose of enabling the *sole* guiding intention, clearly indicated in the *title* of the *whole* of Part I, of attaining the "*transcendental* horizon of the *question* concerning being." All concrete interpretations, above all that of time, are to be evaluated *solely* in the perspective of *enabling* the *question* of being. They have as little to do with modern "dialectical theology" as with medieval Scholasticism.

   If Dasein is here interpreted as that being that in general can pose such a thing as a problem of being as belonging to its existence, then this does *not* mean that this being, which *as Dasein* can exist authentically and inauthentically, is *the* "authentic" being *in general* among all other beings, so that the latter would be only a shadow of the former. Quite on the contrary, the illumination of transcendence is meant to attain *that* horizon within which the concept of being – including the "natural" concept that is often appealed to – can first be philosophically grounded *as a concept*. Ontological interpretation of being in and from out of the transcendence of Dasein does not, however, mean ontic derivation of the sum-total of non-Dasein-like beings from this being qua Dasein.

   As regards the reproach – which is connected with such misinterpretation – of an "anthropocentric standpoint" in *Being and Time*, this objection that is now passed all too readily from hand to hand says nothing so long as one omits to think through the approach, the *entire thrust*, and the *goal* of the development of the problem in *Being and Time* and to comprehend how, precisely through the elaboration of the transcendence of Dasein, "the human being" comes into the "center" in such a way that his nothingness amid beings as a whole can and must become a *problem* in the first place. What dangers are entailed, then, by an "anthropocentric standpoint" that precisely puts its *entire* effort *solely* into showing that the *essence* of Dasein that there stands "at the center" is ecstatic, i.e., "*excentric,*" yet that therefore, in addition, the alleged freedom from any standpoint, which is contrary to the entire meaning of philosophizing as an essentially *finite* possibility of existing, is a delusion? Cf. here the interpretation of the ecstatic-horizonal structure of time as temporality in *Being and Time*, Part I, pp. 316–438.

67 In the present investigation, the Temporal [*temporale*] interpretation of transcendence is intentionally set aside throughout.

68 The first edition of *Wegmarken* simply reads: "as a being" (*als Seiendes*), rather than "as the being that it is" (*als das Seiende, das es ist*). (Trans.)

69   Both the first edition of *Wegmarken* and the *Gesamtausgabe* edition here read "*als dem Entwurf von* Möglichkeit seiner selbst." This appears to be an error. The original publication, in the *Festschrift Edmund Husserl* (1929), reads "*als dem Entwurf von* Möglichkeiten seiner selbst." Here, I have kept to the text of the *Festschrift* and rendered "possibility" in the plural. (Trans.)

On the Essence of Truth

1   Originally published in *Martin Heidegger: Basic Writings*, edited by David Farrell Krell (2nd revised and expanded edition) (New York: HarperCollins, 1993), pp. 115–38. Present version edited and revised by John Sallis and William McNeill.

2   Throughout the translation *das Seiende* is rendered as "being" or "beings," *ein Seiendes* as "a being," *Sein* as "Being," *das Seiende im Ganzen* as "beings as a whole." (Trans.)

3   The first edition of *Wegmarken* reads: "it" (*Sie*); the *Gesamtausgabe* edition reads: "philosophy" (*Die Philosophie*). (Ed.)

4   In the *Gesamtausgabe* edition, the phrase "is thought to need no further special proof" (*bedarf keiner besonderen Begründung mehr*) has been altered to "is considered a foregone conclusion" (*hält man für ausgemacht*). (Ed.)

5   The first edition of *Wegmarken* includes the word *eben*, "indeed," after *Wahrheit*, "truth." The *eben* is deleted in the *Gesamtausgabe* edition. (Ed.)

6   The *Gesamtausgabe* edition here inserts the word *vielmehr*, "rather." (Ed.)

7   The text reads: "ein Offenbares *als ein solches.*" In ordinary German *offenbar* means "evident," "manifest." However, the context that it has here through its link with "open region" (*das Offene*), "open stance" (*Offenständigkeit*), and "openness" (*Offenheit*) already suggests the richer sense that the word has for Heidegger: that of something's being so opened up as to reveal itself, to be manifest (as, for example, a flower in bloom), in contrast to something's being so closed or sealed up within itself that it conceals itself. (Trans.)

8   The phrase "*as the correctness of a statement*" (als Richtigkeit der Aussage verstanden) is an addition to the *Gesamtausgabe* edition. It does not appear in the first edition of *Wegmarken*. (Ed.)

9   The words "i.e., unimpeded" (*d.h. unbehindert*) are an addition that does not appear in the first edition of *Wegmarken*. (Ed.)

10   This variant of the word *Existenz* indicates the ecstatic character of freedom, its standing outside itself. (Trans.)

11   The *Gesamtausgabe* edition adds the words "i.e., openness" (*d.h. die Offenheit*) at this point. They do not appear in the first edition of *Wegmarken*. (Ed.)

12   The text reads, "*Die Gestimmtheit (Stimmung)...*" *Stimmung* refers not only to the kind of attunement that a musical instrument receives by being tuned but also to the kind of attunement that constitutes a mood or a disposition of Dasein. The important etymological connection between *Stimmung* and the various formations based on *stimmen* (to accord) is not retained in the translation. (Trans.)

13 "Resolutely open bearing" seeks to translate *das entschlossene Verhältnis*. *Entschlossen* is usually rendered as "resolute," but such a translation fails to retain the word's structural relation to *verschlossen*, "closed" or "shut up." Significantly, this connection is what makes it possible for Heidegger to transform the sense of the word: he takes the prefix as a privation rather than as indicating establishment of the condition designated by the word to which it is affixed. Thus, as the text here makes quite clear, *entschlossen* signifies just the opposite of that kind of "resolve" in which one makes up one's mind in such fashion as to close off all other possibilities: it is rather a kind of keeping *un-closed*. (Trans.)

14 "To err" may translate *irren* only if it is understood in its root sense derived from the Latin *errare*, "to wander from the right way," and only secondarily in the sense "to fall into error." (Trans.)

Plato's Doctrine of Truth

1 Revised and edited by Thomas Sheehan and William McNeill. A previous translation exists by John Barlow, in *Philosophy in the Twentieth Century*, ed. William Barrett and Henry D. Aiken (New York: Random House, 1962), vol. 3, pp. 251–70.

2 Heidegger appears to use the J. Burnet text of the *Republic*, published by Oxford University Press. (Trans.)

3 The Greek, μὰ Δί᾽ οὐκ ἔγωγ᾽, ἔφη, more literally would be: " 'By Zeus, not I,' he said." (There are only so many ways one can express agreement in a Platonic dialogue.) (Trans.)

4 *Einsichtslosigkeit*: ἀφροσύνη. (Trans.)

5 Literally: "to turn his neck around" (*den Hals umzuwenden*, περιάγειν τὸν αὐχένα). (Trans.)

6 Literally: "those who were chained with him in those days" (*der damals mit ihm Gefesselten*, τῶν τότε συνδεσμωτῶν). (Trans.)

7 More literally: ". . . is not the presenting foreground of ἀλήθεια." (Trans.)

On the Essence and Concept of Φύσις in Aristotle's Physics B, 1

1 Originally published in *Man and World*, vol. 9, no. 3 (August 1976), pp. 219–70. Present version edited and revised by Thomas Sheehan and William McNeill.

2 All parentheses in the translation are Heidegger's. However, *brackets* in the translation represent later interpolations that Heidegger made in his own 1939 text and that appear in the German as: /. . ./. The following are exceptions: (1) If brackets enclose German words, they are my own interpolations for sake of clarity. (2) If brackets appear within parentheses, they are Heidegger's. (3) In one instance (p. [349] *ad initium*) I print Heidegger's parentheses within brackets just as they appear in *Wegmarken*. (Trans.)

3 As in the original translation published in *Man and World*, I have from here on sectioned the text for the sake of clarity according to Roman numerals (I–XIX). Although this sectioning does not appear in the original German, I have retained it here since existing scholarship has used these divisions for the purpose of reference. (Trans.)

4 In the sense of an alteration, i.e., a "change over into something else." (Trans.)
5 The original version in *Il Pensiero* italicizes this entire phrase, including the words "and toward itself." (Trans.)
6 Cf. 193 a9, the beginning of section X. (Trans.)
7 See section XII. (Trans.)

Postscript to "What Is Metaphysics?"

1 The first publication of the "Postscript" (1943) was preceded by the epigraph: " 'Metaphysics,' like the word 'abstract' and almost that of 'thinking' too, is a word from which more or less everyone flees, as though fleeing someone with the plague." Hegel (1770–1831), *Werke* XVII, p. 400. [Neither this note, nor the epigraph itself, appears in the first edition of *Wegmarken*. (Trans.)]
2 An existing translation by Werner Brock in *Existence and Being* (Chicago: H. Regnery, 1949), pp. 349–61, and an unpublished translation by Ferit Güven have also been consulted.
3 The words "metaphysically speaking" (*metaphysisch gesprochen*) do not appear in the first edition of *Wegmarken*. (Trans.)
4 Fourth edition, 1943: "presumably." [a]
5 Fourth edition, 1943: "never, however."
6 ... *als die von jener Stimme gestimmte Stimmung.* Heidegger here plays on the proximity of the German word *Stimme*, meaning "voice," to *Stimmung*, "mood" or "attunement," and *stimmen*, to "attune." (Trans.)
7 Fourth edition, 1943: "Original thanking... [*Das ursprüngliche Danken*]."
8 Fourth edition, 1943: "... in which it [being] is cleared and lets come to pass the singular event:"
9 Fourth edition, 1943: "The speechless response of thanking in sacrifice...."
10 Fourth edition, 1943: "thanking."
11 Fourth edition, 1943: "thinking."
12 Fourth edition, 1943: "thoughtful recollection [*Andenken*]."

Letter on "Humanism"

1 Originally translated by Frank A. Capuzzi in collaboration with John Glenn Gray, edited by David Farrell Krell. Published in *Martin Heidegger: Basic Writings*, edited by David Farrell Krell (2nd, revised and expanded edition) (New York: HarperCollins, 1993), pp. 217–65. Present version edited and revised by William McNeill and David Farrell Krell.
2 The first edition of *Wegmarken* simply reads: "in the element of being." (Ed.)
3 The *Gesamtausgabe* edition alters the German word order in the final clause of this sentence compared to the first edition of *Wegmarken*. There is no difference in meaning. (Ed.)

[a] Fourth edition, 1943: Within the truth of being, beyng prevails as the essence of the difference; such beyng qua beyng, prior to the difference, is the event [*Ereignis*] and for this reason *without* beings.

Fifth edition, 1949: A prefiguring in terms of beyng qua event [*Ereignis*], but not understandable there (in the fourth edition).

4 The word "also" is an addition that does not appear in the first edition of *Wegmarken*. (Ed.)

5 The phrase "does not think being as such" (*denkt nicht das Sein als solches*) is added to the *Gesamtausgabe* edition, and does not appear in the first edition of *Wegmarken*. (Ed.)

6 The first edition of *Wegmarken* reads: "being itself" (*das Sein selbst*); the *Gesamtausgabe* edition reads: "being in each case" (*je Sein*). (Ed.)

7 The first edition of *Wegmarken* here simply reads: "and propriated." (Ed.)

8 The *Gesamtausgabe* edition here inserts the word *einmal*, "once"; this does not appear in the first edition of *Wegmarken*. (Ed.)

9 The first edition of *Wegmarken* reads: *Deus est suum esse*. (Ed.)

10 The first edition of *Wegmarken* reads: "from out of" (*aus*). (Ed.)

11 The first edition of *Wegmarken* does not place the "is" in quotation marks. (Ed.)

12 The word "essentially" (*wesenhaft*) is an addition to the *Gesamtausgabe* edition. It does not appear in the first edition of *Wegmarken*. (Ed.)

13 The first edition of *Wegmarken* here reads: *am weitesten*; the *Gesamtausgabe* reads: *am fernsten*. There is not much difference in meaning. (Ed.)

14 The phrase "than beings" is an addition to the *Gesamtausgabe* edition and does not appear in the first edition of *Wegmarken*. (Ed.)

15 The word "destined" (*geschicklich*) is an addition that does not appear in the first edition of *Wegmarken*. (Ed.)

16 The first edition of *Wegmarken* simply reads: "of the essence of being." (Ed.)

17 The first edition of *Wegmarken* reads: *als eines solchen*; the *Gesamtausgabe* edition reads: *als solchen*. There is little difference in meaning. (Ed.)

18 The first edition of *Wegmarken* reads: *im Wesensgang ... zurückfällt*, "is falling behind in the essential course ..."; the *Gesamtausgabe* edition reads: *hinter dem Wesensgang ... zurückfällt*, "is falling behind the essential course ...". (Ed.)

Introduction to "What Is Metaphysics?"

1 Originally published in *Existentialism from Dostoevsky to Sartre*, edited by Walter Kaufmann (New York: Meridian Books, 1956), Chapter 8. Present translation edited and revised by William McNeill.

2 The first edition of *Wegmarken* simply reads: "of metaphysics." (Ed.)

3 The first edition of *Wegmarken* reads: "which appears as beings" (*das als das Seiende erscheint*). (Ed.)

On the Question of Being

1 An existing translation by William Kluback and Jean T. Wilde, *The Question of Being* (New York: Twayne, 1958), has also been consulted.

2 Here, as in other essays, Heidegger frequently plays on the root of the word *Erörterung* ("discussion") to suggest a "locating" or "situating" of a "locale" (*Ort*) – here the locale of the critical line of nihilism. Cf. the usage of this word in "Phenomenology and Theology" and "Kant's Thesis about Being" in the present volume; also the "Preface to the German Edition." (Trans.)

3 The German word *Arbeit* might be better rendered as "labor" rather than "work," which is closer to *Werk* (as in a "work" of art, or a craft). Because modern usage often employs "work" and "labor" indiscriminately, however, especially with regard to the factory "worker," I have retained the latter term throughout. (Trans.)

4 The German *Wesen*, generally rendered as "essence," traditionally has the nominal sense of *essentia*, referring to the fundamental "whatness" or primary "substance" of something. For Heidegger, the word *Wesen* carries the verbal and temporal sense of being (*Sein*) as the essential unfolding and enduring presencing (*An-wesen*) of something. (Trans.)

5 *Ge-Stell* (sometimes written *Gestell*) is the term by which Heidegger designates the "essence" of modern technology. It is often translated as "enframing." See the essay *"Die Frage nach der Technik"* for further details (*Vorträge und Aufsätze* [5th ed.] [Pfullingen: Neske, 1985], pp. 9–40). [Translated as "The Question Concerning Technology," in *Martin Heidegger: The Question Concerning Technology and Other Essays*, trans. William Lovitt (New York: Harper & Row, 1977), pp. 3–35.] (Trans.)

6 The phrase *Verwindung der Metaphysik* is difficult to render into English. Heidegger uses the word *Verwindung* to suggest something other than a straightforward "overcoming" (*Überwindung*) that would be accomplished by human beings (or by human thinking as subjectivity), and that would simply leave behind it whatever is "overcome." *Verwindung* implies recovery in the sense that metaphysics itself, in its "essence," recovers from the oblivion of its own essence. As Heidegger goes on to clarify, it is not therefore to be taken as implying that human beings recover *from* metaphysics; nor is it human beings in the first instance who "recover" metaphysics in the sense of "retrieving" its essence. In the phrase "recovery of metaphysics," metaphysics is itself the "subject" of the genitive. Elsewhere, Heidegger explains that the *Verwindung* of the "essence of technology" in the direction of its as yet concealed truth "is similar to what happens when, in the human realm, one recovers from grief or pain." See *Die Kehre* (1949), *Gesamtausgabe*, vol. 79, p. 69 (translated by William Lovitt as "The Turning," in *The Question Concerning Technology*, p. 39). *Verwindung* does, therefore, imply an "overcoming," but what is overcome is not left behind or escaped. (Trans.)

7 The first edition of *Wegmarken* simply reads: "a surpassing of beings as such," (*der Überstieg über das Seiende als solches*). (Trans.)

8 In what follows, Heidegger plays on the literal sense of the German *es gibt*, "it gives." The phrase also carries its ordinary meaning, "there is." (Trans.)

Hegel and the Greeks

1 Edited and revised by John Sallis and William McNeill.

2 The phrase "through which the latter reaches completion" (*durch welches dieses sich vollendet*) does not appear in the first edition of *Wegmarken*. (Ed.)

3   So claims P. Friedländer, *Platon*, vol. I (2nd ed.), p. 235 (now 3rd ed. [1964], pp. 233ff., corrected) [This parenthetical reference is an addition to the *Gesamtausgabe* edition (Ed.)], following W. Luther, who in his Göttingen dissertation (1935, pp. 8ff.) sees the matter more clearly.

4   The first edition of *Wegmarken* reads:... *der Thesis und Abstraktion im "Noch nicht,"* while the *Gesamtausgabe* edition reads:... *der Thesis und der Abstraktion im "Noch nicht."* The addition of the definite article indicates that the words "thesis and abstraction" are to be read together; in the first edition, the sentence could conceivably be understood as "... this philosophy remains as the stage of thesis, and [as] abstraction in a 'not yet.'" (Ed.)

5   The first edition of *Wegmarken* reads: *bleibt aus,* "remains absent"; the *Gesamtausgabe* edition reads: *steht noch aus,* "is as yet outstanding." (Ed.)

6   The first edition of *Wegmarken* reads: "and" (*und*); the *Gesamtausgabe* edition reads: "yet at the same time" (*aber zugleich*). (Ed.)

7   The first edition of *Wegmarken* reads: "... to be discussed by thinking" (... *durch das Denken*). (Ed.)

8   The first edition of *Wegmarken* reads: "... in the sense of correctness and of 'being' in the sense of actuality" (... *im Sinne der Richtigkeit und vom "Sein" im Sinne der Wirklichkeit*). (Ed.)

9   The first edition of *Wegmarken* reads: "... to what is enigmatic" (... *auf das Rätselhafte*). (Ed.)

Kant's Thesis about Being

1   Originally published in *Southwestern Journal of Philosophy*, vol. IV, no. 3 (1973), pp. 7–33. Present version edited and revised by William McNeill, Ted E. Klein Jr., and William E. Pohl.

References

Comments on Karl Jaspers's "Psychology of Worldviews." A critical review from the years 1919–21 that the author sent to Karl Jaspers in June of 1921. In this regard, cf. the Foreword to the third edition (1925) of Jaspers's *Psychology of Worldviews*, which without naming names provides a response to Heidegger's critical review:

> This new edition is an unaltered reprint of the second edition. Allow me to make a few purely personal comments as to why a revised edition would be difficult.
>
> The result would be a new book. In representing worldviews as moments or dimensions of the one true worldview, which comprehends the whole only vaguely and never explicitly, I attempted at that time to formulate all this on the basis of intuition, and to communicate it to my readers without any second thoughts. The particulars of what was presented in this manner still seem to me today to be true. I would be unable to do it better today. I could only do it differently. Following this first endeavor that used an immediate, intuitive approach, I have for quite some time been concerned with the methodological issue of venturing the second step of providing a logically precise elucidation of our modern consciousness of existence. Therefore, allowing my youthful undertaking to remain in its original form would seem to be the more natural thing to do. Without my being aware of it or wishing it at the time, my whole approach in the book and my method of analysis expressed a hidden ideal. I fully acknowledge this, now that I have become aware of it. However, the limits found in the nature of this kind of presentation demand that the same content should appear in different forms. I am presently endeavoring to come up with a new form, and the wrong way to do this would be to revise what has already been published. In my subsequent work, I have become a different person not in my cast of mind, but rather in the realm of knowledge and logical form. And I would rather leave my earlier work untouched in the hope that, after this first attempt to provide a psychological explanation and foundation for philosophical existence, I will also be able to be present a logically systematic clarification and foundation.
>
> Another possible result of a revised edition would be damage to the book. Since the book has certain flaws (in its arrangement, methodical comments, and historical digressions, i.e., in matters that should be considered unessential with respect to the purpose of the book), I would want to correct these in a revised edition, taking advantage of my present insights into the book. Pages and sentences that are weak could be deleted, a lot of the terminology could be altered, and above all lacunae could be filled and the systematics of the whole book could be rearranged without affecting the particulars.

But the result would be a hybrid form, and the book would suffer because of this. In return, it would gain only a certain correctness in its outward appearance and in peripheral matters.

Heidegger's "Comments" were first published in Hans Sahner (ed.), *Karl Jaspers in der Diskussion* (Munich: R. Piper Verlag, 1973), pp. 70–100.

Phenomenology and Theology. The lecture was held in Tübingen on March 9, 1927, and again in Marburg on February 14, 1928. The *letter* of March 11, 1964, published as an Appendix, was written for a theological discussion that took place at Drew University, Madison, New Jersey, April 9–11, 1964. Both texts were published for the first time in *Archives de Philosophie*, vol. 32 (1969), pp. 356ff., together with a French translation. They were published separately under the title *Phenomenology and Theology* (Frankfurt am Main: Vittorio Klostermann, 1970), "Dedicated to Rudolf Bultmann, in friendship and remembrance of the Marburg years 1923 to 1928."

From the Last Marburg Lecture Course. Excerpt from the lecture course held in the summer semester of 1928 under the title "Logic," dedicated to the thought of Leibniz. First published as a contribution to *Zeit und Geschichte [Time and History]*, a *Festschrift* for Rudolf Bultmann on his eightieth birthday (Tübingen: I. C. B. Mohr [Paul Siebeck], 1964), pp. 497–507.

What Is Metaphysics? Inaugural public lecture, held on July 24, 1929, in the assembly hall of the University of Freiburg im Breisgau. Published in 1929 by Friedrich Cohen, Bonn. Fourth and subsequent editions published by Vittorio Klostermann, Frankfurt am Main. Since the fifth edition "Dedicated to Hans Carossa – on his seventieth birthday." Eleventh, revised edition published 1975.

On the Essence of Ground. Contribution to a *Festschrift* for Edmund Husserl on his seventieth birthday: *Ergänzungsband* of the *Jahrbuch für Philosophie und phänomenologische Forschung* (Halle [Saale]: Max Niemeyer, 1929), pp. 71–110. Published simultaneously as an offprint by Max Niemeyer, Halle (Saale). Since the third edition (1949) published, together with a Foreword, by Vittorio Klostermann, Frankfurt am Main. Sixth edition published 1973.

On the Essence of Truth. The first edition appeared in 1943 (Vittorio Klostermann, Frankfurt am Main). The essay contains the text – revised several times – of a public lecture conceived in 1930 and delivered on different occasions under the same title (in fall and winter 1930 in Bremen, Marburg an der Lahn, and Freiburg im Breisgau; in summer 1932 in Dresden). The first paragraph of the concluding Note was added in the second edition (1949). Fifth edition published 1967.

Plato's Doctrine of Truth. The train of thought goes back to the Freiburg lecture course of winter semester 1930/31, "On the Essence of Truth." The text was composed in 1940 and first appeared in *Geistige Überlieferung. Das Zweite Jahrbuch* (Berlin: Helmut Küpper, 1942), pp. 96–124. Published as a separate essay, together with the "Letter on Humanism," by A. Francke A. G. (Bern, 1947). Third edition published 1975.

On the Essence and Concept of Φύσις *in Aristotle's* Physics B, 1. Written in 1939. First published in *Il Pensiero*, vol. 3, nos. 2 and 3 (Milan-Varese, 1958). Published separately in *Testi Filosofici*, 1960 (*Biblioteca "Il Pensiero"*).

Postscript to "What Is Metaphysics?" Added in 1943 to the fourth edition of the inaugural lecture. The text of the Postscript was reworked in several places for the fifth edition (1949). The original version of these parts of the text is indicated in the numbered footnotes. Eleventh, revised edition published 1975.

Letter on Humanism. A letter to Jean Beaufret, Paris (fall 1946). The text was revised and expanded in a few places for publication. First published together with "Plato's Doctrine of Truth" by A. Francke A. G. (Bern, 1947). Appeared in 1949 as a separate publication by Vittorio Klostermann, Frankfurt am Main. Seventh edition published 1974.

Introduction to "What Is Metaphysics?" Placed at the beginning of the fifth edition (1949) of the inaugural lecture. Eleventh, revised edition published 1975.

On the Question of Being. First appeared under the title "Concerning 'The Line'" [*Über "Die Linie"*] as a contribution to *Freundschaftliche Begegnungen*, a *Festschrift* for Ernst Jünger on his sixtieth birthday (Frankfurt am Main: Vittorio Klostermann, 1955), pp. 9–45. Published separately in 1956 by Vittorio Klostermann, Frankfurt am Main. Third edition published 1967.

Hegel and the Greeks. Written as a lecture that was held in the general assembly of the Heidelberg Akademie der Wissenschaften on July 26, 1958. First published as a contribution to *Die Gegenwart der Griechen im neueren Denken* [*The Presence of the Greeks in Modern Thought*], a *Festschrift* for Hans-Georg Gadamer on his sixtieth birthday (Tübingen: J. C. B. Mohr [Paul Siebeck], 1960), pp. 43–57. An earlier version of the text was the basis of a lecture in Aix-en-Provence on March 20, 1958, and appeared in a French translation by Jean Beaufret and Pierre-Paul Sagave in *Cahiers du Sud*, vol. 47, no. 349 (January 1959), pp. 355–68.

Kant's Thesis about Being. A lecture held on May 17, 1961, in Kiel. First appeared as a contribution to *Existenz und Ordnung*, a *Festschrift* for Erik Wolf on his sixtieth birthday (Frankfurt am Main: Vittorio Klostermann, 1962), pp. 217–45. Published as a separate essay in 1963 by Vittorio Klostermann, Frankfurt am Main.

Editor's Postscript to the German Edition

The collection *Wegmarken*, in its present form as volume 9 of the *Gesamtausgabe*, has been *extended* by the inclusion of two separate essays and provided with *marginal notes* from the various personal copies belonging to the author.

Newly included are the "Comments on Karl Jaspers's *Psychology of Worldviews*" from 1919/21, and the essay "Phenomenology and Theology" (1927). The encounter with Jaspers, which understands itself as a "positive and illuminating critical review of this work published by Jaspers," is guided by the beginning of the question of being that finds explicit formulation in Heidegger. Here it takes the early form of the question concerning the meaning of the being of the "I *am*" (existence, *Dasein*) as distinct from the meaning of being found in the "something *is* something" that belongs to objectifying thinking.

The essays have been newly ordered in accordance with the chronological principle of when they were written. The volume now contains pathmarks belonging to the period from 1919 to 1961. The correspondence of pagination with that of the first edition (1967) is given in the margins.

Various minor textual corrections that serve only to clarify were incorporated from Heidegger's own editions. According to the author, these corrections were not to be explicitly noted. In addition, all texts were examined for previous printing errors. The "Postscript to 'What Is Metaphysics?'" indicates in its numbered footnotes the original 1943 version of those places in the text that were altered for the fifth edition (1949), and which triggered extensive discussion in the secondary literature.

The *marginal notes* that appear in the footnotes and are indicated by letters (a, b, c) are, by general decision of the author, to be reserved solely for the volumes of the *Gesamtausgabe*. They were drawn from Heidegger's personal editions of separate publications of the texts collected in *Wegmarken*, as well as from his personal copy of the first edition of *Wegmarken*. Martin Heidegger entrusted the editor of this volume with the task of selecting the marginalia, a process that was undertaken in accordance with the guidelines provided by the author. Marginal notes that were meaningful only for the author and would not be transparent to readers were not included. In the majority of cases, there are several personal copies, sometimes even four or five, of different editions of one and the same essay. In the present volume the particular edition, together with its year of publication, is noted before each of the marginalia.

The marginal notes were made in different years and even in different decades – usually beginning with the year of publication of the text and extending to the last years of the philosopher's life – but were not dated. An extrinsic indicator of the approximate period from which they date is provided by the year of each edition. Yet this indicates *only* that the marginalia are not from an earlier period, prior to the date of publication – apart from a few instances in which Heidegger copied marginal notes from an earlier edition into a later one. This does *not* entail, however, that marginalia from an earlier, or even from the first, edition must belong to the period prior to the publication of the later edition. Heidegger on occasion preferred to use his copy of the first, or of an earlier, edition for the insertion of notes, even when he had already acquired his own copy of a more recent edition. There are enough instances of entries being found in his copy of an early edition that stem from a period after the appearance of a later edition, while his own copy of the later edition may contain marginalia that stem from a much earlier period than those found in an earlier edition.

Yet the thought contained in these marginal notes is and remains more decisive for cautiously dating them than this extrinsic indicator. Whoever has read Heidegger's essays attentively and has carefully and thoughtfully followed the path of his thinking – to the extent possible thus far given the much greater amount of unpublished manuscripts – will be able to decide with some degree of certainty the stop along his path of thought to which a particular marginal note belongs. Because the marginalia arose over a period of decades and accompany Heidegger on his path, they too let us detect something of the path that characterizes his thinking.

In terms of their thought-content, the marginal notes fall into three categories. First, there are the elucidatory clarifications immanent to the text, which do not go beyond, in any critical or progressive manner, the horizon of thought belonging to the essay. A second, larger portion of marginalia that belong to the essays relating to *Being and Time* are of a self-critical nature. They are thought from out of the turning that occurs, which Heidegger earlier had designated using the Kantian term "overturning" [*Umkippung*]. These notes often grant us a sudden insight into the movement of a thinking that turns. In a third group of marginal remarks, Heidegger looks back from his later position at what was thought at an earlier stop on the same path, in order to point to the substantive connection between his current and his earlier positions. All marginalia that speak from the perspective of the "event" [*Ereignis*] arose only after 1936, when this word became for Heidegger the guiding word of his thinking.

My sincere thanks are due to Hartmut Tietjen (cand. phil.) and to Murray Miles (cand. phil.) for their careful assistance with corrections.

Friedrich-Wilhelm von Herrmann
Freiburg im Breisgau, July 1976